Creating Mobile Games

Using Java™ ME Platform to Put the Fun into Your Mobile Device and Cell Phone

D1408165

■ ■ ■

Carol Hamer

Apress®

Creating Mobile Games: Using Java™ ME Platform to Put the Fun into Your Mobile Device and Cell Phone

Copyright © 2007 by Carol Hamer

ISBN-13 (pbk): 978-1-59059-880-1

ISBN-10 (pbk): 1-59059-880-6

Printed and bound in the United States of America 9 8 7 6 5 4 3 2 1

Lead Editors: Steve Anglin, Jeff Pepper
Technical Reviewer: Alain Le Guirec
Editorial Board: Steve Anglin, Ewan Buckingham, Gary Cornell, Jonathan Gennick, Jason Gilmore, Jonathan Hassell, Chris Mills, Matthew Moodie, Jeffrey Pepper, Ben Renow-Clarke, Dominic Shakeshaft, Matt Wade, Tom Welsh
Project Manager: Richard Dal Porto
Copy Edit Manager: Nicole Flores
Copy Editor: Liz Welch
Assistant Production Director: Kari Brooks-Copony
Production Editor: Laura Esterman
Compositor: Kinetic Publishing Services, LLC
Proofreader: Elizabeth Berry
Indexer: Carol Burbo
Artist: April Milne
Cover Designer: Kurt Krames
Manufacturing Director: Tom Debolski

Distributed to the book trade worldwide by Springer-Verlag New York, Inc., 233 Spring Street, 6th Floor, New York, NY 10013. Phone 1-800-SPRINGER, fax 201-348-4505, e-mail orders-ny@springer-sbm.com, or visit http://www.springeronline.com.

For information on translations, please contact Apress directly at 2560 Ninth Street, Suite 219, Berkeley, CA 94710. Phone 510-549-5930, fax 510-549-5939, e-mail info@apress.com, or visit http://www.apress.com.

The source code for this book is available to readers at http://www.apress.com in the Source Code/Download section.

To my boys: Nicolas, Léo, and Emmanuel

Contents at a Glance

About the Author xi

Introduction xiii

■CHAPTER 1   Getting Started 1

■CHAPTER 2   Using MIDlets 21

■CHAPTER 3   Using the MIDP 2 Games API 53

■CHAPTER 4   Using Threads and Media 95

■CHAPTER 5   Storing and Retrieving Data 131

■CHAPTER 6   Using Network Communications 193

■CHAPTER 7   Advanced Messaging and Data Access 263

■CHAPTER 8   Securing Your Applications 305

■CHAPTER 9   The Mobile 3D Graphics API 317

■CHAPTER 10   Adding a Professional Look and Feel 351

■INDEX 409

Contents

About the Author xi

Introduction xiii

■CHAPTER 1   **Getting Started** 1

Understanding Java ME 1
    How the CLDC Differs from the Rest of the Java Universe 2
    The Three Versions of MIDP 3
Downloading and Installing the Toolkit 4
Building an Application for MIDP 5
Creating the "Hello, World" Application 6
Using KToolbar 11
Running Your Game on an Actual Cell Phone 14
    Using WAP 14
    Preparing the WML File 15
    Configuring the Server 16
    Accessing the WML File and Downloading Applications 18
Summary 19

■CHAPTER 2   **Using MIDlets** 21

Using the MIDlet Class 22
    Understanding the MIDlet Lifecycle 22
    Using the Displayable and Display Classes 26
    Using Buttons and Menus 28
Using the Form and Item Classes 29
Using the Graphics and Canvas Classes 34
Using the java.util Package 44
Summary 51

■CHAPTER 3   **Using the MIDP 2 Games API** 53

Starting with the MIDlet Class 53
Using the Thread Class 58

Using the GameCanvas Class 62
    How GameCanvas Differs from Canvas 62
    Using the Graphics Class with a GameCanvas 69
Using the LayerManager Class 71
Using the Sprite Class... 77
Using the TiledLayer Class... 89
Summary 94

■CHAPTER 4   **Using Threads and Media** 95

Using Threads 95
    Differences Between CLDC Threads and Threads in
        Standard Java.. 95
    Strategies for Deciding When to Use a New Thread 104
    Avoiding Race Conditions and Deadlock 115
Using Media 118
    Playing Simple Tones 118
    Playing Tones with a Player 122
    Using Audio Files 128
Summary 129

■CHAPTER 5   **Storing and Retrieving Data** 131

Saving Simple Data.. 131
Serializing More Complex Data Using Streams 135
Using Data Types and Byte Arithmetic............................. 136
Applying Data Storage to a Dungeon Game 143
Creating the Complete Example Game 159
Summary 192

■CHAPTER 6   **Using Network Communications** 193

Choosing a Protocol 193
Using the Micro Edition IO API.................................... 194
Using HTTP.. 195
    The Dungeon Example: Downloading the Next Board........... 197
    Writing the Client Code for the Dungeon Example............. 198
    Writing the Server Code for the Dungeon Example 206
Using SMS 209
    Using the Push Registry 210

Creating a Multiplayer Game Example: Checkers 212
    Writing the Communications Code for the Checkers Example. . . . 212
    Writing the Game Logic for the Checkers Example 234
Summary 262

■CHAPTER 7   **Advanced Messaging and Data Access** 263

Using Bluetooth 263
Using the Personal Information Management API 285
Using the File Connection API 297
More Options 302
Summary 303

■CHAPTER 8   **Securing Your Applications** 305

Understanding Protection Domains and Permissions 305
    Requesting Permissions 307
    Using Digital Certificates 308
Setting Up Secure Connections. 311
    Using HTTPS 311
    Using Other Secure Connections. 315
Summary 316

■CHAPTER 9   **The Mobile 3D Graphics API**. 317

Vertex Buffers and Coordinates. 317
    Defining the Polygon 317
    Lights, Camera, Render!. 322
    Textures and Lighting 325
The M3G File Format. 332
    The M3G File Structure. 332
    Creating an M3G File. 333
Nodes and Rendering 335
    Rendering Modes. 336
    A Tour of the World Node 336
Further Tools and Features 345
    Animations 345
    Collisions. 348
    Optimization 349
Summary 349

■CHAPTER 10 **Adding a Professional Look and Feel** 351

Customizing for Multiple Target Platforms 352
  Organizing Custom Resources. 352
  Modifying Image Colors and Transparency 363
Creating a GUI 367
  Starting Off on the Right Foot 367
  Creating Custom Menus. 380
  Implementing Softkeys. 396
Applying Custom Resources to the Game. 398
Summary 407

■INDEX 409

About the Author

CAROL HAMER has worked for more than three years as a software engineer for In-Fusio Mobile Game Connections. She is currently the director of client development for Business Anywhere.

Introduction

When people ask me what I do, in addition to telling them I can show them: I can pull out my cell phone and demonstrate some of the games I've written for it. It's a great time to be a software developer because a pastime that's so much fun—writing games for cell phones and mobile devices—is now a huge growth industry.

The number of cell phones worldwide is well over 2 billion, dwarfing the market of other high-tech items such as personal computers. The number of Java-enabled cell phones is in the hundreds of millions, and, by some counts, the number may already be over a billion. And since cell phones are naturally a personal-use device, many of these users will want to use their phones for fun and entertainment, and you can tap into that market with Java Micro Edition games.

If you're already a software engineer with lots of experience in Java Standard Edition and/or Java Enterprise Edition, learning to use Java Micro Edition isn't too hard. And if you have only a basic knowledge of programming in Java, Java ME is a fine place to start. The main differences you encounter in your day-to-day programming are the limitations of the devices involved and the differences from one device to the next.

Both of these challenges have corresponding advantages. Since a cell phone has limited capabilities (in terms of speed, memory, connectivity, screen size, screen colors, and so forth), you have to work harder to make sure your program is as efficient as possible, and you end up having to manipulate bytes of data in more of a hands-on fashion than other Java programmers. The flip-side advantage is that your application has to be small—and let's face it: being responsible for a big part of a small application is far more fun than writing a fraction of a module doing database queries or something for a giant mainframe application. Refactoring your code to make it more elegant is a priority, so you're less likely to get stuck perpetually patching some old, inefficient code and making it endlessly bigger and uglier. And since the device can only handle fairly simple games, that means that an individual developer or a small studio can write the whole game—a complete, professional product ready for the real game market. It's not like the market for computer or console games where the simple ones are freeware; to write a game people will pay money for, you have to compete against the big boys: huge game studio corporations. Additionally, since a device only has room for so many games, a user who likes games is unlikely to be satisfied with the few that come bundled with the handset and will want to buy more.

The other big challenge—dealing with the differences from one handset to the next—can be a bit of a headache. On the bright side, it gives you plenty of opportunity to show off your troubleshooting skills as you investigate why a program that ran great on one handset has strange bugs or even crashes on another. Differences in capabilities (in terms of display or optional APIs available) make it so that a given game is usually only appropriate for a portion of the total market of Java handsets, even after a costly "porting" phase to produce a range of custom versions for different devices. But as users keep upgrading their devices, they'll want games to take advantage of each new device's capacities, which translates to more programs for you, the developer, to write and sell.

Overall, Java Micro Edition opens up a rich field of exciting opportunities for software developers and helps you put the fun in your mobile device and cell phone.

CHAPTER 1

■■■

Getting Started

This book is all about creating mobile games for the Java platform. With that in mind, it is obviously important to have a working knowledge of the tools involved and to get them installed so that we can tackle the fun stuff later. So, I will start with introducing the tools in the first two sections to give you a general idea of what is involved. Then I will cover what you need to do to set up your computer for Java Micro Edition (Java ME) game development and how to get your games running on an actual target device. Once you have your development environment running, you can start by building and modifying the examples from this book. You can download all the source code for the examples from the Source Code/Download section of the Apress web site (http://www.apress.com). This includes all the image files, descriptor files, and other resource files.

Understanding Java ME

The Java Micro Edition (Java ME) is the version of the Java platform that's designed for use with small devices such as cell phones, personal digital assistants (PDAs), TV set-top boxes (for web browsing and e-mail without a whole computer), and embedded devices. Since these devices vary quite a bit in their capabilities, the Java ME platform has two different *configurations*, each with its own choice of *profiles*. The Connected Limited Device Configuration (CLDC) is the configuration you'll be working with in this book. It's designed for cell phones and low-level PDAs. More precisely, CLDC is intended for devices with a 16-bit or 32-bit processor, with at least 160KB of nonvolatile memory, at least 32KB of volatile memory, and some network connectivity, possibly wireless and intermittent. CLDC's unique profile is the Mobile Information Device Profile (MIDP). This book covers MIDP versions 1, 2, and 3, although the focus will be on MIDP 2 since that is the current industry standard for cell phones and will continue to be the standard for some time. The other configuration possibility associated with Java ME is the Connected Device Configuration (CDC), which isn't specifically covered in this book. Starting with MIDP 3, some CDC devices will be able to run MIDP applications; however, from the MIDP application's perspective, the configuration must behave as if it were CLDC, and therefore, no CDC-specific programming is covered here.

The configuration specifies the type of Java Virtual Machine (JVM) that's used and what will be included in the minimal class libraries (the java.* packages and the javax.microedition.io package in the case of CLDC). CDC specifies a complete JVM, but the JVM of CLDC has some limitations compared to the standard JVM. A profile is added on top of the configuration to define a standard set of libraries (the other javax.microedition.* packages in this case). MIDP contains packages for application lifecycle, a user interface, media control, input/output, data storage, and security.

In addition to its configuration and profile, a Java ME–capable device may also have a set of optional application programming interfaces (APIs) available. Some are proprietary, but many are standard. Standard optional APIs are defined in Java Specification Requests (JSRs), which are submitted, reviewed, and published through the Java Community Process (JCP). You can download the precise specifications for any JSR (free) from the JCP web site (http://jcp.org/). CLDC, CDC, and MIDP are all defined as JSRs through the Java Community Process.

How the CLDC Differs from the Rest of the Java Universe

If you're coming to Java ME from a background of programming for Java Standard Edition (Java SE) or Java Enterprise Edition (Java EE), things should look pretty familiar, but just a little bit different. It's like Java in a parallel universe where everything has been streamlined to be as small and efficient as possible. You have fewer tools at your disposal in terms of built-in libraries, and you need to place greater priority on writing tight, efficient code than a Java SE or Java EE developer would. Those are already good reasons to switch to Java ME if you're one of those people who loves a good challenge. Another motivation for making the switch to Micro Edition is that the applications are so small that you typically get to design most or all of the program yourself instead of being a cog writing a part of an obscure module.

The designers of the CLDC specification have made an effort to make CLDC resemble the standard platform as closely as possible, and they've done a pretty good job of it. Nothing critical to small applications appears to be missing. I'll give a general outline of the changes here, and I'll refer you to later chapters in this book for a more in-depth discussion of the aspects that have changed the most dramatically.

Differences in the JVM

The JVM specified in CLDC is mostly the same as the standard JVM. Unsurprisingly, a few of the costlier noncritical features have been eliminated. One example is the method Object.finalize(). According to the JavaDoc, the Object.finalize() method is called on an object when the JVM determines that it's time to garbage-collect that object. The actions the object can take in its finalize() method aren't restricted, so in particular it can make itself available again to currently active threads! The garbage collection algorithm is already expensive, and this method clearly undermines its efficiency by obligating the JVM to recheck objects that had already been marked as garbage. It's no wonder this method was eliminated in CLDC, since it's not hard at all to keep track of the objects that you're still using without requiring the JVM to check with you before throwing anything away.

Some of the other areas where the JVM's set of features have been reduced are in security, threads, and exceptions/errors. See the "Understanding Protection Domains and Permissions" section in Chapter 8 for a discussion of the differences in the security model. See the "Differences Between CLDC Threads and Threads in Standard Java" section in Chapter 4 for information about threads. The changes in the error-handling system are that CLDC doesn't allow asynchronous exceptions and that the set of error classes has been greatly reduced. Instead of 22 possible errors, you now have only OutOfMemoryError, VirtualMachineError, and Error. On the other hand, almost all the exceptions in the java.lang.* package have been retained.

You may not notice a few changes to the JVM just by looking at the API. In CLDC, the JVM is allowed to perform some optimizations (such as prelinking classes) that were disallowed to the standard JVM. Such changes shouldn't concern the application programmer in general. The one exception is that an additional preverification stage has been added after compilation. The preverification process adds extra information to the class file to make the bytecode veri-fication algorithm easier at runtime when the device checks that your class file is valid before using it. You easily accomplish the preverification step with standard tools (see the "Using KToolbar" section and the "Building with Ant" sidebar later in this chapter). Preverification isn't technically required 100 percent of the time, but it aids in compatibility, and there's no reason not to do it.

One more general item to be aware of is that although a CLDC-compliant platform is required to support Unicode characters, it's required to support only the International Organization for Standardization (ISO) Latin 1 range of characters from the Unicode standard, version 3.0. For more information about character encoding in Java, see http://java.sun.com/javase/6/docs/technotes/guides/intl/encoding.doc.html. Also, the initial version of CLDC (1.0) did not include floating-point numbers as simple data types (double and float). These were added in the newer version, CLDC 1.1.

Differences in the Libraries

As you may guess, the standard libraries have been drastically reduced. It's unfortunate in many cases, but—as I mentioned earlier—doing without some helpful tools is one of your challenges as a Java ME developer. The only java.* packages that you have available to you are java.lang.*, java.util.*, and java.io.*. That means you have to do without java.lang. reflect.*, java.math.*, java.security.*, and many others. Many of the missing packages have been replaced by MIDP packages that are more appropriate for small devices, as you'll see throughout this book.

Although the three remaining java.* packages have been greatly reduced, it's clear that the designers of CLDC have tried to keep as much as possible and create familiar replacements for classes and methods that had to be removed. The java.lang.* package has been pared down to just the classes that correspond to data types (Integer, Boolean, and so on) and a few necessary items: Math, Object, Runnable, String, StringBuffer, System, Thread, and Throwable (plus the exceptions and errors discussed previously). The java.util.* and java.io.* packages have been similarly reduced to their essentials. For examples of how to use the MIDP versions of the java.io.* classes, see the "Serializing More Complex Data Using Streams" section in Chapter 5. For a discussion of the changes to the java.util.* package, see the "Using the java.util Package" section in Chapter 2.

The Three Versions of MIDP

Unlike products where a new version completely replaces an earlier version, different versions of MIDP coexist on the market and likely will continue to do so for some time. It's not just a question of the new version being better or more innovative than an earlier version—in the case of MIDP there's also a question of earlier versions being more appropriate for less-powerful devices. The handset market seems to be constantly evolving toward more power and more features becoming cheaper, and the portion of the market using more advanced versions expands accordingly. On the other hand, there's a market for a range of models, and manufac-turers will continue to make cheap, low-end models as long as they keep selling. Additionally, while people tend to upgrade their cell phones pretty frequently on average, there are still a lot of old handsets out there in the wild—and they're attached to potential customers for your game—so you probably don't want to just dismiss them out of hand.

MIDP 2 is a good level to write games for because it provides big advantages over MIDP 1 for game programming. Plus, if you shoot for MIDP 2 as a target when writing your game, there exist tools such as J2ME Polish to back-port it to MIDP 1 devices (see the sidebar "Using J2ME Polish" in Chapter 10). There's less advantage in specifically targeting MIDP 3 handsets (by writing games that won't run on MIDP 2 handsets) because MIDP 3 doesn't offer all that much over MIDP 2 in terms of tools for games. The biggest difference between MIDP 3 and MIDP 2 is found in terms of how MIDP applications interact with each other. In MIDP 3, `MIDlets` can share libraries and communicate with each other while running concurrently (see the "More Options" section of Chapter 7); plus, the `Permission` class has been changed to be compatible with CDC and the rest of the larger Java universe (see Chapter 8).

It's possible to write some fun basic games using MIDP 1. I wrote the example game in Chapter 2 to be compatible with MIDP 1 so you can see what's available there. It's easy to underestimate the value of simple games, but keep in mind that not only are they cheaper to produce, sometimes they actually sell better than more complicated games since many users just want a familiar diversion when playing a game on a cell phone instead of something cool yet involved, requiring time and attention to learn. But MIDP 2 is loaded with additional features that allow you to create a much richer gaming environment, and the added advantages—not only in terms of making a more exciting game but also in terms of making a simple game look more beautiful, exciting, and professional—shouldn't be underestimated either. The most obvious additional tool you get in MIDP 2 is the package `javax.microedition.lcdui.game`, which is a special package to help you optimize game graphics and controls (see Chapter 3). Also, a version of the Mobile Media API (JSR 135) is a required part of MIDP 2, so you can add music to your game (see the "Using Media" section in Chapter 4).

Much of the difference from one target device to the next is more a question of which optional APIs are supported than of which version of MIDP is being used. The optional APIs can open up new channels of communication (see the sections "Using SMS" in Chapter 6 and "Using Bluetooth" in Chapter 7). And one of the most enticing APIs for a game developer to try out and play with is the (optional but widely supported) Mobile 3D Graphics API, which is defined in JSR 184 (see Chapter 9).

Overall, dealing with the huge range of devices with different capabilities (in terms of both hardware and software) is one of the two big challenges of Micro Edition programming, right up there with the challenge of optimizing your game for small, limited devices. But even though Java's "write once, run anywhere" philosophy works less than perfectly here, Java ME goes a long way toward making it easy for you to write for a wide range of target devices at once. It's a great common platform for keeping up with the hot and fast-paced world of mobile!

Downloading and Installing the Toolkit

If you haven't already downloaded and installed a development toolkit, you can get the Sun Java Wireless Toolkit for CLDC at `http://java.sun.com/javame/downloads/index.jsp`. I downloaded the WTK version 2.2 for this book, but if you've selected a more recent release, it won't be very different. Some handset manufacturers offer specialized Java ME emulators for free download, but they're often based on Sun's Reference Implementation (RI), so for the rest of this chapter I'll assume you're using the Java ME Wireless Toolkit from Sun.

If you have trouble downloading the toolkit from Sun, keep in mind that you need to register at the Sun site and log in. This shouldn't be a problem—it doesn't cost anything. You have to submit your e-mail address, but Sun has never sent me any spam as a result of my registration, so don't worry about anything.

The Java ME Wireless Toolkit contains a minimal MIDlet development environment (called *KToolbar*), a cell phone emulator, and a number of helpful demo applications with source code. It also contains a clear and comprehensive manual in both Hypertext Markup Language (HTML) format and PDF format (the "User Guide" in the WTK docs folder). You should definitely take the time to familiarize yourself with it so that you can find more details on what's available once you've got the basics down.

Building an Application for MIDP

I'll stick with tradition and start with the classic "Hello, World" application. This example will illustrate how to get a minimal MIDlet compiled and running.

When you examine the demo applications that are bundled with the toolkit, you'll notice that they consist of a JAR (Java archive) file and a JAD (Java application descriptor) file. The JAR file contains the class files, the resources, and a manifest file (just as you'd expect to find in any JAR file). The JAD file is a Java properties (text) file that contains information to help the device install and run the application. The manifest file (MANIFEST.MF) found inside the JAR file contains a lot of the same information as the JAD file, and properties that appear in both must have identical values; otherwise (for security reasons), the application can't be installed on any MIDP device, including the WTK emulator. The JAD file and the manifest file contain data that the platform needs to run the application, such as the CLDC version that the application requires. The reason for having two separate files for these same properties is that one goes inside the JAR file and one is outside. So security-critical properties go in the manifest file inside the JAR (where they can be protected from corruption by digitally signing the JAR, as you'll learn in the "Using Digital Certificates" section of Chapter 8), and properties that are needed before the application is installed—to aid in the installation process—go in the JAD file. Notably, the JAD file contains the two installation-specific properties MIDlet-Jar-URL and MIDlet-Jar-Size.

Listing 1-1 is an example of the JAD file I wrote for my "Hello, World" application. I called this file hello.jar.

Listing 1-1. *hello.jar*

```
MIDlet-1: Hello World, /images/hello.png, net.frog_parrot.hello.Hello
MMIDlet-Description: Hello World for MIDP
MIDlet-Jar-URL: hello.jar
MIDlet-Name: Hello World
MIDlet-Permissions:
MIDlet-Vendor: frog-parrot.net
MIDlet-Version: 2.0
MicroEdition-Configuration: CLDC-1.0
MicroEdition-Profile: MIDP-2.0
MIDlet-Jar-Size: 3201
```

The MIDlet-1 (and MIDlet-2, and so on) property gives the name of the MIDlet, the location of the MIDlet's icon, and the fully qualified name of the MIDlet class to run (see the section on "Understanding the MIDlet Lifecycle" in Chapter 2). The first two items describe how the MIDlet will appear on the menu of MIDlets. The icon should be in the JAR file, and its location should be given in the same format as is used by the method Class.getResource(). Thus, in this example, your JAR file should contain a top-level folder called images, which contains an icon called hello.png, as shown in Figure 1-1.

Figure 1-1. *This is the icon hello.png.*

■**Note** The MIDlet-Jar-Size property gives the size of the corresponding JAR file in bytes, which you can find by looking at the properties or long listing of the JAR file. Be aware that if you rebuild the demos or your own applications using the build script or batch file bundled with the toolkit, you must manually update the size of the JAR file in the JAD file. If the MIDlet-Jar-Size property in the JAD file doesn't match the size of the JAR file, the MIDlet won't run. The simplest way to deal with this is just to use the KToolbar application (see the section on "Using KToolbar" later in this chapter). For a more complex project that may require customized build steps, the standard solution is to use Ant (see the "Building with Ant" sidebar later in this chapter).

The MIDlet-Jar-URL property gives the address of the MIDlet jar as a uniform resource locator (URL). According to the MIDP specifications, this can be a relative path (relative to the location of the JAD file, so if the JAR file and the JAD file are kept in the same directory, this is just the name of the JAR file); however, there are some handsets on the market that require an absolute (complete) URL. The "Requesting Permissions" section of Chapter 8 discusses the MIDlet-Permissions property, but for simple games, you can omit it or leave it blank. The other properties are self-explanatory.

Creating the "Hello, World" Application

This section shows the "Hello, World" application. The MIDlet will display the message *Hello World!* on the screen and remove it (or later put it back) when you click the Toggle Msg button. Clicking the Exit button will terminate the MIDlet. The application consists of two classes: the MIDlet subclass called Hello and the Canvas subclass called HelloCanvas. How it works is very simple. The Hello class implements a list of standard methods to receive information from the device. This includes the MIDlet lifecycle methods that the platform calls in order to start and stop the application (see the section on "Understanding the MIDlet Lifecycle" in Chapter 2 for more details) as well as the implementation of the CommandListener interface that the platform calls if the user presses a key while the application is running. The HelloCanvas class repaints the screen with or without the *Hello World!* message when the toggleHello() method is called. Listing 1-2 shows the code for Hello.java.

Listing 1-2. *Hello.java*

```java
package net.frog_parrot.hello;

import javax.microedition.midlet.*;
import javax.microedition.lcdui.*;

/**
 * This is the main class of the "Hello, World" demo.
 *
 * @author Carol Hamer
 */
public class Hello extends MIDlet implements CommandListener {

  /**
   * The canvas is the region of the screen that has been allotted
   * to the game.
   */
  HelloCanvas myCanvas;

  /**
   * The Command objects appear as buttons in this example.
   */
  private Command exitCommand = new Command("Exit", Command.EXIT, 99);

  /**
   * The Command objects appear as buttons in this example.
   */
  private Command toggleCommand = new Command("Toggle Msg", Command.SCREEN, 1);

  /**
   * Initialize the canvas and the commands.
   */
  public Hello() {
    myCanvas = new HelloCanvas();
    myCanvas.addCommand(exitCommand);
    myCanvas.addCommand(toggleCommand);
    // you set one command listener to listen to all
    // of the commands on the canvas:
    myCanvas.setCommandListener(this);
  }

  //-----------------------------------------------------------------
```

```java
// implementation of MIDlet

/**
 * Start the application.
 */
public void startApp() throws MIDletStateChangeException {
  // display my canvas on the screen:
  Display.getDisplay(this).setCurrent(myCanvas);
  myCanvas.repaint();
}

/**
 * If the MIDlet was using resources, it should release
 * them in this method.
 */
public void destroyApp(boolean unconditional)
    throws MIDletStateChangeException {
}

/**
 * This method is called to notify the MIDlet to enter a paused
 * state. The MIDlet should use this opportunity to release
 * shared resources.
 */
public void pauseApp() {
}

//------------------------------------------------------------------
// implementation of CommandListener

/*
 * Respond to a command issued on the Canvas.
 * (either reset or exit).
 */
public void commandAction(Command c, Displayable s) {
  if(c == toggleCommand) {
    myCanvas.toggleHello();
  } else if(c == exitCommand) {
    try {
      destroyApp(false);
      notifyDestroyed();
    } catch (MIDletStateChangeException ex) {
    }
  }
}

}
```

Listing 1-3 shows the code for HelloCanvas.java.

Listing 1-3. *HelloCanvas.java*

```java
package net.frog_parrot.hello;

import javax.microedition.lcdui.*;

/**
 * This class represents the region of the screen that has been allotted
 * to the game.
 *
 * @author Carol Hamer
 */
public class HelloCanvas extends Canvas {

  //-----------------------------------------------------------
  //   fields

  /**
   * whether the screen should currently display the
   * "Hello World" message.
   */
  boolean mySayHello = true;

  //-------------------------------------------------------
  //    initialization and game state changes

  /**
   * toggle the hello message.
   */
  void toggleHello() {
    mySayHello = !mySayHello;
    repaint();
  }

  //--------------------------------------------------------
  // graphics methods

  /**
   * clear the screen and display the "Hello World" message if appropriate.
   */
```

```
public void paint(Graphics g) {
  // get the dimensions of the screen:
  int width = getWidth ();
  int height = getHeight();
  // clear the screen (paint it white):
  g.setColor(0xffffff);
  // The first two args give the coordinates of the top
  // left corner of the rectangle.  (0,0) corresponds
  // to the top-left corner of the screen.
  g.fillRect(0, 0, width, height);
  // display the "Hello World" message if appropriate.
  if(mySayHello) {
    Font font = g.getFont();
    int fontHeight = font.getHeight();
    int fontWidth = font.stringWidth("Hello World!");
    // set the text color to red:
    g.setColor(255, 0, 0);
    g.setFont(font);
    // write the string in the center of the screen
    g.drawString("Hello World!", (width - fontWidth)/2,
                 (height - fontHeight)/2,
                 g.TOP|g.LEFT);
  }
}

}
```

The "Hello, World" application is simple enough to run with MIDP 1 as well as with MIDP 2. Figure 1-2 shows what the "Hello, World" application looks like when running on an early version of the Wireless Toolkit (version 1.0.4) using the DefaultGrayPhone emulator. It is possible to use the WTK 2.2 and later to see how your program works on a MIDP 1 device by changing the target platform in the project settings, as you'll see in the next section.

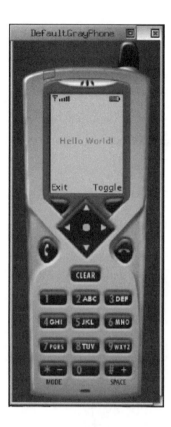

Figure 1-2. *The "Hello, World" application*

Using KToolbar

The MIDlet development environment KToolbar is easy to use, and it's well documented. KToolbar is a "minimal" development environment in the sense that, unlike complete integrated development environments (IDEs) such as JBuilder, it doesn't contain a text editor. But you probably already have a text editor, so if you don't mind using an ordinary text editor to write your source code, KToolbar will take care of the MIDP-specific tasks.

The first thing to do after launching KToolbar is click the New Project button just below the menu bar. This will automatically open some GUI windows that prompt you to fill in information that KToolbar will use to construct the JAD and manifest files as well as the directories for the project (see Figures 1-3 and 1-4).

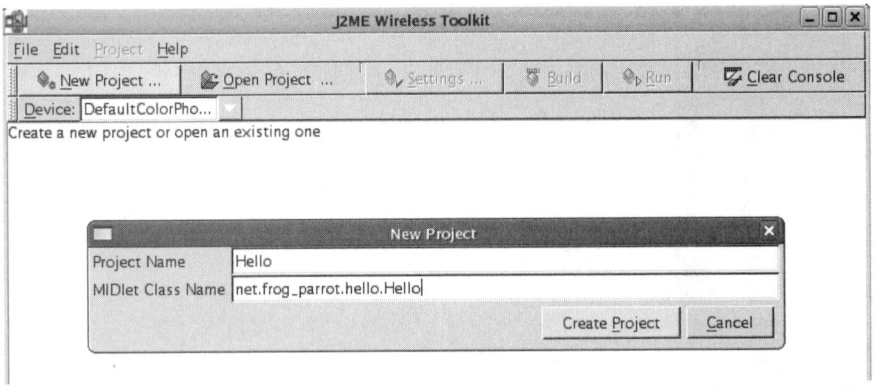

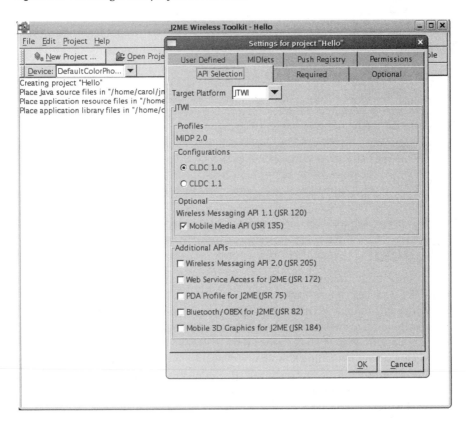

Figure 1-3. *Creating a new project in KToolbar*

Figure 1-4. *Setting up a new project in KToolbar*

Once you've filled in the project settings, KToolbar creates a set of directories for the project under the WTK's apps folder. It creates a src directory (where you place your source code), a res directory (where you place resource files such as images that should be built into the JAR), and a bin directory (where KToolbar places the finished JAR and JAD files it constructs for your project). Note that unlike some IDEs such as JBuilder, it doesn't create its own project file describing your project, so you can open a "project" in KToolbar, even if you created the directory tree for the project yourself, instead of having KToolbar create it for you. All you need to do is make sure your project's root directory is in the right place (in the apps folder inside the WTK2.2 folder), and you can open it as a project in KToolbar.

In addition to setting up your project, KToolbar will preverify and build your project and then run it in the emulator at the click of a GUI button. It also has a whole suite of useful features for debugging and performance monitoring. Plus, it has tools for digitally signing your MIDlet (see the "Using Digital Certificates" section of Chapter 8). If you place a third-party obfuscation tool JAR in the WTK's bin directory, KToolbar will also obfuscate the class files automatically during the build. If you click KToolbar's Build and Run buttons, the current project will be run from the project's directory without building it into a JAR file. However, if you select Project ➤ Package ➤ Create Package, KToolbar will create a JAR and JAD pair that can be run on an actual device. By selecting Project ➤ Run via OTA, you can install the MIDlet on the emulator (via local HTTP) exactly the same way you download and install the MIDlet onto a handset.

The WTK offers a choice of different default emulators to test your MIDlet on, such as the DefaultColorPhone, DefaultGrayPhone, MediaControlSkin, and QwertyDevice. KToolbar has a drop-down menu that allows you to choose which device to use. All of these devices are defined in subdirectories of the WTK's wtklib/devices directory. If you look there, you'll see that each emulator skin has a corresponding properties file, which you can modify if you'd like to change something, such as the emulator's screen size. You can also add new directories there (such as skins offered by manufacturers to emulate their devices), and the new emulators will automatically show up as options in KToolbar. Through KToolbar you can also set parameters such as network speed, Virtual Machine (VM) speed, and heap size in order to better emulate the behavior on specific devices, but in practice it's not terribly effective at reproducing the behavior on specific devices. It's not a real substitute for testing on a number of devices both for optimization and for platform-specific bugs.

BUILDING WITH ANT

For a basic MIDlet, the Wireless Toolkit's KToolbar application is pretty convenient, but as soon as you want to do anything fancy with your build at all (such as add extra steps for style checking, preprocessing, custom resource building, etc.) it's a good idea to set up your build process to use Ant.

The nice thing about Ant is that it's easy to use and it's easy to extend it to do essentially anything you want. The build process is controlled through XML files, which group sets of commands as "targets." The commands themselves (Ant tasks) can be calls to Java classes, so if there's no existing command to perform some task that you'd like to have in your build process, you can write your own Ant task to do it.

An MIDP project has some standard steps (compile, preverify, build the JAD file, write the corresponding JAR), and as you might imagine, other people have already written Ant tasks for all of this. So after installing Ant, the next step for an MIDP project is to download and install a JAR of Java ME–specific build tasks such as those provided by Antenna (http://antenna.sourceforge.net/).

All you really need to do to install Antenna is download the JAR file and drop it into your Ant lib directory. Then the Antenna Home overview page gives you all the details about what Ant tasks are available and describes the corresponding properties and attributes you need to set. If you download the source code as well, it comes with some sample demo build files that are designed to work with example programs in the WTK to get you started.

Running Your Game on an Actual Cell Phone

The emulator is a helpful development tool, but even though it works well, it's no substitute for testing your game on an actual device. Plus, playing your game on your own cell phone is the fun part! The idea of how to load the file onto the phone is pretty simple, but you need to be aware of a few details.

You have two ways to proceed. The first is to transfer files from your PC using a serial/ Universal Serial Bus (USB) cable or an infrared connection or Bluetooth. This option doesn't require the data to even leave your house. The second option is more exciting. It consists of placing the required files on a server on the Internet and downloading them using a data connection from the phone—using Global System for Mobile Communications/General Packet Radio Service (GSM/GPRS).

Both methods have advantages. The first method doesn't require you to make a call from the phone and is therefore completely free (except for the cost of the cable if one isn't included with the phone). Also, since the transfer takes place entirely within your own network (generally behind your firewall), there's no danger of your game being downloaded by unauthorized users. But this technique can place additional requirements on your local system. For example, in the case of Nokia, the software that's used to perform the transfer works only on Windows, and the PC that the data is being loaded from must have an infrared port or a separate USB cable.

The second method, placing the games on a Wireless Application Protocol (WAP)–accessible web page, is clearly preferable if you intend to distribute the game yourself—even if you're distributing it only to your friends. After all, if you set it up so that you can download your game off the Internet, you can tell other people where it is and they can download it as well. For this option you need to be sure that your phone service contract includes WAP access and application downloading. (This is a typical option that's offered with a Java-enabled phone, so the salesperson who sells you the phone will probably suggest it to you before you even have to ask about it.) You'll also need a server on which to place the files. This shouldn't be too difficult to come by since most Internet service providers (ISPs) offer some personal web space with standard Internet access contracts. All additional software needed for this means of data transfer exists in free versions for all platforms.

In this book I'll cover only how to transfer your games to the device through the Internet and not through direct file transfer because transferring the files directly is vendor dependent. If you'd like to transfer the files to your phone directly, the first step is to go to the web site of the phone's manufacturer. In the case of Nokia, for example, the necessary software is easy to find on the site and is well documented. The same should be true of most other makers of CLDC devices.

Using WAP

WAP is the protocol that small devices use to access the Internet. The principle of WAP is that your cell-phone provider makes available a gateway through which your phone can access the Internet. Since small screens make standard browser functions and standard HTML pages unusable on low-end devices, there's another markup language specially designed for cell phones and other small devices called Wireless Markup Language (WML). If your phone contract specifies WAP access and doesn't restrict browsing to some specific portal and sites, you can direct your phone to a WML page listing your MIDlets. From there you can download them. This is similar to a standard HTML web page embedding a Java applet. Many MIDP handsets are capable of loading simple HTML pages, but since the principle is the same, I'll give a WML page as an example. For an example of a corresponding HTML page for MIDlet download, look no further than your project's bin directory, where KToolbar generates an HTML page to go with the JAR and JAD it builds.

To prepare your games for download, you first need to upload them onto a web server. You need to place the WML file on the server as well as the JAR and JAD files. In addition, you may have to perform some configuration so that the web server, when accessed, returns a correct Multipurpose Internet Mail Extensions (MIME) type description for those files. Otherwise, the phone may be unable to recognize them. The following sections explain these steps in detail using the Nokia 6100 as the example phone.

Preparing the WML File

You can use WML to display interesting content by itself, offering user interface (UI) elements such as forms, buttons, and so on. But you don't need to do anything fancy to make a page from which your game can be downloaded. In fact, it's better to resist the temptation to make a complex WML page because of the screen limitations of the target device. Try to keep it small and simple. Listing 1-4 shows a minimal example suitable for a download page. The file is called hello.wml.

Listing 1-4. *hello.wml*

```
<?xml version="1.0"?>
<!DOCTYPE wml PUBLIC "-//WAPFORUM//DTD WML 1.1//EN"
  "http://www.WAPforum.org/DTD/wml_1.1.xml">
<wml>
<card id="hello">
<p>
Hello world!
</p>
<p>
<a href="hello.jad">Hello World App</a>
</p>
</card>
</wml>
```

Here's how it works: The first two lines are mandatory to identify the file as WML. The content of the page must be enclosed between the <wml> opening tag and the </wml> closing tag. The <card> tag delimits one screen of data for the device (not much!). As you may guess if you know some HTML or Extensible Markup Language (XML), this page will display one line containing the text *Hello world!* and another line with a link with the text *Hello World App*, as shown in Figure 1-5.

Figure 1-5. *The hello.wml WAP page running on the Nokia 6100*

For this link to work, the server directory containing the file hello.wml must contain a JAR file called hello.jar and a JAD file called hello.jad.

The page can contain multiple game links, and you add them in the obvious way. For example, inside the enclosing <card> tags, you could add a second triple such as the following:

```
<p>
<a href="maze.jad">Amazing Maze!</a>
</p>
```

on the lines immediately following these lines:

```
<p>
<a href="hello.jad">Hello World App</a>
</p>
```

(Obviously, you must also upload the corresponding JAR and JAD files to the server for this link.) But if you have a large number of downloadable JAR files, you'll probably want to arrange them on a series of separate pages. If you have multiple versions of the same game suite that are optimized for different devices, it's a good idea to make a separate WML page for each device rather than making a page for each game suite and having the page contain the versions for multiple devices. The standard technique for a professional game is to configure the server to return the page with links to the appropriate game versions based on the "user-agent" header sent by the handset when requesting the page (see the "Identifying the Platform" sidebar in Chapter 10).

One word of warning: The <p></p> tags enclosing the links in the previous files aren't optional. In the case of the Nokia 6100, the device failed to recognize the links without the <p></p> tags.

Configuring the Server

MIDP specifies a particular protocol for downloading and installing MIDlets called Over the Air (OTA) provisioning. The protocol requires that the handset first download the JAD file (and do some checking to see if the MIDlet can be installed and if it's replacing another MIDlet) and then download the JAR file and—after some security checks to make sure it conforms to the JAD description—install the MIDlet. Fortunately, the protocol was designed in such a way that any ordinary HTTP server can be used without any special configuration except to be sure that the appropriate file types are recognized. Many web servers aren't configured by default to recognize the file types associated with WAP/WML/Java ME by the file extensions. If you're lucky, just uploading the files (described in the previous section) to a directory in the public area of the server will be sufficient. If you're not, the cell phone will complain that the files are in an unrecognized format (even though the JAD file is just text . . .). If you run into this problem, you'll need to do a little bit of server configuration. I'll explain what to do in the case of the popular Apache server.

If the Apache server is running on your own machine—which is a convenient option if you have cable or Asymmetric Digital Subscriber Line (ADSL)—all you need to do is update the `httpd.conf` file. (On Red Hat 9, this file is located in `/etc/httpd/conf/httpd.conf`.) Just add the following lines to the file:

```
#### WAP/WML/JAD
##
AddType text/vnd.wap.wml wml
AddType text/vnd.wap.wmlscript wmls
AddType application/vnd.wap.wmlc wmlc
AddType application/vnd.wap.wmlscriptc wmlsc
AddType image/vnd.wap.wbmp wbmp
AddType text/vnd.sun.j2me.app-descriptor jad
AddType application/java jar
####
```

Then you must restart the server to make this information available. On Red Hat 9 you can restart the server by typing the following command as root:

```
# service httpd restart
```

If the web server you're using belongs to your ISP, first check if the server is already configured to recognize the required types. (To check, create the page and then try to access it with your cell phone as described in the following section.) If you're using web space made available by the cell-phone provider, then there's a high probability that the ISP has already taken care of the proper configuration.

If the server hasn't been configured correctly, you may be able to fix it yourself. Here's what to do if your ISP uses an Apache server (other servers may have similar tricks that you can find by consulting the documentation or Google): you won't be allowed to change the main configuration file, but you can inform Apache of the correct MIME types by placing the same lines as previously in a file called `.htaccess` somewhere in your web space area. (Note that you must put such a file in every directory in which you place WAP/WML/J2ME files.) Here's the file `.htaccess`:

```
#### WAP/WML/JAD
##
AddType text/vnd.wap.wml wml
AddType text/vnd.wap.wmlscript wmls
AddType application/vnd.wap.wmlc wmlc
AddType application/vnd.wap.wmlscriptc wmlsc
AddType image/vnd.wap.wbmp wbmp
AddType text/vnd.sun.j2me.app-descriptor jad
```

```
AddType application/java jar
####
```

Of course, you can't ask the ISP to restart its server, but it isn't necessary because Apache will notice the new file automatically. It's possible that the main configuration (which you don't control) forbids this type of user-directed overriding. In that case, you'll have to ask the ISP to change its policy or use another ISP.

Accessing the WML File and Downloading Applications

Now for the fun part: downloading the games onto the phone! Recall that in this section I'll use the Nokia 6100 as an example. This is a typical MIDP 1 CLDC-enabled phone, but it works the same as later model devices.

Remember, you need WAP access as mentioned previously. Be sure to check the costs involved in your contract with WAP connections. For friends who simply download your games and keep them in their phones, this is unlikely to be expensive since `MIDlets` are quite small and the time required for downloading them will rarely exceed a single minute. For the developer, however (that's you!), it's best to get a contract that has a fixed price with unlimited WAP usage since you'll certainly have to perform this operation a number of times (unless you're placing your games on your phone using a direct PC connection during the development phase).

Before you start, you must verify that the WAP access is configured on the phone. This should have been done when you got the phone, or you should have documentation from your phone service and WAP provider giving the details. In my case, I configured the phone by going to a particular web site and giving the phone number and a PIN code. The server then sent a Short Message Service (SMS) message containing all required information to the phone, which responded by prompting me through the procedure of entering the correct settings. On the Nokia phone you can view or edit the settings by pressing the Menu softkey and then selecting Services ➤ Settings ➤ Edit Active Service Settings.

You can then connect to the `hello.wml` page by selecting Services ➤ Go To and typing the URL just as you would for a regular web page. So, for example, if your domain name is `frog-parrot.net`, you'd type `http://frog-parrot.net/hello.wml` if the `hello.wml` file is in the top-level directory. (If your `hello.wml` is in a subdirectory, add the names of the subdirectories to the URL just as you would for any other URL.)

If you're using your own server at home and connecting through cable or ADSL, then you may not have a nice domain name, but you should still have an Internet Protocol (IP) address to which the phone can connect. Depending on how your connection works, your IP address may change from time to time. The operating system will tell you what your current IP address is. In the case of Linux you can find out by looking for the `inet addr` in the output you get from typing the following command:

```
$ /sbin/ifconfig ppp0
```

If your address is just a set of numbers, it still works perfectly well in the URL. Suppose, for example, that you entered the previous command and you got the following output:

```
ppp0      Link encap:Point-to-Point Protocol
          inet addr:81.49.195.43  P-t-P:193.253.160.3  Mask:255.255.255.255
          UP POINTOPOINT RUNNING NOARP MULTICAST  MTU:1492  Metric:1
          RX packets:1108 errors:0 dropped:0 overruns:0 frame:0
```

```
TX packets:1097 errors:0 dropped:0 overruns:0 carrier:0
collisions:0 txqueuelen:3
RX bytes:798514 (779.7 Kb)  TX bytes:98348 (96.0 Kb)
```

In this case, the URL to enter into your phone is `http://81.49.195.43/hello.wml`.

Merely typing the URL into the phone can be tricky! In the case of the Nokia 6100 you can get a list of symbols by hitting the asterisk+plus key (*+). Navigate through this list using the right and left arrow keys until you find the desired symbol (such as . or / for a URL), and then select Use. Fortunately, the fact that the period (.) is the default symbol may save you a little effort. If you have a fixed IP address or domain name, you can also save yourself some typing by making a bookmark to your page.

Once the URL is entered, click OK, and the phone should open your WML page! From here you can click the link to your game, and your phone will download and install it.

So you can see that it's easy to get started developing MIDP games and even to get them up and running on your handset. Just download and install the free development toolkit, build a demo and upload it with a few simple files to a web site, then play!

MAKING IMAGE FILES

If you're wondering where all the image files in this book came from, I drew them myself with a free program called *the gimp*, which you can download from `http://www.gimp.org/downloads`. If you decide to draw your image files with the gimp and you'd like them to have transparent backgrounds, be sure to select a transparent background when you first create a new image file. Transparency can be added later, but it's simpler to have it from the beginning. (A transparent background is nice for game objects because you don't want the rectangular frame of one game object obscuring another game object.) Then when you're done with the image, select the transparent part and choose Filters ➤ Colors ➤ Color to Alpha so that the transparency will be correctly recognized; also, make sure you select Save Background Color when you save the file. You should save it with the `.png` extension so that the gimp will save it in the right format to be used by a J2ME game. One thing to keep in mind when making images is that the difference in screen size from one device to another is the factor that's likely to break your game most dramatically when you try to port it from one device to another. With very small screens, every pixel counts, so a screen size difference that seems insignificant can translate to a major problem for a game. To make your game more portable, you should of course avoid using hard-coded numerical values when drawing the graphics. Additionally, it helps to make different versions of your images in different sizes. If you have only a few image files, it's probably OK to have the game dynamically choose which images to use based on screen calculations, but if you have quite a number of image files, it's usually preferable to maintain different versions of the game's JAR file for different devices. Graphics in the PNG format tend to be pretty small, but they can add up quickly and therefore significantly impact the size of your JAR. This type of optimization is covered in detail in Chapter 10.

Summary

In this chapter you've seen how Java Micro Edition works, how it's implemented, and where it fits in the Java universe. Then we've covered what you need to do in order to set up your development environment and to write an actual program and get it installed and running on your handset. Now that you've finished these steps, you're ready to write some real games!

CHAPTER 2

■■■

Using MIDlets

Applications written for the Mobile Internet Device Profile (MIDP) are called MIDlets. This chapter shows you how to develop a MIDlet and places a special emphasis on how to use the graphical user interface (GUI) elements. Even if you've never written a Java GUI before, you don't have to worry about anything. It's simple. In fact, the javax.microedition.lcdui package is a good place to start learning GUI programming because the package is so limited. Yet it contains the same core elements as Standard Edition Java GUI packages such as the java.awt and javax.swing packages, so once you've written a few micro-edition GUIs, you can apply the same ideas and switch to writing Standard Edition GUIs pretty easily.

This chapter's example MIDlet will be a simple maze game that has a size preferences screen that the user can access to modify the maze's size. Figure 2-1 shows this project open in KToolbar and running on the emulator. This example game will illustrate simple MIDlet concepts such as buttons, menus, changing screens, forms, and simple graphics, as well as describe the MIDlet lifecycle and highlight some differences between Java Micro Edition (Java ME) programming and programming for the other two main Java editions (Standard and Enterprise).

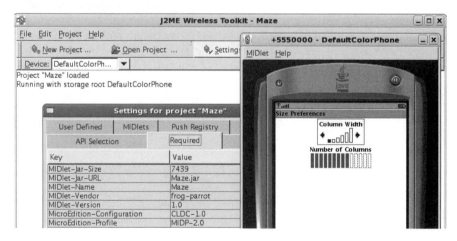

Figure 2-1. *A MIDlet running on the WTK emulator with KToolbar*

Using the MIDlet Class

Your starting point when developing a MIDlet will be to extend the MIDlet class. The MIDlet class is primarily concerned with controlling the application's lifecycle: starting, stopping, and pausing. It also provides the developer with a handle to the device's display so that you can control what appears on the screen.

Understanding the MIDlet Lifecycle

Just as Standard Edition Java GUI packages help you understand Java ME GUI writing, your knowledge of Applets will help you grasp MIDlets easily. (Or vice versa—once you've learned how MIDlets work, you'll discover that you understand Applets, too.) The parallels are striking. Applets and MIDlets are both run by *application management software* that acts as a layer of protection between the (possibly untrusted) Applet or MIDlet and the target Java Virtual Machine (JVM). For Applets, the application management software is generally a browser. In both cases the application management software performs the same role: it controls the Applet or MIDlet's lifecycle, and it provides a sandbox for the Applet or MIDlet to run in that limits access to resources. And in both cases, the program's starting point isn't the public static void main(String[] args) method. An Applet starts with the start() method, and a MIDlet starts with the startApp() method.

After the application management software calls startApp(), it has a couple more methods it uses to control the MIDlet's lifecycle: pauseApp() and destroyApp(). Both of these are signals that the MIDlet needs to free up shared resources, such as input/output (IO) connections, so other applications can use them. You should think of pauseApp() as the method the application management software will call when the user temporarily switches to using another function on the device but wants to go back to your game later. destroyApp() is, of course, the signal that the user is quitting your program. If you disagree with the application management software's decision to start or destroy your MIDlet, you can throw a MIDletStateChangeException to stop it. Bear in mind that if destroyApp() is called with the unconditional argument set to true, your MIDletStateChangeException will be ignored. Since the MIDletStateChangeException is something thrown by the MIDlet developer's code, you can safely ignore any MIDletStateChangeException in a try/catch block (as I've done in Listing 2-1) if you're certain that no such Exception will be thrown.

Listing 2-1. *Maze.java*

```
package net.frog_parrot.maze;

import javax.microedition.midlet.*;
import javax.microedition.lcdui.*;

/**
 * This is the main class of the maze game.
 *
 * @author Carol Hamer
 */
public class Maze extends MIDlet implements CommandListener {

  //-------------------------------------------------------------------
```

```
//  game object fields

/**
 * The canvas that the maze is drawn on.
 */
private MazeCanvas myCanvas;

/**
 * The screen that allows the user to alter the size parameters
 * of the maze.
 */
private SelectScreen mySelectScreen;

//-------------------------------------------------------------------
//  command fields

/**
 * The button to exit the game.
 */
private Command myExitCommand = new Command("Exit", Command.EXIT, 99);

/**
 * The command to create a new maze.  (This command may appear in a menu.)
 */
private Command myNewCommand = new Command("New Maze", Command.SCREEN, 1);

/**
 * The command to dismiss an alert error message.  In MIDP 2.0
 * an Alert set to Alert.FOREVER automatically has a default
 * dismiss command.  This program does not use it in order to
 * allow backward compatibility.
 */
private Command myAlertDoneCommand = new Command("Done", Command.EXIT, 1);

/**
 * The command to go to the screen that allows the user
 * to alter the size parameters.  (This command may appear in a menu)
 */
private Command myPrefsCommand
  = new Command("Size Preferences", Command.SCREEN, 1);

//-------------------------------------------------------------------
//  initialization

/**
 *Empty constructor.
 */
```

```
public Maze() {

}

//-------------------------------------------------------------------
//  implementation of MIDlet

/**
 * Initialize the canvas and the commands and start the application.
 */
public void startApp() throws MIDletStateChangeException {
  try {
    myCanvas = new MazeCanvas(Display.getDisplay(this));
    myCanvas.addCommand(myExitCommand);
    myCanvas.addCommand(myNewCommand);
    myCanvas.addCommand(myPrefsCommand);
    myCanvas.setCommandListener(this);
    myCanvas.start();
  } catch(Exception e) {
    // if there's an error during creation, display it as an alert.
    Alert errorAlert = new Alert("error",
                                 e.getMessage(), null, AlertType.ERROR);
    errorAlert.setCommandListener(this);
    errorAlert.setTimeout(Alert.FOREVER);
    errorAlert.addCommand(myAlertDoneCommand);
    Display.getDisplay(this).setCurrent(errorAlert);
  }

}

/**
 * Clean up.
 */
public void destroyApp(boolean unconditional)
    throws MIDletStateChangeException {
  myCanvas = null;
  System.gc();
}

/**
 * Does nothing since this program occupies no shared resources
 * and little memory.
 */
public void pauseApp() {
}

//-------------------------------------------------------------------
```

```
//  implementation of CommandListener

/*
 * Respond to a command issued on the Canvas.
 * (reset, exit, or change size prefs).
 */
public void commandAction(Command c, Displayable s) {
  if(c == myNewCommand) {
    myCanvas.newMaze();
  } else if(c == myAlertDoneCommand) {
    try {
      destroyApp(false);
      notifyDestroyed();
    } catch (MIDletStateChangeException ex) {
    }
  } else if(c == myPrefsCommand) {
    if(mySelectScreen == null) {
      mySelectScreen = new SelectScreen(myCanvas);
    }
    Display.getDisplay(this).setCurrent(mySelectScreen);
  } else if(c == myExitCommand) {
    try {
      destroyApp(false);
      notifyDestroyed();
    } catch (MIDletStateChangeException ex) {
    }
  }
}

}
```

There's a strange lack-of-parallel to be aware of surrounding the pauseApp() method: while the AMS calls separate methods for when the MIDlet is paused and when it is destroyed, upon returning from a pause it calls exactly the same method—startApp()—as it calls at the very beginning. Since you almost always perform different actions at startup than you would when resuming a game in course, a typical MIDlet maintains a field to keep track of whether or not the game has been started once.

Incidentally, the application management software is allowed to move your application to run in the background at any time without necessarily calling pauseApp(). In such a case, your program would still be running, but it would no longer have control of the screen and also wouldn't receive signals from the buttons. You can find out whether this has happened by calling the isShown() method of your MIDlet's current Displayable or implementing the hideNotify() method if your Displayable is a Canvas (the following section describes the Displayable class). You may expect that you don't need to worry about being sent to the background since a game isn't the sort of program that would be asked to perform its calculations in the background without pausing. But it can certainly happen, especially if your game itself has a set of commands grouped in a menu (see Figure 2-2). When the menu pops up, your program no longer controls the screen, so the game may appear to the user to be paused even though it's still running in the background! If your game is one that performs tasks (such as running a timer) even when the user isn't interacting with it, then you should probably implement the method hideNotify() and have it pause the game. Of course, if the user can pause the game but it can also be paused automatically when hidden, there's a little bit of extra work to do to in the showNotify() method to decide whether the game needs to be unpaused. Also, some handsets call showNotify() when returning from an incoming call, so if the game is one where every second counts, you need to be careful to have the game stay paused until the user is ready to start playing again after finishing a call. The section "Strategies for Deciding When to Use a New Thread" in Chapter 4 contains an example of how to deal with this.

Figure 2-2. *The AMS controls the screen when the command menu is active.*

Listing 2-1 gives some indication of what may be placed in the destroyApp() method. For this game, I put nothing in the pauseApp() method since the program does nothing if the user isn't actively directing the player dot through the maze. This example is simple enough that it has no shared resources that it needs to let go of, but it's occupying memory (which is valuable on a small device!), so it's a good idea to set your MIDlet's object references to null so that any objects your game was using can be garbage collected. Note that calling notifyDestroyed() returns control of the device to the application management software, but it doesn't necessarily cause the JVM to exit (unless the user explicitly stops the Java functions and/or turns the device off). So, particular classes that were loaded by your MIDlet will remain in memory even after your game is done. It's especially important to keep this in mind when using static fields because they may retain their values from one run to the next, and they occupy space in memory when they're no longer in use.

Using the Displayable and Display Classes

Every MIDlet that displays something on the screen has a currently active instance of the Displayable class. It's the object that represents what's currently on the screen. This example game has two Displayable objects. The screen that the maze is drawn on is a subclass of Canvas (which in turn is a subclass of Displayable), and the screen that allows the user to modify the size parameters of the maze is a subclass of Form (which is also a subclass of Displayable through the intermediate subclass Screen). You set the current Displayable by calling setCurrent() on the MIDlet's unique instance of Display. If the Displayable is a Canvas, the call to setCurrent() typically calls the paint() method, so be sure the data of the Canvas is ready before calling this.

The MIDlet's instance of Display is created for you. It manages the display and input devices (buttons) of the hardware. You can get a handle to it by sending your MIDlet instance as an argument to the static method Display.getDisplay(). The setCurrent() method is probably the most important method in this class, but you can do other fun things with this class, such as making the device flash its backlight or vibrate (if the device is capable of doing such things, of course). The Display class is also where you find the isColor() and numColors() methods, which are important if you'd like to write one program that will run on devices with various screen limitations. Yet another useful method is the setCurrentItem() method, which sets the input focus to the requested Item on a Form, first setting the Item's Form to the current Displayable and scrolling to the Item if necessary.

MIDP 1 and 2 assume that the device has only one display, but MIDP 3 allows MIDlets to draw on multiple displays such as the external screen on a clamshell phone. The Display.getDisplay() method still behaves the same way (returning the primary Display), but the MIDlet can find out about other available Displays using Display.getDisplays(). A MIDlet can query each Display for its capabilities and can use setCurrent() to set a Displayable for each Display. The setCurrent() method acts essentially as a request for the AMS to place the MIDlet's chosen Displayable in the foreground for a given Display, and the MIDlet can use the Displayable.isShown() method to find out whether the AMS honored the request. The AMS can move a MIDlet to the background on one Display and to the foreground on another at will, so in MIDP 3, you have more to keep track of to determine whether your MIDlet has been moved completely to the background.

Notice that the example class in Listing 2-1 contains an Alert, which is another subclass of Displayable:

```
} catch(Exception e) {
    // if there's an error during creation, display it as an alert.
    Alert errorAlert = new Alert("error",
                                 e.getMessage(), null, AlertType.ERROR);
    errorAlert.setCommandListener(this);
    errorAlert.setTimeout(Alert.FOREVER);
    errorAlert.addCommand(myAlertDoneCommand);
    Display.getDisplay(this).setCurrent(errorAlert);
}
```

An Alert is a temporary screen that's meant to give the user a punctual message, sort of like a Dialog, except that it takes up the whole screen. In the example program, the Alert is there to warn the user that the screen is too small to create a reasonable maze (although in reality the screen would have to be *extremely* small for this program to refuse to draw a maze on it— smaller than the minimum required size for devices that are compliant with Connected Limited Device Configuration (CLDC). Like other Displayable subclasses, an Alert is displayed by calling setCurrent(). It remains for a fixed period of time (or needs to be dismissed by the user depending on how you construct it), and then the previous Displayable or another Displayable of your choice becomes current. In this case, where I create an error Alert, I call setCommandListener() to set my MIDlet as a command listener for the Alert, and then I deal with the Command myAlertDoneCommand in my implementation of commandAction():

```
  } else if(c == myAlertDoneCommand) {
    try {
      destroyApp(false);
      notifyDestroyed();
    } catch (MIDletStateChangeException ex) {
    }
  } else if(c == myPrefsCommand) {
```

When you create an Alert in MIDP 2.0 and set its timeout to Alert.FOREVER, the Alert automatically contains a Done Command, which corresponds to the default Command Alert.DISMISS_COMMAND. With the default dismiss command, when the user clicks the Done button, the previous Displayable becomes current (or another Displayable of your choice becomes current if you constructed the Alert with a Displayable as an argument). Therefore, it isn't usually necessary to listen for the Alert's dismiss command. However, in this case, I added my own dismiss command for two reasons: First, I'd like this game to be compatible with MIDP 1.0.4, in which the field Alert.DISMISS_COMMAND doesn't exist. Second, if the screen is really the wrong size for the game, I'd like the game to end when the Alert is done rather than just going to another Displayable. But I can't just end the game right after calling Display.getDisplay(this).setCurrent(errorAlert) because that method returns immediately after setting the current display and doesn't wait for the user to be done with the Alert. So, if I end the application immediately after setting the Alert to the current Displayable, it appears for only a split second and then disappears. Instead I listen for my custom Done Command and end the game when the command has been activated. It's a bit of a technical point, and some professional game developers avoid using Alerts because they don't simplify the code much compared to the potential confusion caused by their special behavior.

Using Buttons and Menus

Although the GUI functionality is contained in the javax.microedition.lcdui package, I've organized things by placing some of the main buttons in my MIDlet subclass (called Maze in this example) because the functions of these buttons relate to my MIDlet's lifecycle.

Looking at the Maze class in Listing 2-1, you'll notice that buttons and menu items are instances of javax.microedition.lcdui.Command. There's no Button class and no MenuItem class. This is because your target screen and button configurations vary so much from device to device that it doesn't make sense to have the MIDlet developer decide which commands should be placed in buttons and which should be placed in menus. That's the theory anyway—in practice you generally have to produce different versions of a game for different device groups with different capabilities, so it's common to customize the GUI for different devices as well (see Chapter 10). However, it's good to try to keep the application as portable as possible, and the system of using Command objects that the platform can map to a softkey or a stylus touch or whatever makes it easy to write a GUI that works well on devices with vastly different screen configurations. So you just create a Command object and give the device a bit of information about the Command, and the device does the work of arranging your Commands for you. This is great news for those of you (like me) who would rather go straight to designing the game instead of spending hours or days working out all the intricate ergonomic details of the perfect GUI. The trade-off is, of course, that you're limited in what you can do, but a lot of MIDP devices have limited capabilities anyway, so it's nice that the code is correspondingly simple.

The last two arguments of the constructor give the extra information that the Command object needs in order to decide where it's to be placed. These arguments are the commandType and the priority. The commandType should be a static field code such as Command.BACK or Command.HELP that allows standard types of commands to be mapped to their usual buttons on the device. If you add a Command that isn't one of the standard types provided, then the commandType should be Command.SCREEN. The implementation of the priority argument may vary some from device to device, but in general those commands that have higher priority (indicated by a lower priority value) will be more easily accessible to the user. In Listing 2-1, the Exit command has been given a priority of 99, which means that this command is quite unimportant, whereas the commands New Maze and Size Preferences are both given priority 1. Yet if you run this program in the emulator, you'll see that the Exit command gets its own button whereas the other two commands are hidden away in a menu (see Figure 2-2). How can this be? It's because there's a particular button that the emulator assigns to the Command of type Command.EXIT, so the Exit command was mapped to that one. The Commands of type Command.SCREEN had to fight over what was left.

Then, to respond to the commands, you must implement the interface javax.microedition. lcdui.CommandListener. When the user selects a Command, the application management software calls the CommandListener's commandAction() method. There are two differences between this interface and other GUI listeners such as java.awt.event.ActionListener. First, all the Commands that have been added to a given instance of javax.microedition.lcdui.Displayable have the same CommandListener instead of making every Button and other command element have their own list of ActionListeners. (You associate the CommandListener with a Displayable by calling the Displayable's setCommandListener() method.) Second, when the CommandListener is notified, it receives only a handle to the Command and the corresponding Displayable instead of having the JVM create a separate Event object. As usual, these are memory-saving simplifications that should probably cause you little inconvenience, if any.

Using the Form and Item Classes

The Form class is the subclass of Displayable to use when you want to create a simple GUI screen. (For a professional game you would typically create a custom GUI—see Chapter 10—but for a basic game, the Form and Item classes are easier to use.) The GUI items you place on it are of class Item. Since some target devices may have small screens, you should probably put only a few Items on any one Form. You can put an arbitrary number of Items on a Form, but if you fill it with too many Items, the device may have to make your Form scrollable or fold it into subscreens to fit everything. A multiline TextBox naturally appears alone on the screen because it's a subclass of Screen instead of being an Item that can be placed on a Form.

Since your Form contains only a few Items anyway, you can just append() them to the Form and trust the application management software to lay them out appropriately. But if you have some definite ideas about where you'd like the Items to appear, you can call setLayout() on each Item with one of the static fields of Item, such as LAYOUT_CENTER. Even with layout directives, however, the platform has the final say in where each item is placed, so the same layout will look different on different devices (see Figure 2-3). Also be aware that an Item has only one layout int field, so if you'd like to combine two or more layout directives on your Item, you should call setLayout() only once and combine your layout directives in the argument using the or (|) operator (for example, setLayout(LAYOUT_RIGHT | LAYOUT_VCENTER)). This same use of the or operator appears in the drawString() method of the Graphics class described in the "Using the Graphics and Canvas Classes" section later in this chapter. Also keep in mind that the method setLayout() is new for MIDP 2, so if your program doesn't require MIDP 2 for anything else, you should probably not bother with this method in order to allow backward compatibility.

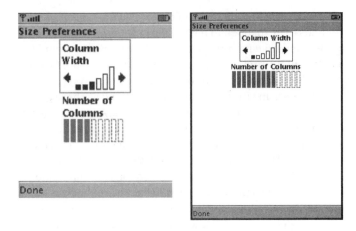

Figure 2-3. *The form that controls the Maze game's preferences as it appears on two different emulators.*

In my example game, the Items I've placed on my Form are both of type Gauge. A Gauge is a convenient Item to use when your target device is a cell phone because it allows the user to increase or decrease a numerical value merely by pressing the arrow keys rather than having to enter something. The corresponding value is represented graphically. In this case, I've placed two related Gauges on the same Form, and I've set the layout for each one to LAYOUT_CENTER. The first one allows the user to modify the width of the maze walls, and the second one (which the user can't control) shows the number of columns that the maze will be divided into, given the width of the walls. To test the various layout possibilities, I tried placing the same two Gauges on the Form using the layout directives setLayout(LAYOUT_LEFT | LAYOUT_TOP) and setLayout(LAYOUT_RIGHT | LAYOUT_VCENTER), shown in Figure 2-4.

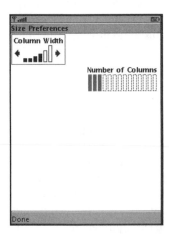

Figure 2-4. *The Form containing the two Gauges, each with custom layout directives*

Once you've placed all of your Items on your Form, you'll need to set an ItemCommandListener on any Item that has a Command of type Command.ITEM associated with it or an ItemStateListener on the whole Form if the Form contains Items into which the user can enter data. Item-specific Commands are new to MIDP 2. You add them to Items using the method Item.addCommand(), and they appear when the user selects the corresponding Item. If the Item is naturally something that the user can modify (such as a TextField or a Gauge), it's generally not necessary to add Item-specific Commands to it. Setting an ItemStateListener should be sufficient, as it's notified with a call to itemStateChanged() when the user makes a change.

Notice that when you add a Command directly to a Form, it will be mapped to a button or menu, as described in the section "Using Buttons and Menus" earlier in this chapter. In the example class in Listing 2-2, this is illustrated by the Done Command, which sets the current Displayable to the MazeCanvas (in other words, it exits the size preferences screen and sends the user to the screen with the maze on it).

Listing 2-2 shows the code for the maze game's Form subclass called SelectScreen.java.

Listing 2-2. *SelectScreen.java*

```
package net.frog_parrot.maze;

import javax.microedition.midlet.*;
import javax.microedition.lcdui.*;

/**
 * This is the screen that allows the user to modify the
 * width of the maze walls.
 *
 * @author Carol Hamer
 */
public class SelectScreen extends Form
  implements ItemStateListener, CommandListener  {

  //-------------------------------------------------------------------
  //  fields

  /**
   * The Done button to exit this screen and return to the maze.
   */
  private Command myExitCommand = new Command("Done", Command.EXIT, 1);

  /**
   * The gauge that modifies the width of the maze walls.
   */
  private Gauge myWidthGauge;
```

```java
/**
 * The gauge that displays the number of columns of the maze.
 */
private Gauge myColumnsGauge;

/**
 * A handle to the main game canvas.
 */
private MazeCanvas myCanvas;

//------------------------------------------------------------------
//  initialization

/**
 * Create the gauges and place them on the screen.
 */
public SelectScreen(MazeCanvas canvas) {
  super("Size Preferences");
  addCommand(myExitCommand);
  setCommandListener(this);
  myCanvas = canvas;
  setItemStateListener(this);
  myWidthGauge = new Gauge("Column Width", true,
                           myCanvas.getMaxColWidth(),
                           myCanvas.getColWidth());
  myColumnsGauge = new Gauge("Number of Columns", false,
                             myCanvas.getMaxNumCols(),
                             myCanvas.getNumCols());
  // Warning: the setLayout method does not exist in
  // MIDP 1.4.  If there is any chance that a target
  // device will be using MIDP 1.4, comment out the
  // following two lines:
  myWidthGauge.setLayout(Item.LAYOUT_CENTER);
  myColumnsGauge.setLayout(Item.LAYOUT_CENTER);
  append(myWidthGauge);
  append(myColumnsGauge);
}

//------------------------------------------------------------------
```

```java
// implementation of ItemStateListener

/**
 * Respond to the user changing the width.
 */
public void itemStateChanged(Item item) {
  if(item == myWidthGauge) {
    int val = myWidthGauge.getValue();
    if(val < myCanvas.getMinColWidth()) {
      myWidthGauge.setValue(myCanvas.getMinColWidth());
    } else {
      int numCols = myCanvas.setColWidth(val);
      myColumnsGauge.setValue(numCols);
    }
  }
}


//-------------------------------------------------------------------
// implementation of CommandListener

/*
 * Respond to a command issued on this screen.
 * (either reset or exit).
 */
public void commandAction(Command c, Displayable s) {
  if(c == myExitCommand) {
    myCanvas.newMaze();
  }
}

}
```

Other types of Items that can be added to a Form include TextFields, ChoiceGroups, and (in MIDP 2) CustomItems. When you place a TextField on a Form, the underlying system provides native support for the user to type in text, possibly providing special functionality so that the user can enter a particular data type such as a password or an e-mail address. A ChoiceGroup is essentially a menu, providing support for familiar types of menu functionality such as EXCLUSIVE (radio buttons) or IMPLICIT (the currently focused item is selected when a command or select key is pressed). A CustomItem allows you to draw anything you want within the CustomItem's region of the screen (in the same way you would draw on a Canvas; see the next section for how to do it) and when the Item is the focused Item on the Form, the CustomItem allows you to respond to keystrokes in the same way you would respond to keystrokes on a Canvas. In fact, a CustomItem is very much like a small Canvas that can be placed on a Form. Similarly, there are corresponding classes for both TextField and ChoiceGroup that allow you to create a menu or text input area that takes up the whole screen rather than being one Item on a Form: TextBox and List. In MIDP 3, you can group all of these different types of GUI screens (Form, TextBox, List, etc.) together in a TabbedPane, thus allowing the user to navigate from one screen to the next by selecting different tabs.

Using the Graphics and Canvas Classes

The Canvas class is the subclass of Displayable that you're really interested in as a game developer since not many games lend themselves to being played on a Form. In Chapter 3, I'll talk about the extra things you can do on a GameCanvas. But a GameCanvas is a subclass of Canvas, and a lot of the important functionality is already here. There's enough to draw a simple game at least, as the example code shows.

The main tasks of the Canvas object are to implement the paint() method, which draws the game on the screen, and to implement the keyPressed() method to respond to the user's keystrokes. Implementing keyPressed() is very straightforward. When the user presses a key, the application management software calls keyPressed(), sending a keyCode as a parameter to indicate which key was pressed. In a game, you then need to translate this keyCode into a gameAction (such as Canvas.UP or Canvas.FIRE) using the method getGameAction(). This translation is necessary for portability because the mapping between keyCodes and gameActions may vary from device to device. Once the method keyPressed() returns, the application management software will call keyRepeated() (if the user is still holding down the key, possibly multiple times) and then keyReleased(). You can also implement these two methods as well if your game is interested in such events. Once the underlying game data has changed, you'll probably want to call repaint() to get the application management software to update the screen with a call to paint().

The Graphics object that the Canvas class receives as an argument carries out most of the work in the paint() method. The Graphics class has four built-in shapes that it can draw: arcs, triangles, rectangles, and round rectangles. It can draw filled shapes or just outlines; it can draw in any Red Green Blue (RGB) value or grayscale color and can use a dotted or solid outline. Using just the built-in shapes, you can already draw quite a lot of things. You'll notice in Listing 2-3 that I drew the maze itself by filling in a series of white and black rectangles, and I drew the player as a red circle by first calling setColor() with the red argument set to its maximum value and then calling fillRoundRect() with the width, height, arcWidth, and arcHeight arguments all set to the same value as each other. Figure 2-5 shows what the maze looks like on the emulator's screen, and Figure 2-6 shows what it looks like on a handset.

Figure 2-5. *The maze on a small device emulator's screen*

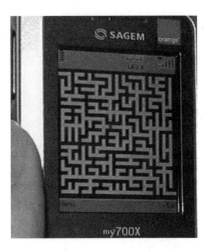

Figure 2-6. *The maze on the Sagem my700x*

Listing 2-3. *MazeCanvas.java*

```
package net.frog_parrot.maze;

import javax.microedition.lcdui.*;

/**
 * This class is the display of the game.
 *
 * @author Carol Hamer
 */
public class MazeCanvas extends javax.microedition.lcdui.Canvas {

  //------------------------------------------------------------
  //   static fields

  /**
   * color constant
   */
  public static final int BLACK = 0;

  /**
   * color constant
   */
  public static final int WHITE = 0xffffff;

  //------------------------------------------------------------
  //   instance fields
```

```
/**
 * a handle to the display.
 */
private Display myDisplay;

/**
 * The data object that describes the maze configuration.
 */
private Grid myGrid;

/**
 * Whether the currently displayed maze has
 * been completed.
 */
private boolean myGameOver = false;

/**
 * maze dimension: the width of the maze walls.
 */
private int mySquareSize;

/**
 * maze dimension: the maximum width possible for the maze walls.
 */
private int myMaxSquareSize;

/**
 * maze dimension: the minimum width possible for the maze walls.
 */
private int myMinSquareSize;

/**
 * top corner of the display: X coordinate
 */
private int myStartX = 0;

/**
 * top corner of the display: Y coordinate
 */
private int myStartY = 0;

/**
 * how many rows the display is divided into.
 */
private int myGridHeight;
```

```java
/**
 * how many columns the display is divided into.
 */
private int myGridWidth;

/**
 * the maximum number columns the display can be divided into.
 */
private int myMaxGridWidth;

/**
 * the minimum number columns the display can be divided into.
 */
private int myMinGridWidth;

/**
 * previous location of the player in the maze: X coordinate
 * (in terms of the coordinates of the maze grid, NOT in terms
 * of the coordinate system of the Canvas.)
 */
private int myOldX = 1;

/**
 * previous location of the player in the maze: Y coordinate
 * (in terms of the coordinates of the maze grid, NOT in terms
 * of the coordinate system of the Canvas.)
 */
private int myOldY = 1;

/**
 * current location of the player in the maze: X coordinate
 * (in terms of the coordinates of the maze grid, NOT in terms
 * of the coordinate system of the Canvas.)
 */
private int myPlayerX = 1;

/**
 * current location of the player in the maze: Y coordinate
 * (in terms of the coordinates of the maze grid, NOT in terms
 * of the coordinate system of the Canvas.)
 */
private int myPlayerY = 1;

//--------------------------------------------------------
//    gets / sets
```

```java
/**
 * Changes the width of the maze walls and calculates how
 * this change affects the number of rows and columns
 * the maze can have.
 * @return the number of columns now that the
 *         width of the columns has been updated.
 */
int setColWidth(int colWidth) {
  if(colWidth < 2) {
    mySquareSize = 2;
  } else {
    mySquareSize = colWidth;
  }
  myGridWidth = getWidth() / mySquareSize;
   if((myGridWidth & 0x1) == 0) {
    myGridWidth -= 1;
  }
  myGridHeight = getHeight() / mySquareSize;
   if((myGridHeight & 0x1) == 0) {
    myGridHeight -= 1;
  }
  myGrid = null;
  return(myGridWidth);
}

/**
 * @return the minimum width possible for the maze walls.
 */
int getMinColWidth() {
  return(myMinSquareSize);
}

/**
 * @return the maximum width possible for the maze walls.
 */
int getMaxColWidth() {
  return(myMaxSquareSize);
}

/**
 * @return the maximum number of columns the display can be divided into.
 */
int getMaxNumCols() {
  return(myMaxGridWidth);
}
```

```
/**
 * @return the width of the maze walls.
 */
int getColWidth() {
  return(mySquareSize);
}

/**
 * @return the number of maze columns the display is divided into.
 */
int getNumCols() {
  return(myGridWidth);
}

//--------------------------------------------------------
//     initialization and game state changes

/**
 * Constructor performs size calculations.
 * @throws Exception if the display size is too
 *          small to make a maze.
 */
public MazeCanvas(Display d) throws Exception {
  myDisplay = d;
  // a few calculations to make the right maze
  // for the current display.
  int width = getWidth();
  int height = getHeight();
  // tests indicate that 5 is a good default square size,
  // but the user can change it...
  mySquareSize = 5;
  myMinSquareSize = 3;
  myMaxGridWidth = width / myMinSquareSize;
  if((myMaxGridWidth & 0x1) == 0) {
    myMaxGridWidth -= 1;
  }
  myGridWidth = width / mySquareSize;
  // the grid width must be odd for the maze-generation
  // algorithm to work
  if((myGridWidth & 0x1) == 0) {
    myGridWidth -= 1;
  }
  myGridHeight = height / mySquareSize;
  // the grid height must be odd for the maze-generation
  // algorithm to work
  if((myGridHeight & 0x1) == 0) {
    myGridHeight -= 1;
  }
```

```
        myMinGridWidth = 15;
        myMaxSquareSize = width / myMinGridWidth;
        if(myMaxSquareSize > height / myMinGridWidth) {
          myMaxSquareSize = height / myMinGridWidth;
        }
        // if the display is too small to make a reasonable maze,
        // then you throw an Exception
        if(myMaxSquareSize < mySquareSize) {
          throw(new Exception("Display too small"));
        }
      }

      /**
       * This is called as soon as the application begins.
       */
      void start() {
        myDisplay.setCurrent(this);
        repaint();
      }

      /**
       * discard the current maze and draw a new one.
       */
      void newMaze() {
        myGameOver = false;
        // throw away the current maze.
        myGrid = null;
        // set the player back to the beginning of the maze.
        myPlayerX = 1;
        myPlayerY = 1;
        myOldX = 1;
        myOldY = 1;
        myDisplay.setCurrent(this);
        // paint the new maze
        repaint();
      }

      //----------------------------------------------------------
      //  graphics methods

      /**
       * Create and display a maze if necessary; otherwise just
       * move the player.  Since the motion in this game is
       * very simple, it is not necessary to repaint the whole
       * maze each time, just the player + erase the square
       * that the player just left.
       */
      protected void paint(Graphics g) {
```

```java
// If there is no current maze, create one and draw it.
if(myGrid == null) {
  int width = getWidth();
  int height = getHeight();
  // create the underlying data of the maze.
  myGrid = new Grid(myGridWidth, myGridHeight);
  // draw the maze:
  // loop through the grid data and color each square the
  // right color
  for(int i = 0; i < myGridWidth; i++) {
    for(int j = 0; j < myGridHeight; j++) {
      if(myGrid.mySquares[i][j] == 0) {
        g.setColor(BLACK);
      } else {
        g.setColor(WHITE);
      }
      // fill the square with the appropriate color
      g.fillRect(myStartX + (i*mySquareSize),
                 myStartY + (j*mySquareSize),
                 mySquareSize, mySquareSize);
    }
  }
  // fill the extra space outside of the maze
  g.setColor(BLACK);
  g.fillRect(myStartX + ((myGridWidth-1) * mySquareSize),
             myStartY, width, height);
  // erase the exit path:
  g.setColor(WHITE);
  g.fillRect(myStartX + ((myGridWidth-1) * mySquareSize),
             myStartY + ((myGridHeight-2) * mySquareSize), width, height);
  // fill the extra space outside of the maze
  g.setColor(BLACK);
  g.fillRect(myStartX,
             myStartY + ((myGridHeight-1) * mySquareSize), width, height);
}
// draw the player (red):
g.setColor(255, 0, 0);
g.fillRoundRect(myStartX + (mySquareSize)*myPlayerX,
                myStartY + (mySquareSize)*myPlayerY,
                mySquareSize, mySquareSize,
                mySquareSize, mySquareSize);
// erase the previous location
if((myOldX != myPlayerX) || (myOldY != myPlayerY)) {
  g.setColor(WHITE);
  g.fillRect(myStartX + (mySquareSize)*myOldX,
             myStartY + (mySquareSize)*myOldY,
             mySquareSize, mySquareSize);
}
```

```
      // if the player has reached the end of the maze,
      // you display the end message.
      if(myGameOver) {
        // perform some calculations to place the text correctly:
        int width = getWidth();
        int height = getHeight();
        Font font = g.getFont();
        int fontHeight = font.getHeight();
        int fontWidth = font.stringWidth("Maze Completed");
        g.setColor(WHITE);
        g.fillRect((width - fontWidth)/2, (height - fontHeight)/2,
                        fontWidth + 2, fontHeight);
        // write in red
        g.setColor(255, 0, 0);
        g.setFont(font);
        g.drawString("Maze Completed", (width - fontWidth)/2,
                    (height - fontHeight)/2,
                        g.TOP|g.LEFT);
      }
    }

    /**
     * Move the player.
     */
    public void keyPressed(int keyCode) {
      if(! myGameOver) {
        int action = getGameAction(keyCode);
        switch (action) {
        case LEFT:
          if((myGrid.mySquares[myPlayerX-1][myPlayerY] == 1) &&
            (myPlayerX != 1)) {
            myOldX = myPlayerX;
            myOldY = myPlayerY;
            myPlayerX -= 2;
            repaint();
          }
          break;
        case RIGHT:
          if(myGrid.mySquares[myPlayerX+1][myPlayerY] == 1) {
            myOldX = myPlayerX;
            myOldY = myPlayerY;
            myPlayerX += 2;
            repaint();
          } else if((myPlayerX == myGrid.mySquares.length - 2) &&
                    (myPlayerY == myGrid.mySquares[0].length - 2)) {
            myOldX = myPlayerX;
            myOldY = myPlayerY;
```

```
        myPlayerX += 2;
        myGameOver = true;
        repaint();
      }
      break;
    case UP:
      if(myGrid.mySquares[myPlayerX][myPlayerY-1] == 1) {
        myOldX = myPlayerX;
        myOldY = myPlayerY;
        myPlayerY -= 2;
        repaint();
      }
      break;
    case DOWN:
      if(myGrid.mySquares[myPlayerX][myPlayerY+1] == 1) {
        myOldX = myPlayerX;
        myOldY = myPlayerY;
        myPlayerY += 2;
        repaint();
      }
      break;
    }
  }
}

}
```

If the built-in shapes of the Graphics class aren't sufficient, you can also draw an Image from a file. But if you're planning to use anything more than the simplest graphics, you'll probably want to use the javax.microedition.lcdui.games package described in Chapter 3 because it contains a lot of additional support for using images.

The X and Y coordinates that are used by the various drawing methods of the Graphics class tell how far (in pixels) a given point is from the top-left corner of the Canvas. The Y value increases as you go *down* and not as you go *up*, which confused me a bit because it's the opposite of what I learned in math class, but I got used to it pretty quickly. To find out how much room you have to paint on, use the getHeight() and getWidth() methods of the Canvas. Using the point (0,0) as your top corner and drawing on a rectangle, whose size is given by the getHeight() and getWidth() methods, will automatically ensure that your drawing is correctly placed on the screen. If you'd like to do a larger drawing according to your own choice of coordinates and then specify which region is shown, you can do it with the "clip" methods (setClip(), and so on). But, again, I'd use the javax.microedition.lcdui.games package when doing such a complex graphical operation since the class javax.microedition.lcdui.games.LayerManager has additional support for moving the view window on a larger drawing.

The one method in the Graphics class that's a little tricky is the drawString() method. The tricky part is to figure out which anchor point you'd like to use. (Actually it's rather simple, but it's one point where I found the JavaDoc explanation a little confusing.) The idea is that when you place a String, you may want to place it by specifying where the top-left corner of the String's bounding rectangle should go. Then again, you may not. For example, if you'd like to place the text near the bottom of the screen, it may be easier to place it by specifying where the bottom of the String's bounding rectangle should go. Or perhaps if you'd like the String to be right justified, you'd prefer to place it in terms of the right side of the String's bounding rectangle. So when you draw a String, its position is based on an anchor point within the String's bounding rectangle. You must choose a horizontal component and a vertical component for your anchor point and then combine them using the or operator (for example, BOTTOM|LEFT). The vertical choices are TOP, BASELINE, and BOTTOM, and the horizontal choices are LEFT, HCENTER, and RIGHT.

You'll notice in Listing 2-3 that I've centered the String "Maze Completed" by specifying the anchor point as TOP|LEFT and then placing the top-left corner of the String at the point that's at the center of the screen minus the adjustment value of half of the length and height of the String. The adjustment is needed because I'm placing the top-left corner of the String instead of placing the center of the String. You may be wondering why I didn't set the anchor point to the center point of the String. I could have done that for the horizontal placement but not the vertical placement since VCENTER isn't one of the choices for a String's anchor point. (Incidentally, the method drawImage(), which uses anchor points in the same way to place images, allows the choice of VCENTER instead of BASELINE.) But since I had to calculate the location for the top-left corner of the String anyway (so that I could first paint a blank white rectangle to write the text on), I decided it'd be simpler to use TOP|LEFT as my anchor point. Also, TOP|LEFT is the safest choice for portability—on some handsets there are problems with the implementation of the other choices.

Using the java.util Package

The java.util package is the place where you'll find the standard utility classes for manipulating standard complex data types. If you're used to programming in Java SE or EE, you may not notice that the java.util package that comes with CLDC is any different from the java.util package you already know and love. I found some of my favorite classes there (Vector and Random), and all the methods I wanted to use were in the usual places. You can see how I used some java.util classes in the code in Listing 2-4 a bit later. But beware! Many of the standard java.util classes are simply not there, and the ones that are there are missing some of their functionality.

Fortunately, most of the core classes are there, so even if you don't have a LinkedHashMap, you can probably make do with a Hashtable, and you can probably get around using a StringTokenizer with a little extra programming.

One big difference is that this micro version of the java.util package doesn't contain localization utilities such as Locale and ResourceBundle for internationalization. Localization for small devices is a little more complex because you have only so much space for resources, and you'd be surprised how much space bundles of strings to display can take up. So you don't necessarily want to simply throw in every set of GUI labels for every language from Icelandic to Swahili willy-nilly the way you might with a desktop application. That doesn't mean you shouldn't worry about localizing your labels, though; it just means it's a bit more complicated. There are a few different strategies for localization discussed in Chapter 10. Until then, however, I'll just stick with English labels in the examples for simplicity.

The example class for this section is the class that contains the maze generation algorithm. It illustrates the use of some standard java.util classes such as Vector and Random. The maze algorithm is also an example of how you can make a fun game that's small and simple enough for even a very limited device by using some familiar ideas. There are a whole lot of familiar types of games in the public domain that you can program in MIDP without worrying about running afoul of someone's copyright. In fact, this game is simple enough that it only requires MIDP 1 classes. Figure 2-7 shows the maze game running on a MIDP 1 handset.

Figure 2-7. *The Maze game running on the Nokia 6100*

Here's the basic idea of how the maze algorithm works. Think of the pathways through the maze as being a graph (in the mathematical sense) where a point at which two pathways join or a point where you might turn is a vertex, and then the pathways connecting the vertices are edges. It's clear that for a maze, you want your graph to be one connected tree—in other words, a graph with no cycles. As long as the entry point and the exit point are part of one connected tree, there will be exactly one path from the beginning to the end.

To apply this idea and create the maze, the first step is to use the screen and graphics dimensions to determine the size of your grid of vertices (how many squares across and how many down). In this implementation, I start by dividing the entire playing field into equal-sized squares, which form part of the maze pathways if colored white and part of the maze wall if colored black. There's a lattice of squares that I know should be black and a lattice that I know should be white, and the trick is to figure out which colors to give to the wildcard squares. In Figure 2-8, I've colored gray all of the squares whose color should be decided by the algorithm (note that this screen never appears in the final game). In graph terms, the white squares are the vertices, and the gray squares are the squares that might potentially be edges by being added to the maze pathway and turned white. You can see from this that the number of rows and number of columns both need to be odd numbers. That's why every time the grid size is calculated (see Listing 2-3) there are a few extra lines to make sure the number is odd. You can check whether a number is even or odd by checking the result of using the % operator with 2, but in this example I've done a bitwise & with the byte of value 1 (0 × 1) because the % operator uses division, which is a costly operation.

Figure 2-8. *An illustration showing which squares need to have their color decided by the maze generation algorithm*

The algorithm works by picking one of the white squares at random from the middle of the grid and growing the tree from there by picking undecided (gray) squares and turning them white. Throughout the algorithm, you maintain a list of all of the white squares (vertices) that are not yet connected to the maze but are only one gray square away from being linked in. At each round of the algorithm, you use the randomizer to pick one square from the list and attach it to the maze (by turning a gray square white, hence adding an edge to the graph). Then just keep going until there are no white squares left that aren't connected to the maze pathway graph, and color the remaining gray squares black.

By only adding edges to connect vertices that weren't already connected to the graph, you can see that you'll never get a cycle. And by growing the graph from one central point, you can be sure that all of the vertices will be connected to the same component. So in the end, for every two white squares in the maze there's exactly one path that leads from one to the other. Notably there's a unique path from the entry square to the exit square.

Listing 2-4 shows the code for `Grid.java`. Note there's nothing CLDC-specific about this code—the same class could be compiled using Java SE.

Listing 2-4. *Grid.java*

```
package net.frog_parrot.maze;

import java.util.Random;
import java.util.Vector;

/**
 * This class contains the data necessary to draw the maze.
 *
```

```
 * @author Carol Hamer
 */
public class Grid {

  /**
   * Random number generator to create a random maze.
   */
  private Random myRandom = new Random();

  /**
   * data for which squares are filled and which are blank.
   * 0 = black
   * 1 = white
   * values higher than 1 are used during the maze creation
   * algorithm.
   * 2 = the square could possibly be appended to the maze this round.
   * 3 = the square will be white but is
   * not close enough to be appended to the maze this round.
   */
  int[][] mySquares;

  //--------------------------------------------------------
  //  maze generation methods

  /**
   * Create a new maze.
   */
  public Grid(int width, int height) {
    mySquares = new int[width][height];
    // initialize all the squares to white except a lattice
    // framework of black squares.
    for(int i = 1; i < width - 1; i++) {
      for(int j = 1; j < height - 1; j++) {
        if(((i & 0x1) != 0) || ((j & 0x1) !=0)) {
          mySquares[i][j] = 1;
        }
      }
    }
    // the entrance to the maze is at (0,1).
    mySquares[0][1] = 1;
    createMaze();
  }

  /**
   * This method randomly generates the maze.
   */
  private void createMaze() {
```

```
// create an initial framework of black squares.
for(int i = 1; i < mySquares.length - 1; i++) {
  for(int j = 1; j < mySquares[i].length - 1; j++) {
    if(((i + j) & 0x1) != 0) {
      mySquares[i][j] = 0;
    }
  }
}
// initialize the squares that will be white and act
// as vertices: set the value to 3 which means the
// square has not been connected to the maze tree.
for(int i = 1; i < mySquares.length - 1; i+=2) {
  for(int j = 1; j < mySquares[i].length - 1; j+=2) {
    mySquares[i][j] = 3;
  }
}
// Then those squares that can be selected to be open
// (white) paths are given the value of 2.
// You randomly select the square where the tree of maze
// paths will begin.  The maze is generated starting from
// this initial square and branches out from here in all
// directions to fill the maze grid.
Vector possibleSquares = new Vector(mySquares.length
                                    * mySquares[0].length);
int[] startSquare = new int[2];
startSquare[0] = getRandomInt(mySquares.length / 2)*2 + 1;
startSquare[1] = getRandomInt(mySquares[0].length / 2)*2 + 1;
mySquares[startSquare[0]][startSquare[1]] = 2;
possibleSquares.addElement(startSquare);
// Here you loop to select squares one by one to append to
// the maze pathway tree.
while(possibleSquares.size() > 0) {
  // the next square to be joined on is selected randomly.
  int chosenIndex = getRandomInt(possibleSquares.size());
  int[] chosenSquare = (int[])possibleSquares.elementAt(chosenIndex);
  // you set the chosen square to white and then
  // remove it from the list of possibleSquares (i.e. squares
  // that can possibly be added to the maze), and you link
  // the new square to the maze.
  mySquares[chosenSquare[0]][chosenSquare[1]] = 1;
  possibleSquares.removeElementAt(chosenIndex);
  link(chosenSquare, possibleSquares);
}
// now that the maze has been completely generated, you
// throw away the objects that were created during the
// maze creation algorithm and reclaim the memory.
possibleSquares = null;
```

```
  System.gc();
}


/**
 * internal to createMaze.  Checks the four squares surrounding
 * the chosen square.  Of those that are already connected to
 * the maze, one is randomly selected to be joined to the
 * current square (to attach the current square to the
 * growing maze).  Those squares that were not previously in
 * a position to be joined to the maze are added to the list
 * of "possible" squares (that can be chosen to be attached
 * to the maze in the next round).
 */
private void link(int[] chosenSquare, Vector possibleSquares) {
  int linkCount = 0;
  int i = chosenSquare[0];
  int j = chosenSquare[1];
  int[] links = new int[8];
  if(i >= 3) {
    if(mySquares[i - 2][j] == 1) {
      links[2*linkCount] = i - 1;
      links[2*linkCount + 1] = j;
      linkCount++;
    } else if(mySquares[i - 2][j] == 3) {
      mySquares[i - 2][j] = 2;
      int[] newSquare = new int[2];
      newSquare[0] = i - 2;
      newSquare[1] = j;
      possibleSquares.addElement(newSquare);
    }
  }
  if(j + 3 <= mySquares[i].length) {
    if(mySquares[i][j + 2] == 3) {
      mySquares[i][j + 2] = 2;
      int[] newSquare = new int[2];
      newSquare[0] = i;
      newSquare[1] = j + 2;
      possibleSquares.addElement(newSquare);
    } else if(mySquares[i][j + 2] == 1) {
      links[2*linkCount] = i;
      links[2*linkCount + 1] = j + 1;
      linkCount++;
    }
  }
  if(j >= 3) {
    if(mySquares[i][j - 2] == 3) {
      mySquares[i][j - 2] = 2;
      int[] newSquare = new int[2];
```

```java
        newSquare[0] = i;
        newSquare[1] = j - 2;
        possibleSquares.addElement(newSquare);
      } else if(mySquares[i][j - 2] == 1) {
        links[2*linkCount] = i;
        links[2*linkCount + 1] = j - 1;
        linkCount++;
      }
    }
    if(i + 3 <= mySquares.length) {
      if(mySquares[i + 2][j] == 3) {
        mySquares[i + 2][j] = 2;
        int[] newSquare = new int[2];
        newSquare[0] = i + 2;
        newSquare[1] = j;
        possibleSquares.addElement(newSquare);
      } else if(mySquares[i + 2][j] == 1) {
        links[2*linkCount] = i + 1;
        links[2*linkCount + 1] = j;
        linkCount++;
      }
    }
    if(linkCount > 0) {
      int linkChoice = getRandomInt(linkCount);
      int linkX = links[2*linkChoice];
      int linkY = links[2*linkChoice + 1];
      mySquares[linkX][linkY] = 1;
      int[] removeSquare = new int[2];
      removeSquare[0] = linkX;
      removeSquare[1] = linkY;
      possibleSquares.removeElement(removeSquare);
    }
  }

  /**
   * a randomization utility.
   * @param upper the upper bound for the random int.
   * @return a random non-negative int less than the bound upper.
   */
  public int getRandomInt(int upper) {
    int retVal = myRandom.nextInt() % upper;
    if(retVal < 0) {
      retVal += upper;
    }
    return(retVal);
  }

}
```

Summary

In this chapter you've seen the structure of a MIDP application (a MIDlet), and how a MIDlet is controlled by the application management system. Following the example in this chapter, you can write a basic game including a simple graphical user interface. These ideas alone are all you need to write a lot of fun games such as the Maze game. But there's plenty more you can do to make your game more fun and exciting, as you'll see in the chapters to come.

CHAPTER 3

■■■

Using the MIDP 2 Games API

Now it's time to look at the most important package you'll be dealing with when writing games with Mobile Internet Device Profile (MIDP), version 2.0 or greater: the package `javax.microedition.lcdui.game.*`. In this chapter, I show you the main parts of a MIDP game by explaining the code of an example game called Tumbleweed. The game (see Figure 3-1) involves a cowboy walking through a prairie jumping over tumbleweeds. It's kind of a silly game, but it illustrates most of the basics you'll need when writing more serious games.

As in the earlier chapters, I've included all of the code necessary to build the example, and you can download the code from the Source Code/Download section of the Apress web site (http://www.apress.com) with all its resources.

Figure 3-1. *The Tumbleweed game*

Starting with the MIDlet Class

As usual, the application starts with the `MIDlet` class. In this case, my `MIDlet` subclass is called Jump. This class is essentially the same as the `MIDlet` subclass from the previous chapter, so if you'd like a detailed explanation of what's going on in it, please see the "Using the MIDlet Class" section in Chapter 2. The only differences here are the use of a separate `GameThread` class and the fact that when the user presses a command button, I have the `MIDlet` change the command that's available on the screen. The command change is because the user can pause the game only when it's unpaused, can unpause the game only when it's paused, and can start over only when the game has ended.

Listing 3-1 shows the game's MIDlet subclass called Jump.java.

Listing 3-1. *Jump.java*

```java
package net.frog_parrot.jump;

import javax.microedition.midlet.*;
import javax.microedition.lcdui.*;

/**
 * This is the main class of the Tumbleweed game.
 *
 * @author Carol Hamer
 */
public class Jump extends MIDlet implements CommandListener {

  //-------------------------------------------------------------
  //    commands

  /**
   * the command to end the game.
   */
  private Command myExitCommand = new Command("Exit", Command.EXIT, 99);

  /**
   * the command to start moving when the game is paused.
   */
  private Command myGoCommand = new Command("Go", Command.SCREEN, 1);

  /**
   * the command to pause the game.
   */
  private Command myPauseCommand = new Command("Pause", Command.SCREEN, 1);

  /**
   * the command to start a new game.
   */
  private Command myNewCommand = new Command("Play Again", Command.SCREEN, 1);

  //-------------------------------------------------------------
```

```java
//   game object fields

/**
 * the canvas that all of the game will be drawn on.
 */
private JumpCanvas myCanvas;

/**
 * the thread that advances the cowboy.
 */
private GameThread myGameThread;

//--------------------------------------------------------
//   initialization and game state changes

/**
 * empty constructor.
 */
public Jump() {
}

/**
 * Switch the command to the play again command.
 */
void setNewCommand () {
  myCanvas.removeCommand(myPauseCommand);
  myCanvas.removeCommand(myGoCommand);
  myCanvas.addCommand(myNewCommand);
}

/**
 * Switch the command to the go command.
 */
private void setGoCommand() {
  myCanvas.removeCommand(myPauseCommand);
  myCanvas.removeCommand(myNewCommand);
  myCanvas.addCommand(myGoCommand);
}

/**
 * Switch the command to the pause command.
 */
private void setPauseCommand () {
  myCanvas.removeCommand(myNewCommand);
  myCanvas.removeCommand(myGoCommand);
  myCanvas.addCommand(myPauseCommand);
}

//----------------------------------------------------------------
```

```
//  implementation of MIDlet
// these methods may be called by the application management
// software at any time, so you always check fields for null
// before calling methods on them.

/**
 * Start the application.
 */
public void startApp() throws MIDletStateChangeException {
  try {
    if(myCanvas == null) {
      myCanvas = new JumpCanvas(this);
      myCanvas.addCommand(myExitCommand);
      myCanvas.addCommand(myPauseCommand);
      myCanvas.setCommandListener(this);
    }
    if(myGameThread == null) {
      myGameThread = new GameThread(myCanvas);
      myCanvas.start();
      myGameThread.start();
    } else {
      myCanvas.removeCommand(myGoCommand);
      myCanvas.addCommand(myPauseCommand);
      myCanvas.flushKeys();
      myGameThread.resumeGame();
    }
  } catch(Exception e) {
    errorMsg(e);
  }
}

/**
 * stop and throw out the garbage.
 */
public void destroyApp(boolean unconditional)
    throws MIDletStateChangeException {
  if(myGameThread != null) {
    myGameThread.requestStop();
  }
  myGameThread = null;
  myCanvas = null;
  System.gc();
}

/**
 * request the thread to pause.
 */
```

```
public void pauseApp() {
  if(myCanvas != null) {
    setGoCommand();
  }
  if(myGameThread != null) {
    myGameThread.pauseGame();
  }
}


//------------------------------------------------------------------
//  implementation of CommandListener

/*
 * Respond to a command issued on the Canvas.
 * (either reset or exit).
 */
public void commandAction(Command c, Displayable s) {
  if(c == myGoCommand) {
    myCanvas.removeCommand(myGoCommand);
    myCanvas.addCommand(myPauseCommand);
    myCanvas.flushKeys();
    myGameThread.resumeGame();
  } else if(c == myPauseCommand) {
    myCanvas.removeCommand(myPauseCommand);
    myCanvas.addCommand(myGoCommand);
    myGameThread.pauseGame();
  } else if(c == myNewCommand) {
    myCanvas.removeCommand(myNewCommand);
    myCanvas.addCommand(myPauseCommand);
    myCanvas.reset();
    myGameThread.resumeGame();
  } else if((c == myExitCommand) || (c == Alert.DISMISS_COMMAND)) {
    try {
      destroyApp(false);
      notifyDestroyed();
    } catch (MIDletStateChangeException ex) {
    }
  }
}


//----------------------------------------------------------
//  error methods

/**
 * Converts an exception to a message and displays
 * the message.
 */
```

```
    void errorMsg(Exception e) {
      if(e.getMessage() == null) {
        errorMsg(e.getClass().getName());
      } else {
        errorMsg(e.getClass().getName() + ":" + e.getMessage());
      }
    }

    /**
     * Displays an error message alert if something goes wrong.
     */
    void errorMsg(String msg) {
      Alert errorAlert = new Alert("error",
                                     msg, null, AlertType.ERROR);
      errorAlert.setCommandListener(this);
      errorAlert.setTimeout(Alert.FOREVER);
      Display.getDisplay(this).setCurrent(errorAlert);
    }

}
```

Using the Thread Class

This game requires only the simplest use of the Thread class. Chapter 4 covers how to use threads. But even in this simple case, I'd like to mention a few points.

In this case, it really is necessary to spawn a new thread. The animation in this game is always moving, even when the user doesn't press a button, so I need to have a game loop that repeats constantly until the end of the game. I can't use the main thread for the game loop because the application management software may need to use the main thread while my game is running. While testing the game in the emulator, I found that if I use the main thread for my game's animation loop, the emulator is unable to respond to keystrokes. Of course, in general, it's good practice to spawn a new thread when you plan to go into a loop that's to be repeated throughout the duration of your program's active lifecycle. Alternately you could use a Timer and a TimerTask, but it's important to be able to write and understand the threading code. It gives you better control over how the scheduling works and how many Threads are spawned (a costly operation).

Here's how my Thread subclass (called GameThread) works: once the thread starts, it goes into the main loop (inside the while(true) block). The first step is to check if the Jump class has called requestStop() since the last cycle. If so, you break out of the loop, and the run() method returns. Otherwise, if the user hasn't paused the game, you prompt the GameCanvas to respond to the user's keystrokes and advance the game animation. Then you do a short pause. This is partially to be sure that your game animation advances no faster than a standard rate, such as 20 frames per second. Usually the worry is to optimize the game so that you're sure to be able to advance the frames fast enough to have a smooth animation, but you can have some unpleasant surprises running a simple game on a high-performance device if you don't keep the animation from advancing too fast.

The pause is also useful to help the keystroke query work correctly. As mentioned, the information about the user's keystrokes is updated on another thread, so it's necessary to put a short wait inside your game loop to make sure that the other thread gets a turn and has the opportunity to update the key state's value in a timely fashion. This allows your game to respond immediately when the user presses a key. Even a millisecond will do the trick. (I earlier wrote a racecar game in which I neglected to put a wait in the main game loop, and I found that the car would go halfway around the track between the time I pressed the lane change key and the time the car actually changed lanes.) But if this threading question were the only concern, it's also possible to use the Thread.yield() method to give the other threads a turn.

Listing 3-2 shows the code for GameThread.java.

Listing 3-2. *GameThread.java*

```java
package net.frog_parrot.jump;

/**
 * This class contains the loop that keeps the game running.
 *
 * @author Carol Hamer
 */
public class GameThread extends Thread {

  //-------------------------------------------------------------
  //   fields

  /**
   * Whether the main thread would like this thread
   * to pause.
   */
  private boolean myShouldPause;

  /**
   * Whether the main thread would like this thread
   * to stop.
   */
  private boolean myShouldStop;

  /**
   * A handle back to the graphical components.
   */
  private JumpCanvas myJumpCanvas;

  /**
   * The System.time of the last screen refresh, used
   * to regulate refresh speed.
   */
  private long myLastRefreshTime;

  //-------------------------------------------------------------
```

```
// initialization

/**
 * standard constructor.
 */
GameThread(JumpCanvas canvas) {
  myJumpCanvas = canvas;
}

//-------------------------------------------------------------
// utilities

/**
 * Get the amount of time to wait between screen refreshes.
 * Normally we wait only a single millisecond just to give
 * the main thread a chance to update the keystroke info,
 * but this method ensures that the game will not attempt
 * to show more than 20 frames per second.
 */
private long getWaitTime() {
  long retVal = 1;
  long difference = System.currentTimeMillis() - myLastRefreshTime;
  if(difference < 50) {
    retVal = 50 - difference;
  }
  return(retVal);
}

//-------------------------------------------------------------
// actions

/**
 * pause the game.
 */
void pauseGame() {
  myShouldPause = true;
}

/**
 * restart the game after a pause.
 */
synchronized void resumeGame() {
  myShouldPause = false;
  notify();
}
```

```java
/**
 * stops the game.
 */
synchronized void requestStop() {
  myShouldStop = true;
  notify();
}

/**
 * start the game.
 */
public void run() {
  // flush any keystrokes that occurred before the
  // game started:
  myJumpCanvas.flushKeys();
  myShouldStop = false;
  myShouldPause = false;
  while(true) {
    myLastRefreshTime = System.currentTimeMillis();
    if(myShouldStop) {
      break;
    }
    synchronized(this) {
      while(myShouldPause) {
        try {
          wait();
        } catch(Exception e) {}
      }
    }
    myJumpCanvas.checkKeys();
    myJumpCanvas.advance();
    // you do a short pause to allow the other thread
    // to update the information about which keys are pressed
    // and regulate the animation speed:
    synchronized(this) {
      try {
        wait(getWaitTime());
      } catch(Exception e) {}
    }
  }
}

}
```

Using the GameCanvas Class

Now you'll look at the class that allows you to paint customized game graphics to the screen.

How GameCanvas Differs from Canvas

The GameCanvas class represents the area of the screen that the device has allotted to your game. The javax.microedition.lcdui.game.GameCanvas class differs from its superclass javax. microedition.lcdui.Canvas in two important ways: graphics buffering and the ability to query key states. Both of these changes give the game developer enhanced control over precisely when the program deals with events such as keystrokes and screen repainting. Another difference to keep in mind is that because implementations vary from one platform to another, some handsets have trouble with GameCanvas and others don't perform correctly in full-screen mode without choosing GameCanvas over Canvas. So as usual you need to consider the limitations of your target handsets.

The graphics buffering allows all the graphical objects to be created behind the scenes and then flushed to the screen all at once when they're ready. This makes animation smoother. I've illustrated how to use it in the method advance() in Listing 3-3 in a moment. (Recall that advance() is called from the main loop of my GameThread object.) Notice that to update and repaint the screen, all you need to do is call paint(getGraphics()) and then call flushGraphics(). To make your program more efficient, there's even a version of the flushGraphics() method that allows you to repaint just a subset of the screen if you know that only part has changed. As an experiment, I tried replacing the calls to paint(getGraphics()) and flushGraphics() with calls to repaint() and then serviceRepaints() as you might if your class extended Canvas instead of GameCanvas. In my simple examples, it didn't make much difference, but if your game has a lot of complicated graphics, the GameCanvas version will undoubtedly make a big difference.

The ability to query key states is helpful for the game's organization. When you extend the Canvas class directly, you must implement keyPressed(int keyCode) if your game is interested in keystrokes. The application management software then calls this method when the user presses a button. But if your program is running on its own thread, this might happen at any point in your game's algorithm. If you're not careful about using synchronized blocks, this could potentially cause errors if one thread is updating data about the game's current state and the other is using that data to perform calculations. The program is simpler and easier to follow if you get the keystroke information when you want it by calling the GameCanvas method getKeyStates().

An additional advantage of the getKeyStates() method is that it can tell you if multiple keys are being pressed simultaneously. The keyCode that's passed to the keyPressed(int keyCode) method can tell you only about a single key and therefore will be called multiple times even if the user presses two keys at the same time. In a game, the precise timing of each keystroke is often important, so the Canvas method keyPressed() loses valuable information. Looking at the method checkKeys() in Listing 3-3, you can see that the value returned by getKeyStates() contains all the keystroke information. All you need to do is perform a bitwise and (&) between the getKeyStates() return value and a static field such as GameCanvas.LEFT_PRESSED to tell if a given key is currently being pressed.

This is a large class file, but you can see the main idea of how it works by recalling that the main loop of the GameThread class first tells my GameCanvas subclass (called JumpCanvas) to query the key states (see the method JumpCanvas.checkKeys() in Listing 3-3 for details). Then once the key events have been dealt with, the main loop of the GameThread class calls

`JumpCanvas.advance()`, which tells the `LayerManager` to make appropriate updates in the graphics (more on that in the next sections) and then paints the screen.

Listing 3-3 shows the code for `JumpCanvas.java`.

Listing 3-3. *JumpCanvas.java*

```java
package net.frog_parrot.jump;

import javax.microedition.lcdui.*;
import javax.microedition.lcdui.game.*;

/**
 * This class is the display of the game.
 *
 * @author Carol Hamer
 */
public class JumpCanvas extends javax.microedition.lcdui.game.GameCanvas {

  //-----------------------------------------------------------
  //   dimension fields
  //   (constant after initialization)

  /**
   * the height of the green region below the ground.
   */
  static final int GROUND_HEIGHT = 32;

  /**
   * a screen dimension.
   */
  static final int CORNER_X = 0;

  /**
   * a screen dimension.
   */
  static final int CORNER_Y = 0;

  /**
   * a screen dimension.
   */
  static int DISP_WIDTH;

  /**
   * a screen dimension.
   */
  static int DISP_HEIGHT;
```

```java
/**
 * a font dimension.
 */
static int FONT_HEIGHT;

/**
 * the default font.
 */
static Font FONT;

/**
 * a font dimension.
 */
static int SCORE_WIDTH;

/**
 * The width of the string that displays the time,
 * saved for placement of time display.
 */
static int TIME_WIDTH;

/**
 * color constant
 */
public static final int BLACK = 0;

/**
 * color constant
 */
public static final int WHITE = 0xffffff;

//-----------------------------------------------------------
//   game object fields

/**
 * a handle to the display.
 */
private Display myDisplay;

/**
 * a handle to the MIDlet object (to keep track of buttons).
 */
private Jump myJump;

/**
 * the LayerManager that handles the game graphics.
 */
private JumpManager myManager;
```

```
/**
 * whether the game has ended.
 */
private boolean myGameOver;

/**
 * the player's score.
 */
private int myScore = 0;

/**
 * How many ticks you start with.
 */
private int myInitialGameTicks = 950;

/**
 * this is saved to determine if the time string needs
 * to be recomputed.
 */
private int myOldGameTicks = myInitialGameTicks;

/**
 * the number of game ticks that have passed.
 */
private int myGameTicks = myOldGameTicks;

/**
 * you save the time string to avoid re-creating it
 * unnecessarily.
 */
private static String myInitialString = "1:00";

/**
 * you save the time string to avoid re-creating it
 * unnecessarily.
 */
private String myTimeString = myInitialString;

//-----------------------------------------------------
//     gets/sets

/**
 * This is called when the game ends.
 */
void setGameOver() {
  myGameOver = true;
  myJump.pauseApp();
}

//-----------------------------------------------------
```

```java
//    initialization and game state changes

/**
 * Constructor sets the data, performs dimension calculations,
 * and creates the graphical objects.
 */
public JumpCanvas(Jump midlet) throws Exception {
  super(false);
  myDisplay = Display.getDisplay(midlet);
  myJump = midlet;
  // calculate the dimensions
  DISP_WIDTH = getWidth();
  DISP_HEIGHT = getHeight();
  Display disp = Display.getDisplay(myJump);
  if(disp.numColors() < 256) {
    throw(new Exception("game requires 256 shades"));
  }
  if((DISP_WIDTH < 150) || (DISP_HEIGHT < 170)) {
    throw(new Exception("Screen too small"));
  }
  if((DISP_WIDTH > 250) || (DISP_HEIGHT > 320)) {
    throw(new Exception("Screen too large"));
  }
  FONT = getGraphics().getFont();
  FONT_HEIGHT = FONT.getHeight();
  SCORE_WIDTH = FONT.stringWidth("Score: 000");
  TIME_WIDTH = FONT.stringWidth("Time: " + myInitialString);
  if(myManager == null) {
    myManager = new JumpManager(CORNER_X, CORNER_Y + FONT_HEIGHT*2,
        DISP_WIDTH, DISP_HEIGHT - FONT_HEIGHT*2 - GROUND_HEIGHT);
  }
}

/**
 * This is called as soon as the application begins.
 */
void start() {
  myGameOver = false;
  myDisplay.setCurrent(this);
  repaint();
}

/**
 * sets all variables back to their initial positions.
 */
void reset() {
  myManager.reset();
```

```
    myScore = 0;
    myGameOver = false;
    myGameTicks = myInitialGameTicks;
    myOldGameTicks = myInitialGameTicks;
    repaint();
  }

  /**
   * clears the key states.
   */
  void flushKeys() {
    getKeyStates();
  }

  /**
   * This version of the game does not deal with what happens
   * when the game is hidden, so I hope it won't be hidden...
   * see the version in the next chapter for how to implement
   * hideNotify and showNotify.
   */
  protected void hideNotify() {
  }

  /**
   * This version of the game does not deal with what happens
   * when the game is hidden, so I hope it won't be hidden...
   * see the version in the next chapter for how to implement
   * hideNotify and showNotify.
   */
  protected void showNotify() {
  }

  //----------------------------------------------------------
  //   graphics methods

  /**
   * paint the game graphic on the screen.
   */
  public void paint(Graphics g) {
    // clear the screen:
    g.setColor(WHITE);
    g.fillRect(CORNER_X, CORNER_Y, DISP_WIDTH, DISP_HEIGHT);
    // color the grass green
    g.setColor(0, 255, 0);
    g.fillRect(CORNER_X, CORNER_Y + DISP_HEIGHT - GROUND_HEIGHT,
               DISP_WIDTH, DISP_HEIGHT);
    // paint the layer manager:
```

```
    try {
      myManager.paint(g);
    } catch(Exception e) {
      myJump.errorMsg(e);
    }
    // draw the time and score
    g.setColor(BLACK);
    g.setFont(FONT);
    g.drawString("Score: " + myScore,
                 (DISP_WIDTH - SCORE_WIDTH)/2,
                 DISP_HEIGHT + 5 - GROUND_HEIGHT, g.TOP|g.LEFT);
    g.drawString("Time: " + formatTime(),
                 (DISP_WIDTH - TIME_WIDTH)/2,
                 CORNER_Y + FONT_HEIGHT, g.TOP|g.LEFT);
    // write game over if the game is over
    if(myGameOver) {
      myJump.setNewCommand();
      // clear the top region:
      g.setColor(WHITE);
      g.fillRect(CORNER_X, CORNER_Y, DISP_WIDTH, FONT_HEIGHT*2 + 1);
      int goWidth = FONT.stringWidth("Game Over");
      g.setColor(BLACK);
      g.setFont(FONT);
      g.drawString("Game Over", (DISP_WIDTH - goWidth)/2,
                   CORNER_Y + FONT_HEIGHT, g.TOP|g.LEFT);
    }
  }

  /**
   * a simple utility to make the number of ticks look like a time...
   */
  public String formatTime() {
    if((myGameTicks / 16) + 1 != myOldGameTicks) {
      myTimeString = "";
      myOldGameTicks = (myGameTicks / 16) + 1;
      int smallPart = myOldGameTicks % 60;
      int bigPart = myOldGameTicks / 60;
      myTimeString += bigPart + ":";
      if(smallPart / 10 < 1) {
        myTimeString += "0";
      }
      myTimeString += smallPart;
    }
    return(myTimeString);
  }

  //---------------------------------------------------------
```

```
// game movements

/**
 * Tell the layer manager to advance the layers and then
 * update the display.
 */
void advance() {
  myGameTicks--;
  myScore += myManager.advance(myGameTicks);
  if(myGameTicks == 0) {
    setGameOver();
  }
  // paint the display
  try {
    paint(getGraphics());
    flushGraphics();
  } catch(Exception e) {
    myJump.errorMsg(e);
  }
}

/**
 * Respond to keystrokes.
 */
public void checkKeys() {
  if(! myGameOver) {
    int keyState = getKeyStates();
    if((keyState & LEFT_PRESSED) != 0) {
      myManager.setLeft(true);
    }
    if((keyState & RIGHT_PRESSED) != 0) {
      myManager.setLeft(false);
    }
    if((keyState & UP_PRESSED) != 0) {
      myManager.jump();
    }
  }
}

}
```

Using the Graphics Class with a GameCanvas

Chapter 2 covered using the Graphics class. In this section, I just go over the main points of
how the Graphics class is used in the example game.

In the Tumbleweed game, I need to draw a cowboy walking through a prairie jumping
over tumbleweeds. Figure 3-2 shows the game.

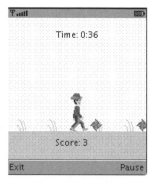

Figure 3-2. *The Tumbleweed game*

As you can see, I've put the score on the bottom and the time remaining on the top. (To simplify the game, I just have it end when the player runs out of time.) As the cowboy is walking along, I'd like his background to scroll to the right or to the left (otherwise, he won't have very far to go on such a small screen . . .), but I'd like the time and the score to stay in place. To accomplish this, I have my JumpCanvas class take care of painting the stable strip on the top and the bottom of the screen, and I delegate the interesting graphics to the LayerManager (more details on that in the next section).

When the JumpCanvas is first created, you start by analyzing the screen with which you have to work. Some of the information about the screen's capacities comes from the Graphics object, some from the display object, and some directly from methods of the GameCanvas. This information calculates where the objects should be placed, including calculating the dimensions of the region that will be painted by the LayerManager subclass (JumpManager). If you'd like to vary the emulator's screen capabilities when testing, remember that each emulator skin has a properties file under the WTK's wtklib/devices directory. If you're interested in maintaining Java's "write once, run anywhere" philosophy, it's obviously better to base the screen layout on the (dynamically determined) dimensions of the current screen rather than basing the dimensions on fixed constants. Of course, if the game graphics are even a little more complex than the very basics, it's better to use resource files to build multiple versions of the game rather than putting all of the code together in a single version and using the display information to determine which version to run (see Chapter 10 for techniques). In my example game, if the screen is too different from the screen I wrote the game for (the emulator that came with the toolkit in this case), I throw an Exception that the Jump class will catch and show it to the user as an Alert. When using this technique professionally, you'd of course make sure the Alert clearly states that the user needs to download a different version of the game for the current device or at least be very careful about serving the right version of the game to the device (see the "Identifying the Platform" sidebar in Chapter 10).

At the risk of belaboring the obvious, I'll point out that once I know the appropriate sizes for the top and bottom regions, the paint(Graphics g) method paints the top one white and the bottom one green with g.fillRect(), and then the method g.drawString() adds the time and the score. Chapter 2 discussed the drawString() method. (Don't ask me why my prairie has both green grass and tumbleweeds; my only excuse is that I know more about Java than I know about the Wild West . . .)

Using the LayerManager Class

The interesting graphical objects in an MIDP game are usually represented by subclasses of the javax.microedition.lcdui.game.Layer class. The background layers could be instances of javax. microedition.lcdui.game.TiledLayer, and the player (and his enemies) would likely be instances of javax.microedition.lcdui.game.Sprite, both of which are subclasses of Layer. The LayerManager class helps you to organize all these graphical layers. The order in which you append your Layers to your LayerManager determines the order in which they'll be painted. (The first one appended is the last one painted.) The top layers will cover the lower layers, but you can allow parts of the lower layers to show through by creating image files that have transparent regions.

Probably the most useful aspect of the LayerManager class is that you can create a graphical painting that's much larger than the screen and then choose which section of it will appear on the screen. Imagine drawing a huge, elaborate drawing and then covering it with a piece of paper that has a small rectangular hole you can move. The whole drawing represents what you can stock into the LayerManager, and the hole is the window showing the part that appears on the screen at any given time. Allowing the possibility of a virtual screen that's much larger than the actual screen is extremely helpful for games on devices with small screens. It'll save you huge amounts of time and effort if, for example, your game involves a player exploring an elaborate dungeon (see Chapter 5 for just such an example). The confusing part is that this means you have to deal with two separate coordinate systems. The Graphics object of the GameCanvas has one coordinate system, but the various Layers need to be placed in the LayerManager according to the LayerManager's coordinate system. So, keep in mind that the method LayerManager. paint(Graphics g, int x, int y) paints the layer on the screen according to the coordinates of the GameCanvas, and the method LayerManager.setViewWindow(int x, int y, int width, int height) sets the visible rectangle of the LayerManager in terms of the LayerManager's coordinate system.

In my example, I have a simple background (it's just a repeating series of patches of grass), but I'd like the cowboy to stay in the middle of the screen as he walks to the right and left, so I need to continuously change which part of the LayerManager's graphical area is visible. I do this by calling the method setViewWindow(int x, int y, int width, int height) from the paint(Graphics g) method of my subclass of LayerManager (called JumpManager). More precisely, what happens is the following: the main loop in the GameThread calls JumpCanvas.checkKeys(), which queries the key states and tells the JumpManager class whether the cowboy should be walking to the right or to the left and whether he should be jumping. JumpCanvas passes this information along to JumpManager by calling the methods setLeft(boolean left) or jump(). If the message is to jump, the JumpManager calls jump() on the cowboy Sprite. If the message is that the cowboy is going to the left (or similarly to the right), then when the GameThread calls the JumpCanvas to tell the JumpManager to advance (in the next step of the loop), the JumpManager tells the cowboy Sprite to move one pixel to the left and compensates by moving the view window one pixel to the right to keep the cowboy in the center of the screen. You can accomplish these two actions by incrementing the field myCurrentLeftX (which is the X coordinate that's sent to the method setViewWindow(int x, int y, int width, int height)) and then calling myCowboy.advance(gameTicks, myLeft). Of course, I could keep the cowboy centered by not moving him and not appending him to the LayerManager but, rather, painting him separately afterward; however, it's easier to keep track of everything by putting all of the moving graphics on one set of layers and then keeping the view window focused on the cowboy Sprite. While telling the cowboy to advance his position, I also have the tumbleweed Sprites advance their positions, and I have the grass TiledLayer advance its animation. Then I check if the cowboy has collided with any tumbleweeds (I'll go into more detail about those steps in the following sections). After moving the game pieces around, the JumpManager calls the method wrap() to see if the view window has reached the edge of the background and, if so, move all of the game objects so that the background appears to continue indefinitely in both directions. Then the JumpCanvas repaints everything, and the game loop begins again.

I'll just add a few words here about the method wrap(). The class LayerManager unfortunately doesn't have a built-in wrapping capability for the case in which you have a simple background you'd like to have repeat indefinitely. The LayerManager's graphical area will appear to wrap when the coordinates sent to setViewWindow(int x, int y, int width, int height) exceed the value Integer.MAX_VALUE, but that's unlikely to help you. Thus, you have to write your own functions to prevent the player Sprite from leaving the region that contains background graphics. In my example, the background grass repeats after the number of pixels given by Grass.TILE_ WIDTH*Grass.CYCLE. So, whenever the X coordinate of the view window (myCurrentLeftX) is an integer multiple of the length of the background, I move the view window back to the center and also move all of the Sprites in the same direction, which seamlessly prevents the player from reaching the edge.

Listing 3-4 shows the code for JumpManager.java.

Listing 3-4. *JumpManager.java*

```
package net.frog_parrot.jump;

import javax.microedition.lcdui.*;
import javax.microedition.lcdui.game.*;

/**
 * This handles the graphics objects.
 *
 * @author Carol Hamer
 */
public class JumpManager extends javax.microedition.lcdui.game.LayerManager {

  //-----------------------------------------------------------
  //   dimension fields
  //   (constant after initialization)

  /**
   * The X coordinate of the place on the game canvas where
   * the LayerManager window should appear, in terms of the
   * coordinates of the game canvas.
   */
  static int CANVAS_X;

  /**
   * The Y coordinate of the place on the game canvas where
   * the LayerManager window should appear, in terms of the
```

```
 * coordinates of the game canvas.
 */
static int CANVAS_Y;

/**
 * The width of the display window.
 */
static int DISP_WIDTH;

/**
 * The height of this object's graphical region. This is
 * the same as the height of the visible part because
 * in this game the layer manager's visible part scrolls
 * only left and right but not up and down.
 */
static int DISP_HEIGHT;

//----------------------------------------------------------
//   game object fields

/**
 * the player's object.
 */
private Cowboy myCowboy;

/**
 * the tumbleweeds that enter from the left.
 */
private Tumbleweed[] myLeftTumbleweeds;

/**
 * the tumbleweeds that enter from the right.
 */
private Tumbleweed[] myRightTumbleweeds;

/**
 * the object representing the grass in the background.
 */
private Grass myGrass;

/**
 * Whether the player is currently going left.
 */
private boolean myLeft;

/**
 * The leftmost X coordinate that should be visible on the
```

```
 * screen in terms of this object's internal coordinates.
 */
private int myCurrentLeftX;

//-------------------------------------------------------
//    gets/sets

/**
 * This tells the player to turn left or right.
 * @param left whether the turn is toward the left.
 */
void setLeft(boolean left) {
  myLeft = left;
}


//-------------------------------------------------------
//    initialization and game state changes

/**
 * Constructor sets the data and constructs the graphical objects.
 * @param x The X coordinate of the place on the game canvas where
 * the LayerManager window should appear, in terms of the
 * coordinates of the game canvas.
 * @param y The Y coordinate of the place on the game canvas where
 * the LayerManager window should appear, in terms of the
 * coordinates of the game canvas.
 * @param width the width of the region that is to be
 * occupied by the LayoutManager.
 * @param height the height of the region that is to be
 * occupied by the LayoutManager.
 */
public JumpManager(int x, int y, int width, int height)
    throws Exception {
  CANVAS_X = x;
  CANVAS_Y = y;
  DISP_WIDTH = width;
  DISP_HEIGHT = height;
  myCurrentLeftX = Grass.CYCLE*Grass.TILE_WIDTH;
  setViewWindow(0, 0, DISP_WIDTH, DISP_HEIGHT);
  // create the player:
  if(myCowboy == null) {
    myCowboy = new Cowboy(myCurrentLeftX + DISP_WIDTH/2,
                          DISP_HEIGHT - Cowboy.HEIGHT - 2);
    append(myCowboy);
  }
  // create the tumbleweeds to jump over:
  if(myLeftTumbleweeds == null) {
    myLeftTumbleweeds = new Tumbleweed[2];
```

```
      for(int i = 0; i < myLeftTumbleweeds.length; i++) {
        myLeftTumbleweeds[i] = new Tumbleweed(true);
        append(myLeftTumbleweeds[i]);
      }
    }
    if(myRightTumbleweeds == null) {
      myRightTumbleweeds = new Tumbleweed[2];
      for(int i = 0; i < myRightTumbleweeds.length; i++) {
        myRightTumbleweeds[i] = new Tumbleweed(false);
        append(myRightTumbleweeds[i]);
      }
    }
    // create the background object:
    if(myGrass == null) {
      myGrass = new Grass();
      append(myGrass);
    }
  }

  /**
   * sets all variables back to their initial positions.
   */
  void reset() {
    if(myGrass != null) {
      myGrass.reset();
    }
    if(myCowboy != null) {
      myCowboy.reset();
    }
    if(myLeftTumbleweeds != null) {
      for(int i = 0; i < myLeftTumbleweeds.length; i++) {
        myLeftTumbleweeds[i].reset();
      }
    }
    if(myRightTumbleweeds != null) {
      for(int i = 0; i < myRightTumbleweeds.length; i++) {
        myRightTumbleweeds[i].reset();
      }
    }
    myLeft = false;
    myCurrentLeftX = Grass.CYCLE*Grass.TILE_WIDTH;
  }

  //-------------------------------------------------------
  //  graphics methods

  /**
```

```
 * paint the game graphic on the screen.
 */
public void paint(Graphics g) {
  setViewWindow(myCurrentLeftX, 0, DISP_WIDTH, DISP_HEIGHT);
  paint(g, CANVAS_X, CANVAS_Y);
}

/**
 * If the cowboy gets to the end of the graphical region,
 * move all of the pieces so that the screen appears to wrap.
 */
private void wrap() {
  if(myCurrentLeftX % (Grass.TILE_WIDTH*Grass.CYCLE) == 0) {
    if(myLeft) {
      myCowboy.move(Grass.TILE_WIDTH*Grass.CYCLE, 0);
      myCurrentLeftX += (Grass.TILE_WIDTH*Grass.CYCLE);
      for(int i = 0; i < myLeftTumbleweeds.length; i++) {
        myLeftTumbleweeds[i].move(Grass.TILE_WIDTH*Grass.CYCLE, 0);
      }
      for(int i = 0; i < myRightTumbleweeds.length; i++) {
        myRightTumbleweeds[i].move(Grass.TILE_WIDTH*Grass.CYCLE, 0);
      }
    } else {
      myCowboy.move(-(Grass.TILE_WIDTH*Grass.CYCLE), 0);
      myCurrentLeftX -= (Grass.TILE_WIDTH*Grass.CYCLE);
      for(int i = 0; i < myLeftTumbleweeds.length; i++) {
        myLeftTumbleweeds[i].move(-Grass.TILE_WIDTH*Grass.CYCLE, 0);
      }
      for(int i = 0; i < myRightTumbleweeds.length; i++) {
        myRightTumbleweeds[i].move(-Grass.TILE_WIDTH*Grass.CYCLE, 0);
      }
    }
  }
}

//---------------------------------------------------------
// game movements

/**
 * Tell all of the moving components to advance.
 * @param gameTicks the remaining number of times that
 *         the main loop of the game will be executed
 *         before the game ends.
 * @return the change in the score after the pieces
 *         have advanced.
 */
int advance(int gameTicks) {
```

```
  int retVal = 0;
  // first you move the view window
  // (so you are showing a slightly different view of
  // the manager's graphical area.)
  if(myLeft) {
    myCurrentLeftX--;
  } else {
    myCurrentLeftX++;
  }
  // now you tell the game objects to move accordingly.
  myGrass.advance(gameTicks);
  myCowboy.advance(gameTicks, myLeft);
  for(int i = 0; i < myLeftTumbleweeds.length; i++) {
    retVal += myLeftTumbleweeds[i].advance(myCowboy, gameTicks,
                  myLeft, myCurrentLeftX, myCurrentLeftX + DISP_WIDTH);
    retVal -= myCowboy.checkCollision(myLeftTumbleweeds[i]);
  }
  for(int i = 0; i < myLeftTumbleweeds.length; i++) {
    retVal += myRightTumbleweeds[i].advance(myCowboy, gameTicks,
          myLeft, myCurrentLeftX, myCurrentLeftX + DISP_WIDTH);
    retVal -= myCowboy.checkCollision(myRightTumbleweeds[i]);
  }
  // now you check if you have reached an edge of the viewable
  // area, and if so, you move the view area and all of the
  // game objects so that the game appears to wrap.
  wrap();
  return(retVal);
}

/**
 * Tell the cowboy to jump.
 */
void jump() {
  myCowboy.jump();
}

}
```

Using the Sprite Class

A Sprite is a graphical object represented by one image (at a time). The fact that a Sprite is composed of only one image is the principal difference between a Sprite and a TiledLayer, which is a region that's covered with images that can be manipulated. (The Sprite class has a few extra features, but the fact that it uses one image rather than filling an area with images is the most obvious difference.) So, a Sprite is generally used for small, active game objects (such as your spaceship and the asteroids that are coming to crash into it), and a TiledLayer would be more likely to be used for an animated background. One cool feature of a Sprite is that even though a Sprite is represented by only one image at a time, it can be easily represented by different images under different circumstances, including by a series of images that make up an animation. In my example game, the cowboy has three different images in which he's walking and one in which he's jumping. All of the images used for a given Sprite need to be stored together in a single image file. (To indicate where to find the image file to use, send the address of the image within the JAR in the same format that's used to find resources in the method Class.getResource(); see Chapter 1 for more details.) Multiple frames are stored in a single Image object, which is a convenience that means you don't have to manipulate multiple Image objects to determine which face your Sprite is wearing at any given time. Figure 3-3 shows the image file for the cowboy Sprite.

Figure 3-3. *The image file to use for the cowboy Sprite*

The tumbleweed image file consists of three frames that give a rolling animation when shown in sequence (see Figure 3-4).

Figure 3-4. *The tumbleweed image*

The way to select which frame is shown at any given time is intuitive. First, if your image file comprises multiple images (as these two do), you should construct the Sprite with the constructor that specifies the width and height (in pixels) that you'd like your Sprite to be. The width and height of the Image should be integer multiples of the width and height you send to the constructor. In other words, the computer should be able to divide your image file evenly into rectangles of the size you specify. As you can see from the previous examples, you can arrange the subimages arranged horizontally or vertically. You can even arrange them in a grid with multiple rows and columns. Then, to identify the individual frames, they're numbered starting with zero at the top-left corner, continuing to the right and then continuing to the lower rows, in the same order in which you're reading the letters on this page. To select the frame that's currently displayed, use the method setFrame(int sequenceIndex), sending the frame number as an argument.

The Sprite class has some added support for animation that allows you to define a frame sequence with the method setFrameSequence(int[] sequence). As you can see in Listing 3-5 a bit later, I've set a frame sequence of { 1, 2, 3, 2 } for my cowboy and { 0, 1, 2 } for my tumbleweed. (Note that for the tumbleweed, the frame sequence I'd like to use is just the default frame sequence, so I don't have to set the Tumbleweed's frame sequence in the code.) To advance your Sprite's animation from one frame to the next, you use the method nextFrame() (or, if you prefer, prevFrame()). This is convenient in cases such as my tumbleweed where all the available frames are used in the animation. It's slightly less convenient in cases such as my cowboy that have an image or images that fall outside of the frame sequence of the animation. This is because once a frame sequence has been set, the argument to the method setFrame (int sequenceIndex) gives the index of an entry in the frame sequence instead of giving the index of the frame itself. What that means is that once I've set my cowboy's frame sequence to { 3, 2, 1, 2 }, if I call setFrame(0), it'll show frame number 1, setFrame(1) will show frame number 2, setFrame(2) will show frame number 3, and setFrame(3) will show frame number 2. But when the cowboy is jumping, I'd like it to show frame number 0, which is no longer accessible. So, when my cowboy jumps, I have to set my frame sequence to null before calling setFrame(0), and then I have to set my frame sequence back to the animation sequence { 1, 2, 3, 2 } afterward. Listing 3-5 shows this in the methods jump() and advance(int tickCount, boolean left). Figure 3-5 shows how the cells of the cowboy sprite are numbered before setting a frame sequence, and Figure 3-6 shows how the cells are numbered after the frame sequence has been defined. Figure 3-6 also shows the order in which the cells will be displayed to animate the cowboy as he is walking.

Figure 3-5. *The default numbering system for the cells of the cowboy Sprite*

Figure 3-6. *The numbering system of the cowboy Sprite's cells after the "walking cowboy animation" frame sequence has been set*

In addition to changing your Sprite's appearance by changing frames, you can change it by applying simple transforms such as rotations or mirror images. Both my cowboy and my tumbleweed in Listings 3-5 and 3-6 can be going either left or right, so of course I need to use the mirror image transform to change from one direction to the other.

Once you start applying transforms, you need to keep track of the Sprite's reference pixel. This is because when you transform your Sprite, the reference pixel is the pixel that doesn't move. You might expect that if your Sprite's image is square, then after a transformation the Sprite's image will continue to occupy the same square of area on the screen. This isn't the case. The best way to illustrate what happens is to imagine an example Sprite of a standing person facing left whose reference pixel has been defined to be the tip of his toe. Then after applying a 90-degree rotation, your person will be in the spot he'd be in if he had tripped and fallen forward. Clearly, this has its applications if your Sprite has a special pixel (such as the tip of an arrow) that should stay put after a transformation. But if you want your Sprite to continue to occupy the same space on the screen after a transformation, then you should first call defineReferencePixel(int x, int y) and set your Sprite's reference pixel to the center of the Sprite, as I did in the Cowboy constructor in Listing 3-5. (Another trick to keep the Sprite from moving after a transformation is to use getX() and getY() to get the absolute coordinates of the Sprite's upper-left corner before the transformation and then, after the transformation, use setPosition() to set the upper-left corner back to the earlier location.)

Be aware that the coordinates in defineReferencePixel(int x, int y) are relative to the top corner of the Sprite whereas the coordinates sent to setRefPixelPosition(int x, int y) tell where to place the Sprite's reference pixel on the screen in terms of the screen's coordinates. To be more precise, the coordinates sent to setRefPixelPosition(int x, int y) refer to the coordinate system of the Canvas if the Sprite is painted directly onto the Canvas, but if the Sprite is painted by a LayerManager, these coordinates should be given in terms of the LayerManager's coordinate system. (I explained how these coordinate systems fit together in the earlier "Using the LayerManager Class" section.) The coordinates in the various methods to set and get the position of the reference pixel or to set and get the position of the pixel in the top-left corner refer to the coordinates of the appropriate Canvas or LayerManager. Also note that if you perform multiple transformations, the later transformations are applied to the original image and not to its current state. In other words, if I apply setTransform(TRANS_MIRROR) twice in a row, the second transform won't mirror my image back to its original position; it'll just repeat the action of setting the Image to being a mirror image of the original Image. If you want to set a transformed Sprite back to normal, use setTransform(TRANS_NONE). This is illustrated in the top of the Cowboy.advance(int tickCount, boolean left) method.

Another great feature of the Layer class (including both Sprites and TiledLayers) is the support it gives you for placing your objects in relative terms instead of in absolute terms. If your Sprite needs to move over three pixels regardless of where it currently is, you can just call move(int x, int y), sending it the x and y distances it should move from its current position, as opposed to calling setRefPixelPosition(int x, int y) with the absolute coordinates of the Sprite's new location. Even more useful is the set of collidesWith() methods. This allows you to check if a Sprite is occupying the same space as another Sprite or TiledLayer or even an Image. It's easy to see that this saves you quite a number of comparisons, especially since when you send the pixelLevel argument as true, it will consider the two Layers as having collided only if their opaque pixels overlap.

In the Tumbleweed game, after advancing all of the Sprites, I check if the cowboy has collided with any tumbleweeds. (This happens in the Cowboy.checkCollision(Tumbleweed tumbleweed) method that's called from `JumpManager.advance(int gameTicks)`.) I check the collisions between the cowboy and all of the tumbleweeds each time because it automatically returns `false` for any tumbleweeds that aren't currently visible anyway, so I'm not really being wasteful by checking the cowboy against tumbleweeds that aren't currently in use. In many cases, however, you can save some effort by checking only for collisions that you know are possible rather than checking all of the `Sprite`s against each other. Note that in my example I don't bother to check if the tumbleweeds collide with each other or if anything collides with the background grass because that's irrelevant. If you're checking for pixel-level collisions, you'll want to be sure your images have a transparent background. (This is also helpful in general so that your `Sprite` doesn't paint an ugly rectangle of background color over another `Sprite` or `Image`.) You can find some discussion of creating the image files correctly in the sidebar "Making Image Files" in Chapter 1.

Listing 3-5 shows the code for `Cowboy.java`.

Listing 3-5. *Cowboy.java*

```java
package net.frog_parrot.jump;

import javax.microedition.lcdui.*;
import javax.microedition.lcdui.game.*;

/**
 * This class represents the player.
 *
 * @author Carol Hamer
 */
public class Cowboy extends Sprite {

  //-----------------------------------------------------------
  //    dimension fields

  /**
   * The width of the cowboy's bounding rectangle.
   */
  static final int WIDTH = 32;

  /**
   * The height of the cowboy's bounding rectangle.
   */
  static final int HEIGHT = 48;

  /**
   * This is the order that the frames should be displayed
   * for the animation.
   */
  static final int[] FRAME_SEQUENCE = { 3, 2, 1, 2 };

  //-----------------------------------------------------------
```

```
//     instance fields

/**
 * the X coordinate of the cowboy where the cowboy starts
 * the game.
 */
private int myInitialX;

/**
 * the Y coordinate of the cowboy when not jumping.
 */
private int myInitialY;

/**
 * The jump index that indicates that no jump is
 * currently in progress.
 */
private int myNoJumpInt = -6;

/**
 * Where the cowboy is in the jump sequence.
 */
private int myIsJumping = myNoJumpInt;

/**
 * If the cowboy is currently jumping, this keeps track
 * of how many points have been scored so far during
 * the jump.  This helps the calculation of bonus points since
 * the points being scored depend on how many tumbleweeds
 * are jumped in a single jump.
 */
private int myScoreThisJump = 0;

//------------------------------------------------------------
//   initialization

/**
 * constructor initializes the image and animation.
 */
public Cowboy(int initialX, int initialY) throws Exception {
  super(Image.createImage("/images/cowboy.png"),
        WIDTH, HEIGHT);
  myInitialX = initialX;
  myInitialY = initialY;
  // you define the reference pixel to be in the middle
```

```java
  // of the cowboy image so that when the cowboy turns
  // from right to left (and vice versa) he does not
  // appear to move to a different location.
  definedReferencePixel(WIDTH/2, 0);
  setRefPixelPosition(myInitialX, myInitialY);
  setFrameSequence(FRAME_SEQUENCE);
}

//------------------------------------------------------------
//   game methods

/**
 * If the cowboy has landed on a tumbleweed, you decrease
 * the score.
 */
int checkCollision(Tumbleweed tumbleweed) {
  int retVal = 0;
  if(collidesWith(tumbleweed, true)) {
    retVal = 1;
    // once the cowboy has collided with the tumbleweed,
    // that tumbleweed is done for now, so you call reset
    // which makes it invisible and ready to be reused.
    tumbleweed.reset();
  }
  return(retVal);
}

/**
 * set the cowboy back to its initial position.
 */
void reset() {
  myIsJumping = myNoJumpInt;
  setRefPixelPosition(myInitialX, myInitialY);
  setFrameSequence(FRAME_SEQUENCE);
  myScoreThisJump = 0;
  // at first the cowboy faces right:
  setTransform(TRANS_NONE);
}

//------------------------------------------------------------
//   graphics

/**
 * alter the cowboy image appropriately for this frame.
 */
void advance(int tickCount, boolean left) {
```

```
    if(left) {
      // use the mirror image of the cowboy graphic when
      // the cowboy is going toward the left.
      setTransform(TRANS_MIRROR);
      move(-1, 0);
    } else {
      // use the (normal, untransformed) image of the cowboy
      // graphic when the cowboy is going toward the right.
      setTransform(TRANS_NONE);
      move(1, 0);
    }
    // this section advances the animation:
    // every third time through the loop, the cowboy
    // image is changed to the next image in the walking
    // animation sequence:
    if(tickCount % 3 == 0) { // slow the animation down a little
      if(myIsJumping == myNoJumpInt) {
        // if he's not jumping, set the image to the next
        // frame in the walking animation:
        nextFrame();
      } else {
        // if he's jumping, advance the jump:
        // the jump continues for several passes through
        // the main game loop, and myIsJumping keeps track
        // of where you are in the jump:
        myIsJumping++;
        if(myIsJumping < 0) {
          // myIsJumping starts negative, and while it's
          // still negative, the cowboy is going up.
          // here you use a shift to make the cowboy go up a
          // lot in the beginning of the jump and ascend
          // more and more slowly as he reaches his highest
          // position:
          setRefPixelPosition(getRefPixelX(),
                          getRefPixelY() - (2<<(-myIsJumping)));
        } else {
          // once myIsJumping is negative, the cowboy starts
          // going back down until he reaches the end of the
          // jump sequence:
          if(myIsJumping != -myNoJumpInt - 1) {
            setRefPixelPosition(getRefPixelX(),
                          getRefPixelY() + (2<<myIsJumping));
          } else {
            // once the jump is done, you reset the cowboy to
            // his nonjumping position:
```

```
            myIsJumping = myNoJumpInt;
            setRefPixelPosition(getRefPixelX(), myInitialY);
            // you set the image back to being the walking
            // animation sequence rather than the jumping image:
            setFrameSequence(FRAME_SEQUENCE);
            // myScoreThisJump keeps track of how many points
            // were scored during the current jump (to keep
            // track of the bonus points earned for jumping
            // multiple tumbleweeds).  Once the current jump is done,
            // you set it back to zero.
            myScoreThisJump = 0;
          }
        }
      }
    }
  }

/**
 * makes the cowboy jump.
 */
void jump() {
  if(myIsJumping == myNoJumpInt) {
    myIsJumping++;
    // switch the cowboy to use the jumping image
    // rather than the walking animation images:
    setFrameSequence(null);
    setFrame(0);
  }
}

/**
 * This is called whenever the cowboy clears a tumbleweed
 * so that more points are scored when more tumbleweeds
 * are cleared in a single jump.
 */
int increaseScoreThisJump() {
  if(myScoreThisJump == 0) {
    myScoreThisJump++;
  } else {
    myScoreThisJump *= 2;
  }
  return(myScoreThisJump);
}

}
```

Listing 3-6 shows the code for Tumbleweed.java.

Listing 3-6. *Tumbleweed.java*

```java
package net.frog_parrot.jump;

import java.util.Random;

import javax.microedition.lcdui.*;
import javax.microedition.lcdui.game.*;

/**
 * This class represents the tumbleweeds that the player
 * must jump over.
 *
 * @author Carol Hamer
 */
public class Tumbleweed extends Sprite {

  //-----------------------------------------------------------
  //   dimension fields

  /**
   * The width of the tumbleweed's bounding square.
   */
  static final int WIDTH = 16;

  //-----------------------------------------------------------
  //   instance fields

  /**
   * Random number generator to randomly decide when to appear.
   */
  private Random myRandom = new Random();

  /**
   * whether this tumbleweed has been jumped over.
   * This is used to calculate the score.
   */
  private boolean myJumpedOver;

  /**
   * whether this tumbleweed enters from the left.
   */
  private boolean myLeft;
```

```
/**
 * the Y coordinate of the tumbleweed.
 */
private int myY;

//------------------------------------------------------------
//   initialization

/**
 * constructor initializes the image and animation.
 * @param left whether this tumbleweed enters from the left.
 */
public Tumbleweed(boolean left) throws Exception {
  super(Image.createImage("/images/tumbleweed.png"),
        WIDTH, WIDTH);
  myY = JumpManager.DISP_HEIGHT - WIDTH - 2;
  myLeft = left;
  if(!myLeft) {
    setTransform(TRANS_MIRROR);
  }
  myJumpedOver = false;
  setVisible(false);
}

//------------------------------------------------------------
//   graphics

/**
 * move the tumbleweed back to its initial (inactive) state.
 */
void reset() {
  setVisible(false);
  myJumpedOver = false;
}

/**
 * alter the tumbleweed image appropriately for this frame.
 * @param left whether the player is moving left
 * @return how much the score should change by after this
 *         advance.
 */
int advance(Cowboy cowboy, int tickCount, boolean left,
            int currentLeftBound, int currentRightBound) {
  int retVal = 0;
```

```
// if the tumbleweed goes outside of the display
// region, set it to invisible since it is
// no longer in use.
if((getRefPixelX() + WIDTH <= currentLeftBound) ||
   (getRefPixelX() - WIDTH >= currentRightBound)) {
  setVisible(false);
}
// If the tumbleweed is no longer in use (i.e. invisible)
// it is given a 1 in 100 chance (per game loop)
// of coming back into play:
if(!isVisible()) {
  int rand = getRandomInt(100);
  if(rand == 3) {
    // when the tumbleweed comes back into play,
    // you reset the values to what they should
    // be in the active state:
    myJumpedOver = false;
    setVisible(true);
    // set the tumbleweed's position to the point
    // where it just barely appears on the screen
    // so that it can start approaching the cowboy:
    if(myLeft) {
      setRefPixelPosition(currentRightBound, myY);
      move(-1, 0);
    } else {
      setRefPixelPosition(currentLeftBound, myY);
      move(1, 0);
    }
  }
} else {
  // when the tumbleweed is active, you advance the
  // rolling animation to the next frame and then
  // move the tumbleweed in the right direction across
  // the screen.
  if(tickCount % 2 == 0) { // slow the animation down a little
    nextFrame();
  }
  if(myLeft) {
    move(-3, 0);
    // if the cowboy just passed the tumbleweed
    // (without colliding with it) you increase the
    // cowboy's score and set myJumpedOver to true
    // so that no further points will be awarded
    // for this tumbleweed until it goes off the screen
    // and then is later reactivated:
```

```
        if((! myJumpedOver) &&
            (getRefPixelX() < cowboy.getRefPixelX())) {
          myJumpedOver = true;
          retVal = cowboy.increaseScoreThisJump();
        }
      } else {
        move(3, 0);
        if((! myJumpedOver) &&
            (getRefPixelX() > cowboy.getRefPixelX() + Cowboy.WIDTH)) {
          myJumpedOver = true;
          retVal = cowboy.increaseScoreThisJump();
        }
      }
    }
    return(retVal);
  }

  /**
   * Gets a random int between
   * zero and the param upper.
   */
  public int getRandomInt(int upper) {
    int retVal = myRandom.nextInt() % upper;
    if(retVal < 0) {
      retVal += upper;
    }
    return(retVal);
  }

}
```

Using the TiledLayer Class

As mentioned, the TiledLayer class is similar to the Sprite class except that a TiledLayer can consist of multiple cells, each of which is painted with an individually set image frame. The other differences between TiledLayer and Sprite are mostly related to functionality missing from TiledLayer; TiledLayer has no transforms, reference pixel, or frame sequence.

Of course, the mere fact that you're simultaneously managing multiple images complicates things a bit. I'll explain it by going over my subclass of TiledLayer, which I've called Grass. This class represents a row of grass in the background that waves back and forth as the game is being played (see Figure 3-7). To make it more interesting, some of the cells in my TiledLayer have animated grasses, and others have no tall grasses and hence just consist of a green line representing the ground at the bottom of the cell.

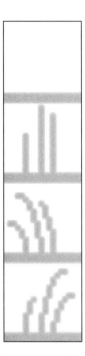

Figure 3-7. *The image file that's used by the Grass TiledLayer*

■Caution The tile index for Sprite starts with 0, but the tile index for TiledLayer starts with 1! This is a little confusing (it caused me to get an IndexOutOfBoundsException the first time I made a Sprite because I assumed that the Sprite images were numbered like the TiledLayer images). Yet the system is completely logical. In a TiledLayer, the tile index 0 indicates a blank tile (in other words, paint nothing in the cell if the cell's tile index is set to 0). A Sprite, however, comprises only one cell, so if you want that cell to be blank, then you can just call setVisible(false), meaning that Sprite doesn't need to reserve a special index to indicate a blank tile. This little confusion in the indexes shouldn't pose a big problem, but it's something to keep in mind if you can't figure out why your animation appears to be displaying the wrong images. Aside from this point, the image file is divided into individual frames or tiles in TiledLayer just as in Sprite, explained previously.

The first step in creating your TiledLayer is to decide how many rows and columns of cells you'll need. If you don't want your layer to be rectangular, it isn't a problem because any unused cells are by default set to being blank, which prevents them from getting in the way of other images. In my example, shown in Listing 3-7 in a moment, I have only one row, and I calculate the number of columns based on the width of the screen.

In the course of the game, the background tiled layer moves to the right and to the left to give the impression that the cowboy is moving (even though in reality he stays in the center of the screen), so to give plenty of room to translate the background, it is calculated to be a little more than three times the width of the screen. You can see that in the constructor Grass() in

Listing 3-7 contains the calculation for how many columns of background tiles are needed to cover three times the width of the screen. Then, since grass is sparse in this cowboy's world, only some of the background tiles have grass. To keep it simple, the sequence of cells repeats after every five columns: the zeroth and second columns contain the image of blades of grass; the others do not. To illustrate, if the screen were just a little narrower than eight cells wide, then the tiled layer of Grass would be one row high and 24 columns wide, and would look like Figure 3-8.

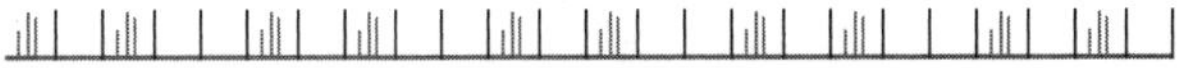

Figure 3-8. *The background tiled layer for a screen 150 pixels wide, with outlines drawn around each cell.*

Once you've set how many rows and columns you'll be using, you can fill each cell with a tile using the method setCell(int col, int row, int tileIndex). The earlier section "Using the Sprite Class" explained the tileIndex argument. If you'd like some of the cells to be filled with animated images, you need to create an animated tile by calling createAnimatedTile(int staticTileIndex), which returns the tile index that has been allotted to your new animated tile. You can make as many animated tiles as you want, but remember that each animated tile can be used in multiple cells if you want the cells to display the same animation simultaneously. In my case, even though all of the cells with the grass image in them are animated, I create only one animated tile and reuse it because I want all of my animated grass to be waving in sync. The cells are set in the constructor of Grass in Listing 3-7. To advance the animation, you don't get built-in frame-sequence functionality as in Sprite, so you have to set the frames with the method setAnimatedTile(int animatedTileIndex, int staticTileIndex). This sets the current frame of the given animated tile. Thus, all the cells that have been set to contain the animated tile corresponding to animatedTileIndex will change to the image given by the argument staticTileIndex. To simplify the animation updates, it's easy to add your own frame-sequence functionality; see the method Grass.advance(int tickCount) for an idea of how to do it.

Listing 3-7 shows the code for the last class, Grass.java.

Listing 3-7. *Grass.java*

```
package net.frog_parrot.jump;

import javax.microedition.lcdui.*;
import javax.microedition.lcdui.game.*;

/**
 * This class draws the background grass.
 *
 * @author Carol Hamer
 */
public class Grass extends TiledLayer {

  //-----------------------------------------------------------
```

```
//    dimension fields
//  (constant after initialization)

/**
 * The width of the square tiles that make up this layer.
 */
static final int TILE_WIDTH = 20;

/**
 * This is the order that the frames should be displayed
 * for the animation.
 */
static final int[] FRAME_SEQUENCE = { 2, 3, 2, 4 };

/**
 * This gives the number of squares of grass to put along
 * the bottom of the screen.
 */
static int COLUMNS;

/**
 * After how many tiles does the background repeat.
 */
static final int CYCLE = 5;

/**
 * the fixed Y coordinate of the strip of grass.
 */
static int TOP_Y;

//-------------------------------------------------------------
//    instance fields

/**
 * Which tile you are currently on in the frame sequence.
 */
private int mySequenceIndex = 0;

/**
 * The index to use in the static tiles array to get the
 * animated tile.
 */
private int myAnimatedTileIndex;

//-------------------------------------------------------------
//    gets / sets

/**
```

```
 * Takes the width of the screen and sets my columns
 * to the correct corresponding number
 */
static int setColumns(int screenWidth) {
  COLUMNS = ((screenWidth / 20) + 1)*3;
  return(COLUMNS);
}


//----------------------------------------------------------
//    initialization

/**
 * constructor initializes the image and animation.
 */
public Grass() throws Exception {
  super(setColumns(JumpCanvas.DISP_WIDTH), 1,
        Image.createImage("/images/grass.png"),
        TILE_WIDTH, TILE_WIDTH);
  TOP_Y = JumpManager.DISP_HEIGHT - TILE_WIDTH;
  setPosition(0, TOP_Y);
  myAnimatedTileIndex = createAnimatedTile(2);
  for(int i = 0; i < COLUMNS; i++) {
    if((i % CYCLE == 0) || (i % CYCLE == 2)) {
      setCell(i, 0, myAnimatedTileIndex);
    } else {
      setCell(i, 0, 1);
    }
  }
}


//----------------------------------------------------------
//    graphics

/**
 * sets the grass back to its initial position.
 */
void reset() {
  setPosition(-(TILE_WIDTH*CYCLE), TOP_Y);
  mySequenceIndex = 0;
  setAnimatedTile(myAnimatedTileIndex, FRAME_SEQUENCE[mySequenceIndex]);
}

/**
 * alter the background image appropriately for this frame.
 * @param left whether the player is moving left
 */
void advance(int tickCount) {
```

```
    if(tickCount % 2 == 0) { // slow the animation down a little
      mySequenceIndex++;
      mySequenceIndex %= 4;
      setAnimatedTile(myAnimatedTileIndex, FRAME_SEQUENCE[mySequenceIndex]);
    }
  }

}
```

One last point to note about using Layers (including Sprite and TiledLayer) is that there is a performance cost on some handsets. In other words, you will often get faster screen painting by writing your own utilities to manage where graphical objects need to appear on the screen and then doing paints using the Graphics.drawImage() method. So you need to consider your project—its complexity and range of target handsets—when deciding whether to use the javax.microedition.lcdui.game package as in this example or write your own optimized implementation. However, even if you're ambitious enough to write your own game utility classes, the javax.microedition.lcdui.game package serves as a good model of how to structure game utility classes for ease of use.

Summary

So, now you've seen a basic game that illustrates how to use all of the classes of the javax.microedition.lcdui.game package: juggling the different coordinate systems of the various layers to create a simple window into your game's universe, and especially how to take advantage of the graphics and animation features. In the next chapter, you'll take the same game and improve it by adding some more threads to play music and to optimize performance.

CHAPTER 4

■■■

Using Threads and Media

In this chapter, you'll improve the Tumbleweed game from the previous chapter by adding some new threads. One of the new threads will make the algorithm that releases the tumbleweeds more efficient, and the other new thread will play background music. You won't need to change some of the classes for this version, and therefore the code for certain classes won't be repeated in this chapter. Please see Chapter 3 if you'd like to review the source code for GameThread.java, Cowboy.java, and Grass.java (which the current example also uses). The following listings include the code for the modified classes.

Using Threads

Working with threads is a standard skill that most Java developers learn pretty quickly. But since threading is tricky and threading errors are difficult to reproduce and often show up unexpectedly when porting from one platform to another, I'll devote nearly the whole chapter to threading strategies and threading issues. If you're already comfortable with threads and you just want to see an example of how to add music to your game, you can skip to the "Using Media" section.

Differences Between CLDC Threads and Threads in Standard Java

Two main thread-related items have been eliminated in CLDC: the class ThreadGroup and the possibility of marking your threads as daemon threads. You won't miss them. This is another case of the CLDC specification authors eliminating something that you didn't need anyway.

Daemon threads can be useful in many programs. Marking a thread as a daemon is a way of telling the program not to wait around for the thread to finish—if the rest of the program is done, just exit. For example, in a game you may use a daemon thread to move around background items. Throughout the game you want the background items to keep moving, but once the player's character is dead, of course you don't want the program to keep going just for the sake of the background animation. But in a Mobile Internet Device Profile (MIDP) program, daemon threads wouldn't work as you may like them to work. Since a MIDlet is run by application management software (AMS), the end of the MIDlet's lifecycle doesn't correspond to the Java Virtual Machine (JVM) exiting. Regardless of how many threads the MIDlet has started, and regardless of whether they're active, the MIDlet's active life ends when it's destroyed. It's therefore not even clear what it would mean for a thread to be a daemon in this case.

The ThreadGroup class, on the other hand, is essentially useless even for versions of Java that allow its use. Its original purpose was to group the threads of a program to simplify pausing, restarting, and stopping them all at once. But as you probably know, the methods Thread.suspend(), Thread.resume(), and Thread.stop() were all deprecated because they're inherently unsafe. ThreadGroup's uncaughtException() method can be useful, but without the thread lifecycle methods, putting your threads in a ThreadGroup isn't significantly more useful than grouping them in a Vector.

You may wonder what you're supposed to do to pause or stop your game if it has multiple threads running. If you've done much programming with threads, you probably already know the answer. Your thread classes should have fields that serve as flags, telling the thread to pause or stop. Other classes can set these fields, and then your Thread subclass can query the fields and pause or stop when it becomes convenient to do so. In fact, this is exactly what I did in the GameThread class of the previous version of the Tumbleweed game. Since that class will not be changed for this version, I won't reprint it here. See the "Using the Thread Class" section in Chapter 3 to review how it works. The pause flags are set by my MIDlet subclass (called Jump). I've included the code for Jump in Listing 4-1 because there are some changes in this version. Basically, since I've added some more threads, I've separated the code to start and stop the threads and grouped it, specifically differentiating between cases where the user has initiated a pause or resume action from when the platform has initiated a pause or resume action (explained just after Listing 4-2). Also, since one of my new threads plays music and since I want to allow the user to turn the music on and off while the game is running, I've added code to just pause and unpause the music alone.

Listing 4-1 shows the code for the new version of Jump.java.

Listing 4-1. *Jump.java*

```java
package net.frog_parrot.jump;

import javax.microedition.midlet.*;
import javax.microedition.lcdui.*;

/**
 * This is the main class of the Tumbleweed game.
 *
 * @author Carol Hamer
 */
public class Jump extends MIDlet implements CommandListener {

  //-------------------------------------------------------------
  //    commands

  /**
   * the command to end the game.
   */
  private Command myExitCommand = new Command("Exit", Command.EXIT, 99);
```

```
/**
 * the command to start moving when the game is paused.
 */
private Command myGoCommand = new Command("Go", Command.SCREEN, 1);

/**
 * the command to pause the game.
 */
private Command myPauseCommand = new Command("Pause", Command.SCREEN, 1);

/**
 * the command to start a new game.
 */
private Command myNewCommand = new Command("Play Again", Command.SCREEN, 1);

/**
 * The command to start/pause the music.  (This command may appear in a menu.)
 */
private Command myMusicCommand = new Command("Music", Command.SCREEN, 2);

//-----------------------------------------------------------
//   game object fields

/**
 * the canvas that all the game will be drawn on.
 */
private JumpCanvas myCanvas;

//-----------------------------------------------------------
//   thread fields

/**
 * the thread that advances the cowboy.
 */
private GameThread myGameThread;

/**
 * The class that plays music if the user wants.
 */
private MusicMaker myMusicMaker;
//private ToneControlMusicMaker myMusicMaker;

/**
 * The thread that sets tumbleweeds in motion at random
 * intervals.
 */
private TumbleweedThread myTumbleweedThread;
```

```java
/**
 * if the user has paused the game.
 */
private boolean myGamePause;

/**
 * if the game is paused because it is hidden.
 */
private boolean myHiddenPause;

//-------------------------------------------------------
//    initialization and game state changes

/**
 * Empty constructor.
 */
public Jump() {

}

/**
 * Switch the command to the play again command.
 */
void setNewCommand() {
  myCanvas.removeCommand(myPauseCommand);
  myCanvas.removeCommand(myGoCommand);
  myCanvas.addCommand(myNewCommand);
}

/**
 * Switch the command to the go command.
 */
private void setGoCommand() {
  myCanvas.removeCommand(myPauseCommand);
  myCanvas.removeCommand(myNewCommand);
  myCanvas.addCommand(myGoCommand);
}

/**
 * Switch the command to the pause command.
 */
private void setPauseCommand() {
  myCanvas.removeCommand(myNewCommand);
  myCanvas.removeCommand(myGoCommand);
  myCanvas.addCommand(myPauseCommand);
}

//-------------------------------------------------------------------
```

```
//  implementation of MIDlet
// these methods may be called by the application management
// software at any time, so you always check fields for null
// before calling methods on them.

/**
 * Start the application.
 */
public void startApp() throws MIDletStateChangeException {
  try {
    // if this is the first call to startApp,
    // initialize the game, otherwise set the
    // game to a paused state (that the user
    // must unpause) since we're returning
    // from a call.
   if(myCanvas == null) {
      myCanvas = new JumpCanvas(this);
      myCanvas.addCommand(myExitCommand);
      myCanvas.addCommand(myMusicCommand);
      myCanvas.addCommand(myPauseCommand);
      myCanvas.setCommandListener(this);
      myCanvas.start();
      myCanvas.flushKeys();
      systemStartThreads();
    } else {
      myCanvas.flushKeys();
      userPauseThreads();
    }
  } catch(Exception e) {
    errorMsg(e);
  }
}

/**
 * stop and throw out the garbage.
 */
public void destroyApp(boolean unconditional)
    throws MIDletStateChangeException {
  try {
    stopThreads();
    myCanvas = null;
    System.gc();
  } catch(Exception e) {
    errorMsg(e);
  }
}
```

```java
/**
 * request the game to pause. This method is called
 * by the application management software, not in
 * response to a user pausing the game.
 */
public void pauseApp() {
  try {
    if(myCanvas != null) {
      setGoCommand();
      systemPauseThreads();
    }
  } catch(Exception e) {
    errorMsg(e);
  }
}

//------------------------------------------------------------------
//  implementation of CommandListener

/*
 * Respond to a command issued on the Canvas.
 * (either reset or exit).
 */
public void commandAction(Command c, Displayable s) {
  try {
    if(c == myGoCommand) {
      myCanvas.removeCommand(myGoCommand);
      myCanvas.addCommand(myPauseCommand);
      myCanvas.flushKeys();
      userStartThreads();
    } else if(c == myPauseCommand) {
      myCanvas.removeCommand(myPauseCommand);
      myCanvas.addCommand(myGoCommand);
      userPauseThreads();
    } else if(c == myNewCommand) {
      myCanvas.removeCommand(myNewCommand);
      myCanvas.addCommand(myPauseCommand);
      System.gc();
      myCanvas.reset();
      myCanvas.flushKeys();
      myHiddenPause = false;
      myGamePause = false;
      startThreads();
    } else if(c == myMusicCommand) {
      if(myMusicMaker != null) {
        myMusicMaker.toggle();
        myCanvas.repaint();
```

```
        myCanvas.serviceRepaints();
      }
    } else if((c == myExitCommand) || (c == Alert.DISMISS_COMMAND)) {
      try {
        destroyApp(false);
        notifyDestroyed();
      } catch (MIDletStateChangeException ex) {
      }
    }
  } catch(Exception e) {
    errorMsg(e);
  }
}


//---------------------------------------------------------
//  thread methods

/**
 * start up all the game's threads.
 * Creates them if necessary.
 * to be called when the user hits the go command.
 */
private synchronized void userStartThreads() throws Exception {
  myGamePause = false;
  if(! myHiddenPause) {
    startThreads();
  }
}


/**
 * start up all the game's threads.
 * Creates them if necessary.
 * used by showNotify
 */
synchronized void systemStartThreads() throws Exception {
  myHiddenPause = false;
  if(! myGamePause) {
    startThreads();
  }
}


/**
 * start up all the game's threads.
 * Creates them if necessary.
 * internal version.
 * note: if this were synchronized, would it cause deadlock?
 */
```

```
private void startThreads() throws Exception {
  if(myGameThread == null) {
    myGameThread = new GameThread(myCanvas);
    myGameThread.start();
  } else {
    myGameThread.resumeGame();
  }
  if(myTumbleweedThread == null) {
    myTumbleweedThread = new TumbleweedThread(myCanvas);
    myTumbleweedThread.start();
  } else {
    myTumbleweedThread.resumeGame();
  }
  if(myMusicMaker == null) {
    //myMusicMaker = new ToneControlMusicMaker();
    myMusicMaker = new MusicMaker();
    myMusicMaker.start();
  } else {
    myMusicMaker.resumeGame();
  }
}

/**
 * Pause all the threads started by this game.
 * to be called when the user hits the pause command.
 */
synchronized void userPauseThreads() {
  myGamePause = true;
  pauseThreads();
}




/**
 * Pause all the threads started by this game.
 * used by hideNotify
 */
void systemPauseThreads() {
  myHiddenPause = true;

  pauseThreads();
}

/**
 * pause all the game's threads.
 * Creates them if necessary.
 * internal version.
```

```
 * note: if this were synchronized, would it cause deadlock?
 */
private void pauseThreads() {
  if(myGameThread != null) {
    myGameThread.pauseGame();
  }
  if(myTumbleweedThread != null) {
    myTumbleweedThread.pauseGame();


  }
  if(myMusicMaker != null) {
    myMusicMaker.pauseGame();
  }
}


/**
 * Stop all the threads started by this game and
 * delete them as they are no longer usable.
 */
private synchronized void stopThreads() {
  if(myGameThread != null) {
    myGameThread.requestStop();
  }
  if(myTumbleweedThread != null) {
    myTumbleweedThread.requestStop();
  }
  if(myMusicMaker != null) {
    myMusicMaker.requestStop();
  }
  myGameThread = null;
  myTumbleweedThread = null;
  myMusicMaker = null;
}

//----------------------------------------------------------
//  error methods

/**
 * Converts an exception to a message and displays
 * the message.
 */
void errorMsg(Exception e) {
  if(e.getMessage() == null) {
    errorMsg(e.getClass().getName());
  } else {
    errorMsg(e.getClass().getName() + ":" + e.getMessage());
  }
}
```

```
/**
 * Displays an error message alert if something goes wrong.
 */
void errorMsg(String msg) {
  Alert errorAlert = new Alert("error",
                               msg, null, AlertType.ERROR);
  errorAlert.setCommandListener(this);
  errorAlert.setTimeout(Alert.FOREVER);
  Display.getDisplay(this).setCurrent(errorAlert);
}

}
```

The other big change you'll encounter when working with CLDC threads is a practical one: the computing power of the device. Most devices that use CLDC don't have the capacity to do parallel processing. So if you're accustomed to dividing your calculations between two threads to get them done faster, don't waste your energy on it here: your threads will merely take turns, and performance won't be enhanced.

Strategies for Deciding When to Use a New Thread

Spawning a new thread and starting it up is a costly operation in MIDP and hence should be done sparingly. A lot of times you can reuse a single thread for related tasks. For example, if you have an animation on one page and another animation on another, you could have a single thread class that is told to switch which animation it is updating when the user flips from one page to another. You can see this strategy in Chapter 10 when the thread class starts by advancing the opening animation and then goes on to advance the game animation (see Listing 10-6 in that chapter). Another example would be to have a single thread for all communications operations since they're generally blocking operations that need to be run on a separate thread. In Chapter 6 the receiver class that interprets incoming SMS messages (Listing 6-5) treats them all on the same thread, interpreting them one by one as they come in. Similarly, in the Bluetooth example (Chapter 7, Listing 7-1), all of the communications in both directions are performed on a single thread.

An important point to keep in mind when choosing whether you need a new thread is that the methods called by the AMS need to return quickly. Some methods to be especially careful with are your MIDlet's constructor, startApp(), pauseApp(), destroyApp(), and commandAction(). No method that might potentially block should ever be called directly from one of these methods. Instead, these methods should set the relevant data and spawn or notify another thread to call the blocking method. You probably already know that any method that is listening for incoming data is a blocking method. But keep in mind that any method that might require the user to give permission to use it is also potentially a blocking method because the AMS may display a permission screen, and the method will block until the user responds (see Chapter 8 for more on permissions). Additionally, many platforms have trouble if you perform nonblocking yet time-consuming operations from the methods called by the AMS. Time-consuming operations can include things like opening or closing the Record Management System, or RMS (see Chapter 5), or loading images from the JAR file (See the "Using the Sprite Class" section of Chapter 3). And failing to return quickly enough from one of the methods called by the AMS will crash many handsets.

In the Tumbleweed example—as with all of the examples in this book—the animations are run by a subclass of `Thread`. Another standard technique for advancing an animation (or other punctual, repeated task) is to use a `Timer` and a `TimerTask`. The `TimerTask` class implements the `Runnable` interface—it's the type of `Runnable` that is designed to be run repeatedly at fixed intervals by scheduling it on a `Timer` object. A typical application would be to implement the run method to contain a simple call to advance the animation and then call `Timer.schedule()` to schedule the task 20 times a second. `Timer` even allows you to choose what to do in case the Virtual Machine is unable to call the task on schedule for some reason. Fixed-rate runs each task according to absolute time—for example, every hour on the hour—and if one run gets delayed for some reason, the next one won't be. This is good for timed alarms but bad for animations because a long delay can cause the animation calls to bunch up and be run too frequently. For animations there's another choice, fixed-delay, which ensures that the delay between calls will never be less than the delay that is set when the task is scheduled. In the section on "Using the Thread Class" from Chapter 3, you saw how to implement the equivalent of a fixed-delay timer using the `Thread` class.

Why reinvent the wheel in these examples? Mostly because I like to have a handle on exactly how many threads are created and when each thread is spawned so I can optimize, but also because it's important to be comfortable with using threads and how they interact with each other, and creating at animation threads is instructive. However, if you have a simple game that has only one animation and no communications, it's simpler just to use a `TimerTask`. In the "Animations" section of Chapter 9, there's an example of an animation that is run by a `Timer`.

In the Tumbleweed example, you spawn three threads, which means there are really at least four threads running (and probably more), counting the threads used by the application management software to query the hardware for keystrokes among other things. Then you have the `GameThread` object, which contains the main game loop that updates the timer, moves all the graphical objects, and then repaints them. Then you have a thread that plays the music. If you use a `Player` to play your game's music, you won't need to spawn a new thread because `Player` will do that for you (see the "Playing Tones with a Player" section later in this chapter). But if you want the music to be synchronized with screen events, one strategy is to devote a thread to playing the music (see the "Playing Simple Tones" section, also later in this chapter) and then keep the music and the screen events aligned by keeping the two threads in contact with each other. The final thread that's spawned by the Tumbleweed game is a loop to decide when to start each new tumbleweed rolling.

In the earlier version of the Tumbleweed game, the technique I used to determine when a tumbleweed should start crossing the screen again once it was done with its previous pass wasn't very efficient. Basically, if the tumbleweed wasn't currently on the screen, then for every game tick (every pass through the main game animation loop), the tumbleweed generated a random number. If the number was the right one, the tumbleweed would start rolling across the screen again. But this means I'm wasting quite a lot of computing power to generate several random numbers for each game tick when I could just generate one random number to select a random length of time to wait before sending another tumbleweed across the screen. So, since the tumbleweeds starting off on their journeys across the screen is a repeated event that doesn't coincide with the repeated events on the other threads, I've created a new thread (called `TumbleweedThread`) to control this event.

The `TumbleweedThread` has a simple, standard design with a main loop where the action takes place and methods that allow the `MIDlet` to pause or stop it. Figure 4-1 shows how it works.

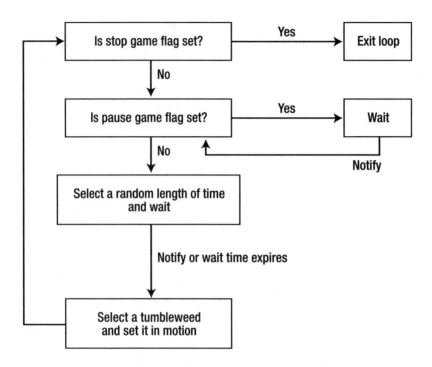

Figure 4-1. *The main loop of the TumbleweedThread class*

Listing 4-2 shows the code for TumbleweedThread.java.

Listing 4-2. *TumbleweedThread.java*

```
package net.frog_parrot.jump;

import java.util.Random;

/**
 * This class contains the loop that sets the tumbleweeds in motion.
 *
 * @author Carol Hamer
 */
public class TumbleweedThread extends Thread {

  //----------------------------------------------------------
  //   fields

  /**
   * Whether the main thread would like this thread
   * to pause.
   */
  private boolean myShouldPause;
```

```java
/**
 * Whether the main thread would like this thread
 * to stop.
 */
private boolean myShouldStop;

/**
 * A handle back to the graphical components.
 */
private Tumbleweed[] myTumbleweeds;

/**
 * Random number generator to randomly decide when to appear.
 */
private Random myRandom = new Random();

//------------------------------------------------------------
//   initialization

/**
 * standard constructor, sets data.
 */
TumbleweedThread(JumpCanvas canvas) throws Exception {
  myTumbleweeds = canvas.getTumbleweeds();
}

//------------------------------------------------------------
//   actions

/**
 * pause the thread.
 */
void pauseGame() {
  myShouldPause = true;
}

/**
 * restart the thread after a pause.
 */
synchronized void resumeGame() {
  myShouldPause = false;
  notify();
}

/**
 * stops the thread.
 */
```

```
synchronized void requestStop() {
  myShouldStop = true;
  notify();
}

/**
 * start the thread.
 */
public void run() {
  myShouldStop = false;
  myShouldPause = false;
  while(true) {
    if(myShouldStop) {
      break;
    }
    synchronized(this) {
      while(myShouldPause) {
        try {
          wait();
        } catch(Exception e) {}
      }
    }
    // wait a random length of time:
    int waitTime = (1 + getRandomInt(10)) * 100;
    synchronized(this) {
      try {
        wait(waitTime);
      } catch(Exception e) {}
    }
    if(!myShouldPause) {
      // randomly select which one to set in motion and
      // tell it to go.  If the chosen tumbleweed is
      // currently visible, it will not be affected
      int whichWeed = getRandomInt(myTumbleweeds.length);
      myTumbleweeds[whichWeed].go();
    }
  }
}

//------------------------------------------------------------
//    randomization utilities

/**
 * Gets a random int between
 * zero and the param upper (exclusive).
 */
public int getRandomInt(int upper) {
```

```java
    int retVal = myRandom.nextInt() % upper;
    if(retVal < 0) {
      retVal += upper;
    }
    return(retVal);
  }

}
```

Listing 4-3 shows the modified version of Tumbleweed.java.

Listing 4-3. *The Modified Tumbleweed.java*

```java
package net.frog_parrot.jump;

import javax.microedition.lcdui.*;
import javax.microedition.lcdui.game.*;

/**
 * This class represents the tumbleweeds that the player
 * must jump over.
 *
 * @author Carol Hamer
 */
public class Tumbleweed extends Sprite {

  //------------------------------------------------------------
  //   dimension fields

  /**
   * The width of the tumbleweed's bounding square.
   */
  static final int WIDTH = 16;

  //------------------------------------------------------------
  //   instance fields

  /**
   * whether this tumbleweed has been jumped over.
   * This calculates the score.
   */
  private boolean myJumpedOver;

  /**
   * whether this tumbleweed enters from the left.
   */
  private boolean myLeft;
```

```
/**
 * the Y coordinate of the tumbleweed.
 */
private int myY;

/**
 * the leftmost visible pixel.
 */
private int myCurrentLeftBound;

/**
 * the rightmost visible pixel.
 */
private int myCurrentRightBound;

//-----------------------------------------------------------
//   initialization

/**
 * constructor initializes the image and animation.
 * @param left whether this tumbleweed enters from the left.
 */
public Tumbleweed(boolean left) throws Exception {
  super(Image.createImage("/images/tumbleweed.png"),
        WIDTH, WIDTH);
  myY = JumpManager.DISP_HEIGHT - WIDTH - 2;
  myLeft = left;
  if(!myLeft) {
    setTransform(TRANS_MIRROR);
  }
  myJumpedOver = false;
  setVisible(false);
}

//-----------------------------------------------------------
//   game actions

/**
 * Set the tumbleweed in motion if it is not currently visible.
 */
synchronized boolean go() {
  boolean retVal = false;
  if(!isVisible()) {
    retVal = true;
    //System.out.println("Tumbleweed.go-->not visible");
    myJumpedOver = false;
    setVisible(true);
```

```
      // set the tumbleweed's position to the point
      // where it just barely appears on the screen
      // to that it can start approaching the cowboy:
      if(myLeft) {
        setRefPixelPosition(myCurrentRightBound, myY);
        move(-1, 0);
      } else {
        setRefPixelPosition(myCurrentLeftBound, myY);
        move(1, 0);
      }
    } else {
      //System.out.println("Tumbleweed.go-->visible");
    }
    return(retVal);
  }


//-----------------------------------------------------------
//   graphics

/**
 * move the tumbleweed back to its initial (inactive) state.
 */
void reset() {
  setVisible(false);
  myJumpedOver = false;
}

/**
 * alter the tumbleweed image appropriately for this frame.
 * @param left whether the player is moving left
 * @return how much the score should change by after this
 *         advance.
 */
synchronized int advance(Cowboy cowboy, int tickCount, boolean left,
             int currentLeftBound, int currentRightBound) {
  int retVal = 0;
  myCurrentLeftBound = currentLeftBound;
  myCurrentRightBound = currentRightBound;
  // if the tumbleweed goes outside of the display
  // region, set it to invisible since it is
  // no longer in use.
  if((getRefPixelX() - WIDTH >= currentRightBound) && (!myLeft)) {
    setVisible(false);
  }
  if((getRefPixelX() + WIDTH <= currentLeftBound) && myLeft) {
    setVisible(false);
  }
```

```
  if(isVisible()) {
    // when the tumbleweed is active, you advance the
    // rolling animation to the next frame and then
    // move the tumbleweed in the right direction across
    // the screen.
    if(tickCount % 2 == 0) { // slow the animation down a little
      nextFrame();
    }
    if(myLeft) {
      move(-3, 0);
      // if the cowboy just passed the tumbleweed
      // (without colliding with it), you increase the
      // cowboy's score and set myJumpedOver to true
      // so that no further points will be awarded
      // for this tumbleweed until it goes off the screen
      // and then is later reactivated:
      if((! myJumpedOver) &&
          (getRefPixelX() < cowboy.getRefPixelX())) {
        myJumpedOver = true;
        retVal = cowboy.increaseScoreThisJump();
      }
    } else {
      move(3, 0);
      if((! myJumpedOver) &&
          (getRefPixelX() > cowboy.getRefPixelX() + Cowboy.WIDTH)) {
        myJumpedOver = true;
        retVal = cowboy.increaseScoreThisJump();
      }
    }
  }
  return(retVal);
}

}
```

Note that the changes to Tumbleweed.java require adding the method shown in Listing 4-4 to JumpManager.java.

Listing 4-4. *Additions to JumpManager.java*

```
/**
 * @return a handle to the tumbleweed objects.
 */
Tumbleweed[] getTumbleweeds() {
  Tumbleweed[] retArray = new Tumbleweed[myLeftTumbleweeds.length
                                  + myRightTumbleweeds.length];
  for(int i = 0; i < myLeftTumbleweeds.length; i++) {
    retArray[i] = myLeftTumbleweeds[i];
  }
```

```
    for(int i = 0; i < myRightTumbleweeds.length; i++) {
      retArray[i + myLeftTumbleweeds.length] = myRightTumbleweeds[i];
    }
    return(retArray);
  }
```

You must also add a corresponding method to `JumpCanvas.java` as well as slightly modify the `setGameOver()` method. Additionally, I've added implementations to `showNotify()` and `hideNotify()`. These two are among the methods where behavior varies from one platform to another, but on most devices the implementation should match the behavior of the emulator. The changes to `showNotify()` and `hideNotify()` are necessary because the added command to toggle the music forced the emulator to put some commands in a menu. When the menu pops up, the game is hidden. Figure 4-2 shows what the game looks like when the user clicks the Menu button and the command menu obscures the game. But it wouldn't be fair for the tumbleweeds to keep rolling by and crashing into the cowboy while the user is busy with the menu. (In fact, while the menu is open, the game doesn't receive keystroke information and the display isn't updated, so the user may think the game is paused even if it's not.) So, I'd like for the game to pause when it's hidden and start again when it's displayed. My first solution was to put a call to `pauseGame()` in `hideNotify()` and a call to `resumeGame()` in `showNotify()`. The problem with this approach is that if the user selects the pause command from the menu, `showNotify()` will be called as soon as the menu goes away, starting the game again against the user's wishes! That's why I've created two distinct functions in the `Jump` code in Listing 4-1: `userPauseThreads()` and `systemPauseThreads()`. That way, the game proceeds only if the user wants it to proceed *and* the application management software verifies that the game isn't hidden.

Figure 4-2. *When the AMS displays the command menu, the game is paused.*

In addition to handling the situation where the platform has hidden the game canvas (either with a command menu or for some other reason), you also need to consider what happens when the device pauses the game because of an incoming call (or other interruption). In this case, the AMS will call `pauseApp()` to pause the game, and will call `startApp()` when the game resumes. Since this is the same `startApp()` method that is called when the application first starts, you need to write the code in such a way that it keeps track of whether the game is just starting or whether you're returning from a pause (see the implementation of `startApp()`

in Listing 4-1). In this example, when returning from a system-initiated pause, you set the game to the state of being in a user-initiated pause. The reason for this is that it may take a second for the user to be ready to return to play at the end of a call, so the game should be paused until the user is ready to unpause it. On the emulator, you can use the F6 and F7 keys to test whether you've implemented your pause/resume functionality correctly.

Listing 4-5 shows the added and modified parts of JumpCanvas.java.

Listing 4-5. *Additions and Changes to JumpCanvas.java*

```
//-------------------------------------------------------
//     gets/sets

  /**
   * This is called when the game ends.
   */
  void setGameOver() {
    myGameOver = true;
    myJump.userPauseThreads();
  }

  /**
   * @return a handle to the tumbleweed objects.
   */
  Tumbleweed[] getTumbleweeds() {
    return(myManager.getTumbleweeds());
  }

  //-------------------------------------------------------
  //     initialization and game state changes

  /**
   * pause the game when it's hidden.
   */
  protected void hideNotify() {
    try {
      myJump.systemPauseThreads();
    } catch(Exception oe) {
      myJump.errorMsg(oe);
    }
  }

  /**
   * When it comes back into view, unpause it.
   */
  protected void showNotify() {
    try {
      myJump.systemStartThreads();
    } catch(Exception oe) {
```

```
        myJump.errorMsg(oe);
    }
}
```

Avoiding Race Conditions and Deadlock

Synchronization issues are some of the hardest problems to locate and debug. This is because the errors they create are often rare and almost impossible to reproduce. You therefore have to do all your thread synchronization debugging by pure thought. To give you an idea of how to do it, I'll go over using the synchronized keyword in this example program and suggest how to keep your program thread safe. This section will contain nothing new for experienced Java programmers, but because keeping your program thread safe is at once tricky and important, I'll include this material for those readers who are new to it.

Recall the basics of how synchronization works: each instance of an object has a lock, and each class has a lock for its static methods. Suppose the instance is called myObject. If a thread enters a method for that instance marked with the synchronized keyword or if the thread enters a block of code contained in a block delineated by synchronized(myObject), then the thread picks up the instance's lock. If one thread is holding the lock for a particular instance, no other thread can enter any method or synchronized block for that particular instance until the thread currently holding the lock exits the synchronized method or block. This is a means of preventing *race conditions* in which two or more threads are at risk of modifying and/or acting on the values of data simultaneously. Clearly there are going to be problems if one thread completes the phrase if(x == y) and then another thread changes the value of x before the first thread executes all the statements in the if block.

Obviously, the problem arises when two or more threads are using the same data at the same time and at least one of those threads might modify that data. A naive solution is to use the synchronized keyword on every method that reads or modifies data. That would force all the threads to take turns using data-related methods. But that strategy would almost certainly lead to frequent *deadlock*, which is when two threads get stuck because each one is waiting for the other to give up a lock.

The best strategy is to analyze each class, method by method, to see where synchronization is needed and where it isn't. That's not as terrible as it sounds since it becomes second nature once you're used to doing it. Here are a few little tips:

- Use local method variables instead of class fields when you can because this avoids the necessity of making the method synchronized (local method variables can't be altered by other threads).

- Make each synchronized segment as small and simple as possible.

- Try to avoid grabbing a second lock from within a synchronized section.

You'll now see how these ideas apply to GameThread. Using synchronization in the other two thread classes is nearly identical to how you use it in GameThread. The run() method has two synchronized blocks and two other synchronized methods. Listing 4-6 shows what they look like.

Listing 4-6. *Synchronized Blocks and Methods*

```
/**
 * restart the game after a pause.
 */
synchronized void resumeGame() {
  myShouldPause = false;
  notify();
}

/**
 * stops the game.
 */
synchronized void requestStop() {
  myShouldStop = true;
  notify();
}

/**
 * start the game.
 */
public void run() {
  // flush any keystrokes that occurred before the
  // game started:
  myJumpCanvas.flushKeys();
  myShouldStop = false;
  myShouldPause = false;
  while(true) {
    if(myShouldStop) {
      break;
    }
    synchronized(this) {
      while(myShouldPause) {
        try {
          wait();
        } catch(Exception e) {}
      }
    }
    myJumpCanvas.checkKeys();
    myJumpCanvas.advance();
    // you do a very short pause to allow the other thread
    // to update the information about which keys are pressed:
    // and regulate the animation speed:
    synchronized(this) {
      try {
        wait(getWaitTime());
```

```
            } catch(Exception e) {}
        }
    }
}
```

The first thing to verify is that none of these synchronized segments can cause deadlock. Clearly they can't. The two methods merely set a data field and then call notify(), so they certainly return without doing anything that would cause the thread to need to grab another lock before it could continue. Similarly, the two blocks in the run() method are safe because all they do is check data and then wait. Waiting with a lock may seem dangerous, but in fact the thread lets go of its lock as soon as it starts waiting (and then grabs it again once it's notified), so in these blocks the thread lets go of the lock almost immediately after grabbing it.

The second thing to analyze is why these particular blocks are synchronized. To begin with, the methods wait() and notify() must always be called from within a synchronized block or method. You must synchronize on the same object that you call the method wait() or notify() on; so, for example, calling myObject.wait() must be done from within a block marked by synchronized(myObject). In most cases, the least confusing thing to do is to synchronize on this as I've done in this example. Of course, you may notice in Listing 4-6 that I included the phrase while(myShouldPause) inside the synchronized block. I did this to avoid a race condition. Imagine what might happen if the synchronized block contained only the call to the method wait(). Suppose that the thread just finished the line while(myShouldPause) and determined that myShouldPause is true. Then, before this thread gets to the next line, another thread calls resumeGame(), which sets myShould Pause to false and then calls notify(). At this point notify() has no effect because the thread isn't waiting. Then the original thread starts up again and executes the next line, which is a call to wait(). The result of all this is that the program has just asked the game to start up again, and the game thread is stuck waiting, which is not what's supposed to happen. Since the call to wait() depends on the data checked on the previous line and that data could potentially be changed on another thread, you group the two within the same synchronized block.

The final question is, why is there so little synchronization in the rest of the code? Many of the classes have places where the action on one line depends strongly on data checked on the previous line. But the difference is that only a single thread can modify the data in the graphical game objects. You can see in Listing 4-6 that GameThread first prompts the GameCanvas to query for keystrokes (which prompts all the keystroke-related data updates) and then prompts the GameCanvas to advance the animation accordingly. No other thread can modify the data objects concurrently to mess up things.

I have one last comment to add about thread scheduling: as I mentioned previously, a cell phone or other small device generally doesn't have parallel processors and hence must run the threads one at a time. In fact, it turns out that in most CLDC implementations the processor switches from one thread to another only when the currently active thread waits or finishes. This means that if one of your threads has an infinite loop, it needs to occasionally wait, as described in the "Using the Thread Class" section in Chapter 3. It also means that none of the race condition or deadlock situations discussed should ever create problems in practice even if you're sloppy with the synchronized keyword. But it's good practice to synchronize correctly anyway.

Using Media

Starting from MIDP 2, the MIDP API includes a subset of the Mobile Media API (JSR 135). The full Mobile Media API specifies how to play media resources such as tones, music files, and video files. A given device may support the entire Mobile Media API; however, the capacity to display video is not required by MIDP.

The Mobile Media API provides two possible strategies for adding music to your game: either you can play music from a music file, or you can create your own music by playing tones. Playing tones generally does not produce professional-quality music, so for a professional game you would normally use recorded music files in some standard format, such as Musical Instrument Digital Interface (MIDI). However, since a tone sequence can be written to a byte array that can be played in the same way as playing back any other audio file, and since tone sequences are the only type of music files that a MIDP 2 device is required to support, the new Tumbleweed example illustrates how to construct music through tones. Then, in the "Playing Tones with a Player" section the same tone sequence will be written to a byte array in order to illustrate how to play back music using the Player class. Finally, the "Using Audio Files" section completes the illustration of how to read a music file from a JAR and then play it.

Playing Simple Tones

Playing tonal music with MIDP is the easiest thing you can possibly imagine. As usual, the situation is that the target devices have limited abilities. The disadvantage is that your possibilities are limited, and the advantage is that what you can do is really simple. All you need to do is call the static method `javax.microedition.media.Manager.playTone()` with the note, volume, and time duration you'd like.

The trickiest part is figuring out which integer value corresponds to which note. For fun, I'll quote to you the JavaDoc on the subject:

[SEMITONE_CONST = 17.31234049066755 = 1/(ln(2^(1/12)))

note = ln(freq/8.176)*SEMITONE_CONST

The musical note A = MIDI note 69 (0x45) = 440 Hz.]

I imagine this formula would be useful for the people writing JVM implementations, and I assume that's who the audience is for this part of the JavaDoc. But allow me to explain how it works in English, assuming that (like me) you haven't done any advanced studies in music theory. As the previous quote states, the number 69 is the note A. To find the number corresponding to another note, count how many piano keys it is away from the note A, including the black keys (the sharps and flats). For example, the following are two scales in the key of A: { 57, 59, 61, 62, 64, 66, 68, 69 } and { 69, 71, 73, 74, 76, 78, 80, 81 }.

Keep in mind that the method `playTone()` is *nonblocking*, which means the thread returns as soon as the note *starts* playing, not when the note finishes playing. The easiest strategy is therefore to have one thread devoted to playing music and, as soon as it plays a note, have it wait for the same length of time that the note is played before starting the next note. That's what I've done in the example code in Listing 4-7.

But what do you do if you need the musical notes to be synchronized with game/animation events? Unfortunately, no version of playTone() allows you to say to the machine, "Play this note until I tell you to stop." So if you want the music and the game events to line up, you have to match the game events to the music, not vice versa. It's probably better that way anyway since you don't really want the rhythm of the music to depend on how the calculations in your game loop are going. What I recommend in that case is to still use a separate music thread and game/animation thread. Then, when the animation thread gets to the point where it shouldn't do anything more until the beginning of the next note, have that thread wait until the music thread notifies it that the next note is about to start. The one thing to be careful of is that the game/animation calculations may occasionally take longer than expected, and that thread may not be waiting yet when the music thread calls notify(). But that's easy to deal with by creating and setting appropriate flags.

Listing 4-7 shows the code for MusicMaker.java.

Listing 4-7. *MusicMaker.java*

```java
package net.frog_parrot.jump;

import javax.microedition.media.*;

/**
 * This is the class that plays a little tune while you
 * play the game.
 *
 * @author Carol Hamer
 */
public class MusicMaker extends Thread {

  //-----------------------------------------------------------
  //   fields

  /**
   * Whether the main thread would like this thread
   * to stop.
   */
  public static final int NOTE_LENGTH = 250;

  /**
   * Whether the main thread would like this thread
   * to pause.
   */
  private boolean myShouldPause;

  /**
   * If the whole game is paused, you pause the music, too.
   */
  private boolean myGamePause;
```

```java
/**
 * Whether the main thread would like this thread
 * to stop.
 */
private static boolean myShouldStop;

/**
 * The tune played by the game, stored as an array
 * of notes and durations.
 *
 * NOTE: 69 is A. To get other notes, just add or subtract
 * their difference from A on the keyboard including the
 * black keys in the calculation.  See the following scales
 * for an idea.
 *
 */
private byte[][] myTune = { { 69, 1 }, { 69, 1 }, { 69, 1 }, { 71, 1 },
                { 73, 2 }, { 71, 2 }, { 69, 1 }, { 73, 1 },
                { 71, 1 }, { 71, 1 }, { 69, 4 },
                { 69, 1 }, { 69, 1 }, { 69, 1 }, { 71, 1 },
                { 73, 2 }, { 71, 2 }, { 69, 1 }, { 73, 1 },
                { 71, 1 }, { 71, 1 }, { 69, 4 },
                { 71, 1 }, { 71, 1 }, { 71, 1 }, { 71, 1 },
                { 66, 2 }, { 66, 2 }, { 71, 1 }, { 69, 1 },
                { 68, 1 }, { 66, 1 }, { 64, 4 },
                { 69, 1 }, { 69, 1 }, { 69, 1 }, { 71, 1 },
                { 73, 2 }, { 71, 2 }, { 69, 1 }, { 73, 1 },
                { 71, 1 }, { 71, 1 }, { 69, 4 }
};

/**
 * An example "tune" that is just a scale.
 * not used.
 */
private byte[][] myScale = { { 69, 1 }, { 71, 1 }, { 73, 1 }, { 74, 1 },
                { 76, 1 }, { 78, 1 }, { 80, 1 }, { 81, 1 } };

/**
 * An example "tune" that is just a scale.
 * not used.
 */
private byte[][] myScale2 = { { 57, 1 }, { 59, 1 }, { 61, 1 }, { 62, 1 },
                { 64, 1 }, { 66, 1 }, { 68, 1 }, { 69, 1 } };

//-------------------------------------------------------------
```

```java
//    actions

/**
 * call this when the game pauses.
 */
void pauseGame() {
  myGamePause = true;
}

/**
 * call this when the game resumes.
 */
synchronized void resumeGame() {
  myGamePause = false;
  this.notify();
}

/**
 * toggle the music.
 * (pause it if it's going, start it again if it's paused).
 */
synchronized void toggle() {
  myShouldPause = !myShouldPause;
  this.notify();
}

/**
 * stops the music.
 */
synchronized void requestStop() {
  myShouldStop = true;
  this.notify();
}

/**
 * start the music.
 */
public void run() {
  myShouldStop = false;
  myShouldPause = true;
  myGamePause = false;
  int counter = 0;
  while(true) {
    if(myShouldStop) {
      break;
    }
    synchronized(this) {
```

```
      while((myShouldPause) || (myGamePause)) {
        try {
          wait();
        } catch(Exception e) {}
      }
    }
    try {
      Manager.playTone(myTune[counter][0],
                       myTune[counter][1]*NOTE_LENGTH, 50);
    } catch(Exception e) {
      // the music isn't necessary, so you ignore exceptions.
    }
    synchronized(this) {
      try {
        wait(myTune[counter][1]*NOTE_LENGTH);
      } catch(Exception e) {}
    }
    counter++;
    if(counter >= myTune.length) {
      counter = 0;
    }
  }
}

}
```

Playing Tones with a Player

Now you'll see how to create a `Player` to take over some of the work of playing the music.

Just as with the previous version, the most important part of creating the music is writing an array of data to describe the tune. In this case, to pass the data to the `Player`, you call `setSequence()` on the `ToneControl` object associated with the `Player`.

The tune data used by a `Player` needs to be stored in a particular format, called *augmented BNF notation*. This notation is pretty simple. It's essentially a sequence of pairs of bytes that give the note and the length of time the note should be played. The correspondence between numbers and notes works in the same way for a `Player` as it did in the previous section when playing the notes with the `Manager` (in other words, 69 is A, and you can find the numbers of the other notes by counting how many piano keys there are from A and adding or subtracting that number from 69). In addition to the notes and their lengths, you have a few extra components to add to the data array, such as codes for the version and the tempo, as you can see in Listing 4-8 (in the field `myTune`). Also, you can define the tune in terms of blocks, which is convenient for the tune I used because the tune has one line that's repeated three times. But it isn't necessary to define the music data in terms of blocks of notes, and if you do use blocks of notes, you can alternate them with sequences of notes that aren't defined as blocks. If you don't want to do anything too fancy, you can more or less work from the example in Listing 4-8 in a moment. For more details, the precise syntax of the augmented BNF notation is given in the JavaDoc of the `javax.microedition.media.control.ToneControl` class.

In addition to using the `ToneControl` interface in the example class, I used the `VolumeControl` to set the volume. All I did was set the volume to its maximum (100), but you could easily write code that would allow the user to access a `Form` screen containing a `Gauge` that uses a `VolumeControl` to control the volume. See the section "Using the Form and Item Classes" in Chapter 2 for a review of using MIDP GUI components.

One main structural difference to notice between this version of the `MusicMaker` code and the version from the previous section is that by using a `Player` I avoid having to create a separate thread for the music. When you call `start()` on the `Player`, the method returns immediately, and the music runs on its own thread. So I have one less thread to keep track of myself. If I want the music to repeat, the simplest way to do it is to call `setLoopCount()`. In a professional game, I would have made the music repeat indefinitely by setting the loop count to -1. But instead I decided to illustrate the use of the `PlayerListener` interface to make the music repeat. With the `PlayerListener` interface, you can listen for state changes in the `Player` such as starting, stopping, changing volume, and so on. In Listing 4-8, I have it listen for `END_OF_MEDIA`, and when the end of the tune is reached, I tell it to play it again.

One more point in the fields of this class may require some explanation. Just as in the other version, I maintain two different fields to keep track of whether the music has been paused by the system or by the user. This is necessary because I don't want to start the music after a pause unless both the system and the user want the music to be unpaused. An example of what can go wrong without this double-checking is that the user might decide to turn off the music, but then later when the game is hidden by a menu and then unhidden, the method `showNotify()` (called by the application management software) may trigger the music to start up again if you're not keeping track of the user's desire to have the music stay turned off.

Note that to have the game use this version of the `MusicMaker` class instead of the one from the previous section, you must make a small change in the `Jump` class. You must change the field `myMusicMaker` from being declared as a `MusicMaker` to being declared as a `ToneControlMusicMaker`. This change involves modifying only two lines, and I've provided the alternate lines (commented out) in the `Jump` code in the "Differences Between CLDC Threads and Threads in Standard Java" section earlier in this chapter.

Listing 4-8 shows the code for `ToneControlMusicMaker.java`.

Listing 4-8. *ToneControlMusicMaker.java*

```java
package net.frog_parrot.jump;

import javax.microedition.media.*;
import javax.microedition.media.control.*;

/**
 * This is the class that plays a little tune while you
 * play the game. This version uses the Player and
 * Control interfaces.
 *
 * @author Carol Hamer
 */
public class ToneControlMusicMaker implements PlayerListener {

  //-----------------------------------------------------------
```

```
//   fields

/**
 * The player object that plays the tune.
 */
private Player myPlayer;

/**
 * Whether the player wants to pause the music.
 */
private boolean myShouldPause;

/**
 * Whether the system wants to pause the music.
 */
private boolean myGamePause;

/**
 * The tune played by the game, stored as an array
 * of bytes in BNF notation.
 */
private byte[] myTune = {
    // first set the version
    ToneControl.VERSION, 1,
    // set the tempo
    ToneControl.TEMPO, 30,
    // define the first line of the song
    ToneControl.BLOCK_START, 0,
    69,8, 69,8, 69,8, 71,8,
    73,16, 71,16, 69,8, 73,8,
    71,8, 71,8, 69,32,
    ToneControl.BLOCK_END, 0,
    // define the other line of the song
    ToneControl.BLOCK_START, 1,
    71,8, 71,8, 71,8, 71,8,
    66,16, 66,16, 71,8, 69,8,
    68,8, 66,8, 64,32,
    ToneControl.BLOCK_END, 1,
    // play the song
    ToneControl.PLAY_BLOCK, 0,
    ToneControl.PLAY_BLOCK, 0,
    ToneControl.PLAY_BLOCK, 1,
    ToneControl.PLAY_BLOCK, 0,
};

//-----------------------------------------------------------
```

```
//    actions

/**
 * call this when the game pauses.
 * This method does not affect the field
 * myShouldPause because this method is called only
 * when the system pauses the music, not when the
 * player pauses the music.
 */
void pauseGame() {
  try {
    myGamePause = true;
    myPlayer.stop();
    // when the application pauses the game, resources
    // are supposed to be released, so you close the
    // player and throw it away.
    myPlayer.close();
    myPlayer = null;
  } catch(Exception e) {
    // the music isn't necessary, so you ignore exceptions.
  }
}

/**
 * call this when the game resumes.
 * This method does not affect the field
 * myShouldPause because this method is called only
 * when the system resumes the music, not when the
 * player pauses the music.
 */
synchronized void resumeGame() {
  try {
    myGamePause = false;
    if(! myShouldPause) {
      // if the player is null, you create a new one.
      if(myPlayer == null) {
        start();
      }
      // start the music.
      myPlayer.start();
    }
  } catch(Exception e) {
    // the music isn't necessary, so you ignore exceptions.
  }
}
```

```java
/**
 * toggle the music.
 * (pause it if it's going, start it again if it's paused).
 */
synchronized void toggle() {
  try {
    myShouldPause = !myShouldPause;
    if(myShouldPause) {
      if(myPlayer != null) {
        myPlayer.stop();
      }
    } else if(! myGamePause) {
      // if the player is null, you create a new one.
      if(myPlayer == null) {
        start();
      }
      // start the music.
      myPlayer.start();
    }
  } catch(Exception e) {
    // the music isn't necessary, so you ignore exceptions.
  }
}

/**
 * stops the music.
 */
synchronized void requestStop() {
  try {
    myPlayer.stop();
    // this is called when the game is over to close
    // up the player to release the resources.
    myPlayer.close();
  } catch(Exception e) {
    // the music isn't necessary, so you ignore exceptions.
  }
}

//------------------------------------------------------------
```

```
//    initialization

/**
 * start the music.
 * Here the method is "start" instead of "run" because
 * it is not necessary to create a thread for the Player.
 * the Player runs on its own thread.
 */
public void start() {
  ToneControl control = null;
  try {
    myPlayer = Manager.createPlayer(Manager.TONE_DEVICE_LOCATOR);
    // do the preliminary setup:
    myPlayer.realize();
    // set a listener to listen for the end of the tune:
    myPlayer.addPlayerListener(this);
    // get the ToneControl object in order to set the tune data:
    control = (ToneControl)myPlayer.getControl("ToneControl");
    control.setSequence(myTune);
    // set the volume to the highest possible volume:
    VolumeControl vc = (VolumeControl)myPlayer.getControl("VolumeControl");
    vc.setLevel(100);
  } catch(Exception e) {
    // the music isn't necessary, so you ignore exceptions.
  }
}


//------------------------------------------------------------
//    implementation of PlayerListener

/**
 * If you reach the end of the song, play it again...
 */
public void playerUpdate(Player player, String event, Object eventData) {
  if(event.equals(PlayerListener.END_OF_MEDIA)) {
    if((! myShouldPause) && (! myGamePause)) {
      try {
        myPlayer.start();
      } catch(Exception e) {
        // the music isn't necessary, so you ignore exceptions.
      }
    }
  }
}


}
```

FINDING PUBLIC DOMAIN MUSIC

If you're planning to distribute your game, don't forget that the background music can potentially give you some legal headaches if you're not careful about the copyright. A tune that you reproduce from memory in tones could easily be owned by someone who may not want you reselling it along with your game. This goes double for reproducing tunes from copyrighted sheet music or for using music files of uncertain origin. Unless using a particular tune is really important for your game and your company is big enough to have a legal department, you probably should avoid using copyrighted music.

Ideally, you're a brilliant composer in addition to being a brilliant game developer, in which case you can just compose a tune yourself, and your problem is solved. If you're not, the easiest solution is to use music that's in the public domain. If you play the Tumbleweed game with music, you may recognize that it plays an old French folk tune called *Au Clair de la Lune* instead of some modern (copyrighted) piece.

Fortunately, plenty of resources exist on the Web that will help you find public domain music. The site at http://www.pdinfo.com/ is full of helpful legal information about how the public domain works, plus it has a list of titles of more than 3,500 public domain songs, many with sheet music you can order. And of course you can find plenty of other resources by typing public domain music into Google.

Using Audio Files

By playing music files instead of creating music through tones, you can give your game a much richer musical background. Unfortunately, playing music files has several drawbacks that make them inappropriate for many applications, especially on small devices such as cell phones. First, devices that run only MIDP 2 aren't required to support playback of audio files, so low-end target devices won't even give you this option. Second, the audio files can be quite large, especially compared to the total amount of storage space on the device. Third, playing an audio file requires a lot of effort on the part of the processor and will likely slow down your game's animation and response time. A fourth drawback is that it's hard to synchronize the music with the game. (You can use the getMediaTime() method of the Player interface to find out where you are in the music file, but it's not guaranteed to work.)

Dealing with memory and processor consumption is a serious issue. Your target device must be a high-end MIDP device to even consider it. Verify that even with the audio file in the JAR your program doesn't take up too much of the device's memory. Having the game download the audio file at runtime is generally not a good solution for keeping the JAR size down since having the device download data during the game and/or read the whole audio file into a buffer will dramatically diminish the computing resources available for your game.

The one situation where playing audio from an audio file is typically appropriate for a game on a small device is when it is played along with a few seconds of introductory animation before your game starts. That way, you can start by impressing your customer with a cool startup sequence without having the music eat up your computing power during the game itself. But even for this use it's important to verify that your target device can handle it.

Once you've decided you want to use an audio file in your game, it's easy to implement. Listing 4-9 shows an example code block to demonstrate.

Listing 4-9. *Playing an Audio File*

```
/**
 * Read the audio file from the JAR and play it.
 */
void playMusic() {
  try {
    // create an input stream that can be used to read the
    // music data from a file called music.wav in a directory
    // called resources in this program's JAR file.

    InputStream is = getClass().getResourceAsStream("/resources/music.wav");
    // create a media player to play the music file, and
    // inform the player that the format is "audio/X-wav"
    Player player = Manager.createPlayer(is, "audio/X-wav");

    // start the music
    player.start();
  } catch (IOException ioe) {
    // deal with the exception
  } catch (MediaException me) {
    // deal with the exception
  }
}
```

Before creating the `Player`, you can verify that the implementation supports playback of files in your chosen format by calling `Manager.getSupportedContentTypes()`. Some common types include .wav audio files (MIME type: audio/x-wav), .au audio files (MIME type: audio/basic), .mp3 audio files (MIME type: audio/mpeg), and .midi files (MIME type: audio/midi). Once you have an instance of `Player`, you have a number of methods at your disposition for controlling the `Player`'s lifecycle. Using `realize()`, you can tell the player to do any preliminary construction steps without acquiring device resources, and the methods `prefetch()` and `deallocate()` allow you to instruct the `Player` to acquire (and release) the resources that the player needs in order to play. Then you can start and stop the music using the aptly named `start()` and `stop()` methods and close the player down with the method `close()`.

Summary

It's important to have a good grasp of how the different threads of an application interact because a lot of troubleshooting has to be done by pure thought. Threading errors are notorious for showing up intermittently and being difficult to consistently reproduce, which makes them difficult to debug. The example game in this chapter illustrates how to get the different threads of a game—for running the animation, music, and handling the user's input—to work together during standard game play as well as when the game is interrupted.

CHAPTER 5

■■■

Storing and Retrieving Data

It turns out that storing bytes of data locally on a device that's equipped for the Mobile Internet Device Profile (MIDP) is easy. Therefore, this chapter starts with an extremely simple example: you'll take the maze game example from Chapter 2 and store the user's preferred size information. Then, each time the user restarts the game, the game will automatically create the maze with walls of the user's chosen width rather than starting at the default width.

The hard part of data storage and retrieval is when you have more complicated data to store. MIDP allows you to store arrays of bytes only. But what if the data you want to store isn't in the form of bytes? The simplest thing to do is to use the classes `java.io.DataInputStream` and `java.io.DataOutputStream` to convert other types of data to bytes. But since memory can be scarce on a small device, it's a good idea to understand how you convert integers to bytes, and vice versa, so you can compact your data to store it more efficiently. Therefore, in this chapter, you'll see a utility class that converts `int`s to `byte`s and back again, compacting the data appropriately if it falls within a certain size range. Then you'll see a complete game example (using the utility class) in which the user can save a game that's currently in play and start it again later from that point. This example illustrates how to store complex data in a real game situation.

Saving Simple Data

The MIDP Record Management System (RMS) is simple. Its package `javax.microedition.rms` has only one class: `RecordStore`. A `RecordStore` is a collection of records, which are in fact just byte arrays. A `RecordStore` is identified by the property `MIDlet-Vendor` and the property `MIDlet-Name` in the JAD file, as well as by the name given to the `RecordStore` by the `MIDlet` that created it. This means that within a `MIDlet` *suite* (a group of `MIDlet`s in the same JAR file), the `MIDlet`s share the `RecordStore`s they've created, but `MIDlet` suites don't share `RecordStore`s with other `MIDlet` suites (unless they're explicitly given permission to do so; you'll learn more about that in the sidebar "Using Secure Connections While Selling Your Game" in Chapter 8). A `RecordStore` is identified by the `MIDlet-Vendor` and the `MIDlet-Name` properties in addition to the store's name, so you don't have to start your `RecordStore`'s name with your own package name to keep it in a separate namespace from the `RecordStore`s of other unrelated `MIDlet`s. It's a good thing, too, because the name of the `RecordStore` can be only 32 (case-sensitive) characters long, so you don't want to waste too many of them.

To create a `RecordStore`, all you have to do is call the `static` method `RecordStore.openRecordStore()` with the name of the `RecordStore` you want to create and the value `true` as arguments. The second argument `true` answers the question of whether to create the `RecordStore` if it doesn't already exist. Once you have a handle to a `RecordStore` (either by creating it or by opening an existing `RecordStore`), you can get or set the records. Note that a *record* isn't a separate class; it's merely a byte array. The RMS assigns each record an integer record ID that you use to get or replace the data array using `getRecord()` or `setRecord()`. The first record is assigned the ID of one, and the record IDs go up incrementally from there. If you don't like hard-coding numerical constants into your code (a reasonable inhibition), you can call `enumerateRecords` to get a `RecordEnumerator` to help you. The `RecordEnumerator` won't necessarily give you the records in the same order they'd appear in if you had gotten them by number using `getRecord()`. If you'd like to traverse the records in a particular order, you can create a `RecordFilter` and/or a `RecordComparator`, which allows you to define, respectively, which subset of the records will be returned and in what order to return them. Both `RecordFilter` and `RecordComparator` are interfaces you must implement yourself if you'd like to use them. These interfaces were obviously designed with address book–type applications in mind rather than games, but you may find a use for them.

In this first example, you'll create the simplest possible `RecordStore`. It'll contain only one record, and that record will contain only 1 byte. The example works as follows: you start with the maze game from Chapter 2. After the user selects the preferred width for the maze walls and clicks Done, the game calls the new class (`PrefsStorage`) with the preferred size information, and the `PrefsStorage` class then saves that information in a `RecordStore`. The game also consults the `PrefsStorage` class when the user first opens the game to check for a stored size preference to use when building the maze. If no preferred size has been stored, the `PrefsStorage` returns the default value.

In addition to adding the `PrefsStorage` class listed next, you need to modify a few other classes a bit. In the class `MazeCanvas` (Listing 2-3), you need to replace this line:

```
mySquareSize = 5;
```

with this line:

```
mySquareSize = PrefsStorage.getSquareSize();
```

Next, in the class `SelectScreen` (Listing 2-2), you need to add the following line:

```
PrefsStorage.setSquareSize(myWidthGauge.getValue());
```

to the method `commandAction`, as follows:

```
public void commandAction(Command c, Displayable s) {
  if(c == myExitCommand) {
    PrefsStorage.setSquareSize(myWidthGauge.getValue());
    myCanvas.newMaze();
  }
}
```

Aside from those changes, the code for this example is identical to the code of the maze example from Chapter 2.

Listing 5-1 shows the code for PrefsStorage.java.

Listing 5-1. *PrefsStorage.java*

```java
package net.frog_parrot.maze;

import javax.microedition.rms.*;

/**
 * This class helps to store and retrieve the data about
 * the maze size preferences.
 *
 * This is a utility class that does not contain instance data,
 * so to simplify access, all the methods are static.
 *
 * @author Carol Hamer
 */
public class PrefsStorage {

  //-----------------------------------------------------------
  //    static fields

  /**
   * The name of the datastore.
   */
  public static final String STORE = "SizePrefs";

  //-----------------------------------------------------------
  //    business methods

  /**
   * This gets the preferred square size from the stored data.
   */
  static int getSquareSize() {
    // if data retrieval fails, the default value is 5
    int retVal = 5;
    RecordStore store = null;
    try {
      // if the record store does not yet exist, the second
      // arg "true" tells it to create.
      store = RecordStore.openRecordStore(STORE, true);
      int numRecords = store.getNumRecords();
      if(numRecords > 0) {
        // the first record has id number 1
        // (In fact this program stores only one record)
        byte[] rec = store.getRecord(1);
        retVal = rec[0];
      }
```

```
      } catch(Exception e) {
        // data storage is not critical for this game and you're
        // not creating a log, so if data retrieval fails, you
        // just skip it and move on.
      } finally {
        try {
          store.closeRecordStore();
        } catch(Exception e) {
          // if the record store is open, this shouldn't throw.
        }
      }
      return(retVal);
    }

    /**
     * This saves the preferred square size.
     */
    static void setSquareSize(int size) {
      RecordStore store = null;
      try {
        // since you're storing the int as a single byte,
        // it's important that its value be less than
        // 128.  In fact, in real life the value would never
        // get anywhere near this high, but I'm adding this
        // little size check as a last line of defense against
        // errors:
        if(size > 127) {
          size = 127;
        }
        // if the record store doesn't yet exist, the second
        // arg "true" tells it to create.
        store = RecordStore.openRecordStore(STORE, true);
        byte[] record = new byte[1];
        record[0] = (byte)(size);
        int numRecords = store.getNumRecords();
        if(numRecords > 0) {
          store.setRecord(1, record, 0, 1);
        } else {
          store.addRecord(record, 0, 1);
        }
      } catch(Exception e) {
        // data storage isn't critical for this game and you're
        // not creating a log, so if data storage fails, you
        // just skip it and move on.
      } finally {
        try {
          store.closeRecordStore();
```

```
    } catch(Exception e) {
      // if the record store is open, this shouldn't throw.
    }
  }
}


}
```

I need to mention one last point before you're done with this little example—namely, the technique for converting back and forth between int values and byte values. The value I'm saving is an int, yet I save it in the form of a byte with little regard for the fact that an int and a byte in Java aren't the same thing at all. (In particular, an int occupies 4 bytes of memory!) Yet you'll notice that in the method setSquareSize() I get a byte value for the argument size merely by calling byteValue(), and in the other direction (in the method getSquareSize()) I convert the byte rec[0] to an int without any sort of conversion operation at all. What's going on here? The answer is, I know the argument size is between -128 and 127 in value, so I know it can be stored and cast as a single byte without losing any data. This simple conversion between ints and bytes is useful, but only if you're 100 percent certain your int isn't going to fall outside the appropriate range. If you'd like to store your int value with more precision, you can use alternate conversion techniques, discussed in the next section.

Serializing More Complex Data Using Streams

Java doesn't make it easy for the programmer to take one kind of data and directly reinterpret it as another type of data. This can be frustrating if you've done any programming in C and are used to looking at data in terms of bytes. But maintaining strongly typed data is integral to Java's internal security, so if you want to program in Java, you might as well get used to it.

You can easily convert all of Java's simple data types into byte arrays and back again using the classes java.io.ByteArrayInputStream, java.io.ByteArrayOutputStream, java.io.DataInputStream, and java.io.DataOutputStream. The pair of methods shown in Listing 5-2 demonstrates how you can use these classes to convert between byte arrays and ints.

Listing 5-2. *Converting Between Arrays and Ints*

```
/**
 * Uses an input stream to convert an array of bytes to an int.
 */
public static int parseInt(byte[] data) throws IOException {
  DataInputStream stream
    = new DataInputStream(new ByteArrayInputStream(data));
  int retVal = stream.readInt();
  stream.close();
  return(retVal);
}
```

```
/**
 * Uses an output stream to convert an int to four bytes.
 */
public static byte[] intToFourBytes(int i) throws IOException {
  ByteArrayOutputStream baos = new ByteArrayOutputStream(4);
  DataOutputStream dos = new DataOutputStream(baos);
  dos.writeInt(i);
  baos.close ();
  dos.close();
  byte[] retArray = baos.toByteArray();
  return(retArray);
}
```

This same technique works for all of Java's simple data types. For Strings, you can use the methods readUTF() and writeUTF(). One design note in Listing 5-2 is that in most applications you wouldn't want to make multiple calls to utility functions like these because each call creates two stream objects that clutter memory and will later need to be garbage collected. Usually, if you plan to save a record that comprises multiple chunks of data, you'd create the appropriate OutputStream as you did previously and then write the entire record to it before closing it. My example game uses the previous methods because, as you'll see next, each record contains only one int that needs to be saved using a stream.

Using Data Types and Byte Arithmetic

Using InputStream and OutputStream to encode and decode your data for storage purposes would be sufficient if your target device had an infinite amount of memory, which is far from the case for many small devices. And the DataOutputStream uses a full byte to record a single Boolean when of course you could squeeze eight Booleans into the same space, and as mentioned previously, DataOutputStream uses 4 bytes to store an int when you often know in advance that the value will be small enough to fit into 1 or 2 bytes. Of course, you have a little bit of design strategy to consider when deciding whether to store your data in the standard way or compact it. Compacting your data not only complicates your program, but it makes your data less portable. If you're using custom compression algorithms, it's easier to render your data completely unsalvageable with a small error than it is when your data is serialized in a standard format. Therefore, if you're storing only a little data, it's generally better to serialize it using the standard methods. In the case of this chapter's example program, however, data compression makes a nontrivial difference. In the game, a player is exploring a maze-like dungeon that's created by a 16×16 square grid. I'd like to allow for the possibility of having a large series of different boards for this game, and each board is stored as a chunk of data that tells which squares of the grid should be empty and which should be filled. Therefore, you create the background of this game with a 16×16 two-dimensional array of ones and zeros—or, in other words, with 256 Booleans. If I plan to store multiple boards, I'd prefer not to store this as an array of 256 bytes (or worse, as 256 ints that would equal 1024 bytes!) when I could store it compactly as 32 bytes. Figure 5-1 shows a couple of the boards that were designed for this game.

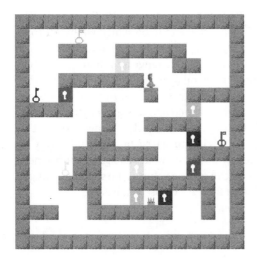
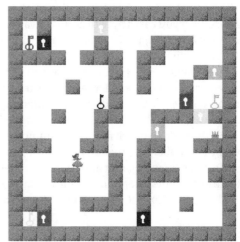

Figure 5-1. *Two complete boards of the Dungeon game*

It's not hard to compact data if you know a bit about byte arithmetic. And Java Micro Edition (Java ME) programmers naturally need to use byte arithmetic more than the average Java programmer. Recall that you use the bitwise or operator for placing strings and images (see the "Using the Graphics and Canvas Classes" section in Chapter 2) and for layout directives (see the "Using the Form and Item Classes" section, also in Chapter 2), and you use a bitwise and operator to get all the information about the current key states (see the "Using the GameCanvas Class" section in Chapter 3).

Another useful tool for bitwise arithmetic is the shift operator. The shift operators are written in Java code as >> and <<, where the operand on the left is the byte to shift and the operand on the right is the number of places to shift it. They have the effect of multiplying the value of the byte by a power of 2. For example, the result of myval >> 1 is the same as dividing myval by 2. All the shift operator is really doing is moving the values of the byte— shifting them all in unison to the left or to the right—so they can be used to make it easier to access each individual value (1 or 0) in the byte. So to stock eight Booleans into a byte, all you need to do is add the ones and zeros to the byte, one by one, and use the shift operator to shift the result up one bit between each new addition. To get the data out again, you just perform a bitwise and between the byte and a series of appropriate flag bytes. For example, 128 corresponds to the top bit of a byte, so to find out if the top bit of a given byte is set, all you have to do is perform a bitwise and with your chosen byte and a flag byte whose value is equal to 128. The value returned by the operation will be nonzero if and only if the top bit of your byte was set. You can get all the other flag bytes easily from the initial flag by shifting down the flag byte.

The class in Listing 5-3 is the complete version of my integer compression utility class (called DataConverter). It contains methods to pack eight Booleans into a byte as described previously, as well as methods to convert integers in various size ranges to bytes. I've even included methods that will convert an int to an array of 4 bytes giving exactly the same values as you'd get using DataInputStream.

The only tricky part in any of the algorithms in Listing 5-3 is dealing with when a byte of data is considered to be signed and when it's considered to be unsigned. Signed bytes range in value from –128 to 127, and unsigned bytes range in value from 0 to 255. Any byte can be regarded as signed or unsigned; it's just a question of whether you consider the top bit to indicate a negative sign or 128. If you cast a byte to an int, Java will consider the byte to be signed when returning the value. If you wanted its value as an unsigned byte, then you can fix it by adding 256 if the value is negative (that is, add 128 to get the value into the positive range and then add another 128 for the value of the top bit that was set). An integer obviously needs only one sign, so when Java represents an integer internally as 4 bytes, only the high byte (which is the first of the 4 bytes) is regarded as signed. Dealing with the interplay between signed and unsigned bytes is a little bit confusing, but I hope that the code example in Listing 5-3 will help clarify how it works. I've written the code to check for positive or negative values because it's a fairly intuitive way of making it clear that the program is converting between viewing the values as signed or unsigned. Keep in mind, however, that as discussed earlier, you can get the value of the sign bit through bitwise arithmetic: just perform a bitwise and (&) with the byte whose value is 128.

Listing 5-3 shows the code for DataConverter.java.

Listing 5-3. *DataConverter.java*

```java
package net.frog_parrot.util;

import java.io.*;

/**
 * This class is a set of simple utility functions that
 * can be used to convert standard data types to bytes
 * and back again. It is used especially for data storage,
 * but also for sending and receiving data.
 *
 * @author Carol Hamer
 */
public class DataConverter {

  //-----------------------------------------------------------
  //  utilities to encode small, compactly stored small ints.

  /**
   * Encodes a coordinate pair into a byte.
   * @param coordPair a pair of integers to be compacted into
   * a single byte for storage.
   * WARNING: each of the two values MUST BE
   * between 0 and 15 (inclusive).  This method does not
   * verify the length of the array (which must be 2!)
   * and it doesn't verify that the ints are of the right size.
   */
  public static byte encodeCoords(int[] coordPair) {
    // get the byte value of the first coordinate:
    byte retVal = (byte)(coordPair[0]);
    // move the first coordinate's value up to the top
    // half of the storage byte:
    retVal = (byte)(retVal << 4);
```

```java
    // store the second coordinate in the lower half
    // of the byte:
    retVal += (byte)(coordPair[1]);
    return(retVal);
}


/**
 * Encodes eight ints into a byte.
 * This could be easily modified to encode eight Booleans.
 * @param eight an array of at least eight ints.
 * WARNING: all values must be 0 or 1!  This method does
 * not verify that the values are in the correct range
 * and it doesn't verify that the array is long enough.
 * @param offset the index in the array eight to start
 * reading data from.  (should usually be 0)
 */
public static byte encode8(int[] eight, int offset) {
    // get the byte value of the first int:
    byte retVal = (byte)(eight[offset]);
    // progressively move the data up one bit in the
    // storage byte and then record the next int in
    // the lowest spot in the storage byte:
    for(int i = offset + 1; i < 8 + offset; i++) {
        retVal = (byte)(retVal << 1);
        retVal += (byte)(eight[i]);
    }
    return(retVal);
}


//----------------------------------------------------------
// utilities to decode small, compactly stored small ints.

/**
 * Turns a byte into a pair of coordinates.
 */
public static int[] decodeCoords(byte coordByte) {
    int[] retArray = new int[2];
    // you perform a bitwise and with the value 15
    // in order to just get the bits of the lower
    // half of the byte:
    retArray[1] = coordByte & 15;
    // To get the bits of the upper half of the
    // byte, you perform a shift to move them down:
    retArray[0] = coordByte >> 4;
    // bytes in Java are generally assumed to be
    // signed, but in this coding algorithm you
    // would like to treat them as unsigned:
    if(retArray[0] < 0) {
```

```java
      retArray[0] += 16;
    }
    // The above block is equivalent to the (more efficient)
    // bitwise operation retArray[0] & 0xf
    return(retArray);
  }


  /**
   * Turns a byte into eight ints.
   */
  public static int[] decode8(byte data) {
    int[] retArray = new int[8];
    // The flag allows us to look at each bit individually
    // to determine if it is 1 or 0.  The number 128
    // corresponds to the highest bit of a byte, so you
    // start with that one.
    int flag = 128;
    // You use a loop that checks
    // the data bit by bit by performing a bitwise
    // and (&) between the data byte and a flag:
    for(int i = 0; i < 8; i++) {
      if((flag & data) != 0) {
        retArray[i] = 1;
      } else {
        retArray[i] = 0;
      }
      // move the flag down one bit so you can
      // check the next bit of data on the next pass
      // through the loop:
      flag = flag >> 1;
    }
    return(retArray);
  }



  //-----------------------------------------------------------
  //   standard integer interpretation

  /**
   * Uses an input stream to convert an array of bytes to an int.
   */
  public static int parseInt(byte[] data) throws IOException {
    DataInputStream stream
      = new DataInputStream(new ByteArrayInputStream(data));
    int retVal = stream.readInt();
    stream.close();
    return(retVal);
  }
```

```
/**
 * Uses an output stream to convert an int to four bytes.
 */
public static byte[] intToFourBytes(int i) throws IOException {
  ByteArrayOutputStream baos = new ByteArrayOutputStream(4);
  DataOutputStream dos = new DataOutputStream(baos);
  dos.writeInt(i);
  baos.close();
  dos.close();
  byte[] retArray = baos.toByteArray();
  return(retArray);
}


//---------------------------------------------------------
//   integer interpretation illustrated

/**
 * Java appears to treat a byte as being signed when
 * returning it as an int--this function converts from
 * the signed value to the corresponding unsigned value.
 * This method is used by nostreamParseInt.
 */
public static int unsign(int signed) {
  int retVal = signed;
  if(retVal < 0) {
    retVal += 256;
  }
  return(retVal);
}

/**
 * Takes an array of bytes and returns an int.
 * This version will return the same value as the
 * method parseInt previously.  This version is included
 * in order to illustrate how Java encodes int values
 * in terms of bytes.
 * @param data an array of 1, 2, or 4 bytes.
 */
public static int nostreamParseInt(byte[] data) {
  // byte 0 is the high byte, which is assumed
  // to be signed.  As you add the lower bytes
  // one by one, you unsign them because
  // a single byte alone is interpreted as signed,
  // but in an int only the top byte should be signed.
  // (note that the high byte is the first one in the array)
  int retVal = data[0];
  for(int i = 1; i < data.length; i++) {
    retVal = retVal << 8;
```

```
      retVal += unsign(data[i]);
    }
    return(retVal);
  }


/**
 * Takes an arbitrary int and returns
 * an array of 4 bytes.
 * This version will return the same byte array
 * as the method intToFourBytes previous. This version
 * is included in order to illustrate how Java encodes
 * int values in terms of bytes.
 */
public static byte[] nostreamIntToFourBytes(int i) {
  byte[] fourBytes = new byte[4];
  // when you take the byte value of an int, it
  // only gives you the lowest byte. So you
  // get all 4 bytes by taking the lowest
  // byte four times and moving the whole int
  // down by one byte between each one.
  // (note that the high byte is the first one in the array)
  fourBytes[3] = (byte)(i);
  i = i >> 8;
  fourBytes[2] = (byte)(i);
  i = i >> 8;
  fourBytes[1] = (byte)(i);
  i = i >> 8;
  fourBytes[0] = (byte)(i);
  return(fourBytes);
}



/**
 * Takes an int between -32768 and 32767 and returns
 * an array of 2 bytes. This does not verify that
 * the argument is of the right size. If the absolute
 * value of i is too high, it will not be encoded
 * correctly.
 */
public static byte[] nostreamIntToTwoBytes(int i) {
  byte[] twoBytes = new byte[2];
  // when you take the byte value of an int, it
  // only gives you the lowest byte. So you
  // get the lower two bytes by taking the lowest
  // byte twice and moving the whole int
  // down by one byte between each one.
  twoBytes[1] = (byte)(i);
  i = i >> 8;
```

```
    twoBytes[0] = (byte)(i);
    return(twoBytes);
  }

}
```

Applying Data Storage to a Dungeon Game

In this section, you'll see how the example game works. As I mentioned previously, the game involves a character (in fact, a princess) exploring a dungeon that's made up of a 16×16 grid. To make it more interesting, the maze is a vertical cross section of the dungeon, so the princess gets around by jumping up and falling down in addition to running around. Also, to add to the challenge, four keys on each board open eight locked doors. Each key is a different color and opens doors of the corresponding color. Each board has two doors of each color. The player can hold only one key at a time. The goal is to find a crown that's locked away somewhere in the maze. Figure 5-1 shows what some of the possible boards look like if you could see the whole board at once, but only part of the board is visible to the player at a time. Figure 5-2 shows what the player sees when playing the game.

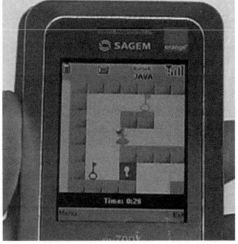

Figure 5-2. *The game in action*

In this version, data storage comes into play because the user can save a game that's currently in progress and start again later from that point. All the saved game information is serialized and deserialized by the GameInfo class (see Listing 5-4). As you'll see in the code, the GameInfo class stores the number of the board that the player is currently on, the current location of the player, the current locations of the keys, the key (if any) that's currently in the player's hand, the doors that are already open, and the time on the clock. All the locations are in terms of their coordinates on a 16×16 grid, so they're integers from 0 to 15 (inclusive). Therefore, to save memory, I've stocked the coordinates two to a byte using the DataConverter class in Listing 5-3. The time on the clock, however, may be a very large number, so I use all 4 bytes to store it. Listing 5-4 shows the code for GameInfo.java.

Listing 5-4. *GameInfo.java*

```
package net.frog_parrot.dungeon;

import javax.microedition.lcdui.*;
import javax.microedition.lcdui.game.*;
import javax.microedition.rms.*;

import net.frog_parrot.util.DataConverter;

/**
 * This class contains the data for a game currently in progress.
 * used to store a game and to resume a stored game.
 *
 * @author Carol Hamer
 */
public class GameInfo {

  //----------------------------------------------------------
  //  fields

  /**
   * The name of the datastore.
   */
  public static final String STORE = "GameInfo";

  /**
   * This is set to true if an attempt is made to
   * read a game when no game has been saved.
   */
  private boolean myNoDataSaved;

  /**
   * The number that indicates which board the player
   * is currently on.
   */
  private int myBoardNum;

  /**
   * The amount of time that has passed.
   */
  private int myTime;

  /**
   * The coordinates of where the player is on the board.
   * coordinate values must be between 0 and 15.
   */
  private int[] myPlayerSquare;
```

```
/**
 * The coordinates of where the keys are currently found.
 * MUST BE four sets of two integer coordinates.
 * coordinate values must be between 0 and 15.
 */
private int[][] myKeyCoords;

/**
 * The list of which doors are currently open.
 * 0 = open
 * 1 = closed
 * WARNING: this array MUST have length 8.
 */
private int[] myDoorsOpen;

/**
 * The number of the key that is currently being held
 * by the player.  if no key is held, then the value is -1.
 */
private int myHeldKey;

//----------------------------------------------------------
//  data gets/sets

/**
 * @return true if no saved game records were found.
 */
boolean getIsEmpty() {
  return(myNoDataSaved);
}

/**
 * @return The number that indicates which board the player
 * is currently on.
 */
int getBoardNum() {
  return(myBoardNum);
}

/**
 * @return The number of the key that is currently being held
 * by the player.  if no key is held, then the value is -1.
 */
int getHeldKey() {
  return(myHeldKey);
}
```

```
/**
 * @return The amount of time that has passed.
 */
int getTime() {
  return(myTime);
}

/**
 * @return The coordinates of where the player is on the board.
 * coordinate values must be between 0 and 15.
 */
int[] getPlayerSquare() {
  return(myPlayerSquare);
}

/**
 * @return The coordinates of where the keys are currently found.
 * MUST BE four sets of two integer coordinates.
 * coordinate values must be between 0 and 15.
 */
int[][] getKeyCoords() {
  return(myKeyCoords);
}

/**
 * @return The list of which doors are currently open.
 * 0 = open
 * 1 = closed
 * WARNING: this array MUST have length 8.
 */
int[] getDoorsOpen() {
  return(myDoorsOpen);
}

//-----------------------------------------------------------
//  constructors

/**
 * This constructor records the game info of a game currently
 * in progress.
 */
GameInfo(int boardNum, int time, int[] playerSquare, int[][] keyCoords,
         int[] doorsOpen, int heldKey) throws Exception {
  myBoardNum = boardNum;
  myTime = time;
  myPlayerSquare = playerSquare;
  myKeyCoords = keyCoords;
  myDoorsOpen = doorsOpen;
```

```
    myHeldKey = heldKey;
    encodeInfo();
}


/**
 * This constructor reads the game configuration from memory.
 * This is used to reconstruct a saved game.
 */
GameInfo() {
  RecordStore store = null;
  try {
    // if the record store does not yet exist, don't
    // create it
    store = RecordStore.openRecordStore(STORE, false);
    if((store != null) && (store.getNumRecords() > 0)) {
      // the first record has id number 1
      // it should also be the only record since this
      // particular game stores only one game.
      byte[] data = store.getRecord(1);
      myBoardNum = data[0];
      myPlayerSquare = DataConverter.decodeCoords(data[1]);
      myKeyCoords = new int[4][];
      myKeyCoords[0] = DataConverter.decodeCoords(data[2]);
      myKeyCoords[1] = DataConverter.decodeCoords(data[3]);
      myKeyCoords[2] = DataConverter.decodeCoords(data[4]);
      myKeyCoords[3] = DataConverter.decodeCoords(data[5]);
      myDoorsOpen = DataConverter.decode8(data[6]);
      myHeldKey = data[7];
      byte[] fourBytes = new byte[4];
      System.arraycopy(data, 8, fourBytes, 0, 4);
      myTime = DataConverter.parseInt(fourBytes);
    } else {
      myNoDataSaved = true;
    }
  } catch(Exception e) {
    // this throws when the record store doesn't exist.
    // for that or any error, you assume no data is saved:
    myNoDataSaved = true;
  } finally {
    try {
      if(store != null) {
        store.closeRecordStore();
      }
    } catch(Exception e) {
      // if the record store is open this shouldn't throw.
    }
  }
}
```

```
//------------------------------------------------------------
// encoding method

/**
 * Turn the data into a byte array and save it.
 */
private void encodeInfo() throws Exception {
  RecordStore store = null;
  try {
    byte[] data = new byte[12];
    data[0] = (byte)(myBoardNum);
    data[1] = DataConverter.encodeCoords(myPlayerSquare);
    data[2] = DataConverter.encodeCoords(myKeyCoords[0]);
    data[3] = DataConverter.encodeCoords(myKeyCoords[1]);
    data[4] = DataConverter.encodeCoords(myKeyCoords[2]);
    data[5] = DataConverter.encodeCoords(myKeyCoords[3]);
    data[6] = DataConverter.encode8(myDoorsOpen, 0);
    data[7] = (byte)(myHeldKey);
    byte[] timeBytes = DataConverter.intToFourBytes(myTime);
    System.arraycopy(timeBytes, 0, data, 8, 4);
    // if the record store does not yet exist, the second
    // arg "true" tells it to create.
    store = RecordStore.openRecordStore(STORE, true);
    int numRecords = store.getNumRecords();
    if(numRecords > 0) {
      store.setRecord(1, data, 0, data.length);
    } else {
      store.addRecord(data, 0, data.length);
    }
  } catch(Exception e) {
    throw(e);
  } finally {
    try {
      if(store != null) {
        store.closeRecordStore();
      }
    } catch(Exception e) {
      // if the record store is open this shouldn't throw.
    }
  }
}

}
```

In this version of the game, I'm not storing the floor plan of each board in memory records on the device. That's because the dungeons themselves aren't created by the user's interaction with the game; they're created in advance. In the next chapter, you'll use the same basic game, but you'll store the various boards in memory as the user downloads them from a game site. In this version, I've compacted all the information for the boards into bytes in anticipation of the next version in which the boards themselves will be downloaded and stored locally. Listing 5-5 shows the class that converts an array of bytes to a dungeon (BoardDecoder.java).

Listing 5-5. *BoardDecoder.java*

```java
package net.frog_parrot.dungeon;

import javax.microedition.lcdui.*;
import javax.microedition.lcdui.game.*;

import net.frog_parrot.util.DataConverter;

/**
 * This class contains the data for the map of the dungeon.
 *
 * @author Carol Hamer
 */
public class BoardDecoder {

  //----------------------------------------------------------
  //  fields

  /**
   * The coordinates of where the player starts on the map
   * in terms of the array indices.
   */
  private int[] myPlayerSquare;


  /**
   * The coordinates of the goal (crown).
   */
  private int[] myGoalSquare;

  /**
   * The coordinates of the doors.
   * the there should be two in a row of each color,
   * following the same sequence as the keys.
   */
  private int[][] myDoors;

  /**
   * The coordinates of the Keys.
   * they should be of each color,
   * following the same sequence as the doors.
   */
  private int[][] myKeys;
```

```java
/**
 * The coordinates of the stone walls of the maze,
 * encoded bit by bit.
 */
private TiledLayer myLayer;

/**
 * The data in bytes that gives the various boards.
 * This was created using EncodingUtils...
 * This is a two-dimensional array: Each of the four
 * main sections corresponds to one of the four
 * possible boards.
 */
private static byte[][] myData = {
    { 0, 0, -108, -100, -24, 65, 21, 58, 53, -54, -116, -58, -56,
      -84, 115, -118,
      -1, -1, -128, 1, -103, -15, -128, 25, -97, -127, -128, 79, -14,
      1, -126, 121, -122, 1, -113, -49, -116, 1, -100, -3, -124, 5,
      -25, -27, -128, 1, -1, -1 },
    { 0, 1, 122, 90, -62, 34, -43, 72, -59, -29, 56, -55, 98, 126,
      -79, 61,
      -1, -1, -125, 1, -128, 17, -26, 29, -31, 57, -72, 1, -128, -51,
      -100, 65, -124, 57, -2, 1, -126, 13, -113, 1, -97, 25, -127,
      -99, -8, 1, -1, -1 },
    { 0, 2, 108, -24, 18, -26, 102, 30, -58, 46, -28, -88, 34,
      -98, 97, -41,
      -1, -1, -96, 1, -126, 57, -9, 97, -127, 69, -119, 73, -127,
      1, -109, 59, -126, 1, -26, 103, -127, 65, -103, 115, -127,
      65, -25, 73, -128, 1, -1, -1 },
    { 0, 3, -114, 18, -34, 27, -39, -60, -76, -50, 118, 90, 82,
      -88, 34, -74,
      -1, -1, -66, 1, -128, 121, -26, 125, -128, -123, -103, 29,
      -112, 1, -109, 49, -112, 1, -116, -31, -128, 5, -122, 5,
      -32, 13, -127, -51, -125, 1, -1, -1 },
};

//------------------------------------------------------------
// initialization

/**
 * Constructor fills data fields by interpreting
 * the data bytes.
 */
public BoardDecoder(int boardNum) throws Exception {
    // you start by selecting the two dimensional
    // array corresponding to the desired board:
    byte[] data = myData[boardNum];
    // The first two bytes give the version number and
```

```
  // the board number, but you ignore them because
  // they are assumed to be correct.
  // The third byte of the first array is the first one
  // you read: it gives the player's starting coordinates:
  myPlayerSquare = DataConverter.decodeCoords(data[2]);
  // the next byte gives the coordinates of the crown:
  myGoalSquare = DataConverter.decodeCoords(data[3]);
  // the next 4 bytes give the coordinates of the keys:
  myKeys = new int[4][];
  for(int i = 0; i < myKeys.length; i++) {
    myKeys[i] = DataConverter.decodeCoords(data[i + 4]);
  }
  // the next 8 bytes give the coordinates of the doors:
  myDoors = new int[8][];
  for(int i = 0; i < myDoors.length; i++) {
    myDoors[i] = DataConverter.decodeCoords(data[i + 8]);
  }
  // now you create the TiledLayer object that is the
  // background dungeon map:
  myLayer = new TiledLayer(16, 16,
        Image.createImage("/images/stone.png"),
        DungeonManager.SQUARE_WIDTH, DungeonManager.SQUARE_WIDTH);
  // now you call an internal utility that reads the array
  // of data that gives the positions of the blocks in the
  // walls of this dungeon:
  decodeDungeon(data, myLayer, 16);
}


//-----------------------------------------------------------
// get/set data

/**
 * @return the number of boards currently stored in
 * this class.
 */
public static int getNumBoards() {
  return(myData.length);
}

/**
 * get the coordinates of where the player starts on the map
 * in terms of the array indices.
 */
public int[] getPlayerSquare() {
  return(myPlayerSquare);
}
```

```
/**
 * get the coordinates of the goal crown
 * in terms of the array indices.
 */
public int[] getGoalSquare() {
  return(myGoalSquare);
}

/**
 * get the tiled layer that gives the map of the dungeon.
 */
public TiledLayer getLayer() {
  return(myLayer);
}

/**
 * Creates the array of door sprites. (call this only once to avoid
 * creating redundant sprites).
 */
DoorKey[] createDoors() {
  DoorKey[] retArray = new DoorKey[8];
  for(int i = 0; i < 4; i++) {
    retArray[2*i] = new DoorKey(i, false, myDoors[2*i]);
    retArray[2*i + 1] = new DoorKey(i, false, myDoors[2*i + 1]);
  }
  return(retArray);
}

/**
 * Creates the array of key sprites. (call this only once to avoid
 * creating redundant sprites.)
 */
DoorKey[] createKeys() {
  DoorKey[] retArray = new DoorKey[4];
  for(int i = 0; i < 4; i++) {
    retArray[i] = new DoorKey(i, true, myKeys[i]);
  }
  return(retArray);
}

//----------------------------------------------------------
//  decoding utilities

/**
 * Takes a dungeon given as a byte array and uses it
 * to set the tiles of a tiled layer.
 *
 * The TiledLayer in this case is a 16x16 grid
 * in which each square can be either blank
```

```
 * (value of 0) or can be filled with a stone block
 * (value of 1). Therefore each square requires only
 * one bit of information.  Each byte of data in
 * the array called "data" records the frame indices
 * of eight squares in the grid.
 */
private static void decodeDungeon(byte[] data, TiledLayer dungeon,
      int offset) throws Exception {
  if(data.length + offset < 32) {
    throw(new Exception(
            "BoardDecoder.decodeDungeon-->not enough data!!!"));
  }
  // a frame index of zero indicates a blank square
  // (this is always true in a TiledLayer).
  // This TiledLayer has only one possible (nonblank)
  // frame, so a frame index of 1 indicates a stone block
  int frame = 0;
  // Each of the 32 bytes in the data array records
  // the frame indices of eight block in the 16x16
  // grid. Two bytes give one row of the dungeon,
  // so you have the array index go from zero to 16
  // to set the frame indices for each of the 16 rows.
  for(int i = 0; i < 16; i++) {
    // The flag allows you to look at each bit individually
    // to determine if it is one or zero. The number 128
    // corresponds to the highest bit of a byte, so you
    // start with that one.
    int flag = 128;
    // Here you check two bytes at the same time
    // (the two bytes together correspond to one row
    // of the dungeon). You use a loop that checks
    // the bytes bit by bit by performing a bitwise
    // and (&) between the data byte and a flag:
    for(int j = 0; j < 8; j++) {
      if((data[offset + 2*i] & flag) != 0) {
        frame = 1;
      } else {
        frame = 0;
      }
      dungeon.setCell(j, i, frame);
      if((data[offset + 2*i + 1] & flag) != 0) {
        frame = 1;
      } else {
        frame = 0;
      }
      dungeon.setCell(j + 8, i, frame);
      // move the flag down one bit so you can
      // check the next bit of data on the next pass
```

```
        // through the loop:
        flag = flag >> 1;
      }
    }
  }
}
```

In case you're wondering where the byte arrays in the previous class came from, Listing 5-6 shows the utility class I used to encode them. Keep in mind that this class is merely a tool I used to create the data for the game. Once the data has been created, this class is no longer used. It would certainly not be distributed to users with the game. Listing 5-6 shows EncodingUtils.java. The class as it appears in Listing 5-6 is encoding the data that defines the board shown in Figure 5-3.

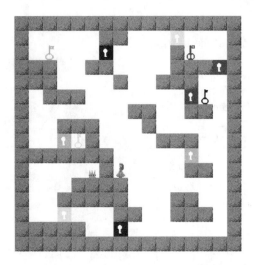

Figure 5-3. *The board that corresponds to the data encoded in Listing 5-6*

Listing 5-6. *EncodingUtils.java*

```java
package net.frog_parrot.dungeon;

import  net.frog_parrot.util.DataConverter;

/**
 * This class contains the data for the map of the dungeon.
 * This is a utility class that allows a developer to write
 * the data for a board in a simple format, then this class
 * encodes the data in a format that the game can use.
 *
 * Note that the data that this class encodes is hard-coded.
 * That is because this class is intended to be used only a
 * few times to encode the data. Once the board data has been
 * encoded, it never needs to be encoded again. The encoding
```

```
 * methods used in this class could be generalized to be used
 * to create a board editor that would allow a user to easily
 * create new boards, but that is an exercise for another day...
 *
 * @author Carol Hamer
 */
public class EncodingUtils {

    //-----------------------------------------------------------
    //  fields

    /**
     * data for which squares are filled and which are blank.
     * 0 = empty
     * 1 = filled
     */
    private int[][] mySquares = {
      { 1, 1, 1, 1, 1, 1, 1, 1, 1, 1, 1, 1, 1, 1, 1, 1 },
      { 1, 0, 0, 0, 0, 0, 1, 1, 0, 0, 0, 0, 0, 0, 0, 1 },
      { 1, 0, 0, 0, 0, 0, 0, 0, 0, 0, 0, 1, 0, 0, 0, 1 },
      { 1, 1, 1, 0, 0, 1, 1, 0, 0, 0, 0, 1, 1, 1, 0, 1 },
      { 1, 1, 1, 0, 0, 0, 0, 1, 0, 0, 1, 1, 1, 0, 0, 1 },
      { 1, 0, 1, 1, 1, 0, 0, 0, 0, 0, 0, 0, 0, 0, 0, 1 },
      { 1, 0, 0, 0, 0, 0, 0, 0, 1, 1, 0, 0, 1, 1, 0, 1 },
      { 1, 0, 0, 1, 1, 1, 0, 0, 0, 1, 0, 0, 0, 0, 0, 1 },
      { 1, 0, 0, 0, 0, 1, 0, 0, 0, 0, 1, 1, 1, 0, 0, 1 },
      { 1, 1, 1, 1, 1, 1, 1, 0, 0, 0, 0, 0, 0, 0, 0, 1 },
      { 1, 0, 0, 0, 0, 0, 1, 0, 0, 0, 0, 0, 1, 1, 0, 1 },
      { 1, 0, 0, 0, 1, 1, 1, 1, 0, 0, 0, 0, 0, 0, 0, 1 },
      { 1, 0, 0, 1, 1, 1, 1, 1, 0, 0, 0, 1, 1, 0, 0, 1 },
      { 1, 0, 0, 0, 0, 0, 0, 1, 1, 0, 0, 1, 1, 1, 0, 1 },
      { 1, 1, 1, 1, 1, 0, 0, 0, 0, 0, 0, 0, 0, 0, 0, 1 },
      { 1, 1, 1, 1, 1, 1, 1, 1, 1, 1, 1, 1, 1, 1, 1, 1 },
    };

    /**
     * The coordinates of where the player starts on the map
     * in terms of the array indices.
     */
    private int[] myPlayerSquare = { 7, 10 };

    /**
     * The coordinates of the goal (crown).
     */
    private int[] myGoalSquare = { 5, 10 };
```

```
//-----------------------------------------------------------
//  get/set data

/**
 * Creates the array of door sprites. (call this only once to avoid
 * creating redundant sprites).
 */
int[][] getDoorCoords() {
  int[][] retArray = new int[8][];
  for(int i = 0; i < retArray.length; i++) {
    retArray[i] = new int[2];
  }
  // red
  retArray[0][0] = 12;
  retArray[0][1] = 5;
  retArray[1][0] = 14;
  retArray[1][1] = 3;
  // green
  retArray[2][0] = 3;
  retArray[2][1] = 8;
  retArray[3][0] = 12;
  retArray[3][1] = 9;
  // blue
  retArray[4][0] = 6;
  retArray[4][1] = 2;
  retArray[5][0] = 7;
  retArray[5][1] = 14;
  // yellow
  retArray[6][0] = 11;
  retArray[6][1] = 1;
  retArray[7][0] = 3;
  retArray[7][1] = 13;
  return(retArray);
}

/**
 * Creates the array of key sprites. (call this only once to avoid
 * creating redundant sprites.)
 */
int[][] getKeyCoords() {
  int[][] retArray = new int[4][];
  for(int i = 0; i < retArray.length; i++) {
    retArray[i] = new int[2];
  }
  // red
  retArray[0][0] = 12;
  retArray[0][1] = 2;
  // green
```

```java
  retArray[1][0] = 2;
  retArray[1][1] = 2;
  // blue
  retArray[2][0] = 13;
  retArray[2][1] = 5;
  // yellow
  retArray[3][0] = 4;
  retArray[3][1] = 8;
  return(retArray);
}


//----------------------------------------------------------
//  encoding / decoding utilities

/**
 * Encodes the entire dungeon.
 */
byte[][] encodeDungeon() {
  byte[][] retArray = new byte[2][];
  retArray[0] = new byte[16];
  // the first byte is the version number:
  retArray[0][0] = 0;
  // the second byte is the board number:
  retArray[0][1] = 0;
  // the player's start square:
  retArray[0][2] = DataConverter.encodeCoords(myPlayerSquare);
  // the goal (crown) square:
  retArray[0][3] = DataConverter.encodeCoords(myGoalSquare);
  //encode the keys:
  int[][] keyCoords = getKeyCoords();
  for(int i = 0; i < keyCoords.length; i++) {
    retArray[0][i + 4] = DataConverter.encodeCoords(keyCoords[i]);
  }
  //encode the doors:
  int[][] doorCoords = getDoorCoords();
  for(int i = 0; i < doorCoords.length; i++) {
    retArray[0][i + 8] = DataConverter.encodeCoords(doorCoords[i]);
  }
  //encode the maze:
  try {
    retArray[1] = encodeDungeon(mySquares);
  } catch(Exception e) {
    e.printStackTrace();
  }
  return(retArray);
}
```

```
/**
 * Takes a dungeon given in terms of an array of ones and zeros
 * and turns it into an array of bytes.
 * WARNING: the array MUST BE 16x16.
 */
static byte[] encodeDungeon(int[][] dungeonMap) throws Exception {
  if((dungeonMap.length != 16) || (dungeonMap[0].length != 16)) {
    throw(new Exception("EncodingUtils.encodeDungeon-->must be 16x16!!!"));
  }
  byte[] retArray = new byte[32];
  for(int i = 0; i < 16; i++) {
    retArray[2*i] = DataConverter.encode8(dungeonMap[i], 0);
    retArray[2*i + 1] = DataConverter.encode8(dungeonMap[i], 8);
  }
  return(retArray);
}


//----------------------------------------------------------
//  main prints the bytes to standard out.
// (note that this class is not intended to be run as a MIDlet)

/**
 * Prints the byte version of the board to standard out.
 */
public static void main(String[] args) {
  try {
    EncodingUtils map = new EncodingUtils();
    byte[][] data = map.encodeDungeon();
    System.out.println("EncodingUtils.main-->dungeon encoded");
    System.out.print("{\n    " + data[0][0]);
    for(int i = 1; i < data[0].length; i++) {
      System.out.print(", " + data[0][i]);
    }
    for(int i = 1; i < data[1].length; i++) {
      System.out.print(", " + data[1][i]);
    }
    System.out.println("\n};");
  } catch(Exception e) {
    e.printStackTrace();
  }
}


}
```

Creating the Complete Example Game

All the classes you've seen to encode and store data aren't much use without a game to go with them. This section shows you the code for the fun part of the game. I've discussed all the programming ideas used in this game in previous chapters, so I'm leaving the explanation for the comments.

Listing 5-7 shows the code for the MIDlet subclass Dungeon.java.

Listing 5-7. *Dungeon.java*

```
package net.frog_parrot.dungeon;

import javax.microedition.midlet.*;
import javax.microedition.lcdui.*;

/**
 * This is the main class of the dungeon game.
 *
 * @author Carol Hamer
 */
public class Dungeon extends MIDlet implements CommandListener {

  //-------------------------------------------------------
  //    game object fields

  /**
   * The canvas that the dungeon is drawn on.
   */
  private DungeonCanvas myCanvas;

  /**
   * the thread that advances the game clock.
   */
  private GameThread myGameThread;

  //-------------------------------------------------------
  //    command fields

  /**
   * The button to exit the game.
   */
  private Command myExitCommand = new Command("Exit", Command.EXIT, 99);

  /**
   * The command to save the game in progress.
   */
  private Command mySaveCommand = new Command("Save Game", Command.SCREEN, 2);
```

```java
/**
 * The command to restore a previously saved game.
 */
private Command myRestoreCommand
  = new Command("Restore Game", Command.SCREEN, 2);

/**
 * the command to start moving when the game is paused.
 */
private Command myGoCommand = new Command("Go", Command.SCREEN, 1);

/**
 * the command to pause the game.
 */
private Command myPauseCommand = new Command("Pause", Command.SCREEN, 1);

/**
 * the command to start a new game.
 */
private Command myNewCommand = new Command("Next Board", Command.SCREEN, 1);

//----------------------------------------------------
//    initialization and game state changes

/**
 * Empty constructor.
 */
public Dungeon() {
}


/**
 * Switch the command to the play again command.
 * (removing other commands that are no longer relevant)
 */
void setNewCommand() {
  myCanvas.removeCommand(myPauseCommand);
  myCanvas.removeCommand(myGoCommand);
  myCanvas.addCommand(myNewCommand);
}

/**
 * Switch the command to the go command.
 * (removing other commands that are no longer relevant)
 */
void setGoCommand() {
  myCanvas.removeCommand(myPauseCommand);
  myCanvas.removeCommand(myNewCommand);
```

```
  myCanvas.addCommand(myGoCommand);
}


/**
 * Switch the command to the pause command.
 * (removing other commands that are no longer relevant)
 */
void setPauseCommand() {
  myCanvas.removeCommand(myNewCommand);
  myCanvas.removeCommand(myGoCommand);
  myCanvas.addCommand(myPauseCommand);
}


//------------------------------------------------------------------
//   implementation of MIDlet
// these methods may be called by the application management
// software at any time, so you always check fields for null
// before calling methods on them.


/**
 * Start the application.
 */
public void startApp() throws MIDletStateChangeException {
    try {
      if(myCanvas == null) {
        // create the canvas and set up the commands:
        myCanvas = new DungeonCanvas(this);
        myCanvas.addCommand(myExitCommand);
        myCanvas.addCommand(mySaveCommand);
        myCanvas.addCommand(myRestoreCommand);
        myCanvas.addCommand(myPauseCommand);
        myCanvas.setCommandListener(this);
      }
      if(myGameThread == null) {
        // create the thread and start the game:
        myGameThread = new GameThread(myCanvas);
        myCanvas.start();
        myGameThread.start();
      } else {
        // in case this gets called again after
        // the application has been started once:
        myCanvas.removeCommand(myGoCommand);
        myCanvas.addCommand(myPauseCommand);
        myCanvas.flushKeys();
        myGameThread.resumeGame();
      }
    } catch(Exception e) {
      // if there's an error during creation, display it as an alert.
```

```
      errorMsg(e);
    }
  }


  /**
   * Stop the threads and throw out the garbage.
   */
  public void destroyApp(boolean unconditional)
      throws MIDletStateChangeException {
    myCanvas = null;
    if(myGameThread != null) {
      myGameThread.requestStop();
    }
    myGameThread = null;
    System.gc();
  }


  /**
   * Pause the game.
   */
  public void pauseApp() {
    if(myCanvas != null) {
      setGoCommand();
    }
    if(myGameThread != null) {
      myGameThread.pause();
    }
  }


  //----------------------------------------------------------------
  //  implementation of CommandListener


  /*
   * Respond to a command issued on the Canvas.
   * (reset, exit, or change size prefs).
   */
  public void commandAction(Command c, Displayable s) {
    try {
      //myCanvas.setNeedsRepaint();
      if(c == myGoCommand) {
        myCanvas.setNeedsRepaint();
        myCanvas.removeCommand(myGoCommand);
        myCanvas.addCommand(myPauseCommand);
        myCanvas.flushKeys();
        myGameThread.resumeGame();
      } else if(c == myPauseCommand) {
        myCanvas.setNeedsRepaint();
        myCanvas.removeCommand(myPauseCommand);
```

```
      myCanvas.addCommand(myGoCommand);
      myGameThread.pause();
    } else if(c == myNewCommand) {
      myCanvas.setNeedsRepaint();
      // go to the next board and restart the game
      myCanvas.removeCommand(myNewCommand);
      myCanvas.addCommand(myPauseCommand);
      myCanvas.reset();
      myGameThread.resumeGame();
    } else if(c == Alert.DISMISS_COMMAND) {
      // if there was a serious enough error to
      // cause an alert, then we end the game
      // when the user is done reading the alert:
      // (Alert.DISMISS_COMMAND is the default
      // command that is placed on an Alert
      // whose timeout is FOREVER)
      destroyApp(false);
      notifyDestroyed();
    } else if(c == mySaveCommand) {
      myCanvas.setNeedsRepaint();
      myCanvas.saveGame();
    } else if(c == myRestoreCommand) {
      myCanvas.setNeedsRepaint();
      myCanvas.removeCommand(myNewCommand);
      myCanvas.removeCommand(myGoCommand);
      myCanvas.addCommand(myPauseCommand);
      myCanvas.revertToSaved();
    } else if(c == myExitCommand) {
      destroyApp(false);
      notifyDestroyed();
    }
  } catch(Exception e) {
    errorMsg(e);
  }
}

//----------------------------------------------------------
//   error methods

/**
 * Converts an exception to a message and displays
 * the message.
 */
void errorMsg(Exception e) {
  if(e.getMessage() == null) {
    errorMsg(e.getClass().getName());
  } else {
    errorMsg(e.getClass().getName() + ":" + e.getMessage());
```

```
    }
  }

  /**
   * Displays an error message alert if something goes wrong.
   */
  void errorMsg(String msg) {
    Alert errorAlert = new Alert("error",
                                  msg, null, AlertType.ERROR);
    errorAlert.setCommandListener(this);
    errorAlert.setTimeout(Alert.FOREVER);
    Display.getDisplay(this).setCurrent(errorAlert);
  }

}
```

Listing 5-8 shows the code for the GameCanvas subclass DungeonCanvas.java.

Listing 5-8. *DungeonCanvas.java*

```
package net.frog_parrot.dungeon;

import javax.microedition.lcdui.*;
import javax.microedition.lcdui.game.*;

/**
 * This class is the display of the game.
 *
 * @author Carol Hamer
 */
public class DungeonCanvas extends GameCanvas {

  //----------------------------------------------------------
  //   dimension fields
  //   (constant after initialization)

  /**
   * the height of the black region below the play area.
   */
  static int TIMER_HEIGHT = 32;

  /**
   * the top-corner X coordinate according to this
   * object's coordinate system:
   */
  static final int CORNER_X = 0;
```

```
/**
 * the top-corner Y coordinate according to this
 * object's coordinate system:
 */
static final int CORNER_Y = 0;

/**
 * the width of the portion of the screen that this
 * canvas can use.
 */
static int DISP_WIDTH;

/**
 * the height of the portion of the screen that this
 * canvas can use.
 */
static int DISP_HEIGHT;

/**
 * the height of the font used for this game.
 */
static int FONT_HEIGHT;

/**
 * the font used for this game.
 */
static Font FONT;

/**
 * color constant
 */
public static final int BLACK = 0;

/**
 * color constant
 */
public static final int WHITE = 0xffffff;

//------------------------------------------------------------
//    game object fields

/**
 * a handle to the display.
 */
private Display myDisplay;

/**
 * a handle to the MIDlet object (to keep track of buttons).
 */
```

```
    */
  private Dungeon myDungeon;

  /**
   * the LayerManager that handles the game graphics.
   */
  private DungeonManager myManager;

  /**
   * whether the game has ended.
   */
  private static boolean myGameOver;

  /**
   * The number of ticks on the clock the last time the
   * time display was updated.
   * This is saved to determine if the time string needs
   * to be recomputed.
   */
  private int myOldGameTicks = 0;

  /**
   * the number of game ticks that have passed since the
   * beginning of the game.
   */
  private int myGameTicks = myOldGameTicks;

  /**
   * you save the time string to avoid re-creating it
   * unnecessarily.
   */
  private static String myInitialString = "0:00";

  /**
   * you save the time string to avoid re-creating it
   * unnecessarily.
   */
  private String myTimeString = myInitialString;

  //-------------------------------------------------------
  //    gets/sets

  /**
   * This is called when the game ends.
   */
  void setGameOver() {
    myGameOver = true;
```

```
    myDungeon.pauseApp();
}

/**
 * Find out if the game has ended.
 */
static boolean getGameOver() {
  return(myGameOver);
}

/**
 * Tell the layer manager that it needs to repaint.
 */
public void setNeedsRepaint() {
  myManager.setNeedsRepaint();
}

//--------------------------------------------------------
//     initialization and game state changes

/**
 * Constructor sets the data, performs dimension calculations,
 * and creates the graphical objects.
 */
public DungeonCanvas(Dungeon midlet) throws Exception {
  super(false);
  myDisplay = Display.getDisplay(midlet);
  myDungeon = midlet;
  // calculate the dimensions
  DISP_WIDTH = getWidth();
  DISP_HEIGHT = getHeight();
  if((!myDisplay.isColor()) || (myDisplay.numColors() < 256)) {
    throw(new Exception("game requires full-color screen"));
  }
  if((DISP_WIDTH < 150) || (DISP_HEIGHT < 170)) {
    throw(new Exception("Screen too small"));
  }
  if((DISP_WIDTH > 250) || (DISP_HEIGHT > 320)) {
    throw(new Exception("Screen too large"));
  }
  // since the time is painted in white on black,
  // it shows up better if the font is bold:
  FONT = Font.getFont(Font.FACE_SYSTEM,
                             Font.STYLE_BOLD, Font.SIZE_MEDIUM);
  // calculate the height of the black region that the
  // timer is painted on:
  FONT_HEIGHT = FONT.getHeight();
  TIMER_HEIGHT = FONT_HEIGHT + 8;
```

```
    // create the LayerManager (where all the interesting
    // graphics go!) and give it the dimensions of the
    // region it is supposed to paint:
    if(myManager == null) {
      myManager = new DungeonManager(CORNER_X, CORNER_Y,
          DISP_WIDTH, DISP_HEIGHT - TIMER_HEIGHT, this);
    }
  }

  /**
   * This is called as soon as the application begins.
   */
  void start() {
    myGameOver = false;
    myDisplay.setCurrent(this);
    setNeedsRepaint();
  }

  /**
   * sets all variables back to their initial positions.
   */
  void reset() throws Exception {
    // most of the variables that need to be reset
    // are held by the LayerManager:
    myManager.reset();
    myGameOver = false;
    setNeedsRepaint();
  }

  /**
   * sets all variables back to the positions
   * from a previously saved game.
   */
  void revertToSaved() throws Exception {
    // most of the variables that need to be reset
    // are held by the LayerManager, so we
    // prompt the LayerManager to get the
    // saved data:
    myGameTicks = myManager.revertToSaved();
    myGameOver = false;
    myOldGameTicks = myGameTicks;
    myTimeString = formatTime();
    setNeedsRepaint();
  }

  /**
   * save the current game in progress.
   */
```

```
void saveGame() throws Exception {
  myManager.saveGame(myGameTicks);
}

/**
 * clears the key states.
 */
void flushKeys() {
  getKeyStates();
}

/**
 * If the game is hidden by another app (or a menu)
 * ignore it since not much happens in this game
 * when the user is not actively interacting with it.
 * (you could pause the timer, but it's not important
 * enough to bother with when the user is just pulling
 * up a menu for a few seconds)
 */
protected void hideNotify() {
}

/**
 * When it comes back into view, just make sure the
 * manager knows that it needs to repaint.
 */
protected void showNotify() {
  setNeedsRepaint();
}

//----------------------------------------------------------
//  graphics methods

/**
 * paint the game graphics on the screen.
 */
public void paint(Graphics g) {
  // color the bottom segment of the screen black
  g.setColor(BLACK);
  g.fillRect(CORNER_X, CORNER_Y + DISP_HEIGHT - TIMER_HEIGHT,
            DISP_WIDTH, TIMER_HEIGHT);
  // paint the LayerManager (which paints
  // all the interesting graphics):
  try {
    myManager.paint(g);
  } catch(Exception e) {
    myDungeon.errorMsg(e);
  }
```

```
    // draw the time
    g.setColor(WHITE);
    g.setFont(FONT);
    g.drawString("Time: " + formatTime(), DISP_WIDTH/2,
                 CORNER_Y + DISP_HEIGHT - 4, g.BOTTOM|g.HCENTER);
    // write "Dungeon Completed" when the user finishes a board:
    if(myGameOver) {
      myDungeon.setNewCommand();
      // clear the top region:
      g.setColor(WHITE);
      g.fillRect(CORNER_X, CORNER_Y, DISP_WIDTH, FONT_HEIGHT*2 + 1);
      int goWidth = FONT.stringWidth("Dungeon Completed");
      g.setColor(BLACK);
      g.setFont(FONT);
      g.drawString("Dungeon Completed", (DISP_WIDTH - goWidth)/2,
                   CORNER_Y + FONT_HEIGHT, g.TOP|g.LEFT);
    }
  }

  /**
   * a simple utility to make the number of ticks look like a time...
   */
  public String formatTime() {
    if((myGameTicks / 16) != myOldGameTicks) {
      myTimeString = "";
      myOldGameTicks = (myGameTicks / 16) + 1;
      int smallPart = myOldGameTicks % 60;
      int bigPart = myOldGameTicks / 60;
      myTimeString += bigPart + ":";
      if(smallPart / 10 < 1) {
        myTimeString += "0";
      }
      myTimeString += smallPart;
    }
    return(myTimeString);
  }

  //--------------------------------------------------------
  //  game movements

  /**
   * update the display.
   */
  void updateScreen() {
    myGameTicks++;
    // paint the display
    try {
```

```
      paint(getGraphics());
      flushGraphics(CORNER_X, CORNER_Y, DISP_WIDTH, DISP_HEIGHT);
    } catch(Exception e) {
      myDungeon.errorMsg(e);
    }
  }

  /**
   * Respond to keystrokes.
   */
  public void checkKeys() {
    if(! myGameOver) {
      int vertical = 0;
      int horizontal = 0;
      // determine which moves the user would like to make:
      int keyState = getKeyStates();
      if((keyState & LEFT_PRESSED) != 0) {
        horizontal = -1;
      }
      if((keyState & RIGHT_PRESSED) != 0) {
        horizontal = 1;
      }
      if((keyState & UP_PRESSED) != 0) {
        vertical = -1;
      }
      if((keyState & DOWN_PRESSED) != 0) {
        // if the user presses the down key,
        // we put down or pick up a key object
        // or pick up the crown:
        myManager.putDownPickUp();
      }
      // tell the manager to move the player
      // accordingly if possible:
      myManager.requestMove(horizontal, vertical);
    }
  }

}
```

Listing 5-9 shows the code for the LayerManager subclass DungeonManager.java.

Listing 5-9. *DungeonManager.java*

```
package net.frog_parrot.dungeon;

import javax.microedition.lcdui.*;
import javax.microedition.lcdui.game.*;
```

```java
/**
 * This class handles the graphics objects.
 *
 * @author Carol Hamer
 */
public class DungeonManager extends LayerManager {

  //-----------------------------------------------------------
  //   dimension fields
  //   (constant after initialization)

  /**
   * The X coordinate of the place on the game canvas where
   * the LayerManager window should appear, in terms of the
   * coordinates of the game canvas.
   */
  static int CANVAS_X;

  /**
   * The Y coordinate of the place on the game canvas where
   * the LayerManager window should appear, in terms of the
   * coordinates of the game canvas.
   */
  static int CANVAS_Y;

  /**
   * The width of the display window.
   */
  static int DISP_WIDTH;

  /**
   * The height of this object's visible region.
   */
  static int DISP_HEIGHT;

  /**
   * the (right or left)  distance the player
   * goes in a single keystroke.
   */
  static final int MOVE_LENGTH = 8;

  /**
   * The width of the square tiles that this game is divided into.
   * This is the width of the stone walls as well as the princess and
   * the ghost.
   */
  static final int SQUARE_WIDTH = 24;
```

```
/**
 * The jump index that indicates that no jump is
 * currently in progress.
 */
static final int NO_JUMP = -6;

/**
 * The maximum speed for the player's fall.
 */
static final int MAX_FREE_FALL = 3;

//-----------------------------------------------------------
//   game object fields

/**
 * the handle back to the canvas.
 */
private DungeonCanvas myCanvas;

/**
 * the background dungeon.
 */
private TiledLayer myBackground;

/**
 * the player.
 */
private Sprite myPrincess;

/**
 * the goal.
 */
private Sprite myCrown;

/**
 * the doors.
 */
private DoorKey[] myDoors;

/**
 * the keys.
 */
private DoorKey[] myKeys;

/**
 * the key currently held by the player.
 */
private DoorKey myHeldKey;
```

```
/**
 * The leftmost X coordinate that should be visible on the
 * screen in terms of this object's internal coordinates.
 */
private int myViewWindowX;

/**
 * The top Y coordinate that should be visible on the
 * screen in terms of this object's internal coordinates.
 */
private int myViewWindowY;

/**
 * Where the princess is in the jump sequence.
 */
private int myIsJumping = NO_JUMP;

/**
 * Whether the screen needs to be repainted.
 */
private boolean myModifiedSinceLastPaint = true;

/**
 * Which board we're playing on.
 */
private int myCurrentBoardNum = 0;

//-------------------------------------------------------
//    gets/sets

/**
 * Tell the layer manager that it needs to repaint.
 */
public void setNeedsRepaint() {
  myModifiedSinceLastPaint = true;
}

//-------------------------------------------------------
//    initialization
//    set up or save game data.

/**
 * Constructor merely sets the data.
 * @param x The X coordinate of the place on the game canvas where
 * the LayerManager window should appear, in terms of the
 * coordinates of the game canvas.
 * @param y The Y coordinate of the place on the game canvas where
```

```
 * the LayerManager window should appear, in terms of the
 * coordinates of the game canvas.
 * @param width the width of the region that is to be
 * occupied by the LayoutManager.
 * @param height the height of the region that is to be
 * occupied by the LayoutManager.
 * @param canvas the DungeonCanvas that this LayerManager
 * should appear on.
 */
public DungeonManager(int x, int y, int width, int height,
                      DungeonCanvas canvas) throws Exception {
  myCanvas = canvas;
  CANVAS_X = x;
  CANVAS_Y = y;
  DISP_WIDTH = width;
  DISP_HEIGHT = height;
  // create a decoder object that creates the dungeon and
  // its associated Sprites from data.
  BoardDecoder decoder = new BoardDecoder(myCurrentBoardNum);
  // get the background TiledLayer
  myBackground = decoder.getLayer();
  // get the coordinates of the square that the princess
  // starts on.
  int[] playerCoords = decoder.getPlayerSquare();
  // create the player sprite
  myPrincess = new Sprite(Image.createImage("/images/princess.png"),
                      SQUARE_WIDTH, SQUARE_WIDTH);
  myPrincess.setFrame(1);
  // you define the reference pixel to be in the middle
  // of the princess image so that when the princess turns
  // from right to left (and vice versa) she does not
  // appear to move to a different location.
  myPrincess.defineReferencePixel(SQUARE_WIDTH/2, 0);
  // the dungeon is a 16x16 grid, so the array playerCoords
  // gives the player's location in terms of the grid, and
  // then you multiply those coordinates by the SQUARE_WIDTH
  // to get the precise pixel where the player should be
  // placed (in terms of the LayerManager's coordinate system)
  myPrincess.setPosition(SQUARE_WIDTH * playerCoords[0],
                      SQUARE_WIDTH * playerCoords[1]);
  // you append all the Layers (TiledLayer and Sprite)
  // so that this LayerManager will paint them when
  // flushGraphics is called.
  append(myPrincess);
  // get the coordinates of the square where the crown
  // should be placed.
  int[] goalCoords = decoder.getGoalSquare();
```

```
    myCrown = new Sprite(Image.createImage("/images/crown.png"));
    myCrown.setPosition((SQUARE_WIDTH * goalCoords[0]) + (SQUARE_WIDTH/4),
                        (SQUARE_WIDTH * goalCoords[1]) + (SQUARE_WIDTH/2));
    append(myCrown);
    // The decoder creates the door and key sprites and places
    // them in the correct locations in terms of the LayerManager's
    // coordinate system.
    myDoors = decoder.createDoors();
    myKeys = decoder.createKeys();
    for(int i = 0; i < myDoors.length; i++) {
      append(myDoors[i]);
    }
    for(int i = 0; i < myKeys.length; i++) {
      append(myKeys[i]);
    }
    // append the background last so it will be painted first.
    append(myBackground);
    // this sets the view screen so that the player is
    // in the center.
    myViewWindowX = SQUARE_WIDTH * playerCoords[0]
      - ((DISP_WIDTH - SQUARE_WIDTH)/2);
    myViewWindowY = SQUARE_WIDTH * playerCoords[1]
      - ((DISP_HEIGHT - SQUARE_WIDTH)/2);
    // a number of objects are created in order to set up the game,
    // but they should be eliminated to free up memory:
    decoder = null;
    System.gc();
  }

  /**
   * sets all variables back to their initial positions.
   */
  void reset() throws Exception {
    // first get rid of the old board:
    for(int i = 0; i < myDoors.length; i++) {
      remove(myDoors[i]);
    }
    myHeldKey = null;
    for(int i = 0; i < myKeys.length; i++) {
      remove(myKeys[i]);
    }
    remove(myBackground);
    // now create the new board:
    myCurrentBoardNum++;
    // in this version you go back to the beginning if
    // all boards have been completed.
    if(myCurrentBoardNum == BoardDecoder.getNumBoards()) {
```

```
    myCurrentBoardNum = 0;
  }
  // you create a new decoder object to read and interpret
  // all the data for the current board.
  BoardDecoder decoder = new BoardDecoder(myCurrentBoardNum);
  // get the background TiledLayer
  myBackground = decoder.getLayer();
  // get the coordinates of the square that the princess
  // starts on.
  int[] playerCoords = decoder.getPlayerSquare();
  // the dungeon is a 16x16 grid, so the array playerCoords
  // gives the player's location in terms of the grid, and
  // then you multiply those coordinates by the SQUARE_WIDTH
  // to get the precise pixel where the player should be
  // placed (in terms of the LayerManager's coordinate system)
  myPrincess.setPosition(SQUARE_WIDTH * playerCoords[0],
                         SQUARE_WIDTH * playerCoords[1]);
  myPrincess.setFrame(1);
  // get the coordinates of the square where the crown
  // should be placed.
  int[] goalCoords = decoder.getGoalSquare();
  myCrown.setPosition((SQUARE_WIDTH * goalCoords[0]) + (SQUARE_WIDTH/4),
                      (SQUARE_WIDTH * goalCoords[1]) + (SQUARE_WIDTH/2));
  // The decoder creates the door and key sprites and places
  // them in the correct locations in terms of the LayerManager's
  // coordinate system.
  myDoors = decoder.createDoors();
  myKeys = decoder.createKeys();
  for(int i = 0; i < myDoors.length; i++) {
    append(myDoors[i]);
  }
  for(int i = 0; i < myKeys.length; i++) {
    append(myKeys[i]);
  }
  // append the background last so it will be painted first.
  append(myBackground);
  // this sets the view screen so that the player is
  // in the center.
  myViewWindowX = SQUARE_WIDTH * playerCoords[0]
    - ((DISP_WIDTH - SQUARE_WIDTH)/2);
  myViewWindowY = SQUARE_WIDTH * playerCoords[1]
    - ((DISP_HEIGHT - SQUARE_WIDTH)/2);
  // a number of objects are created in order to set up the game,
  // but they should be eliminated to free up memory:
  decoder = null;
  System.gc();
}
```

```
/**
 * sets all variables back to the position in the saved game.
 * @return the time on the clock of the saved game.
 */
int revertToSaved() throws Exception {
  int retVal = 0;
  // first get rid of the old board:
  for(int i = 0; i < myDoors.length; i++) {
    remove(myDoors[i]);
  }
  myHeldKey = null;
  for(int i = 0; i < myKeys.length; i++) {
    remove(myKeys[i]);
  }
  remove(myBackground);
  // now get the info of the saved game
  // only one game is saved at a time, and the GameInfo object
  // will read the saved game's data from memory.
  GameInfo info = new GameInfo();
  if(info.getIsEmpty()) {
    // if no game has been saved, you start from the beginning.
    myCurrentBoardNum = 0;
    reset();
  } else {
    // get the time on the clock of the saved game.
    retVal = info.getTime();
    // get the number of the board the saved game was on.
    myCurrentBoardNum = info.getBoardNum();
    // create the BoradDecoder that gives the data for the
    // desired board.
    BoardDecoder decoder = new BoardDecoder(myCurrentBoardNum);
    // get the background TiledLayer
    myBackground = decoder.getLayer();
    // get the coordinates of the square that the princess
    // was on in the saved game.
    int[] playerCoords = info.getPlayerSquare();
    myPrincess.setPosition(SQUARE_WIDTH * playerCoords[0],
                           SQUARE_WIDTH * playerCoords[1]);
    myPrincess.setFrame(1);
    // get the coordinates of the square where the crown
    // should be placed (this is given by the BoardDecoder
    // and not from the data of the saved game because the
    // crown does not move during the game).
    int[] goalCoords = decoder.getGoalSquare();
    myCrown.setPosition((SQUARE_WIDTH * goalCoords[0]) + (SQUARE_WIDTH/4),
                        (SQUARE_WIDTH * goalCoords[1]) + (SQUARE_WIDTH/2));
    // The decoder creates the door and key sprites and places
    // them in the correct locations in terms of the LayerManager's
```

```
    // coordinate system.
    myDoors = decoder.createDoors();
    myKeys = decoder.createKeys();
    // get an array of ints that lists whether each door is
    // open or closed in the saved game
    int[] openDoors = info.getDoorsOpen();
    for(int i = 0; i < myDoors.length; i++) {
      append(myDoors[i]);
      if(openDoors[i] == 0) {
        // if the door was open, make it invisible
        myDoors[i].setVisible(false);
      }
    }
    // the keys can be moved by the player, so you get their
    // coordinates from the GameInfo saved data.
    int[][] keyCoords = info.getKeyCoords();
    for(int i = 0; i < myKeys.length; i++) {
      append(myKeys[i]);
      myKeys[i].setPosition(SQUARE_WIDTH * keyCoords[i][0],
                            SQUARE_WIDTH * keyCoords[i][1]);
    }
    // if the player was holding a key in the saved game,
    // you have the player hold that key and set it to invisible.
    int heldKey = info.getHeldKey();
    if(heldKey != -1) {
      myHeldKey = myKeys[heldKey];
      myHeldKey.setVisible(false);
    }
    // append the background last so it will be painted first.
    append(myBackground);
    // this sets the view screen so that the player is
    // in the center.
    myViewWindowX = SQUARE_WIDTH * playerCoords[0]
      - ((DISP_WIDTH - SQUARE_WIDTH)/2);
    myViewWindowY = SQUARE_WIDTH * playerCoords[1]
      - ((DISP_HEIGHT - SQUARE_WIDTH)/2);
    // a number of objects are created in order to set up the game,
    // but they should be eliminated to free up memory:
    decoder = null;
    System.gc();
  }
  return(retVal);
}


/**
 * save the current game in progress.
 */
void saveGame(int gameTicks) throws Exception {
```

```
      int[] playerSquare = new int[2];
      // the coordinates of the player are given in terms of
      // the 16x16 dungeon grid. You divide the player's
      // pixel coordinates to get the right grid square.
      // If the player was not precisely aligned with a
      // grid square when the game was saved, the difference
      // will be shaved off.
      playerSquare[0] = myPrincess.getX()/SQUARE_WIDTH;
      playerSquare[1] = myPrincess.getY()/SQUARE_WIDTH;
      // save the coordinates of the current locations of
      // the keys, and if a key is currently held by the
      // player, we save the info of which one it was.
      int[][] keyCoords = new int[4][];
      int heldKey = -1;
      for(int i = 0; i < myKeys.length; i++) {
        keyCoords[i] = new int[2];
        keyCoords[i][0] = myKeys[i].getX()/SQUARE_WIDTH;
        keyCoords[i][1] = myKeys[i].getY()/SQUARE_WIDTH;
        if((myHeldKey != null) && (myKeys[i] == myHeldKey)) {
          heldKey = i;
        }
      }
      // save the information of which doors were open.
      int[] doorsOpen = new int[8];
      for(int i = 0; i < myDoors.length; i++) {
        if(myDoors[i].isVisible()) {
          doorsOpen[i] = 1;
        }
      }
      // take all the information you've gathered and
      // create a GameInfo object that will save the info
      // in the device's memory.
      GameInfo info = new GameInfo(myCurrentBoardNum, gameTicks,
                                   playerSquare, keyCoords,
                                   doorsOpen, heldKey);
  }


  //-----------------------------------------------------------
  //  graphics methods

  /**
   * paint the game graphic on the screen.
   */
  public void paint(Graphics g) throws Exception {
    // only repaint if something has changed:
    if(myModifiedSinceLastPaint) {
      g.setColor(DungeonCanvas.WHITE);
      // paint the background white to cover old game objects
```

```
      // that have changed position since last paint.
      // here coordinates are given
      // with respect to the graphics (canvas) origin:
      g.fillRect(0, 0, DISP_WIDTH, DISP_HEIGHT);
      // here coordinates are given
      // with respect to the LayerManager origin:
      setViewWindow(myViewWindowX, myViewWindowY, DISP_WIDTH, DISP_HEIGHT);
      // call the paint function of the superclass LayerManager
      // to paint all the Layers
      paint(g, CANVAS_X, CANVAS_Y);
      // don't paint again until something changes:
      myModifiedSinceLastPaint = false;
  }
}


//----------------------------------------------------------
//  game movements

/**
 * respond to keystrokes by deciding where to move
 * and then moving the pieces and the view window correspondingly.
 */
void requestMove(int horizontal, int vertical) {
  if(horizontal != 0) {
    // see how far the princess can move in the desired
    // horizontal direction (if not blocked by a wall
    // or closed door)
    horizontal = requestHorizontal(horizontal);
  }
  // vertical < 0 indicates that the user has
  // pressed the UP button and would like to jump.
  // therefore, if you're not currently jumping,
  // you begin the jump.
  if((myIsJumping == NO_JUMP) && (vertical < 0)) {
    myIsJumping++;
  } else if(myIsJumping == NO_JUMP) {
    // if you're not jumping at all, you need to check
    // if the princess should be falling:
    // you (temporarily) move the princess down and see if that
    // causes a collision with the floor:
    myPrincess.move(0, MOVE_LENGTH);
    // if the princess can move down without colliding
    // with the floor, then we set the princess to
    // be falling.  The variable myIsJumping starts
    // negative while the princess is jumping up and
    // is zero or positive when the princess is coming
    // back down. You therefore set myIsJumping to
    // zero to indicate that the princess should start
```

```java
      // falling.
      if(! checkCollision()) {
        myIsJumping = 0;
      }
      // you move the princess Sprite back to the correct
      // position she was at before you (temporarily) moved
      // her down to see if she would fall.
      myPrincess.move(0, -MOVE_LENGTH);
    }
    // if the princess is currently jumping or falling,
    // you calculate the vertical distance she should move
    // (taking into account the horizontal distance that
    // she is also moving).
    if(myIsJumping != NO_JUMP) {
      vertical = jumpOrFall(horizontal);
    }
    // now that you've calculated how far the princess
    // should move, you move her. (this is a call to
    // another internal method of this method
    // suite, it is not a built-in LayerManager method):
    move(horizontal, vertical);
  }

  /**
   * Internal to requestMove.  Calculates what the
   * real horizontal distance moved should be
   * after taking obstacles into account.
   * @return the horizontal distance that the
   * player can move.
   */
  private int requestHorizontal(int horizontal) {
    // you (temporarily) move her to the right or left
    // and see if she hits a wall or a door:
    myPrincess.move(horizontal * MOVE_LENGTH, 0);
    if(checkCollision()) {
      // if she hits something, then she's not allowed
      // to go in that direction, so you set the horizontal
      // move distance to zero and then move the princess
      // back to where she was.
      myPrincess.move(-horizontal * MOVE_LENGTH, 0);
      horizontal = 0;
    } else {
      // if she doesn't hit anything then the move request
      // succeeds, but you still move her back to the
      // earlier position because this was just the checking
      // phase.
      myPrincess.move(-horizontal * MOVE_LENGTH, 0);
      horizontal *= MOVE_LENGTH;
```

```
  }
  return(horizontal);
}


/**
 * Internal to requestMove.  Calculates the vertical
 * change in the player's position if jumping or
 * falling.
 * this method should only be called if the player is
 * currently jumping or falling.
 * @return the vertical distance that the player should
 * move this turn. (negative moves up, positive moves down)
 */
private int jumpOrFall(int horizontal) {
  // by default you do not move vertically
  int vertical = 0;
  // The speed of rise or descent is computed using
  // the int myIsJumping. Since you are in a jump or
  // fall, you advance the jump by one (which simulates
  // the downward pull of gravity by slowing the rise
  // or accelerating the fall) unless the player is
  // already falling at maximum speed. (a maximum
  // free fall speed is necessary because otherwise
  // it is possible for the player to fall right through
  // the bottom of the maze...)
  if(myIsJumping <= MAX_FREE_FALL) {
    myIsJumping++;
  }
  if(myIsJumping < 0) {
    // if myIsJumping is negative, that means that
    // the princess is rising. You calculate the
    // number of pixels to go up by raising 2 to
    // the power myIsJumping (absolute value).
    // note that you make the result negative because
    // the up and down coordinates in Java are the
    // reverse of the vertical coordinates we learned
    // in math class: as you go up, the coordinate
    // values go down, and as you go down the screen,
    // the coordinate numbers go up.
    vertical = -(2<<(-myIsJumping));
  } else {
    // if myIsJumping is positive, the princess is falling.
    // you calculate the distance to fall by raising 2
    // to the power of the absolute value of myIsJumping.
    vertical = (2<<(myIsJumping));
  }
  // now you temporarily move the princess the desired
  // vertical distance (with the corresponding horizontal
```

```
   // distance also thrown in), and see if she hits anything:
   myPrincess.move(horizontal, vertical);
   if(checkCollision()) {
     // here you're in the case where she did hit something.
     // you move her back into position and then see what
     // to do about it.
     myPrincess.move(-horizontal, -vertical);
     if(vertical > 0) {
       // in this case the player is falling.
       // so you need to determine precisely how
       // far she can fall before she hit the bottom
       vertical = 0;
       // you temporarily move her the desired horizontal
       // distance while calculating the corresponding
       // vertical distance.
       myPrincess.move(horizontal, 0);
       while(! checkCollision()) {
         vertical++;
         myPrincess.move(0, 1);
       }
       // now that you've calculated how far she can fall,
       // you move her back to her earlier position
       myPrincess.move(-horizontal, -vertical);
       // you subtract 1 pixel from the distance calculated
       // because once she has actually collided with the
       // floor, she's gone one pixel too far...
       vertical--;
       // now that she's hit the floor, she's not jumping
       // anymore.
       myIsJumping = NO_JUMP;
     } else {
       // in this case you're going up, so she
       // must have hit her head.
       // This next if is checking for a special
       // case where there's room to jump up exactly
       // one square. In that case you increase the
       // value of myIsJumping in order to make the
       // princess not rise as high. The details
       // of the calculation in this case were found
       // through trial and error:
       if(myIsJumping == NO_JUMP + 2) {
         myIsJumping++;
         vertical = -(2<<(-myIsJumping));
         // now you see if the special shortened jump
         // still makes her hit her head:
         // (as usual, temporarily move her to test
         // for collisions)
         myPrincess.move(horizontal, vertical);
```

```java
      if(checkCollision()) {
        // if she still hits her head even
        // with this special shortened jump,
        // then she was not meant to jump...
        myPrincess.move(-horizontal, -vertical);
        vertical = 0;
        myIsJumping = NO_JUMP;
      } else {
        // now that you've checked for collisions,
        // you move the player back to her earlier
        // position:
        myPrincess.move(-horizontal, -vertical);
      }
    } else {
      // if she hit her head, then she should not
      // jump up.
      vertical = 0;
      myIsJumping = NO_JUMP;
    }
  }
} else {
  // since she didn't hit anything when you moved
  // her, then all you have to do is move her back.
  myPrincess.move(-horizontal, -vertical);
}
return(vertical);
}

/**
 * Internal to requestMove. Once the moves have been
 * determined, actually perform the move.
 */
private void move(int horizontal, int vertical) {
  // repaint only if you actually change something:
  if((horizontal != 0) || (vertical != 0)) {
    myModifiedSinceLastPaint = true;
  }
  // if the princess is moving left or right, you set
  // her image to be facing the right direction:
  if(horizontal > 0) {
    myPrincess.setTransform(Sprite.TRANS_NONE);
  } else if(horizontal < 0) {
    myPrincess.setTransform(Sprite.TRANS_MIRROR);
  }
  // if she's jumping or falling, you set the image to
  // the frame where the skirt is inflated:
  if(vertical != 0) {
    myPrincess.setFrame(0);
```

```
      // if she's just running, you alternate between the
      // two frames:
    } else if(horizontal != 0) {
      if(myPrincess.getFrame() == 1) {
        myPrincess.setFrame(0);
      } else {
        myPrincess.setFrame(1);
      }
    }
    // move the position of the view window so that
    // the player stays in the center:
    myViewWindowX += horizontal;
    myViewWindowY += vertical;
    // after all that work, you finally move the
    // princess for real!!!
    myPrincess.move(horizontal, vertical);
  }

  //-----------------------------------------------------------
  //   sprite interactions

  /**
   * Drops the currently held key and picks up another.
   */
  void putDownPickUp() {
    // you do not want to allow the player to put
    // down the key in the air, so you verify that
    // you're not jumping or falling first:
    if((myIsJumping == NO_JUMP) &&
       (myPrincess.getY() % SQUARE_WIDTH == 0)) {
      // since you're picking something up or putting
      // something down, the display changes and needs
      // to be repainted:
      setNeedsRepaint();
      // if the thing you're picking up is the crown,
      // you're done, the player has won:
      if(myPrincess.collidesWith(myCrown, true)) {
        myCanvas.setGameOver();
        return;
      }
      // keep track of the key you're putting down in
      // order to place it correctly:
      DoorKey oldHeld = myHeldKey;
      myHeldKey = null;
      // if the princess is on top of another key,
      // that one becomes the held key and is hence
      // made invisible:
      for(int i = 0; i < myKeys.length; i++) {
```

```
      // you check myHeldKey for null because you don't
      // want to accidentally pick up two keys.
      if((myPrincess.collidesWith(myKeys[i], true)) &&
         (myHeldKey == null)) {
        myHeldKey = myKeys[i];
        myHeldKey.setVisible(false);
      }
    }
    if(oldHeld != null) {
      // place the key you're putting down in the princess's
      // current position and make it visible:
      oldHeld.setPosition(myPrincess.getX(), myPrincess.getY());
      oldHeld.setVisible(true);
    }
  }
}


/**
 * Checks if the player hits a stone wall or a door.
 */
boolean checkCollision() {
  boolean retVal = false;
  // the "true" arg means to check for a pixel-level
  // collision (so merely an overlap in image
  // squares does not register as a collision)
  if(myPrincess.collidesWith(myBackground, true)) {
    retVal = true;
  } else {
    // Note: it is not necessary to synchronize
    // this block because the thread that calls this
    // method is the same as the one that puts down the
    // keys, so there's no danger of the key being put down
    // between the moment you check for the key and
    // the moment you open the door:
    for(int i = 0; i < myDoors.length; i++) {
      // if she's holding the right key, then open the door
      // otherwise bounce off
      if(myPrincess.collidesWith(myDoors[i], true)) {
        if((myHeldKey != null) &&
           (myDoors[i].getColor() == myHeldKey.getColor())) {
          setNeedsRepaint();
          myDoors[i].setVisible(false);
        } else {
          // if she's not holding the right key, then
          // she has collided with the door just the same
          // as if she had collided with a wall:
          retVal = true;
        }
```

```
        }
      }
    }
    return(retVal);
  }

}
```

The princess and the crown Sprites were too simple to warrant making whole subclasses for them (similarly I didn't bother to subclass TiledLayer for the background this time). But for the doors and keys, I wanted to store their colors in the Sprite object itself, so I created a subclass, DoorKey.java (see Listing 5-10).

Listing 5-10. *DoorKey.java*

```java
package net.frog_parrot.dungeon;

import javax.microedition.lcdui.*;
import javax.microedition.lcdui.game.*;

/**
 * This class represents doors and keys.
 *
 * @author Carol Hamer
 */
public class DoorKey extends Sprite {

  //-----------------------------------------------------------
  //    fields

  /**
   * The image file shared by all doors and keys.
   */
  public static Image myImage;

  /**
   * A code int that indicates the door or key's color.
   */
  private int myColor;

  //-----------------------------------------------------------
  //    get/set data

  /**
   * @return the door or key's color.
   */
  public int getColor() {
```

```
    return(myColor);
  }

  //----------------------------------------------------------
  //    constructor and initializer

  static {
    try {
      myImage = Image.createImage("/images/keys.png");
    } catch(Exception e) {
      throw(new RuntimeException(
          "DoorKey.<init>-->failed to load image, caught "
          + e.getClass() + ": " + e.getMessage())));
    }
  }

  /**
   * Standard constructor sets the image to the correct frame
   * (according to whether this is a door or a key and what
   * color it should be) and then puts it in the correct location.
   */
  public DoorKey(int color, boolean isKey, int[] gridCoordinates) {
    super(myImage, DungeonManager.SQUARE_WIDTH, DungeonManager.SQUARE_WIDTH);
    myColor = color;
    int imageIndex = color * 2;
    if(isKey) {
      imageIndex++;
    }
    setFrame(imageIndex);
    setPosition(gridCoordinates[0] * DungeonManager.SQUARE_WIDTH,
                gridCoordinates[1] * DungeonManager.SQUARE_WIDTH);
  }

}
```

And, of course, you don't want to forget about the Thread subclass GameThread.java (see Listing 5-11).

Listing 5-11. *GameThread.java*

```
package net.frog_parrot.dungeon;

/**
 * This class contains the loop that keeps the game running.
 *
 * @author Carol Hamer
 */
public class GameThread extends Thread {
```

```
//------------------------------------------------------------
//    fields

/**
 * Whether the main thread would like this thread
 * to pause.
 */
private boolean myShouldPause;

/**
 * Whether the main thread would like this thread
 * to stop.
 */
private static boolean myShouldStop;

/**
 * A handle back to the graphical components.
 */
private DungeonCanvas myDungeonCanvas;

/**
 * The System.time of the last screen refresh, used
 * to regulate refresh speed.
 */
private long myLastRefreshTime;

//------------------------------------------------------------
//    initialization

/**
 * standard constructor.
 */
GameThread(DungeonCanvas canvas) {
  myDungeonCanvas = canvas;
}

//------------------------------------------------------------
//    utilities

/**
 * Get the amount of time to wait between screen refreshes.
 * Normally we wait only a single millisecond just to give
 * the main thread a chance to update the keystroke info,
 * but this method ensures that the game will not attempt
 * to show more than 20 frames per second.
 */
private long getWaitTime() {
  long retVal = 1;
```

```java
    long difference = System.currentTimeMillis() - myLastRefreshTime;
    if(difference < 50) {
      retVal = 50 - difference;
    }
    return(retVal);
  }

  //-----------------------------------------------------------
  //   actions

  /**
   * pause the game.
   */
  void pause() {
    myShouldPause = true;
  }

  /**
   * restart the game after a pause.
   */
  synchronized void resumeGame() {
    myShouldPause = false;
    notify();
  }

  /**
   * stops the game.
   */
  synchronized void requestStop() {
    myShouldStop = true;
    this.notify();
  }

  /**
   * start the game..
   */
  public void run() {
    // flush any keystrokes that occurred before the
    // game started:
    myDungeonCanvas.flushKeys();
    myShouldStop = false;
    myShouldPause = false;
    while(true) {
      myLastRefreshTime = System.currentTimeMillis();
      if(myShouldStop) {
        break;
      }
```

```
      myDungeonCanvas.checkKeys();
      myDungeonCanvas.updateScreen();
      // you do a very short pause to allow the other thread
      // to update the information about which keys are pressed:
      // and regulate the animation speed:
      synchronized(this) {
        try {
          wait(getWaitTime());
        } catch(Exception e) {}
      }
      if(myShouldPause) {
        synchronized(this) {
          try {
            wait();
          } catch(Exception e) {}
        }
      }
    }
  }

}
```

Summary

In this chapter you've seen how easy it is to store and retrieve data, and you've seen some of the basics of how to optimize your data storage by interpreting complex data types as bits and bytes. Storing your data locally on the device isn't the only application of transforming your object data into byte arrays (and later converting it back), though. You can use the same functions that prepare your data to be stored to prepare your data to be transmitted over a network, and you can use the functions that interpret the bytes of data without modification to interpret data that the device receives from a server. In the next chapter, you'll see how to add a little bit of communications code to this same example game to allow a remote server to update the. data used by the game.

CHAPTER 6

■■■

Using Network Communications

One of the big strengths of a device that runs the Connected Limited Device Configuration (CLDC) is the "connected" aspect. Most CLDC devices are handsets, so for all the limitations of a limited device, communicating over a network is something it's made to do, and something you'll usually want to take advantage of when developing a game.

The most standard data-transfer protocols for a handset are Hypertext Transfer Protocol (HTTP) and Short Message Service (SMS). If you're asking "What about Wireless Application Protocol (WAP)?" keep in mind that WAP is similar to and related to HTTP. In this chapter we'll cover how to use HTTP using the dungeon example from the previous chapter, and SMS effectively in a game of checkers; then Chapter 7 will cover some of the more advanced and optional protocols such as Bluetooth and plain sockets, and Chapter 8 will discuss the security concerns.

Choosing a Protocol

The first question to ask when choosing a protocol is whether the protocol is supported. You need to worry not only about whether the platform (handset + Virtual Machine) supports the protocol, but also whether your server supports it (if you're doing client-server communications) and whether the operator's network supports it. This is not a trivial concern. Both HTTP and SMS are the two most widely supported, but neither one is guaranteed to work 100 percent of the time.

In theory HTTP should always be available to you as long as your application is granted permission to use it (see Chapter 8). HTTP is required by both MIDP 1 and MIDP 2. In practice, however, the platform needs some information about how to make the jump from the operator's network to the open Internet. This data (regarding proxies and such) is called a *profile*. It is not to be confused with Java profiles such as MIDP—it is a completely different thing—the naming overlap is just a coincidence. The HTTP profile available to the Java Virtual Machine (JVM) should normally be configured correctly by default, but unfortunately it is not always the case. The profile can generally be configured by hand or by SMS. For example, I explained how I got the configuration for my Nokia 6100 via SMS in the "Accessing the WML File and Downloading Applications" section of Chapter 1, but my Sagem my700x was already configured correctly for HTTP when I bought it. Some handsets have a separate profile for the WAP browser and for the JVM, and in that case you can sometimes correct the JVM's profile (if it's not working) by changing it to match the profile used by the WAP browser. Mobile operators don't generally permit independent game design studios to send out SMS messages to configure the HTTP profiles of handsets out in nature, so you have to leave it up to the operators and your users to get their HTTP-from-Java configurations working correctly—and most of them do.

SMS is the protocol that is most likely to work in practice. SMS support is actually part of an optional API (the Wireless Messaging API, JSR 120), which may be implemented on top of MIDP 1.0 or MIDP 2.0. But even though it's optional, it's widely supported. Additionally, there's no extra configuration or setup required on the handset in order for it to work. The drawback to SMS for independent developers and small studios is that it's costly and inconvenient to send and receive SMS messages from a computer unless you have an agreement with the operator. On the other hand, if you do have an agreement with an operator, SMS is the most convenient way to bill your customers for services because the operators' networks are typically set up to use SMS in this way. Since handset-to-handset SMS is available to even independent developers, in this book the SMS example game will be a two-player game using SMS to transfer the moves from one player to the other. Programming the handset to exchange SMS messages with a server is the same.

Once you start looking at protocols other than these two, it starts getting a little iffy. I've found that even attempting to send HTTP on a port other than the default port isn't always allowed by the operator's network. But other options are sometimes useful depending on the circumstances.

Using the Micro Edition IO API

Network communications in Java ME use a suite of `InputStream` and `OutputStream` classes that should be familiar to anyone who has done network programming in Java. And once you've gotten the hang of programming for one type of connection, it's easy to learn to use another since they all follow the same pattern: you get the input and output streams from a `Connection` that is returned by the static method `Connector.open()`.

All of the different types of connection protocols are represented by different subinterfaces of the base interface `javax.microedition.io.Connection`. The virtual machine chooses what type of connection to give you based on the URL you send as an argument to `Connector.open()`. The URL should be of the format described in RFC 2396 (see `http://rfc-editor.org`). In general, the URL consists of the protocol string (such as `http`), then a colon, then routing information, and then additional arguments.

It's convenient that the Java communication APIs are so consistent regardless of underlying technologies and implementations. It means not only that it's easy to learn to use new protocols once you've learned one, but it is also easier to write a program that can use more than one protocol. You'll see this in the examples as the SMS-based checkers game illustrated in this chapter will be modified to use Bluetooth in the next chapter.

In terms of programming techniques, the distinction that generally makes the most difference is whether the protocol is synchronous or asynchronous—that is, whether a response to each request is required by the protocol. HTTP is synchronous; SMS isn't.

With synchronous communications, generally one device acts as a client (making the request), and the other device acts as a server (filling the request). Typically a mobile device acts as a client—but not always. It's easier to act as a client because all you need is the correct URL to initiate the connection with the server. To act as a server, the application needs to find a way to advertise its availability to perform a service and also needs to find a way to receive and handle client requests. In MIDP this is often done through the Push Registry (see the section "Using the Push Registry" later in this chapter), but that's not always the case. Some protocols define their own separate registry services—for example, the Bluetooth API (JSR 82) and the Content Handler API (JSR 211).

With asynchronous communication, the division of labor is between sender and receiver. In terms of establishing a connection, sender code is the same as client code and receiver code is the same as server code. So in practice the difference is that for asynchronous communications you normally expect to have to program both sides, whereas with synchronous communications you often code only one side or the other.

Using HTTP

Using the interface `javax.microedition.io.HttpConnection` is probably the easiest way to use the MIDP API to communicate with a server. Listing 6-1 is a code segment that will create an instance of `HttpConnection` and use it to send a message to a server and read a response.

Listing 6-1. *Creating an Instance of HttpConnection*

```
/**
 * Makes a connection to the server and reads the data.
 */
public void run() {
  // you sync on the class because you don't want multiple
  // instances simultaneously attempting to download
  ContentConnection connection = null;
  DataInputStream dis = null;
  DataOutputStream dos = null;
  byte dataToSend = 3;
  try {
    // the method Connector.open() uses the URL argument
    // to decide what protocol to use (and hence what type
    // of Connection interface to return) in addition to
    // using the URL to determine the address of the
    // program to contact.
    connection = (ContentConnection)Connector.open(
            "http://frog-parrot.net:8080/servlet/ExampleServlet");
    ((HttpConnection)connection).setRequestMethod(HttpConnection.POST);
    dos = connection.openDataOutputStream();
    dos.write(dataToSend);
    // flush sends the message
    dos.flush();
    // some implementations give errors if you open the data input stream
    // without first reading the response code:
    int responseCode = ((HttpConnection)connection).getResponseCode();
    dis = connection.openDataInputStream();
    byte received = dis.readByte();
  } catch(Exception e) {
    // normally you would add some code here to send
    // the user an error message.
```

```
    } finally {
      // even if there is a communications error, you need
      // to close the connection and the streams:
      try {
        if(dis != null) {
          dis.close();
        }
        if(dos != null) {
          dos.close();
        }
        if(connection != null) {
          connection.close();
        }
      } catch(Exception e) {
        // normally you would add some code here to send
        // the user an error message.
      }
    }
  }
}
```

Several points in Listing 6-1 require some further explanation. First, it wasn't an accident that I called the method run() as if the previous code were from a subclass of Thread. Since reading from a socket may cause the current thread to block, it's a good idea to spawn a new thread for communications rather than using the main thread. This is good practice for essentially all Java networking code—it should be running on a dedicated thread. Another thing to notice is that I set the HTTP method to POST. I did this because the program sends data to the server (see the sidebar "GET, POST, and HEAD" later in this chapter for more explanation).

Another thing to notice is that in Listing 6-1 I read one byte of data from the stream regardless of how much data is available. If no data is available, the thread could block and stay blocked until the program terminates. It's a good idea to have the server set the Content-Length HTTP header so that your program will know precisely how much data to read from the stream. (You can get the value of the Content-Length header by calling getLength().) If your client program has to figure out for itself how much data to read, it's a good idea to call the read() method (with a byte array to read the data into). Unlike readFully(), read() won't block if it can't fill the whole array (although it will block if there's no data to read at all and the server hasn't yet closed the stream). As long as there's at least one byte of data to read, the method read() reads as many bytes of data as it can and then returns the number of bytes it read. To make sure you got all the data, you can call read() multiple times (specifying an offset to avoid overwriting the data you've already read) until the method returns a value of -1 to indicate that the end of the stream has been reached. Another trick is to use the available() method of the java.io. DataInputStream to determine how many bytes of data are available before reading them in. That way, you can call readFully() with no danger of blocking. The only problem with using available() is that in my tests I've found it has an annoying tendency to return zero even when there are bytes available to read, so I generally don't use it.

The corresponding server code for HTTP is also easy because most of the work has been done for you. All you need to do is write a Servlet and run it on a web server that will direct the client to the Servlet (using the URL that was used when creating the HttpConnection).

If you don't have a web server that will run Servlets, you can download Tomcat free from http://jakarta.apache.org/tomcat/. The download contains all of the information you need to configure and run the Tomcat Servlet container.

Don't forget that if you want to run your HTTP code on a real device, you'll need to have your Servlet running on a machine that can be accessed from the Internet. It's better to use a domain name (such as frog-parrot.net) instead of a numerical Internet Protocol (IP) address (such as 80.13.176.79) in the contact URL (sent as an argument to Connector.open()) because a numerical IP address can change. But for testing it shouldn't be a problem to use a numerical IP address. If you don't know what your machine's IP address is, see the "Accessing the WML File and Downloading Applications" section in Chapter 1. If your test environment isn't connected to the Internet, you can still test your code with the emulator as long as the emulator and the Servlet container are running on the same network. That's how I did most of my debugging for the examples in this chapter. The emulator is perfectly willing to accept a URL that contains the local machine's name in place of a domain name or IP address.

Servlets aren't hard to write. If you want to know all of the theory behind them and all of the cool things you can do with them, you can find whole books written on the subject (plenty of them). But if you're content with a simple Servlet, you can just follow the example in the "Writing the Server Code for the Dungeon Example" section a bit later. As you can see from the example, all you need to do is implement the method doGet() if you want your Servlet to handle GET requests and implement the method doPost() if you want your Servlet to handle POST requests. Both of these methods receive Request and Response objects as arguments, which you can query to get input and output streams to use to read from and write to the client just as the client uses input and output streams to communicate with the server.

Of course, just because the server-side code can be taken care of with just a simple Servlet, that doesn't mean it's your only option. In real-world applications the server component is generally far more complex, but since the focus of this book is on programming for the device itself, I'll keep the server side of the examples in this chapter as simple as possible.

The Dungeon Example: Downloading the Next Board

As an example of how to use HTTP in a typical game situation, you'll now improve the dungeon example from the previous chapter. This time, instead of hard-coding the data that describes the various boards, you'll have only one hard-coded board ship with the game and have the user download the other boards. That way, the number of possible boards for the game is unlimited because you can always add more boards to your Servlet. Plus, this example shows one way to implement the business model in which you freely distribute the first segment of the game, and then the users who like it can pay to download more (see the sidebar "Using Secure Connections While Selling Your Game" in Chapter 8 for more about that marketing strategy). Figure 6-1 shows the user selecting the command to download the next board.

Figure 6-1. *Selecting the download command to get new boards*

Now I'll go over in detail the changes necessary to make the dungeon game use HTTP to download board data.

Writing the Client Code for the Dungeon Example

The biggest change to the client program is the addition of the class BoardReader, which contacts a server and downloads the data for the remaining boards that the user doesn't have yet and stores them in the device's memory.

Here's how it works. First, you add a command to the MIDlet subclass (Dungeon) to allow the user to tell the game to contact the server to download boards. This means that in the "command fields" section of the Dungeon class, you add the following command:

```
/**
 * The command to download new boards.
 */
private Command myDownloadCommand
  = new Command("Download boards", Command.SCREEN, 10);
```

Then of course you need to add the new command to the canvas, so you should change the startApp() method of Dungeon to the following:

```
/**
 * Start the application, initializing as necessary.
 */
public void startApp() throws MIDletStateChangeException {
  try {
    if(myCanvas == null) {
      // create the canvas and set up the commands:
      myCanvas = new DungeonCanvas(this);
      myCanvas.addCommand(myExitCommand);
```

```
        myCanvas.addCommand(mySaveCommand);
        myCanvas.addCommand(myRestoreCommand);
        myCanvas.addCommand(myPauseCommand);
        myCanvas.setCommandListener(this);
      }
      if(myGameThread == null) {
        // create the thread and start the game:
        myGameThread = new GameThread(myCanvas);
        myCanvas.start();
        myGameThread.start();
      } else {
        // in case this gets called again after
        // the application has been started once:
        myCanvas.removeCommand(myGoCommand);
        myCanvas.addCommand(myPauseCommand);
        myCanvas.flushKeys();
        myGameThread.resumeGame();
      }
    } catch(Exception e) {
      // if there's an error during creation, display it as an alert.
      errorMsg(e);
    }
  }
```

Lastly, when the user selects Download Boards from the command menu, the program needs to create an instance of the new BoardReader class and start it up. So, in the commandAction() method of the Dungeon class, you need to add the following additional else if block to the list of else if blocks:

```
} else if(c == myDownloadCommand) {
  // spawn a new BoardReader thread to
  // connect and download new boards:
  BoardReader br = new BoardReader(this, myCanvas);
  br.start();
```

In the previous code block, you call br.start() because BoardReader is a subclass of Thread, as discussed in the "Using HTTP" section earlier. When the BoardReader starts (in the run() method), the first thing it does is open a connection to the server. Then it checks the local record store to see how many boards are currently stored on the device. BoardReader opens the output stream and tells the server how many boards the device already has. The server then sends the data for the boards that the client doesn't have yet. Then BoardReader reads the data from the Connection's output stream and stores it locally in a series of records. Each record contains all the data needed to construct one board.

Most of the action of BoardReader takes place in the run() method, but also some helper methods store and retrieve the boards from local memory. I made all the local memory methods static since they may be called by other classes even if the user doesn't download any boards in a given game session. Making them static avoids instantiating Thread objects that won't be used.

Listing 6-2 shows the code for BoardReader.java.

Listing 6-2. *BoardReader.java*

```
package net.frog_parrot.dungeon;

import java.io.*;
import javax.microedition.io.*;
import javax.microedition.lcdui.*;
import javax.microedition.rms.*;

import net.frog_parrot.util.DataConverter;

/**
 * This class contacts a remote server in order to
 * downolad data for new game boards and stores
 * them locally.
 *
 * @author Carol Hamer
 */
public class BoardReader extends Thread {

  //----------------------------------------------------------
  //  fields

  /**
   * This is the name of the local datastore on the CLDC device.
   */
  public static final String LOCAL_DATASTORE = "BoardData";

  /**
   * This is the URL to contact.
   * IMPORTANT: change the domain name in the following URL
   * from "frog-parrot.net" to the domain name of the
   * server that the corresponding servlet is running on!!!!
   * (The "/games/DungeonDownload" part of the URL
   * may also need to be changed, depending on how servlet
   * URLs are configured on the web server.)
   */
  public static final String SERVER_URL
    = "http://frog-parrot.net:8080/games/DungeonDownload";

  /**
   * This is the size of the byte array containing
   * all the info for one board.
```

```
   */
  public static final int DATA_LENGTH = 48;


  //-----------------------------------------------------------
  // instance fields
  //   these are used by the thread when downloading
  //   boards to display a possible error message.

  /**
   * The MIDlet subclass, used to set the Display
   * in the case where an error message needs to be sent.
   */
  private Dungeon myDungeon;

  /**
   * The Canvas subclass, used to set the Display
   * in the case where an error message needs to be sent.
   */
  private DungeonCanvas myCanvas;


  //-----------------------------------------------------------
  // initialization

  /**
   * Constructor is used only when the program wants
   * to spawn a data-fetching thread, not for merely
   * reading local data with static methods.
   */
  BoardReader(Dungeon dungeon, DungeonCanvas canvas) {
    myDungeon = dungeon;
    myCanvas = canvas;
  }


  //-----------------------------------------------------------
  // local data methods
  //   note that these methods are static and do
  //   not run on a separate thread even though this
  //   class is a subclass of Thread

  /**
   * @return the number of boards currently stored in the
   * device memory. (this does not include the hard-coded board)
   */
  static int getNumBoards() {
    RecordStore store = null;
```

```
    int retVal = 0;
    try {
      // if the record store does not yet exist, don't
      // create it
      store = RecordStore.openRecordStore(LOCAL_DATASTORE, false);
      if(store != null) {
        retVal = store.getNumRecords();
      }
    } catch(Exception e) {
    } finally {
      try {
        if(store != null) {
          store.closeRecordStore();
        }
      } catch(Exception e) {
        // if the record store is open, this shouldn't throw.
      }
    }
    return(retVal);
  }

  /**
   * @return the byte array that gives the board that
   * has the number boardNum (if it is found). returns null
   * if there is no board in memory that has the given number.
   */
  static byte[] getBoardData(int boardNum) {
    RecordStore store = null;
    byte[] retArray = null;
    try {
      // if the record store does not yet exist, don't
      // create it
      store = RecordStore.openRecordStore(LOCAL_DATASTORE, false);
      if((store != null) && (store.getNumRecords() >= boardNum)) {
        retArray = store.getRecord(boardNum);
      }
    } catch(Exception e) {
    } finally {
      try {
        if(store != null) {
          store.closeRecordStore();
        }
      } catch(Exception e) {
        // if the record store is open, this shouldn't throw.
      }
    }
    return(retArray);
  }
```

```
/**
 * Saves the data of a board being downloaded from the Internet
 */
static void saveBoardData(byte[] data) throws Exception {
  RecordStore store = null;
  try {
    // if the record store does not yet exist,
    // create it
    store = RecordStore.openRecordStore(LOCAL_DATASTORE, true);
    store.addRecord(data, 0, data.length);
  } finally {
    try {
      if(store != null) {
        store.closeRecordStore();
      }
    } catch(Exception e) {
      // if the record store is open, this shouldn't throw.
    }
  }
}


//-----------------------------------------------------------
// download methods

/**
 * Makes an HTTP connection to the server and gets data
 * for more boards.
 */
public void run() {
  // you sync on the class because you don't want multiple
  // instances simultaneously attempting to download
  synchronized(this.getClass()) {
    ContentConnection connection = null;
    DataInputStream dis = null;
    DataOutputStream dos = null;
    try {
      connection = (ContentConnection)Connector.open(SERVER_URL);
      // send the number of local boards to the server
      // so the server will know which boards to send:
      int numBoards = getNumBoards();
      dos = connection.openDataOutputStream();
      // munBoards is an int but it is transferred as a
      // byte.  It should therefore not be more than 15.
      dos.write(numBoards);
      // flush to send the message:
      dos.flush();
      // connection.getLength() returns the value of the
```

```java
            // content-length header, not the number of bytes
            // available to read.  The server must set this header
            // if the client wants to use it.
            // Here numBoards is the number
            // of boards that will be read from the downloaded data.
            numBoards = ((int)connection.getLength())/DATA_LENGTH;
            int responseCode = ((HttpConnection)connection).getResponseCode();
            dis = connection.openDataInputStream();
            for(int i = 0; i < numBoards; i++) {
              byte[] data = new byte[DATA_LENGTH];
              dis.readFully(data);
              saveBoardData(data);
            }
          } catch(Exception e) {
            // if this fails, it is almost undoubtedly
            // a communication problem (server down, etc.)
            // you need to give the right message to the user:
            Alert alert = new Alert("download failed",
                      "please try again later", null, AlertType.INFO);
            // You set the timeout to forever so this Alert will
            // have a default dismiss command. When the user
            // presses the Alert.DISMISS_COMMAND, the displayable
            // myCanvas will become current (see setCurrent() below):
            alert.setTimeout(Alert.FOREVER);
            myCanvas.setNeedsRepaint();
            // the second arg tells the Display to go to
            // myCanvas when the user dismisses the alert
            Display.getDisplay(myDungeon).setCurrent(alert, myCanvas);
          } finally {
            try {
              if(dis != null) {
                dis.close();
              }
              if(dos != null) {
                dos.close();
              }
              if(connection != null) {
                connection.close();
              }
            } catch(Exception e) {
              // if this throws, at least you made your best effort
              // to close everything up....
            }
          }
        }
      }
    }


  }
```

To use the BoardReader class, you have to make a couple of other small changes in other parts of the code. Most of the rest of the changes are in the BoardDecoder. Essentially, you change BoardDecoder so that it no longer reads the board data from an internal (hard-coded) data array but rather calls BoardReader to get the board data from memory. The changes are pretty small compared to the size of the class, so I'll list just the changes rather than listing the whole class and having you search for the differences. First, you eliminate the parts that are related to the local data storage: the field myData and the method getNumBoards(). Instead, you store only the data for the first board by adding the following field:

```
/**
 * This is the array of bytes for just the first board.
 * Encodes where to place the various items
 * in the dungeon and the placement of the walls.
 */
static byte[] myFirstBoard = {
    0, 0, -108, -100, -24, 65, 21, 58, 53, -54, -116, -58, -56,
    -84, 115, -118,
    -1, -1, -128, 1, -103, -15, -128, 25, -97, -127, -128, 79, -14,
    1, -126, 121, -122, 1, -113, -49, -116, 1, -100, -3, -124, 5,
    -25, -27, -128, 1, -1, -1,
};
```

Second, in the beginning of the BoardDecoder constructor, you consult the BoardReader class to get the board data by replacing this line:

```
byte[] data = myData[boardNum];
```

with these lines:

```
byte[] data = null;
if(boardNum < 1) {
  data = myFirstBoard;
} else {
  data = BoardReader.getBoardData(boardNum);
}
```

The final change that's needed to make this example work is to have DungeonManager consult BoardReader instead of BoardDecoder to get the number of possible boards by changing this line:

```
if(myCurrentBoardNum == BoardDecoder.getNumBoards()) {
```

to the following:

```
if(myCurrentBoardNum >= BoardReader.getNumBoards()) {
```

With these changes, the dungeon example will run just as before, except that now a potentially unlimited number of boards could be downloaded for the game instead of just using the boards that came with the original JAR file.

Writing the Server Code for the Dungeon Example

The other half of a client-server exchange is of course the server. Since you're using HTTP, the easiest way to implement the server side is to write a `Servlet` and run it on a web server. I've written a simple `Servlet` called `DungeonDownload`. In my tests, I ran the `Servlet` on a Tomcat server. Figure 6-2 shows the permission screen the WTK emulator will display before opening a connection to communicate with a `Servlet`.

Figure 6-2. *The AMS takes over the screen and requests permission from the user before performing a restricted action such as network communications.*

`DungeonDownload` first redirects all requests to the `doPost()` method and handles the requests from there. If you followed the client half of the conversation in the previous section, you should be able to guess what the server needs to do in this exchange. It reads the data from the client's message. The data consists of an integer that gives the number of boards currently stored locally on the client. If the server has more game boards than the client has, the server sends the remaining boards to the client. Before sending the data, the server determines precisely how many bytes of data it will send and passes this information along to the client by calling `setContentLength()`.

Listing 6-3 shows the code for `DungeonDownload.java`.

Listing 6-3. *DungeonDownload.java*

```
package net.frog_parrot.servlet;

import java.io.*;
import javax.servlet.*;
import javax.servlet.http.*;
```

```java
/**
 * This is the servlet that a small device running the
 * dungeon game can call to download more boards for the game.
 *
 * @author Carol Hamer
 */
public class DungeonDownload extends HttpServlet {

  //--------------------------------------------------------
  //   data

  /**
   * The data in bytes that gives the various boards.
   * No more than 127 boards should be sent to the device
   * in this version because the value that gives the
   * number of remote boards in the transaction is
   * stored in a byte.  If the value is greater than
   * 127, there will be errors when transforming it to a byte.
   */
  static byte[][]myData = {
    { 0, 1, 122, 90, -62, 34, -43, 72,
      -59, -29, 56, -55, 98, 126, -79, 61,
      -1, -1, -125, 1, -128, 17, -26, 29, -31, 57, -72, 1, -128, -51,
      -100, 65, -124, 57, -2, 1, -126, 13, -113, 1, -97, 25, -127,
      -99, -8, 1, -1, -1 },
    { 0, 2, 108, -24, 18, -26, 102, 30, -58, 46, -28, -88, 34,
      -98, 97, -41,
      -1, -1, -96, 1, -126, 57, -9, 97, -127, 69, -119, 73, -127,
      1, -109, 59, -126, 1, -26, 103, -127, 65, -103, 115, -127,
      65, -25, 73, -128, 1, -1, -1 },
    { 0, 3, -114, 18, -34, 27, -39, -60, -76, -50, 118, 90, 82,
      -88, 34, -74,
      -1, -1, -66, 1, -128, 121, -26, 125, -128, -123, -103, 29,
      -112, 1, -109, 49, -112, 1, -116, -31, -128, 5, -122, 5,
      -32, 13, -127, -51, -125, 1, -1, -1 },
  };

  //--------------------------------------------------------
  //   implementation of servlet

  /**
   * send the doPut requests to doPost.
   */
  public void doPut(HttpServletRequest request, HttpServletResponse response)
      throws ServletException, IOException {
    doPost(request, response);
  }
```

```java
/**
 * send the doGet requests to doPost.
 */
public void doGet(HttpServletRequest request, HttpServletResponse response)
    throws ServletException, IOException {
  doPost(request, response);
}

/**
 * send the data.
 */
public void doPost(HttpServletRequest request, HttpServletResponse response)
  throws ServletException, IOException {
  try {
    InputStream is = request.getInputStream();
    // read the number of boards currently on the device.
    int remoteBoards = is.read();
    OutputStream os = response.getOutputStream();
    // use the number of remote boards to decide how many
    // boards to send:
    if(myData.length > remoteBoards) {
      response.setContentLength(
          myData[0].length*(myData.length - remoteBoards));
      for(int i = remoteBoards; i < myData.length; i++) {
        os.write(myData[i]);
      }
    } else {
      response.setContentLength(0);
    }
    // send the message
    os.close();
    response.flushBuffer();
    // if this fails, you try to send the client as much info
    // as possible about what the failure might have been:
    // (The numerical arguments in the sendError() method
    // below are HTTP error codes.)
  } catch(EOFException eofe) {
    System.err.println("DungeonDownload.doPost-->caught " + eofe.getClass()
                       + ": " + eofe.getMessage());
    eofe.printStackTrace();
    response.sendError(408, eofe.getMessage());
  } catch(IOException ioe) {
    System.err.println("DungeonDownload.doPost-->caught " + ioe.getClass()
                       + ": " + ioe.getMessage());
    ioe.printStackTrace();
    response.sendError(500, ioe.getClass() + ": " + ioe.getMessage());
  } catch(Exception e) {
```

```
        System.err.println("DungeonDownload.doPost-->caught " + e.getClass()
                           + ": " + e.getMessage());
        e.printStackTrace();
        response.sendError(500, e.getClass() + ": " + e.getMessage());
      }
    }


}
```

GET, POST, AND HEAD

When you use the class HttpConnection, you can choose which HTTP request method to use by calling the method setRequestMethod(). Your choices are GET, POST, and HEAD. Which one to use depends on what you need to do.

HEAD is the most limited. The idea of the HEAD request is to ask the server for just the HTTP headers from the URL. A Servlet can't even handle a HEAD request in a custom way since there's no doHead() method in the Servlet class. It'll merely return the headers that would be returned by a GET request without returning the content.

GET and POST are similar. They both allow the client to transmit data to the server and receive the server's response data. The difference is how the client's message is encoded as it's sent to the server. As the names of the methods suggest, the purpose of the GET method is to merely request (get) data from the server, whereas POST is used when the client wants to send (post) data to the server (and receive a response from the server). Behind the scenes, a client GET request has no body. Any data sent to the server must be encoded in the URL (which limits the type and amount of data that can be sent). In a POST request, the client can fill the body of the message with whatever data it wants to send to the server. So, if the client needs to send data to the server, it's better to go with POST. Otherwise, you can just stick with the default method, which is GET.

Using SMS

Every mobile developer should be familiar with this protocol because it is so widely accepted and supported, and because it's such an important part of the revenue stream, conveniently tied in with the operators' billing systems. Despite the arrival of more evolved standards like Multimedia Messaging Service (MMS) and Enhanced Messaging Service (EMS), plain old SMS is likely to be with us for some time.

The main challenge with SMS is that it fits so little data per message—only 140 bytes of payload! So it's good for sending small things like a URL, a short message, or a signal that the user has paid to use a bonus feature of your application. It's less useful for sending more data-intensive items (like a whole new board for a game) unless you really optimize. Of course you can send more data by concatenating multiple SMSs, but this has limited utility. Sending too many leads to a bad user experience (costly in time and money). It takes three just to send a tiny favicon (a 16×16 pixel icon), so it's not terribly practical for sending whole images. It's more useful for sending signals than for sending content.

In order to send and receive SMS messages, the handset must support the optional API defined in JSR 120, the Wireless Messaging API (WMA). However, as mentioned in the "Choosing a Protocol" section earlier, this API is widely supported. In fact, in terms of what the operators' networks are set up to handle, SMS is more useful in practice than the User Datagram Protocol (UDP), so it's not clear why UDP is the one that is required by MIDP (as opposed to SMS). However, in terms of programming strategy SMS and UDP are very similar to each other, so if you'd like to use UDP datagrams, the example program in this section is easily adapted from one to the other.

Using the Push Registry

Receiving inbound communications is a little more complicated than sending outbound messages. Whether your application is acting as a server or whether it's just receiving individual messages, you need to make sure the right communications get routed to you, and then you need a listener set up to receive the data. That's where the push registry comes in.

The push registry is exactly what you might guess from its name: it's a central list where applications can register the URLs on which they'd like to receive communications that are pushed to them from outside sources (as opposed to "pulling" data by initiating the request).

The push registry is run by the AMS. When the AMS receives a signal that a MIDlet has registered for, it launches the MIDlet (if the MIDlet is not running) and then makes the corresponding connection available through the PushRegistry class. The signal doesn't need to originate outside the device—it can be a local signal such as communication from another program on the same device (see the "More Options" section of Chapter 7) or an alarm.

Once the AMS has launched the MIDlet, it's up to the MIDlet to go find out whether there's a connection waiting for it. The push registry list maps URLs to MIDlets, but the MIDlet class doesn't have a built-in listener method to implement that the AMS can call to tell the MIDlet "I woke you up to handle this connection" or "There's a live connection waiting for you." So the MIDlet has to actively query the PushRegistry class using the static method PushRegistry. listConnections() to find out what connections are available for the MIDlet to listen on.

When you call PushRegistry.listConnections(), what you get back is an array of strings, which are just the URLs that the AMS has mapped to the current MIDlet. From there, the MIDlet has to open the connection and listen on it. This is where we hit familiar territory because you get the connection in the usual way: by calling Connector.open() with the desired URL. This connection may or may not have message data on it at launch time, and message data may arrive while the MIDlet is running. To find out (and read the data), you generally have a listener method that blocks until a message arrives, so you create a dedicated thread that listens and handles messages as they come in. That's what you'll do in the SMS Checkers example. The precise behavior depends a little on the type of connection (for a ServerSocketConnection you call the method acceptAndOpen(), whereas for an SMS MessageConnection you call receive()), but the basic technique is the same.

If you'd like to just start a thread to handle each message as it comes in rather than maintaining a thread to constantly listen for messages, you can have the push registry tell you when new data is available. When you first get your list of available connections from the push registry, you can tell which ones have data waiting on them by using the boolean argument to the listConnections() method—true to return only those that have input waiting, and false to get all connections that the current MIDlet is registered to listen on. Then while the MIDlet is running, at least in the case of SMS you can set a MessageListener on the connection that will be notified when an incoming message is received. This isn't necessary, though, as you'll see in the SMS Checkers example.

■**Caution** Once you've opened the connection corresponding to a given push URL, all communications bound for that URL will be routed to that same connection. So be careful not to close the connection unless you're sure that you won't be receiving any more messages on it. If you need to close the connection for some reason (such as the game being paused), then you need to open a new connection object for that URL when you're ready to start listening for messages again; otherwise, any further communications addressed to that URL will be lost.

Now that you have the idea of how the push registry works, the remaining question is "How does the MIDlet get listed in the registry?" The AMS just needs some basic data in order to sign your MIDlet up: the routing address (which includes the protocol and the port number requested) and the fully qualified name of the MIDlet class to launch, plus optionally some restrictions on what senders the MIDlet is willing to receive communications from. This information can be passed to the AMS in two ways: statically (by putting the push registration data in the MIDlet's JAD file) or dynamically (by calling PushRegistry.registerConnection). For more details, see the sidebar "Static vs. Dynamic Push Registration."

STATIC VS. DYNAMIC PUSH REGISTRATION

Your MIDlet can either register itself with the push registry statically at install time or dynamically from within the code. Either way, the effect is the same: once the MIDlet has been successfully registered once on a given URL, it is permanently registered to receive messages on that URL (and will be launched to handle the message if it is received when the MIDlet is not running). The MIDlet will only be taken off the push registry list if it calls PushRegistry.unregisterConnection or if it is deleted from the device.

Even though these two ways to register have the same result when successful, they allow for two very different ways of handling error cases. The device's operating system assigns a series of port numbers in order to route communications to the correct application (just as a larger computer does). The port number appears in the URL, generally after the second colon (for example, sms://:65402 is the URL you'd use to listen for SMS messages directed at the port 65402). But what if the port you've requested is already in use?

If your MIDlet's push port request is in the JAD file but the corresponding port is already occupied, your MIDlet will not install on the device. If you request a port dynamically from within the code, you can keep trying to register on different ports until you find one that isn't taken. The problem with that strategy is that the company that distributed the MIDlet doesn't know in advance what port the MIDlet will be listening on, and hence doesn't know the full address for sending messages to the application.

In general, dynamic registration is the way to go if you're sending messages from a central server with a database of users and you've written your MIDlet to contact your server first—giving the port number—before any messages are sent to the device. If it's not convenient to store a phone-number-to-port-number mapping (especially if messages are sent from one device to another as in the Checkers example), you essentially have to go with static registration and hope no other popular application picks the same port number you've chosen.

Creating a Multiplayer Game Example: Checkers

Since SMS is an asynchronous protocol—and not terribly rapid in practice—it doesn't lend itself to the type of multiplayer games where the players compete in real time and speed is of the essence. It's better for games such as checkers where the players take turns and a little network lag time won't be noticed.

Figure 6-3 shows what our Checkers game looks like.

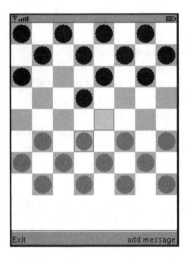

Figure 6-3. *The Checkers example game in action*

Writing the Communications Code for the Checkers Example

The Checkers game itself is very simple. The interesting part is the interaction between the two players, coding and sending the local player's move and then receiving and interpreting the remote player's move.

Each move is coded on four bytes: two giving the coordinates of the piece to move and two giving the coordinates of the destination square. The payload of each message starts with either a 4-byte block of move data or a 1-byte flag that signals a change of game state such as "start game" or "game over." Each SMS message will typically contain only one 4-byte block of move data, but in the case where the move is a double jump it will contain two or more. So the end of the move data segment is signaled by a 1-byte "end turn" flag.

There's enough room in each SMS that we could actually code all of the move data and game state flags into strings and then have the game send and receive text-format SMS messages. But you can save space by tightly packing the data into binary SMS messages. The space you save can then be used to allow the player to send a message to the other player along with the move. Figure 6-4 shows the screen in the Checkers game where the user enters a message. This is a nice bonus feature for the players because typically a user has to pay for each SMS and/or has a fixed number of SMS messages prepaid per month, so this way the user can get the familiar service of being able to send a text message with each SMS sent by the game. The user's message is placed in the payload immediately after the "end turn" flag.

Figure 6-4. *The Checkers game allows the user to enter a message to be sent to the opponent along with the move data.*

The communications code for this example is divided into four classes: MoveManager, SMSManager, SMSSender, and SMSReceiver. The MoveManager keeps track of the game state and separates the game logic from the communications logic. Isolating the communication logic in this manner makes it easier to unplug one communication protocol and replace it with another, as you'll do in Chapter 7. The SMSSender and the SMSReceiver are coded into separate classes in order to make it easier to run them on separate threads. The SMSManager then controls the lifecycle of the SMSSender and the SMSReceiver.

Let's start by having a look at the SMSSender (Listing 6-4).

Listing 6-4. *SMSSender.java*

```java
package net.frog_parrot.net;

import java.io.*;
import javax.microedition.io.*;
import javax.wireless.messaging.*;

import net.frog_parrot.checkers.MoveManager;

/**
 * This class handles the details of sending the
 * SMS message.
 *
 * @author Carol Hamer
 */
public class SMSSender implements Runnable {
```

```
//---------------------------------------------------------
//  static fields

/**
 * The protocol string.
 */
public static final String SMS_PROTOCOL = "sms://";


//---------------------------------------------------------
//  data fields

/**
 * The string with the routing information to send an
 * SMS to the right destination.
 */
private String myAddress;

/**
 * The data to send.
 */
private byte[] myPayload;

/**
 * The class that directs the data from the communications
 * module to the game logic module and vice versa.
 */
private MoveManager myManager;

//---------------------------------------------------------
//  initialization and lifecycle

/**
 * Initialize the main data.
 */
public SMSSender(String phoneNum, String portNum,
      MoveManager manager) {
  myManager = manager;
  // Construct the address url for routing the
  // message, of the form
  // sms://<phonenum>:<pushportnum>
  StringBuffer buff = new StringBuffer(SMS_PROTOCOL);
  if(phoneNum != null) {
    buff.append(phoneNum);
  }
  buff.append(":");
  if(portNum != null) {
    buff.append(portNum);
```

```
  }
  myAddress = buff.toString();
}

/**
 * Set the current move.
 */
public synchronized void setPayload(byte[] data) {
  myPayload = data;
}

//------------------------------------------------------------
//  sending methods.

/**
 * Sends the move data to the remote player.
 */
public void run() {
  MessageConnection conn = null;
  byte[] currentPayload = null;
  // synchronize it so each payload
  // gets sent exactly once:
  synchronized(this) {
    if(myPayload != null) {
      currentPayload = myPayload;
      myPayload = null;
    } else {
      return;
    }
  }
  try {
    // open the SMS connection and create the
    // message instance:
    conn = (MessageConnection)Connector.open(myAddress);

    BinaryMessage msg = (BinaryMessage)conn.newMessage(
        MessageConnection.BINARY_MESSAGE);
    msg.setAddress(myAddress);
    msg.setPayloadData(currentPayload);
    conn.send(msg);
    myManager.doneSending();
  } catch(Exception e) {
    e.printStackTrace();
  }
  if (conn != null) {
    try {
      conn.close();
```

```
      } catch (IOException ioe) {
        ioe.printStackTrace();
      }
    }
  }

}
```

You can see that it's quite simple: construct the URL, create the connection and message, set the data, and send.

Throughout this game, I've hard-coded the port number so that the game doesn't have to try to guess what port to direct the message to on the opponent's handset. For this example, the port number I'm using is 16474. So if the remote opponent's phone number is +5550001 (which is a default phone number for the WTK emulator), the sending URL will be sms://+5550001:16474 and the receiving URL will be sms://:16474. For SMS, the push-port number should be between 16000 and 16999. For more information on how the port numbers are allocated, see the IANA Port Number Registry (http://www.iana.org/).

Figure 6-5 shows the screen of the Checkers game where the user enters the opponent's phone number. Note that the phone number used in the sending URL should not contain spaces or hyphens. As you can see in Figure 6-5, the WTK emulator's phone number entry field automatically displays the phone number with dividing spaces added so that the user won't be tempted to type divider characters into the phone number.

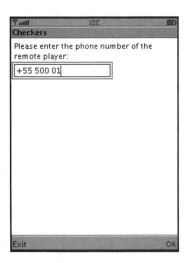

Figure 6-5. *The screen of the Checkers game where the user enters the opponent's phone number*

Notice that this class is a Runnable that sends exactly one message per thread. Since creating a thread is a costly operation, it would be more efficient to put a loop in the run() method and use wait() and notify() to reuse the same thread for each sending operation. However, if there's a chance that the game may be sending multiple SMS messages in a row without a pause in between, it's better practice to send each one on a separate thread as I have done here. The sending operation blocks for a long time, so if you're not careful with synchronization, you might accidentally overwrite one payload with another. If you are careful with synchronization, and you set the payload data from a thread that needs to return quickly, then making the thread wait outside of a synchronized block can cause the program to crash.

Now let's take a look at the receiving code (Listing 6-5).

Listing 6-5. *SMSReceiver.java*

```
package net.frog_parrot.net;

import java.io.*;
import javax.microedition.io.*;
import javax.wireless.messaging.*;

/**
 * This class handles listening for the SMS messages
 * from the remote player.
 *
 * @author Carol Hamer
 */
public class SMSReceiver implements Runnable {

  //----------------------------------------------------------
  //  game instance fields

  /**
   * The class to report back to.
   */
  private SMSManager mySMSManager;

  /**
   * The connection to listen for messages on.
   */
  private MessageConnection myConnection;

  /**
   * whether it's time to clean up.
   */
  private boolean myShouldStop;
```

```
//---------------------------------------------------------
// lifecycle

/**
 * Find connections and start up the listener thread.
 *
 * @returns true if the game was initiated by the remote player.
 */
boolean init(SMSManager manager) throws IOException {
  myShouldStop = false;
  mySMSManager = manager;
  boolean retVal = false;
  // We start by checking for a connection with data to read
  // to see if the application was launched because of
  // receiving an invitation.
  String[] connections = PushRegistry.listConnections(true);
  if (connections != null && connections.length > 0) {
    retVal = true;
  }
  // Here we get the name of all connections that are open
  // to this application, whether they have data or not.
  connections = PushRegistry.listConnections(false);
  if (connections == null || connections.length == 0) {
    throw(new IOException("No push-port registered"));
  }
  myConnection = (MessageConnection)Connector.open(connections[0]);
  // Since listening for messages is a blocking operation,
  // we need to start a new thread to do it:
  Thread thread = new Thread(this);
  thread.start();
  return(retVal);
}

/**
 * Set this thread to die, then close the connection.
 */
void shutDown() {
  myShouldStop = true;
  try {
    myConnection.close();
  } catch (IOException e) {}
}

//---------------------------------------------------------
// listen for messages
```

```
/**
 * Start the listener thread.
 */
public void run() {
  try {
    while(true) {
      Message msg = myConnection.receive();
      if (msg != null) {
        String senderAddress = msg.getAddress();
        // accept only binary messages from the player
        // we're currently playing with -- ignore
        // messages from other players.
        if((mySMSManager.checkPhoneNum(senderAddress))
          && (msg instanceof BinaryMessage)) {
          byte[] data = ((BinaryMessage)msg).getPayloadData();
          int index = 0;
          String taunt = null;
          while(index < data.length) {
            switch(data[index]) {
              // if we've just received an invitation to
              // start the game, then we set the phone
              // number of the other player
              case SMSManager.START_GAME_FLAG:
                index++;
                if(index != data.length) {
                  taunt = new String(data, index, data.length - index);
                }
                index = data.length;
                mySMSManager.receiveInvitation(taunt);
                break;
              case SMSManager.END_GAME_FLAG:
                index++;
                if(index != data.length) {
                  taunt = new String(data, index, data.length - index);
                }
                index = data.length;
                mySMSManager.receiveGameOver(taunt);
                break;
              case SMSManager.END_TURN_FLAG:
                index++;
                if(index != data.length) {
                  taunt = new String(data, index, data.length - index);
                }
                index = data.length;
                mySMSManager.endTurn(taunt);
                break;
              default:
                // the default case is that we've received
```

```
              // some move data to pass along to the
              // game logic.
              byte[] move = new byte[4];
              System.arraycopy(data, index, move, 0, 4);
              mySMSManager.setMove(move);
              index += 4;
              break;
            }
          }
        }
      } // if (msg != null) {
    }
  } catch (IOException e) {
    e.printStackTrace();
  } finally {
    try {
      myConnection.close();
    } catch (Exception e) {}
  }
}

}
```

The first thing the receiver does is check the push registry and get the connections avail-able to this MIDlet. The PushRegistry.listConnections method will return a one-element array containing the string "sms://:16474" because the MIDlet has registered for exactly one connec-tion by placing the following line in the JAD file:

```
MIDlet-Push-1: sms://:16474, net.frog_parrot.checkers.Checkers, *
```

Once you have the connection URL, you open the connection and listen on it. This is accomplished with a while(true) loop so that the listener thread will listen for messages and treat them one by one as long as the MIDlet is running (and not paused).

Figure 6-6 shows the first steps of communication between the two opponents in the Checkers game. Once the first player has sent the invitation SMS, he sees a waiting screen. Meanwhile, receiving the invitation SMS prompts the AMS to launch the Checkers game on the second player's handset. First the AMS uses a system screen to request permission to launch the game, and once the second player grants the AMS permission to launch the Checkers game, the game displays the first player's message along with the first player's phone number (so the sec-ond player can be sure that the first player is someone she knows).

To test the game on two emulators at once using KToolbar, be sure to launch the game using Project ➤ Run Via OTA instead of just clicking KToolbar's Run button. See the "Using KToolbar" section of Chapter 1.

Figure 6-6. *The initial communication steps in the Checkers game*

In the SMSReceiver's main loop, the payload data of the SMS message is interpreted and passed along to the SMSManager. The SMSManager doesn't have much to do when the opponent's move is received. The SMSManager's more interesting jobs are to control the lifecycle of the sending and receiving threads and to construct the payload data to send the local moves to the opponent, as you can see in Listing 6-6.

Listing 6-6. *SMSManager.java*

```java
package net.frog_parrot.net;import java.io.*;

import net.frog_parrot.checkers.MoveManager;

/**
 * This class keeps track of transferring local and
 * remote moves from one player to the other.
 *
 * @author Carol Hamer
 */
public class SMSManager {

  //-----------------------------------------------------------
  //  static fields

  /**
   * The int to signal that the game is to begin.
   */
  public static final byte START_GAME_FLAG = -4;

  /**
   * The byte to signal that the game is to end.
   */
  public static final byte END_GAME_FLAG = -3;

  /**
   * The byte to signal the end of a turn.
   */
  public static final byte END_TURN_FLAG = -2;

  /**
   * The default port number to send to.
   */
  private static final String PORT_NUM = "16474";

  //-----------------------------------------------------------
  //  game instance fields

  /**
   * The class that directs the data from the communications
```

```
 * module to the game logic module and vice versa.
 */
private MoveManager myManager;

/**
 * The class that receives and reads the SMSMessages.
 */
private SMSReceiver myReceiver;

/**
 * The class that sends the SMSMessages.
 */
private SMSSender mySender;

//----------------------------------------------------------
//  data exchange instance fields

/**
 * The data from the local player that is to
 * be sent to the opponent.
 */
private byte[] myMove;

/**
 * The phone number of the opponent:
 */
private String myPhoneNum;

//----------------------------------------------------------
//  lifecycle

/**
 * Start the processes to send and receive messages.
 * @return whether the game was started by receiving
 * an invitation from another player.
 */
public boolean init(MoveManager manager)
    throws IOException {
  myManager = manager;
  myReceiver = new SMSReceiver();
  return(myReceiver.init(this));
}

/**
 * Stop the receiver and sender threads.
 * This method is called alone from pauseApp or destroyApp
 * since sending one last message is too time-consuming.
```

```java
  */
  public void shutDown() {
    myReceiver.shutDown();
  }

  /**
   * Sets the current opponent if none is set, and verifies
   * that subsequent messages came from the right opponent.
   * We cut the first six characters off the beginning of
   * the phone number because these are just the SMS protocol
   * string.
   *
   * @returns true if the message can be accepted.
   */
  public boolean checkPhoneNum(String phoneNumber) {
    if(myPhoneNum == null) {
      myPhoneNum = phoneNumber.substring(6);
      return true;
    } else if (myPhoneNum.equals(phoneNumber.substring(6))) {
      return true;
    } else {
      return false;
    }
  }

  /**
   * This is called when the game is started by receiving
   * an invitation from a remote player.  This triggers the
   * game logic to let the local player make the first move.
   */
  public void receiveInvitation(String taunt) {
    int state = myManager.getState();
    if((state == MoveManager.NOT_STARTED)
        || (state == MoveManager.FOUND_REMOTE_PLAYER)) {
      mySender = new SMSSender(myPhoneNum, PORT_NUM, myManager);
      myManager.receiveInvitation(taunt, myPhoneNum);
    }
  }

  //----------------------------------------------------------
  //  sending methods.

  /**
   * Send the game invitation SMS.
   */
  public void sendInvitation(String phoneNumber) {
    myPhoneNum = phoneNumber;
```

```
  mySender = new SMSSender(myPhoneNum, PORT_NUM, myManager);
  byte[] invitation = new byte[1];
  invitation[0] = START_GAME_FLAG;
  invitation = addTaunt(invitation);
  mySender.setPayload(invitation);
  Thread thread = new Thread(mySender);
  thread.start();
}

/**
 * Send the message to the other
 * player that this player has quit.
 */
public void sendGameOver() {
  byte[] data = new byte[1];
  data[0] = END_GAME_FLAG;
  data = addTaunt(data);
  mySender.setPayload(data);
  Thread thread = new Thread(mySender);
  thread.start();
}

/**
 * Records the local move in a byte array to prepare it
 * to be sent to the remote player.
 */
public void setLocalMove(byte[] move) {
  if(myMove == null) {
    myMove = new byte[5];
    System.arraycopy(move, 0, myMove, 0, 4);
    myMove[4] = END_TURN_FLAG;
  } else {
    // here we're dealing with the case of a
    // series of jumps.  This isn't the typical case, so
    // it shouldn't be too inefficient to just
    // create a new, larger array each time
    // we enlarge the move payload.
    byte[] newMove = new byte[myMove.length + 4];
    System.arraycopy(myMove, 0, newMove, 0, myMove.length);
    System.arraycopy(move, 0, newMove, myMove.length - 1, 4);
    newMove[newMove.length - 1] = END_TURN_FLAG;
    myMove = newMove;
  }
}

/**
 * Sends the current local move to the remote player
```

```
 * then clears the move data.
 */
public void sendLocalMove() {
  if(myMove != null) {
    myMove = addTaunt(myMove);
    mySender.setPayload(myMove);
    myMove = null;
    Thread thread = new Thread(mySender);
    thread.start();
  }
}

//----------------------------------------------------------
//  receiving methods

/**
 * Pass the remote player's move data to the game logic.
 */
public void setMove(byte[] move) {
  myManager.receiveRemoteMove(move);
}

/**
 * Signal that the remote player's turn is over.
 */
public void endTurn(String taunt) {
  myManager.endRemoteTurn(taunt);
}

/**
 * Signal that the remote player has ended the game.
 */
public void receiveGameOver(String taunt) {
  myManager.receiveGameOver(taunt);
}

//----------------------------------------------------------
//  utilities

/**
 * Adds the taunt message data to the message being sent.
 */
public byte[] addTaunt(byte[] data) {
  String taunt = myManager.getTaunt();
  if(taunt != null) {
    try {
      byte[] tauntdata = taunt.getBytes("utf-8");
```

```
      byte[] retData = new byte[tauntdata.length + data.length];
      System.arraycopy(data, 0, retData, 0, data.length);
      System.arraycopy(tauntdata, 0, retData, data.length,
                       tauntdata.length);
      return retData;
    } catch (UnsupportedEncodingException e) {
      // if the encoding is not supported, ignore message.
    }
  }
  return data;
}


}
```

All of the game state data is handled by the MoveManager class. It starts the game communications up and shuts them down. It keeps track of whose turn it is, and it handles the pause mechanism so that during a pause the communications functionality is shut down, and then sets everything back to the correct state when the game resumes.

Note that either player can initiate the game and that the player who receives the invitation to play is the one who moves first (see Figure 6-7).

Figure 6-7. *The first player waits while the second player makes the first move.*

The user who initiates the game sends a message string along with the invitation, and the player who receives the invitation sees the message as well as the phone number of the other player as mentioned earlier and seen in Figure 6-6. Another nice feature is that if one player decides to quit before the end of the game, the MIDlet will try to send one last SMS to the opponent to let him know the game is over. All of these state-control features can be seen in Listing 6-7.

Listing 6-7. *MoveManager.java*

```java
package net.frog_parrot.checkers;

import java.io.*;

import net.frog_parrot.net.SMSManager;

/**
 * This class keeps track of transferring local and
 * remote moves from one player to the other.
 *
 * @author Carol Hamer
 */
public class MoveManager {

  //----------------------------------------------------------
  //  game instance fields

  /**
   * The MIDlet subclass, used to set the Display
   * in the case where an error message needs to be sent.
   */
  private Checkers myCheckers;

  /**
   * The Canvas subclass, used to set the Display
   * in the case where an error message needs to be sent.
   */
  private CheckersCanvas myCanvas;

  /**
   * The game logic class that we send the opponent's
   * moves to.
   */
  private CheckersGame myGame;

  /**
   * The class that performs the actual network connections.
   */
  private SMSManager mySMSManager;
```

```
//----------------------------------------------------------
//  state fields

/**
 * A possible game state.
 */
public static final int NOT_STARTED = 0;

/**
 * A possible game state.
 */
public static final int FOUND_REMOTE_PLAYER = 1;

/**
 * A possible game state.
 */
public static final int LOCAL_TURN = 2;

/**
 * A possible game state.
 */
public static final int SENDING_LOCAL_TURN = 3;

/**
 * A possible game state.
 */
public static final int REMOTE_TURN = 4;

 /**
 * A possible game state.
 */
public static final int GAME_OVER = 5;

 /**
 * A possible game state.
 */
public static final int PAUSED = 6;

/**
 * The code for the state the game is currently in.
 */
private int myState = NOT_STARTED;

/**
 * The code for the state to return to after a pause.
```

```
   */
  private int myPreviousState = NOT_STARTED;

  //------------------------------------------------------------
  //  lifecycle

  /**
   * Constructor initializes the handles back to other
   * game objects.
   */
  MoveManager(Checkers checkers, CheckersCanvas canvas,
                  CheckersGame game) {
    myCheckers = checkers;
    myCanvas = canvas;
    myGame = game;
    mySMSManager = new SMSManager();
    try {
      if(mySMSManager.init(this)) {
        myState = FOUND_REMOTE_PLAYER;
      }
    } catch(IOException e) {
      myCheckers.errorMsg("communications error");
    }
    myCanvas.repaint();
    myCanvas.serviceRepaints();
  }

  /**
   * Stop the receiver.
   * This method is called alone from destroyApp
   * since sending one last message is too time-consuming.
   */
  public void shutDown() {
    myState = GAME_OVER;
    mySMSManager.shutDown();
  }

  /**
   * Stop the receiver and enter the paused state.
   * This method is called alone from pauseApp
   * since sending one last message is too time-consuming.
   */
  public void pause() {
    myPreviousState = myState;
    myState = PAUSED;
    mySMSManager.shutDown();
  }
```

```java
/**
 * If we're returning from a pause, restart the listner.
 */
public void wakeUp() throws IOException {
  if(myState == PAUSED) {
    myState = myPreviousState;
    mySMSManager.init(this);
  }
}

/**
 * Gets the current game state.
 */
public int getState() {
  return(myState);
}

//---------------------------------------------------------
// sending methods

/**
 * Send the game invitation SMS.
 */
public void sendInvitation(String phoneNumber) {
  mySMSManager.sendInvitation(phoneNumber);
  myCanvas.setWaitScreen(true);
  myCanvas.start();
  myCanvas.repaint();
  myCanvas.serviceRepaints();
}

/**
 * This is called when the player moves a piece.
 */
synchronized void move(byte sourceX, byte sourceY, byte destinationX,
                byte destinationY) {
  byte[] move = new byte[4];
  move[0] = sourceX;
  move[1] = sourceY;
  move[2] = destinationX;
  move[3] = destinationY;
  myState = LOCAL_TURN;
  mySMSManager.setLocalMove(move);
}

/**
 * This is called when the local player's turn is over.
```

```
    */
  synchronized void endTurn() {
    myState = SENDING_LOCAL_TURN;
    mySMSManager.sendLocalMove();
  }

  /**
   * Gets the message that the user has entered for the remote
   * player, if any.  Then clears the text.
   */
  public String getTaunt() {
    return myCheckers.getTauntMessage();
  }

  /**
   * Stop the game entirely.  Notify the remote player that
   * the user is exiting the game.
   */
  synchronized void endGame() {
    mySMSManager.shutDown();
    if(myState != GAME_OVER) {
      myState = GAME_OVER;
      mySMSManager.sendGameOver();
      myCanvas.repaint();
      myCanvas.serviceRepaints();
    } else {
      myCheckers.quit();
    }
  }

  /**
   * End the game because the local player has no more moves.
   */
  void loseGame() {
    myCheckers.setWinTaunt();
    endGame();
  }

  /**
   * This method is called by the message sending utility
   * to indicate that the move has been sent.
   */
  public void doneSending() {
    if(myState == GAME_OVER) {
      myCheckers.quit();
    } else {
      myState = REMOTE_TURN;
```

```java
  }
}

//----------------------------------------------------------
//  receiving methods

/**
 * Receive the game invitation SMS.
 */
public synchronized void receiveInvitation(String taunt,
      String phoneNum) {
  myState = LOCAL_TURN;
  myCanvas.setWaitScreen(false);
  myCanvas.start();
  myCanvas.repaint();
  myCanvas.serviceRepaints();
  StringBuffer buff = new StringBuffer(phoneNum);
  buff.append(" invites you to play checkers");
  if(taunt != null) {
    buff.append(": ");
    buff.append(taunt);
  }
  myCheckers.displayTauntMessage(buff.toString());
}

/**
 * Interpret one move by the remote player.
 */
public synchronized void receiveRemoteMove(byte[] fourBytes) {
  myState = REMOTE_TURN;
  myGame.moveOpponent(fourBytes);
}

/**
 * Set the game to ended upon receiving the end game
 * signal from the remote player.
 */
public synchronized void receiveGameOver(String taunt) {
  myState = GAME_OVER;
  mySMSManager.shutDown();
  myCanvas.repaint();
  myCanvas.serviceRepaints();
  if(taunt != null) {
    myCheckers.displayTauntMessage(taunt);
  }
}
```

```
/**
 * Receive the signal that the remote player is done
 * moving (no more jumps possible).
 */
public synchronized void endRemoteTurn(String taunt) {
  myState = LOCAL_TURN;
  myGame.endOpponentTurn();
  myCanvas.setWaitScreen(false);
  myCanvas.repaint();
  myCanvas.serviceRepaints();
  if(taunt != null) {
    myCheckers.displayTauntMessage(taunt);
  }
}

}
```

Note that none of the code up to this point has been specific to the game of checkers. By modularizing the code, you make it reusable. In the next chapter you'll see how to replace the SMS communications code with Bluetooth communications code, adapting the same game code to a different protocol. By the same token, all of the code so far could easily be adapted (with very little modification) to any SMS-based two-player game where the players take turns.

Writing the Game Logic for the Checkers Example

Now let's have a look at the code that makes this game Checkers. Listing 6-8 shows the CheckersCanvas class.

Listing 6-8. *CheckersCanvas.java*

```
package net.frog_parrot.checkers;

import javax.microedition.lcdui.*;

/**
 * This class is the display of the game.
 *
 * @author Carol Hamer
 */
public class CheckersCanvas extends Canvas {

  //-----------------------------------------------------------
  //    static fields

  /**
   * color constant
   */
  public static final int BLACK = 0;
```

```java
/**
 * color constant
 */
public static final int WHITE = 0xffffff;

/**
 * color constant.
 * (not quite bright red)
 */
public static final int RED = 0xf96868;

/**
 * color constant
 */
public static final int GRAY = 0xc6c6c6;

/**
 * color constant
 */
public static final int LT_GRAY = 0xe5e3e3;

/**
 * how many rows and columns the display is divided into.
 */
public static final int GRID_WIDTH = 8;

//-----------------------------------------------------------
//   instance fields

/**
 * The black crown to draw on the red pieces.
 */
private Image myBlackCrown;

/**
 * The red crown to draw on the black pieces.
 */
private Image myWhiteCrown;

/**
 * a handle to the object that stores the game logic
 * and game data.
 */
private CheckersGame myGame;
```

```java
/**
 * checkers dimension: the width of the squares of the checkerboard.
 */
private int mySquareSize;

/**
 * checkers dimension: the minimum width possible for the
 * checkerboard squares.
 */
private int myMinSquareSize = 15;

/**
 * whether or not you're waiting for another player to join
 * the game.
 */
private boolean myIsWaiting;

//--------------------------------------------------------
//     gets / sets

/**
 * @return a handle to the class that holds the logic of the
 * checkers game.
 */
CheckersGame getGame() {
  return(myGame);
}

/**
 * Display a screen to prompt the player to invite
 * another player.
 */
void setInvitationScreen() {
  myIsWaiting = true;
}

/**
 * Display a screen to inform the player of an error.
 */
void setErrorScreen(String errMsg) {
}
```

```
/**
 * Display a screen to tell the local player that
 * the game is waiting for a response from the remote
 * player.
 */
void setWaitScreen(boolean wait) {
  myIsWaiting = wait;
}


//-------------------------------------------------------
//    initialization and game state changes

/**
 * Constructor performs size calculations.
 * @throws Exception if the display size is too
 *         small to make a checkers.
 */
CheckersCanvas(Display d) throws Exception {
  myGame = new CheckersGame();
  // a few calculations to make the right checkerboard
  // for the current display.
  int width = getWidth();
  int height = getHeight();
  // get the smaller dimension fo the two possible
  // screen dimensions in order to determine how
  // big to make the checkerboard.
  int screenSquareWidth = height;
  if(width < height) {
    screenSquareWidth = width;
  }
  mySquareSize = screenSquareWidth / GRID_WIDTH;
  // if the display is too small to make a reasonable checkerboard,
  // then you throw an Exception
  if(mySquareSize < myMinSquareSize) {
    throw(new Exception("Display too small"));
  }
  // initialize the crown images:
  myBlackCrown = Image.createImage("/images/blackCrown.png");
  myWhiteCrown = Image.createImage("/images/whiteCrown.png");
}
```

```
/**
 * This is called as soon as the game begins or when you
 * receive an invitation.
 */
void start() {
  // prepare the game data for the first move:
  myGame.start();
}


//----------------------------------------------------------
//  graphics methods

/**
 * Repaint the checkerboard.
 */
protected void paint(Graphics g) {
  int width = getWidth();
  int height = getHeight();
  g.setColor(WHITE);
  // clear the board (including the region around
  // the board, which can get menu stuff and other
  // garbage painted onto it...)
  g.fillRect(0, 0, width, height);
  // If you need to wait for another player to join the
  // game before you can start, this displays the appropriate
  // message:
  if(myIsWaiting) {
    // perform some calculations to place the text correctly:
    Font font = g.getFont();
    int fontHeight = font.getHeight();
    int fontWidth = font.stringWidth("waiting for another player");
    g.setColor(WHITE);
    g.fillRect((width - fontWidth)/2, (height - fontHeight)/2,
                      fontWidth + 2, fontHeight);
    // write in black
    g.setColor(BLACK);
    g.setFont(font);
    g.drawString("waiting for another player", (width - fontWidth)/2,
                (height - fontHeight)/2,
                      g.TOP|g.LEFT);
    return;
  }
  // now draw the checkerboard:
  // first the dark squares:
  byte offset = 0;
  for(byte i = 0; i < 4; i++) {
    for(byte j = 0; j < 8; j++) {
```

```
// the offset is used to handle the fact that in every
// other row the dark squares are shifted one place
// to the right.
if(j % 2 != 0) {
  offset = 1;
} else {
  offset = 0;
}
// now if this is a selected square, you draw it lighter
// and outline it:
if(myGame.isSelected(i, j)) {
  g.setColor(LT_GRAY);
  g.fillRect((2*i + offset)*mySquareSize, j*mySquareSize,
               mySquareSize, mySquareSize);
  g.setColor(RED);
  g.drawRect((2*i + offset)*mySquareSize, j*mySquareSize,
               mySquareSize - 1, mySquareSize - 1);
} else {
  // if it's not selected, you draw it dark gray:
  g.setColor(GRAY);
  g.fillRect((2*i + offset)*mySquareSize, j*mySquareSize,
             mySquareSize, mySquareSize);
}
// now put the pieces in their places:
g.setColor(RED);
int piece = myGame.getPiece(i, j);
int circleOffset = 2;
int circleSize = mySquareSize - 2*circleOffset;
if(piece < 0) {
  // color the piece in black
  g.setColor(BLACK);
  g.fillRoundRect((2*i + offset)*mySquareSize + circleOffset,
                   j*mySquareSize + circleOffset,
             circleSize, circleSize, circleSize, circleSize);
  // if the player is a king, draw a crown on:
  if(piece < -1) {
    g.drawImage(myWhiteCrown,
             (2*i + offset)*mySquareSize + mySquareSize/2,
             j*mySquareSize + 1 + mySquareSize/2,
             Graphics.VCENTER|Graphics.HCENTER);
  }
} else if(piece > 0) {
  // color the piece in red
  g.fillRoundRect((2*i + offset)*mySquareSize + circleOffset,
                   j*mySquareSize + circleOffset,
             circleSize, circleSize, circleSize, circleSize);
  // if the player is a king, draw a crown on:
```

```
        if(piece > 1) {
          g.drawImage(myBlackCrown,
                    (2*i + offset)*mySquareSize + mySquareSize/2,
                    j*mySquareSize + 1 + mySquareSize/2,
                    Graphics.VCENTER|Graphics.HCENTER);
        }
      }
    }
  }
  // now the blank squares:
  // actually, this part is probably not necessary...
  g.setColor(WHITE);
  for(int i = 0; i < 4; i++) {
    for(int j = 0; j < 8; j++) {
      if(j % 2 == 0) {
        offset = 1;
      } else {
        offset = 0;
      }
      g.fillRect((2*i + offset)*mySquareSize, j*mySquareSize,
                 mySquareSize, mySquareSize);
    }
  }
  // if the player has reached the end of the game,
  // you display the end message.
  if(myGame.getGameOver()) {
    //System.out.println("paint-->gameOver");
    // perform some calculations to place the text correctly:
    Font font = g.getFont();
    int fontHeight = font.getHeight();
    int fontWidth = font.stringWidth("Game Over");
    g.setColor(WHITE);
    g.fillRect((width - fontWidth)/2, (height - fontHeight)/2,
                    fontWidth + 2, fontHeight);
    // write in black
    g.setColor(BLACK);
    g.setFont(font);
    g.drawString("Game Over", (width - fontWidth)/2,
                 (height - fontHeight)/2,
                    g.TOP|g.LEFT);
  }
}


//----------------------------------------------------------
//  handle keystrokes

/**
```

```
 * Move the player.
 */
public void keyPressed(int keyCode) {
  if(myGame.isMyTurn()) {
    int action = getGameAction(keyCode);
    switch (action) {
    case LEFT:
      myGame.leftPressed();
      break;
    case RIGHT:
      myGame.rightPressed();
      break;
    case FIRE:
    case UP:
      myGame.upPressed();
      break;
    case DOWN:
      myGame.deselect();
      break;
    }
    repaint();
    serviceRepaints();
  }
}

}
```

The CheckersCanvas class is a standard application of the Canvas class (see the "Using the Graphics and Canvas Classes" section in Chapter 2 for details about how you use the Canvas class). For this game, I didn't even bother to use GameCanvas since the graphics are simple, and I don't need to synchronize the keystroke queries with any game animations.

The part that's unique to the checkers game is in the paint() method. You can see that there are two possibilities: either it just writes a message and returns or it paints the whole checkerboard. To make it a little easier on the eyes, I made the checkerboard gray and white, rather than red and black, and then made the pieces themselves red and black. (I made a point to verify that the color scheme looks OK on a grayscale screen.) Then whichever square is currently selected is painted a slightly lighter shade of gray than the other dark squares and put a red outline around it.

The only point that may require some explanation is the use of the local variable offset. This variable keeps track of the fact that in every other row of the grid the set of dark squares shifts over one square. So, when painting the grid, you first determine whether you're in an even row or an odd row and (keeping track of it in offset) to determine which four squares should be colored of the eight squares in the row.

Also notice that I always have the local player be the red pieces that start on the bottom half of the screen. So when you're playing, it'll look to you like you moved a red piece, but on your opponent's cell phone it'll appear that you moved one of the black pieces (see Figure 6-8). I can get away with this since the board is symmetric.

Figure 6-8. *The two players' checkerboards are displayed in such a way that the local player's pieces always start at the bottom of the screen.*

The logic of the game itself is in the CheckersGame class (Listing 6-9).

Listing 6-9. *CheckersGame.java*

```java
package net.frog_parrot.checkers;

import java.util.Vector;

/**
 * This class takes care of the underlying logic and data of
 * the checkers game being played.  That includes where
 * all of the pieces are on the board and where it is OK
 * for them to move to.
 *
 * @author Carol Hamer
```

```java
 */
public class CheckersGame {

  //----------------------------------------------------------
  //    static fields

  /**
   * The length of the checkerboard in the x-direction.
   */
  public static final byte X_LENGTH = 4;

  /**
   * The length of the checkerboard in the y-direction.
   */
  public static final byte Y_LENGTH = 8;

  //----------------------------------------------------------
  //    instance fields

  /**
   * a handle to the move manager that keeps track of taking
   * turns with the other player.
   */
  private MoveManager myMoveManager;

  /**
   * This array represents the black squares of the
   * checkerboard.  The two dimensions of the array
   * represent the two dimensions of the checkerboard.
   * The value represents what type of piece is on
   * the square.
   * 0 = empty
   * 1 = local player's piece
   * 2 = local player's king
   * -1 = remote player's piece
   * -2 = remote player's king
   */
  private byte[][] myGrid;

  /**
   * If the user has currently selected a piece to move,
   * this is its X grid coordinate. (-1 if none selected)
   */
  private byte mySelectedX = -1;
```

```
/**
 * If the user has currently selected a piece to move,
 * this is its Y grid coordinate.(-1 if none selected)
 */
private byte mySelectedY = -1;

/**
 * If the user has currently selected a possible
 * destination square for a move, this is its X coordinate.
 * (-1 if none selected)
 */
private byte myDestinationX = -1;

/**
 * If the user has currently selected a possible
 * destination square for a move, this is its Y coordinate.
 * (-1 if none selected)
 */
private byte myDestinationY = -1;

/**
 * This Vector contains the coordinates of all of the
 * squares that the player could currently move to.
 */
private Vector myPossibleMoves = new Vector(4);

/**
 * This is true if the player has just jumped and can
 * jump again.
 */
private boolean myIsJumping = false;

//---------------------------------------------------------
//   get/set data

/**
 * get the piece on the given grid square.
 */
byte getPiece(byte x, byte y) {
  return(myGrid[x][y]);
}

/**
 * This is called by CheckersCanvas to determine if
 * the square is currently selected (as containing
 * a piece to move or a destination square).
 */
```

```
boolean isSelected(byte x, byte y) {
  boolean retVal = false;
  if((x == mySelectedX) && (y == mySelectedY)) {
    retVal = true;
  } else if((x == myDestinationX) && (y == myDestinationY)) {
    retVal = true;
  }
  return(retVal);
}

/**
 * This tells whether or not the keystrokes should currently
 * be taken into account.
 */
boolean isMyTurn() {
  return(myMoveManager.getState() == MoveManager.LOCAL_TURN);
}

/**
 * This tells whether or not the game has ended.
 */
boolean getGameOver() {
  return(myMoveManager.getState() == MoveManager.GAME_OVER);
}

/**
 * set the MoveManager object.
 */
void setMoveManager(MoveManager manager) {
  myMoveManager = manager;
}

//---------------------------------------------------------
//    initialization

/**
 * Constructor puts the pieces in their initial positions:
 */
CheckersGame() {
  myGrid = new byte[X_LENGTH][];
  for(byte i = 0; i < myGrid.length; i++) {
    myGrid[i] = new byte[Y_LENGTH];
    for(byte j = 0; j < myGrid[i].length; j++) {
      if(j < 3) {
        // fill the top of the board with remote players
        myGrid[i][j] = -1;
      } else if(j > 4) {
```

```
          // fill the bottom of the board with local players
          myGrid[i][j] = 1;
        }
      }
    }
  }


  /**
   * This is called just before the player makes the
   * first move.
   */
  void start() {
    mySelectedX = 0;
    mySelectedY = 5;
    getMoves(mySelectedX, mySelectedY, myPossibleMoves, false);
  }


  //--------------------------------------------------------
  //    move the opponent
  // to be called by MoveManager


  /**
   * This is called when the opponent wants to move
   * its piece.
   * @param moveData an array of four bytes:
   * moveData[0] = opponent's initial X coordinate
   * moveData[1] = opponent's initial Y coordinate
   * moveData[2] = opponent's destination X coordinate
   * moveData[3] = opponent's destination Y coordinate
   */
  void moveOpponent(byte[] moveData) {
    // since both players appear on their own screens
    // as the red side (bottom of the screen), you need
    // to invert the opponent's move:
    moveData[0] = (new Integer(X_LENGTH - moveData[0] - 1)).byteValue();
    moveData[2] = (new Integer(X_LENGTH - moveData[2] - 1)).byteValue();
    moveData[1] = (new Integer(Y_LENGTH - moveData[1] - 1)).byteValue();
    moveData[3] = (new Integer(Y_LENGTH - moveData[3] - 1)).byteValue();
    myGrid[moveData[2]][moveData[3]]
      = myGrid[moveData[0]][moveData[1]];
    myGrid[moveData[0]][moveData[1]] = 0;
    // deal with an opponent's jump:
    if((moveData[1] - moveData[3] > 1) ||
       (moveData[3] - moveData[1] > 1)) {
      int jumpedY = (moveData[1] + moveData[3])/2;
      int jumpedX = moveData[0];
      int parity = moveData[1] % 2;
```

```
    if((parity > 0) && (moveData[2] > moveData[0])) {
      jumpedX++;
    } else if((parity == 0) && (moveData[0] > moveData[2])) {
      jumpedX--;
    }
    myGrid[jumpedX][jumpedY] = 0;
  }
  // if the opponent reaches the far side,
  // make him a king:
  if(moveData[3] == Y_LENGTH - 1) {
    myGrid[moveData[2]][moveData[3]] = -2;
  }
}

/**
 * This is called when the opponent's turn is over.
 * Note that the turn doesn't automatically end after
 * the opponent moves because the opponent may make
 * a double or triple jump.
 */
void endOpponentTurn() {
  // Now begin the local player's turn:
  // First select the first local piece that can be
  // moved. (rightPressed will select an appropriate
  // piece or end the game if the local player has
  // no possible moves to make)
  mySelectedX = 0;
  mySelectedY = 0;
  myDestinationX = -1;
  myDestinationY = -1;
  rightPressed();
  // the local player's thread has been waiting
  // for the opponent's turn to end.
  synchronized(this) {
    notify();
  }
}

//---------------------------------------------------------
//    handle keystrokes
// to be called by CheckersCanvas

/**
 * if the left button is pressed, this method takes
 * the correct course of action depending on the situation.
 */
void leftPressed() {
```

```
      // in the first case the user has not yet selected a
      // piece to move:
      if(myDestinationX == -1) {
        // find the next possible piece (to the left)
        // that can move:
        selectPrevious();
        // if selectPrevious fails to fill myPossibleMoves, that
        // means that the local player cannot move, so the game
        // is over:
        if(myPossibleMoves.size() == 0) {
          myMoveManager.loseGame();
        }
      } else {
        // if the user has already selected a piece to move,
        // you give the options of where the piece can move to:
        for(byte i = 0; i < myPossibleMoves.size(); i++) {
          byte[] coordinates = (byte[])myPossibleMoves.elementAt(i);
          if((coordinates[0] == myDestinationX) &&
            (coordinates[1] == myDestinationY)) {
            i++;
            i = (new Integer(i % myPossibleMoves.size())).byteValue();
            coordinates = (byte[])myPossibleMoves.elementAt(i);
            myDestinationX = coordinates[0];
            myDestinationY = coordinates[1];
            break;
          }
        }
      }
    }

    /**
     * if the left button is pressed, this method takes
     * the correct course of action depending on the situation.
     */
    void rightPressed() {
      // in the first case the user has not yet selected a
      // piece to move:
      if(myDestinationX == -1) {
        // find the next possible piece that can
        // move:
        selectNext();
        // if selectNext fails to fill myPossibleMoves, that
        // means that the local player cannot move, so the game
        // is over:
        if(myPossibleMoves.size() == 0) {
          myMoveManager.loseGame();
        }
```

```
    } else {
      // if the user has already selected a piece to move,
      // you give the options of where the piece can move to:
      for(byte i = 0; i < myPossibleMoves.size(); i++) {
        byte[] coordinates = (byte[])myPossibleMoves.elementAt(i);
        if((coordinates[0] == myDestinationX) &&
          (coordinates[1] == myDestinationY)) {
          i++;
          i = (new Integer(i % myPossibleMoves.size())).byteValue();
          coordinates = (byte[])myPossibleMoves.elementAt(i);
          myDestinationX = coordinates[0];
          myDestinationY = coordinates[1];
          break;
        }
      }
    }
  }
}

/**
 * If no piece is selected, you select one.  If a piece
 * is selected, you move it.
 */
void upPressed() {
  // in the first case the user has not yet selected a
  // piece to move:
  if(myDestinationX == -1) {
    fixSelection();
  } else {
    // if the source square and destination square
    // have been chosen, you move the piece:
    move();
  }
}

/**
 * If the user decided not to move the selected piece
 * (and instead wants to select again), this undoes
 * the selection. This corresponds to pressing the
 * DOWN key.
 */
void deselect() {
  // if the player has just completed a jump and
  // could possibly jump again but decides not to
  // (i.e. deselects), then the turn ends:
  if(myIsJumping) {
    mySelectedX = -1;
    mySelectedY = -1;
```

```
      myDestinationX = -1;
      myDestinationY = -1;
      myIsJumping = false;
      myMoveManager.endTurn();
    } else {
      // setting the destination coordinates to -1
      // is the signal that the the choice of which
      // piece to move can be modified:
      myDestinationX = -1;
      myDestinationY = -1;
    }
  }


//------------------------------------------------------------
//    internal square selection methods

/**
 * When the player has decided that the currently selected
 * square contains the piece he really wants to move, this
 * is called. This method switches to the mode where
 * the player selects the destination square of the move.
 */
private void fixSelection() {
  byte[] destination = (byte[])myPossibleMoves.elementAt(0);
  // setting the destination coordinates to valid
  // coordinates is the signal that the user is done
  // selecting the piece to move and now is choosing
  // the destination square:
  myDestinationX = destination[0];
  myDestinationY = destination[1];
}

/**
 * This method starts from the currently selected square
 * and finds the next square that contains a piece that
 * the player can move.
 */
private void selectNext() {
  // Test the squares one by one (starting from the
  // currently selected square) until you find a square
  // that contains one of the local player's pieces
  // that can move:
  byte testX = mySelectedX;
  byte testY = mySelectedY;
  while(true) {
    testX++;
```

```java
    if(testX >= X_LENGTH) {
      testX = 0;
      testY++;
      testY = (new Integer(testY % Y_LENGTH)).byteValue();
    }
    getMoves(testX, testY, myPossibleMoves, false);
    if((myPossibleMoves.size() != 0) ||
        ((testX == mySelectedX) && (testY == mySelectedY))) {
      mySelectedX = testX;
      mySelectedY = testY;
      break;
    }
  }
}


/**
 * This method starts from the currently selected square
 * and finds the next square (to the left) that contains
 * a piece that the player can move.
 */
private void selectPrevious() {
  // Test the squares one by one (starting from the
  // currently selected square) until you find a square
  // that contains one of the local player's pieces
  // that can move:
  byte testX = mySelectedX;
  byte testY = mySelectedY;
  while(true) {
    testX--;
    if(testX < 0) {
      testX += X_LENGTH;
      testY--;
      if(testY < 0) {
        testY += Y_LENGTH;
      }
    }
    getMoves(testX, testY, myPossibleMoves, false);
    if((myPossibleMoves.size() != 0) ||
      ((testX == mySelectedX) && (testY == mySelectedY))) {
      mySelectedX = testX;
      mySelectedY = testY;
      break;
    }
  }
}
```

```java
//--------------------------------------------------------
//    internal utilities

/**
 * Once the user has selected the move to make, this
 * updates the data accordingly.
 */
private void move() {
  // the piece that was on the source square is
  // now on the destination square:
  myGrid[myDestinationX][myDestinationY]
    = myGrid[mySelectedX][mySelectedY];
  // the source square is emptied:
  myGrid[mySelectedX][mySelectedY] = 0;
  if(myDestinationY == 0) {
    myGrid[myDestinationX][myDestinationY] = 2;
  }
  // tell the communicator to inform the other player
  // of this move:
  myMoveManager.move(mySelectedX, mySelectedY,
                     myDestinationX, myDestinationY);
  // deal with the special rules for jumps:
  if((mySelectedY - myDestinationY > 1) ||
    (myDestinationY - mySelectedY > 1)) {
    int jumpedY = (mySelectedY + myDestinationY)/2;
    int jumpedX = mySelectedX;
    int parity = mySelectedY % 2;
    // the coordinates of the jumped square depend on
    // what row you're in:
    if((parity > 0) && (myDestinationX > mySelectedX)) {
      jumpedX++;
    } else if((parity == 0) && (mySelectedX > myDestinationX)) {
      jumpedX--;
    }
    // remove the piece that was jumped over:
    myGrid[jumpedX][jumpedY] = 0;
    // now get ready to jump again if possible:
    mySelectedX = myDestinationX;
    mySelectedY = myDestinationY;
    myDestinationX = -1;
    myDestinationY = -1;
    // see if another jump is possible.
    // The "true" argument tells the program to return
    // only jumps because the player can go again ONLY
    // if there's a jump:
    getMoves(mySelectedX, mySelectedY, myPossibleMoves, true);
    // if there's another jump possible with the same piece,
```

```
      // allow the player to continue jumping:
      if(myPossibleMoves.size() != 0) {
        myIsJumping = true;
        byte[] landing = (byte[])myPossibleMoves.elementAt(0);
        myDestinationX = landing[0];
        myDestinationY = landing[1];
      } else {
        myIsJumping = false;
        myMoveManager.endTurn();
      }
    } else {
      // since it's not a jump, you just end the turn
      // by deselecting everything.
      mySelectedX = -1;
      mySelectedY = -1;
      myDestinationX = -1;
      myDestinationY = -1;
      myPossibleMoves.removeAllElements();
      // tell the other player you're done:
      myIsJumping = false;
      myMoveManager.endTurn();
    }
}

/**
 * Given a square on the grid, get the coordinates
 * of one of the adjoining (diagonal) squares.
 * 0 = top left
 * 1 = top right
 * 2 = bottom left
 * 3 = bottom right.
 * @return the coordinates or null if the desired corner
 * is off the board.
 */
private byte[] getCornerCoordinates(byte x, byte y, byte corner) {
  byte[] retArray = null;
  if(corner < 2) {
    y--;
  } else {
    y++;
  }
  // Where the corner is on the grid depends on
  // whether this is an odd row or an even row:
  if((corner % 2 == 0) && (y % 2 != 0)) {
    x--;
  } else if((corner % 2 != 0) && (y % 2 == 0)) {
    x++;
```

```
    }
    try {
      if(myGrid[x][y] > -15) {
        // you don't really care about the value, this
        // if statement is just there to get it to
        // throw if the coordinates aren't on the board.
        retArray = new byte[2];
        retArray[0] = x;
        retArray[1] = y;
      }
    } catch(ArrayIndexOutOfBoundsException e) {
      // this throws if the coordinates do not correspond
      // to a square on the board. It's not a problem,
      // so you do nothing--you just return null instead
      // of returning coordinates since no valid
      // coordinates correspond to the desired corner.
    }
    return(retArray);
  }

  /**
   * Determines where the piece in the given
   * grid location can move.  Clears the Vector
   * and fills it with the locations that
   * the piece can move to.
   * @param jumpsOnly if you should return only moves that
   *        are jumps.
   */
  private void getMoves(byte x, byte y, Vector toFill, boolean jumpsOnly) {
    toFill.removeAllElements();
    // if the square does not contain one of the local player's
    // pieces, then there are no corresponding moves and you just
    // return an empty vector.
    if(myGrid[x][y] <= 0) {
      return;
    }
    // check each of the four corners to see if the
    // piece can move there:
    for(byte i = 0; i < 4; i++) {
      byte[] coordinates = getCornerCoordinates(x, y, i);
      // if the coordinate array is null, then the corresponding
      // corner is off the board and you don't deal with it.
      // The later two conditions in the following if statement
      // ensure that either the move is a forward move or the
      // current piece is a king:
      if((coordinates != null) &&
         ((myGrid[x][y] > 1) || (i < 2))) {
```

```
        // if the corner is empty (and you're not looking
        // for just jumps), then this is a possible move
        // so you add it to the vector of moves:
        if((myGrid[coordinates[0]][coordinates[1]] == 0) && (! jumpsOnly)) {
          toFill.addElement(coordinates);
          // if the space is occupied by an opponent,
          // see if you can jump it:
        } else if(myGrid[coordinates[0]][coordinates[1]] < 0) {
          byte[] jumpLanding = getCornerCoordinates(coordinates[0],
                                        coordinates[1], i);
          // if the space on the far side of the opponent's piece
          // is on the board and is unoccupied, then a jump
          // is possible, so you add it to the vector of moves:
          if((jumpLanding != null) &&
            (myGrid[jumpLanding[0]][jumpLanding[1]] == 0)) {
            toFill.addElement(jumpLanding);
          }
        }
      }
    }
  } // end for loop
}


}
```

Nothing in this class is specifically MIDP related. This class could easily be used to keep track of all the pieces on a checkerboard for a checkers game written for J2SE and/or a game in which the opponent is the computer (in the form of some additional class) rather than having a remote opponent.

One important consideration I had to think about before writing this code was how the user interface would work. More precisely, how will the player decide which piece to move and where to move it? There is no one correct answer to this question, but I think I came up with a relatively intuitive system. In the beginning of the turn (triggered by the method endOpponentTurn()), the program finds a square that contains one of the player's pieces that is capable of making a move and marks the square as selected. Then, by pressing the left and right keys, the user can select a different square. The methods rightPressed() and leftPressed() find the next square to the left (or respectively to the right) that contains one of the local player's pieces that has possible moves to make. Once the user has finalized the choice of which piece to move, she presses the up or the select key. As soon as the up or select key is pressed, then the next thing to select is the destination square. Choosing the destination square works in exactly the same way. One of the possible moves starts out appearing selected, and the user moves the selection frame through the list of possible moves by using the right and left keys. To finalize the selection of the destination square, the user presses the up key again. If the user selects a piece to move but then changes her mind before choosing a destination square, she can deselect the piece to move by pressing the down key. It sounds rather complicated when I write it out in words, but in practice the system is very simple to use. Behind the scenes, the square selection algorithm required quite a number of methods working together. The methods leftPressed, rightPressed, upPressed, deselect, fixSelection, selectNext, and selectPrevious, as well as some of the internal utilities, all work together just to allow the user to choose a move.

There were a few additional points in the game of Checkers that required a little extra thought. The first one was the fact that the game is played only on the dark squares. So even though a checkerboard is an 8×8 square, if you only look only at the dark squares, it ends up being eight rows of four columns each. (That's why in the following code after the value of X_LENGTH is 4, and the value of Y_LENGTH is 8.) But if you represent it that way, the columns aren't really lined up. Which squares you can move a given piece to depends on whether the piece is on an even row or an odd row. That's why I needed to write some rather complicated methods near the bottom (getCornerCoordinates() and getMoves()) to figure out all of the possible moves for each piece.

Another point that required some extra effort was dealing with the fact that usually a player can move only once, but if the player jumps, he may be allowed to jump again, possibly multiple times. Dealing with the fact that a turn may consist of multiple moves is what motivated a large portion of the code. Most of the move() method is devoted to dealing with what happens when the player can jump again, and as I mentioned in the discussion of the communications code, double jumps are what made me create separate functions to end the players' turns rather than just having the turn end as soon as the player has moved.

Aside from the points mentioned earlier, the workings of the CheckersGame are very straightforward. The class has a two-dimensional array myGrid that keeps track of where all of the pieces are on the checkerboard. The remote player can update this internal set of data through the MoveManager calling the methods moveOpponent() and endOpponentTurn(). And the local player can also update the data (taking turns correctly, of course!) by pressing keys to select moves.

The last class you need to complete this example is the MIDlet class, Checkers (Listing 6-10).

Listing 6-10. *Checkers.java*

```java
package net.frog_parrot.checkers;

import javax.microedition.midlet.*;
import javax.microedition.lcdui.*;

/**
 * This is the main class of the checkers game.
 *
 * @author Carol Hamer
 */
public class Checkers extends MIDlet implements CommandListener {

  //---------------------------------------------------------
  //    game object fields

  /**
   * The canvas that the checkerboard is drawn on.
   */
  private CheckersCanvas myCanvas;
```

```java
/**
 * The class that handles turn taking and communication.
 */
private MoveManager myMoveManager;

/**
 * The field that takes in the remote player's phone number.
 */
private TextField myPhoneNumberField;

/**
 * The screen where the local player enters a message for
 * the remote player.
 */
private TextBox myTauntBox;

//---------------------------------------------------------
//     command fields

/**
 * The button to exit the game.
 */
private Command myExitCommand = new Command("Exit", Command.EXIT, 99);

/**
 * The button to cancel a message in progress.
 */
private Command myCancelCommand = new Command("Cancel", Command.CANCEL, 99);

/**
 * The button to send the initial invitation.
 */
private Command myOkCommand = new Command("Ok", Command.OK, 0);

/**
 * The button to enter a message for the remote player.
 */
private Command myTauntCommand = new Command("add message",
    Command.SCREEN, 1);

//---------------------------------------------------------
//     initialization and data

/**
 * Initialize the canvas and the commands.
 */
public Checkers() {
```

```java
    try {
      //create the canvas and set up the commands:
      myCanvas = new CheckersCanvas(Display.getDisplay(this));
      myCanvas.addCommand(myExitCommand);
      myCanvas.addCommand(myTauntCommand);
      myCanvas.setCommandListener(this);
      CheckersGame game = myCanvas.getGame();
      myMoveManager = new MoveManager(this, myCanvas, game);
      game.setMoveManager(myMoveManager);
      myTauntBox = new TextBox("message", null, 100, TextField.ANY);
      myTauntBox.addCommand(myOkCommand);
      myTauntBox.addCommand(myCancelCommand);
      myTauntBox.setCommandListener(this);
    } catch(Exception e) {
      // if there's an error during creation, display it as an alert.
      errorMsg(e);
    }
  }

  //-----------------------------------------------------------------
  //   implementation of MIDlet
  // these methods may be called by the application management
  // software at any time, so we always check fields for null
  // before calling methods on them.

  /**
   * Start the application.
   */
  public void startApp() {
    // If the game wasn't launched by receiving an invitation,
    // start with a screen to prompt the user to send an
    // invitation to another player.
    if(myMoveManager.getState() == MoveManager.NOT_STARTED) {
      Display.getDisplay(this).setCurrent(myTauntBox);
    } else {
      try {
        myMoveManager.wakeUp();
      } catch(Exception e) {
        errorMsg(e);
      }
    }
  }

  /**
   * Throw out the garbage.
   */
  public void destroyApp(boolean unconditional)
```

```
      throws MIDletStateChangeException {
    // tell the communicator to send the end game
    // message to the other player and then disconnect:
    if(myMoveManager != null) {
      myMoveManager.shutDown();
    }
    // throw the larger game objects in the garbage:
    myMoveManager = null;
    myCanvas = null;
  }

  /**
   * End the program now.
   */
  public void quit() {
    try {
      destroyApp(false);
      notifyDestroyed();
    } catch (MIDletStateChangeException ex) {
    }
  }

  /**
   * Pause the game.
   * This closes the receiving thread.
   */
  public void pauseApp() {
    myMoveManager.pause();
  }

  //------------------------------------------------------------------
  //  implementation of CommandListener

  /*
   * Respond to a command issued on the Canvas.
   */
  public void commandAction(Command c, Displayable s) {
    if(c == myCancelCommand) {
      myTauntBox.setString(null);
    }
    if(s == myTauntBox) {
      if(myMoveManager.getState() == MoveManager.NOT_STARTED) {
        Form invitationForm = new Form("Checkers");
        myPhoneNumberField = new TextField(null, null, 15,
                                        TextField.PHONENUMBER);
        invitationForm.append("Please enter the phone number "
                          + "of the remote player:");
```

```
        invitationForm.append(myPhoneNumberField);
        invitationForm.addCommand(myOkCommand);
        invitationForm.addCommand(myExitCommand);
        invitationForm.setCommandListener(this);
        Display.getDisplay(this).setCurrent(invitationForm);
      } else {
        Display.getDisplay(this).setCurrent(myCanvas);
      }
    } else if((c == myExitCommand) || (c == Alert.DISMISS_COMMAND)) {
      if((myMoveManager != null)
          && (myMoveManager.getState() != MoveManager.NOT_STARTED)) {
        myMoveManager.endGame();
      } else {
        quit();
      }
    } else if(c == myOkCommand) {
      myMoveManager.sendInvitation(myPhoneNumberField.getString());
      myPhoneNumberField = null;
      myCanvas.setWaitScreen(true);
      myCanvas.start();
      myCanvas.repaint();
      myCanvas.serviceRepaints();
      Display.getDisplay(this).setCurrent(myCanvas);
    } else if(c == myTauntCommand) {
      Display.getDisplay(this).setCurrent(myTauntBox);
    }
  }

//-------------------------------------------------------
//  message methods

/**
 * Displays the remote player's message as an Alert.
 */
public void displayTauntMessage(String taunt) {
  Alert tauntScreen = new Alert("message");
  tauntScreen.setString(taunt);
  Display.getDisplay(this).setCurrent(tauntScreen,
      myCanvas);
}

/**
 * Gets the message that the user has entered for the remote
 * player, if any.  Then clears the text.
```

```
  */
  public String getTauntMessage() {
    String retVal = myTauntBox.getString();
    myTauntBox.setString(null);
    return retVal;
  }

  /**
   * Manually set the taunt message to tell the remote
   * player that he has won.
   */
  public void setWinTaunt() {
    myTauntBox.setString("You Win!");
  }

  //-----------------------------------------------------------
  //  error methods

  /**
   * Converts an exception to a message and displays
   * the message.
   */
  void errorMsg(Exception e) {
    e.printStackTrace();
    if(e.getMessage() == null) {
      errorMsg(e.getClass().getName());
    } else {
      errorMsg(e.getMessage());
    }
  }

  /**
   * Displays an error message alert if something goes wrong.
   */
  void errorMsg(String msg) {
    Alert errorAlert = new Alert("error",
                                 msg, null, AlertType.ERROR);
    errorAlert.setCommandListener(this);
    errorAlert.setTimeout(Alert.FOREVER);
    Display.getDisplay(this).setCurrent(errorAlert);
  }

}
```

There's nothing really new in this class. The only real point to note is that I've added an extra command to the Canvas to allow the user to go to the TextField to enter a "taunt" message for the other player at any time.

Summary

So far you've seen the two most common protocols—HTTP and SMS—as they're typically used in a professional game. At this point you're almost ready to run a game that uses network communications—but not quite. Since any network communications may cost the user money, your game has to get permission to send and receive messages. To find out how to get networking permissions, see Chapter 8.

CHAPTER 7

■■■

Advanced Messaging and Data Access

The same programming techniques you use for HTTP and SMS can be applied to a lot of other types of communications and data storage applications to create a richer game—more exciting as well as more profitable. On top of MIDP, many devices typically have additional APIs built in that you'll want to put to good use.

Using Bluetooth

Bluetooth is a popular technology that allows devices to communicate with other nearby devices without being cabled together. And thanks to the Bluetooth API (JSR 82), you can access your device's Bluetooth capabilities from Java. This immediately makes me think of one thing: multi-player games!

With Bluetooth, you have the chance to create a game where players are competing in real time, which you can't do with slower technologies like SMS or routing communications through a central server via HTTP. Still there can be some lag, so it's a good idea to test some concepts on target devices before investing a lot of time and money on a multiplayer game where it's critical that the players receive each other's moves instantaneously. Writing a game where the players take turns is always a safe bet, so for this chapter I'll show you how to take the Checkers example from the previous chapter and convert it to Bluetooth.

Bluetooth is a little more challenging and complicated to program than SMS. Part of the reason for that is that SMS uses the operators' standard way of routing communications to a handset. With SMS, you find the right destination by typing in the right phone number. And it's the same phone number you'd use to route other communications to that device. So you don't have to reinvent the wheel to find, identify, and authenticate the handset you're looking for.

Bluetooth allows you to find all active, Bluetooth-enabled devices within range and see what kind of services they offer. Each server offering a Bluetooth service publishes a set of detailed service records describing the services available. So you have a fair amount of work on the server side creating useful descriptions and on the client side reading the descriptions and choosing the right service on the right device. Add to that the fact that you have the option of choosing a plain socket type connection or discrete packets, different authentication and/or encryption schemes, and even object-oriented communications using the Java Object Exchange Protocol (OBEX), and you have practically unlimited potential to customize (and complicate) your application according to your needs.

In the Checkers example (as with most game applications) you don't really need all the bells and whistles. It's reasonable to assume—since Bluetooth is a protocol for local communications—that the two players are in the same room together and have verbally agreed to start up a game of checkers on their handsets. The Checkers game is fundamentally a peer-to-peer type game, but Bluetooth is a client-server protocol, so this game includes both the client-side code and the server-side code. It starts with a screen where the user can choose whether his handset will be acting as the client or as the server (the first player selects server and the second client as seen in Figure 7-1).

Figure 7-1. *When the Bluetooth Checkers game begins, one player chooses to act as the server and the other chooses to act as the client.*

The first hurdle is writing the code so that the two devices will find each other instead of finding other random Bluetooth devices and services. Fortunately—with simple services like this one—all you really need is a Universally Unique Identifier (UUID). You can create your own UUID (in both Linux and Windows) using the uuidgen command. Then on the server side, all you need to do is construct your Bluetooth URL using your UUID and open the connection and wait for clients to call you up.

For the Checkers game, the server URL looks like this:

```
btspp://localhost:2BBC2D287C8C11DBA1500040F45842EF;name=Checkers;authorize=false
```

The `btspp` indicates that I'd like to use the Bluetooth streaming (socket-like) protocol; the `localhost` makes me a server; then I add on my UUID (what the `uuidgen -t` command returned with the hyphens removed), then some attributes (the application name and the fact that I don't want to require authorization).

Opening this connection creates the corresponding service record, which you can get a handle to and add attributes to if you like. The WTK's BluetoothDemo shows a good example of how to add additional descriptive attributes. The BluetoothDemo has a server that makes images available for Bluetooth clients to download, and there you can see the programmer has added a custom attribute to give the name of the image being offered. As you can see in the `ServiceRecord` JavaDoc, there are a number of common standard attributes that you can use as well. The attributes aren't too complicated to use—you just need to keep in mind that different attributes' values can be of different types, so the values are wrapped in `DataElements` that allow you to handle all the different types of values in a consistent way.

Once your server is up and running, the next thing is to program the client to find it and connect to it. Basically, all you need to do is grab a handle to the local `DiscoveryAgent` and send it off in search of devices and services. It does its work on its own thread while looking for them, then it calls the assigned `DiscoveryListener` when it's done.

Discovery is a two-step procedure. First you gather a list of devices, and then you search the devices for the service you want. (Since I didn't bother with any special service record attributes on the server side, when I started searching my device list for services I sent a null `attrSet` to the `searchServices()` method.) Note that if you're writing a program where the client frequently reconnects to the same set of known servers, you can optimize discovery by caching a list of known devices. Listing 7-1 shows what the discovery code looks like in practice.

Listing 7-1. *BluetoothManager.java*

```java
package net.frog_parrot.net;

import java.io.*;
import java.util.Vector;

import javax.microedition.io.*;

import javax.bluetooth.*;

import net.frog_parrot.checkers.MoveManager;

/**
 * This class keeps track of transferring local and
 * remote moves from one player to the other.
 *
 * @author Carol Hamer
 */
public class BluetoothManager extends Thread
    implements DiscoveryListener {
```

```
//-------------------------------------------------------
//  static fields

/**
 * The int to signal that the game is to begin.
 */
public static final byte START_GAME_FLAG = -4;

/**
 * The byte to signal that the game is to end.
 */
public static final byte END_GAME_FLAG = -3;

/**
 * The byte to signal the end of a turn.
 */
public static final byte END_TURN_FLAG = -2;

/**
 * The byte to signal the remote connection has
 * been closed.
 */
public static final byte EOF_FLAG = -1;

/**
 * A possible connection mode.
 */
public static final byte SERVER_MODE = 0;

/**
 * A possible connection mode.
 */
public static final byte CLIENT_MODE = 1;

/**
 * The protocol string for the bluetooth stream protocol.
 */
public static final String BLUETOOTH_PROTOCOL = "btspp://";

/**
 * The string that uniquely identifies this Bluetooth service:
 */
private static final String CHECKERS_UUID
    = "2bbc2d287c8c11dba1500040f45842ef";

/**
 * The user-friendly name of the service:
```

```java
    */
private static final String CHECKERS_NAME = "Checkers";

//---------------------------------------------------------
//  game instance fields

/**
 * Whether the MIDlet will be acting as a client or as a
 * server for this round.
 */
private int myMode;

/**
 * The results of the client search for available services.
 */
private int myDiscoveryType;

/**
 * The results of the client search for available devices.
 */
private Vector myRemoteDevices = new Vector();

/**
 * The results of the client search for available devices.
 */
private ServiceRecord myRemoteServiceRecord;

/**
 * Whether to break out of the communications loop and
 * end the game.
 */
private boolean myShouldStop;

/**
 * The class that directs the data from the communications
 * module to game logic module and vice versa.
 */
private MoveManager myManager;

/**
 * The instance of the BlueTooth UUID class that is needed to
 * make the connection.
 */
private UUID myUUID = new UUID(CHECKERS_UUID, false);

/**
 * The network connection.
```

```java
 */
private StreamConnection myStreamConnection;

/**
 * The corresponding input stream.
 */
private InputStream myInputStream;

/**
 * The corresponding output stream.
 */
private OutputStream myOutputStream;

//-----------------------------------------------------------
//  data exchange instance fields

/**
 * The data from the local player that is to
 * be sent to the opponent.
 */
private byte[] myMove;

//-----------------------------------------------------------
//  lifecycle

/**
 * Start the processes to send and receive messages.
 */
public void setMode(int mode, MoveManager manager) {
  myManager = manager;
  myMode = mode;
  start();
}

/**
 * Start the thread that communicates with the remote
 * player.
 */
public void run() {
  try {
    if(myMode == SERVER_MODE) {
      serverRun();
    } else {
      clientRun();
    }
  } catch(Exception e) {
    myManager.errorMsg("failed: " + e.getMessage());
```

```
    }
  }

  /**
   * Stop the receiver.
   * This method is called alone from pauseApp or destroyApp
   * since sending one last message is too time-consuming.
   */
  public synchronized void shutDown() {
    myShouldStop = true;
    notify();
  }

  /**
   * Close all of the streams.
   */
  public void cleanUp() {
    try {
      if(myInputStream == null) {
        myInputStream.close();
      }
      if(myOutputStream == null) {
        myOutputStream.close();
      }
      if(myStreamConnection == null) {
        myStreamConnection.close();
      }
    } catch(Exception e) {
    }
  }

  /**
   * This is called when the game is in server mode and has been
   * contacted by a remote client player.  This triggers the
   * game logic to let the local player make the first move.
   */
  public void receiveInvitation() {
    int state = myManager.getState();
    if(state == MoveManager.NOT_STARTED) {
      myManager.receiveInvitation();
    }
  }

  //----------------------------------------------------------
  // server methods.
```

```
/**
 * Perform the initial steps to start up a very simple
 * server connection that accepts only one client connection.
 */
void serverRun() {
  StreamConnectionNotifier notifier;
  try {
    // get a handle to the local device and set it
    // to accept client connections:
    LocalDevice localDevice = LocalDevice.getLocalDevice();
    // GIAC is the standard general discovery mode:
    localDevice.setDiscoverable(DiscoveryAgent.GIAC);

    // create the URL and the server connection
    StringBuffer buff = new StringBuffer(BLUETOOTH_PROTOCOL);
    // setting the host to localhost opens this as a
    // server connection.
    buff.append("localhost").append(':');
    buff.append(myUUID.toString());
    buff.append(";name=");
    buff.append(CHECKERS_NAME);
    buff.append(";authorize=false");

    // Since this is a server connection, Connector.open
    // returns a connection notifier rather than a
    // simple connection
    notifier
        = (StreamConnectionNotifier)Connector.open(buff.toString());

    // accept exactly one client connection:
    myStreamConnection = notifier.acceptAndOpen();
    myInputStream = myStreamConnection.openInputStream();
    // the client player starts by sending the start game
    // flag, triggering the server player to take a turn:
    byte[] oneByte = new byte[1];
    myInputStream.read(oneByte);
    myManager.receiveInvitation();
     // we don't want any more clients to try to connect,
    // so we close up the notifier:
    notifier.close();
    // Even though the stream is closed, it's cleaner to
    // set the server to "not discoverable" so further
    // clients don't query this service and attempt to connect:
    localDevice.setDiscoverable(DiscoveryAgent.NOT_DISCOVERABLE);
    myOutputStream = myStreamConnection.openOutputStream();
    runGame(myOutputStream, myInputStream);
  } catch (IOException e) {
```

```
      myManager.errorMsg("failed: " + e.getMessage());
    }
}


//----------------------------------------------------------
//  client methods.

/**
 * Perform the initial steps to start up a very simple
 * client connection.
 */
void clientRun() {
  try {
    // start looking for available Bluetooth services:
    LocalDevice localDevice = LocalDevice.getLocalDevice();
    DiscoveryAgent discoveryAgent = localDevice.getDiscoveryAgent();
    // Set this as the discovery listener, then wait for
    // the inquiryCompleted call:
    discoveryAgent.startInquiry(DiscoveryAgent.GIAC, this);
    synchronized(this) {
      wait();
    }
    if(myDiscoveryType == INQUIRY_COMPLETED) {
      // now for each device, we search for services:
      for(int i = 0; i < myRemoteDevices.size(); i++) {
        RemoteDevice rd = (RemoteDevice)myRemoteDevices.elementAt(i);
        // we assume that the user has arranged to have
        // exactly one player in range, so we search until
        // we find a checkers service and stop:
        UUID[] uuids = new UUID[2];
        // this indicates socket communications:
        uuids[0] = new UUID(0x1101);
        // and this is the Checkers service specifically:
        uuids[1] = new UUID(CHECKERS_UUID, false);
        // The return value of the search call is an id int
        // that can be used to cancel the search if
        // something goes wrong:
        int id = discoveryAgent.searchServices(null, uuids,
                      rd, this);
        // now wait to see if we found the service:
        synchronized(this) {
          wait();
        }
        if(myRemoteServiceRecord != null) {
          break;
        }
      }
```

```
      if(myRemoteServiceRecord != null) {
        // now let's open the connection:
        String url = myRemoteServiceRecord.getConnectionURL(
            ServiceRecord.NOAUTHENTICATE_NOENCRYPT, false);
        myStreamConnection = (StreamConnection)Connector.open(url);
        myOutputStream = myStreamConnection.openOutputStream();
        byte[] oneByte = new byte[1];
        oneByte[0] = (byte)START_GAME_FLAG;
        myOutputStream.write(oneByte);
        myManager.foundOpponent();
        myInputStream = myStreamConnection.openInputStream();
        runGame(myOutputStream, myInputStream);
      } else {
        myManager.errorMsg("failed to find remote player");
      }
    } else {
      myManager.errorMsg("failed to find remote player");
    }
  } catch (Exception e) {
    myManager.errorMsg("failed: " + e.getMessage());
  }
}

/**
 * Implementation of DiscoveryListener.
 */
public void deviceDiscovered(RemoteDevice device, DeviceClass dc) {
  myRemoteDevices.addElement(device);
}

/**
 * Implementation of DiscoveryListener.
 */
public void inquiryCompleted(int discoveryType) {
  myDiscoveryType = discoveryType;
  synchronized(this) {
    notify();
  }
}

/**
 * Implementation of DiscoveryListener.
 * For a given remote device, find its services.
 */
public synchronized void servicesDiscovered(int id,
    ServiceRecord[] sr) {
  if(myRemoteServiceRecord == null) {
```

```
      myRemoteServiceRecord = sr[0];
      notify();
    }
  }


  /**
   * Implementation of DiscoveryListener.
   * For a given remote device, find its services.
   */
  public synchronized void serviceSearchCompleted(int id, int respCode) {
    // if none were found, notify that the search for services
    // on this device is done.
    if(myRemoteServiceRecord == null) {
      notify();
    }
  }


  //----------------------------------------------------------
  //  main game method

  /**
   * This is the main loop that controls the game play
   * back and forth.
   */
  void runGame(OutputStream os, InputStream is) throws IOException {
    byte[] fourBytes = new byte[4];
    while(! myShouldStop) {
      int state = myManager.getState();
      if(state == MoveManager.LOCAL_TURN) {
        try {
          synchronized(this) {
            wait();
          }
        } catch(InterruptedException e) {
        }
        try {
          if(myMove != null) {
            os.write(myMove);
          }
        } catch(IOException e) {
          // if we can't write anymore, the remote
          // player has probably closed the connection:
          myManager.errorMsg("remote player has quit");
        }
        myMove = null;
      } else if(state == MoveManager.REMOTE_TURN) {
        byte moveData = (byte)is.read();
```

```
      if((moveData == END_GAME_FLAG)
          || (moveData == EOF_FLAG)) {
        myShouldStop = true;
        myManager.receiveGameOver();
      } else if (moveData == END_TURN_FLAG) {
        myManager.endRemoteTurn();
      } else {
        fourBytes[0] = moveData;
        for(int i = 1; i < 4; i++) {
          moveData = (byte)is.read();
          fourBytes[i] = moveData;
        }
        myManager.receiveRemoteMove(fourBytes);
      }
    } else {
      myShouldStop = true;
    }
  }
  cleanUp();
}


//----------------------------------------------------------
//   sending methods.

/**
 * Send the message to the other
 * player that this player has quit.
 */
public synchronized void sendGameOver() {
  myMove = new byte[1];
  myMove[0] = END_GAME_FLAG;
  notify();
}

/**
 * Records the local move in a byte array to prepare it
 * to be sent to the remote player.
 */
public void setLocalMove(byte[] move) {
  if(myMove == null) {
    myMove = new byte[5];
    System.arraycopy(move, 0, myMove, 0, 4);
    myMove[4] = END_TURN_FLAG;
  } else {
    // here we're dealing with the case of a
    // series of jumps.  This isn't the typical case, so
    // it shouldn't be too inefficient to just
```

```
      // create a new, larger array each time
      // we enlarge the move payload.
      byte[] newMove = new byte[myMove.length + 4];
      System.arraycopy(myMove, 0, newMove, 0, myMove.length);
      System.arraycopy(move, 0, newMove, myMove.length - 1, 4);
      newMove[newMove.length - 1] = END_TURN_FLAG;
      myMove = newMove;
    }
  }

  /**
   * Sends the current local move to the remote player.
   */
  public synchronized void sendLocalMove() {
    notify();
  }

}
```

Here all the communications code is in the same class—code for connecting, sending, and interpreting moves—unlike with the SMS Checkers example.

The first step is to select either server or client mode, and then the setMode() method starts a new thread to open the correct type of connection.

In the server case, as you can see in the serverRun() method, this is pretty simple. Just construct the URL, open the connection, and wait. In typical server fashion, the Notifier. acceptAndOpen method blocks until a client connection is found, which can be passed along to the runGame() method. If this were a game where multiple players were connecting to a central player, then the acceptAndOpen() method would be placed in a loop to await more connections, but since a Checkers player only needs one opponent, we clean up the server and registry before proceeding.

The client case is a little trickier because we need to use a DiscoveryAgent. Since the Checkers game knows exactly what service it's looking for (identified by its UUID), it seems like it would be nice to have a simple, blocking method you could call to say "go out and find me a server for this service or return null if there is none." Actually, there is such a method: selectService(). However, the implementation of this method varies in quality from one platform to the next, so the surest bet is to go through the little dance of wait and notify with the DiscoveryListener that queries first for devices and then queries each device for the desired service, as illustrated in the method clientRun() and the four DiscoveryListener methods following it (in Listing 7-1).

Since the Checkers game itself is logically a peer-to-peer type game, once the client and server have found each other, both sides can use the same runGame() method to send and receive moves. As with the SMS Checkers example, the player who initiated the game (in this case, the server player) goes first and is presented with a checkerboard as soon as the remote player connects. Then runGame() method handles the communications for the local and remote turns first by waiting for the player to set the move and send it, then by interpreting the remote player's move when it comes in.

There are a few additional changes in other classes to convert the SMS Checkers game to a Bluetooth Checkers game. First, I've eliminated the "taunt" message feature entirely since it's not useful for players who are in the same room together. So the Checkers MIDlet starts with a List screen offering the player the choice of "client" or "server" instead of prompting the user to set the remote player's phone number and a message. Another simplification is that I've changed it to just quit and clean up in the case of a pause. It would be possible to try to reconnect and resume the game, but in the Bluetooth case—where the players are constantly coupled on a socket-like connection—this adds a mountain of additional complexity, which obscures the main points of the example.

Since the communications code was pretty well isolated, the game didn't need any major refactoring. However, there were little changes throughout the Checkers (MIDlet) class and the MoveManager class, so I'm including them as Listings 7-2 and 7-3 for completeness. The two remaining classes for this example are the same as they appear in Listings 6-8 and 6-9.

Listing 7-2. *Checkers.java*

```
package net.frog_parrot.checkers;

import javax.microedition.midlet.*;
import javax.microedition.lcdui.*;
import java.util.Vector;

import net.frog_parrot.net.*;
/**
 * This is the main class of the checkers game.
 *
 * @author Carol Hamer
 */
public class Checkers extends MIDlet implements CommandListener {

    //-------------------------------------------------------
    //    game object fields

    /**
     * The canvas that the checkerboard is drawn on.
     */
    private CheckersCanvas myCanvas;

    /**
     * The class that handles turn taking and communication.
     */
    private MoveManager myMoveManager;

    /**
     * The List that allows the user to choose
     * between server mode and client mode.
     */
    private List myModeList;
```

```
//---------------------------------------------------------
//    command fields

/**
 * The button to exit the game.
 */
private Command myExitCommand = new Command("Exit", Command.EXIT, 99);

/**
 * The button to send the initial invitation.
 */
private Command myOkCommand = new Command("Ok", Command.OK, 0);

//-----------------------------------------------------
//    initialization and data

/**
 * Initialize the canvas and the commands.
 */
public Checkers() {
  try {
    // create the canvas and set up the commands:
    myCanvas = new CheckersCanvas(Display.getDisplay(this));
    myCanvas.addCommand(myExitCommand);
    myCanvas.setCommandListener(this);
    CheckersGame game = myCanvas.getGame();
    myMoveManager = new MoveManager(this, myCanvas, game);
    game.setMoveManager(myMoveManager);
    String[] modes = { "server mode", "client mode"
    };
    myModeList = new List("Choose Mode", Choice.IMPLICIT,
        modes, null);
    myModeList.addCommand(myExitCommand);
    myModeList.setCommandListener(this);
  } catch(Exception e) {
    // if there's an error during creation,
    // display it as an alert.
    errorMsg(e);
  }
}


//------------------------------------------------------------------
//   implementation of MIDlet
// these methods may be called by the application management
// software at any time, so we always check fields for null
// before calling methods on them.
```

```java
/**
 * Start the application.
 */
public void startApp() {
  // This version doesn't come back after a pause, so
  // we assume this is the initial startup:
  Display.getDisplay(this).setCurrent(myModeList);
}

/**
 * Throw out the garbage.
 */
public void destroyApp(boolean unconditional)
    throws MIDletStateChangeException {
  // tell the communicator to send the end game
  // message to the other player and then disconnect:
  if(myMoveManager != null) {
    myMoveManager.shutDown();
  }
  // throw the larger game objects in the garbage:
  myMoveManager = null;
  myCanvas = null;
}

/**
 * End the program now.
 */
public void quit() {
  try {
    destroyApp(false);
    notifyDestroyed();
  } catch (MIDletStateChangeException ex) {
  }
}

/**
 * Pause the game.
 * Because of the complexity of restarting a game in course,
 * this method merely ends the game.
 */
public void pauseApp() {
  quit();
}
```

```
//-------------------------------------------------------------------
//  implementation of CommandListener

/*
 * Respond to a command issued on the Canvas.
 */
public void commandAction(Command c, Displayable s) {
  if((c == myExitCommand) || (c == Alert.DISMISS_COMMAND)) {
    if((myMoveManager != null)
        && (myMoveManager.getState() != MoveManager.NOT_STARTED)) {
      myMoveManager.endGame();
    } else {
      quit();
    }
  } else if(s == myModeList) {
    myMoveManager.setMode(myModeList.getSelectedIndex());
    Display.getDisplay(this).setCurrent(myCanvas);
  }
}

//---------------------------------------------------------
//  error methods

/**
 * Converts an exception to a message and displays
 * the message.
 */
void errorMsg(Exception e) {
  e.printStackTrace();
  if(e.getMessage() == null) {
    errorMsg(e.getClass().getName());
  } else {
    errorMsg(e.getMessage());
  }
}

/**
 * Displays an error message alert if something goes wrong.
 */
void errorMsg(String msg) {
  Alert errorAlert = new Alert("error",
                               msg, null, AlertType.ERROR);
  errorAlert.setCommandListener(this);
  errorAlert.setTimeout(Alert.FOREVER);
  Display.getDisplay(this).setCurrent(errorAlert);
}

}
```

Listing 7-3. *MoveManager.java*

```java
package net.frog_parrot.checkers;

import java.io.*;

import net.frog_parrot.net.BluetoothManager;

/**
 * This class keeps track of transferring local and
 * remote moves from one player to the other.
 *
 * @author Carol Hamer
 */
public class MoveManager {

  //----------------------------------------------------------
  //  game instance fields

  /**
   * The MIDlet subclass, used to set the Display
   * in the case where an error message needs to be sent.
   */
  private Checkers myCheckers;

  /**
   * The Canvas subclass, used to set the Display
   * in the case where an error message needs to be sent.
   */
  private CheckersCanvas myCanvas;

  /**
   * The game logic class that we send the opponent's
   * moves to.
   */
  private CheckersGame myGame;

  /**
   * The class that performs the actual network connections.
   */
  private BluetoothManager myBluetoothManager;

  //----------------------------------------------------------
  //  state fields

  /**
   * A possible game state.
```

```
 */
public static final int NOT_STARTED = 0;


/**
 * A possible game state.
 */
public static final int LOCAL_TURN = 2;


/**
 * A possible game state.
 */
public static final int REMOTE_TURN = 4;


/**
 * A possible game state.
 */
public static final int GAME_OVER = 5;

/**
 * The code for the state the game is currently in.
 */
private int myState = NOT_STARTED;


//----------------------------------------------------------
//  lifecycle

/**
 * Constructor initializes the handles back to other
 * game objects.
 */
MoveManager(Checkers checkers, CheckersCanvas canvas,
            CheckersGame game) {
  myCheckers = checkers;
  myCanvas = canvas;
  myGame = game;
  myBluetoothManager = new BluetoothManager();
}

/**
 * Stop the receiver.
 * This method is called alone from destroyApp
 * since sending one last message is too time-consuming.
 */
public void shutDown() {
  myState = GAME_OVER;
  if(myBluetoothManager != null) {
    myBluetoothManager.shutDown();
```

```
  }
}

/**
 * Gets the current game state.
 */
public int getState() {
  return(myState);
}

/**
 * End the game with an error screen.
 */
public void errorMsg(String msg) {
  myCheckers.errorMsg(msg);
  myBluetoothManager.cleanUp();
}

//--------------------------------------------------------
//   sending methods

/**
 * Set mode.
 * This method triggers the BluetoothManager to start seeking
 * a remote player, either in client mode or server mode.
 */
public void setMode(int mode) {
  myBluetoothManager.setMode(mode, this);
  myCanvas.setWaitScreen(true);
  myCanvas.start();
  myCanvas.repaint();
  myCanvas.serviceRepaints();
}

/**
 * This is called when the client player finds a server
 * player.
 */
public void foundOpponent() {
  myState = REMOTE_TURN;
}

/**
 * This is called when the player moves a piece.
 */
synchronized void move(byte sourceX, byte sourceY, byte destinationX,
                  byte destinationY) {
```

```
  byte[] move = new byte[4];
  move[0] = sourceX;
  move[1] = sourceY;
  move[2] = destinationX;
  move[3] = destinationY;
  myState = LOCAL_TURN;
  myBluetoothManager.setLocalMove(move);
}

/**
 * This is called when the local player's turn is over.
 */
synchronized void endTurn() {
  myState = REMOTE_TURN;
  myBluetoothManager.sendLocalMove();
}

/**
 * Stop the game entirely.  Notify the remote player that
 * the user is exiting the game.
 */
synchronized void endGame() {
  myBluetoothManager.shutDown();
  if(myState != GAME_OVER) {
    myState = GAME_OVER;
    myBluetoothManager.sendGameOver();
    myCanvas.repaint();
    myCanvas.serviceRepaints();
  } else {
    myCheckers.quit();
  }
}

/**
 * End the game because the local player has no more moves.
 */
void loseGame() {
  endGame();
}

/**
 * This method is called by the message sending utility
 * to indicate that the move has been sent.
 */
public void doneSending() {
  if(myState == GAME_OVER) {
    myCheckers.quit();
```

```java
    } else {
      myState = REMOTE_TURN;
    }
  }

  //----------------------------------------------------------
  //  receiving methods

  /**
   * Receive the game invitation message.
   */
  public synchronized void receiveInvitation() {
    myState = LOCAL_TURN;
    myCanvas.setWaitScreen(false);
    myCanvas.start();
    myCanvas.repaint();
    myCanvas.serviceRepaints();
  }

  /**
   * Interpret one move by the remote player.
   */
  public synchronized void receiveRemoteMove(byte[] fourBytes) {
    myState = REMOTE_TURN;
    myGame.moveOpponent(fourBytes);
  }

  /**
   * Set the game to ended upon receiving the end game
   * signal from the remote player.
   */
  public synchronized void receiveGameOver() {
    myState = GAME_OVER;
    myBluetoothManager.shutDown();
    myCanvas.repaint();
    myCanvas.serviceRepaints();
  }

  /**
   * Receive the signal that the remote player is done
   * moving (no more jumps possible).
   */
  public synchronized void endRemoteTurn() {
    myState = LOCAL_TURN;
    myGame.endOpponentTurn();
    myCanvas.setWaitScreen(false);
    myCanvas.repaint();
```

```
    myCanvas.serviceRepaints();
  }

}
```

The last thing to note is that since we don't use the push registry, we don't need a special push registry attribute in the JAD file. The only thing to add is the request for permission to use Bluetooth, as explained in the next chapter.

COMMUNICATIONS AND BUSINESS STRATEGY

Both of the Checkers examples in this book involve players finding opponents on their own and connecting directly to each other. This kind of multiplayer experience is a nice perk that may make your game more fun (and hence more popular). However, unless you've been hired by an operator to increase SMS traffic, you won't make money off it the way you can if you route your communications through a central server that monitors every interaction.

There are a number of standard ways of earning money through having your game call up your server: selling additional boards and features (see the "Using Secure Connections While Selling Your Game" sidebar in Chapter 8), sending ads along with new content, or charging a fee for a subscription to your service, to name a few of the most popular. These techniques apply to single-player games as well as to multiplayer games, but multiplayer games have the advantage that the user is motivated to interact with your server more often.

Hosting an online multiplayer game doesn't just benefit the developer (or whoever it is collecting the money), though; it also makes it easier for the player to find opponents whenever she feels like playing instead of having to wait until real-life friends are interested. These days people expect the Internet to connect them with other people with similar interests, and you can be there to provide the service. A typical fun way to do that is to have a game where all the players are wandering around the same imaginary universe simultaneously and may encounter one another.

Another popular strategy to get users hooked on your game is to allow them the opportunity to upload their own content. Something as simple as providing a tool for the user to design a character or scene by combining choices from a series of graphical menus allows players to create something personalized and fun that they'll want to share with friends. You can get a boost by tying your gaming community in with an existing Internet community (by creating the mobile version of an existing online game, with permission of course), or you can build your own community from scratch—both strategies have been shown to be successful.

When it comes to collecting the payment, it's easy for even a small-time operation to set up a website and bill through PayPal (again, see the "Using Secure Connections While Selling Your Game" sidebar in Chapter 8 for more details). I used to recommend distributing games for free and then asking the users nicely to send in money (I know people who have made money doing that), but these days people expect that everything you download off the Internet is free. So I recommend attracting users by offering something fun for free, and once they're interested, sell them something even better.

Using the Personal Information Management API

Another useful and widely supported JSR you'll want to have a look at is JSR 75: the PDA Optional Packages. This JSR is actually a set of two separate APIs: the Personal Information

Management API and the File Connection API (covered in the next section). The two APIs aren't that closely related to each other except for the fact that they both allow you to access parts of the device's memory that you can't normally access.

The PIM API allows you to access the user's contact list, calendar, and to-do list. The most interesting item for games is the list of contacts and their phone numbers. In the "Communications and Business Strategy" sidebar, I focused on the value you add by helping players find opponents. But the user's own contacts are obviously a valuable source of potential players for your game.

It's quite simple to present the user with a menu of his own contacts to choose an opponent from—that's what you'll see in the Checkers Plus example in a moment. And if the player's friend doesn't already have your game installed on his handset, it's an opportunity rather than a setback. It's easy to write a little utility that steps the user through the process of sending a text SMS to his friend containing a link to where the friend can download your game. To send a message to the phone's standard inbox (instead of to an application), all you need to do is leave off the port number in the sending URL.

Whether you want to write to the user's contact list or just read from it, you'll need the user's permission. (See the next chapter for more on permissions.) This is largely to prevent your application from doing unethical things such as sending the contents of the user's address book back to your server for the purpose of creating SMS spamming lists. It is possible to do that if you can convince the user to give your application one access to the contact list and then one HTTP connection back to your site. However, I highly recommend against this practice if you're at all interested in having a quality product and satisfied customers.

The PIM API is designed to make it easy to access the contact information in a uniform way across a range of platforms that may be storing the underlying data in various different ways. So the record objects have query methods to allow the application to discover which fields are supported. The API has a vast selection of named constants to allow you to find what you want.

A typical game application would be to create a list of names and phone numbers for the user to choose from, so it's just a question of using the static `PIM.getInstance()` method to get a handle to the contact list and then checking each item in the list for the desired fields, as you can see in Listing 7-4.

Listing 7-4. *PIMRunner.java*

```
package net.frog_parrot.net;

import java.util.Enumeration;
import java.util.Vector;
import javax.microedition.pim.*;

/**
 * A simple PIM utility to load a list of contacts.
 */
public class PIMRunner extends Thread {

  /**
   * A callback listener for this
   * class to call when the PIM list is filled.
```

```java
  */
ContactListener myListener;

/**
 * The list of name fields to check to try to find the name
 * to display to the user.
 */
int[] NAME_INDICES = {
  Contact.NAME,
  Contact.FORMATTED_NAME,
  Contact.NAME_GIVEN,
  Contact.NAME_FAMILY,
};

/**
 * The constructor just sets the callback listener for this
 * class to call when the PIM list is filled.
 */
public PIMRunner(ContactListener listener) {
  myListener = listener;
}

/**
 * The method that fills the data fields.
 */
public void run() {
  ContactList addressbook = null;
  Contact contact = null;
  Enumeration items = null;
  Vector names = new Vector();
  Vector phoneNumbers = new Vector();
  try {
    addressbook = (ContactList)(PIM.getInstance(
        ).openPIMList(PIM.CONTACT_LIST, PIM.READ_ONLY));
    items = addressbook.items();
  } catch(Exception e) {
    // if the addressbook can't be opened, then we're done.
    myListener.setContactList(names, phoneNumbers);
  }
  // Now load the contents of the addressbook:
  while(items.hasMoreElements()) {
    try {
      contact = (Contact)(items.nextElement());
      // only continue if the contact has at least one
      // phone number listed:
      int phoneNumCount = contact.countValues(Contact.TEL);
      if(phoneNumCount > 0) {
        String phoneNum = null;
```

```
      for(int i = 0; i < phoneNumCount; i++) {
        int attr = contact.getAttributes(Contact.TEL, i);
        if(i == 0 || attr == Contact.ATTR_MOBILE) {
          phoneNum = contact.getString(Contact.TEL, i);
        }
      }
      // now we assume that this handset lists all
      // mobile phone numbers with the MOBILE attribute,
      // so if we didn't find a mobile number, we skip
      // this contact:
      if(phoneNum != null) {
        // now try to find the name.
        // since we don't know which name fields this
        // handset supports, we keep trying until we
        // find something:
        int fieldIndex = -1;
        for(int i = 0; i < NAME_INDICES.length; i++) {
          if(addressbook.isSupportedField(NAME_INDICES[i])
              && contact.countValues(NAME_INDICES[i]) > 0) {
            fieldIndex = NAME_INDICES[i];
            break;
          }
        }
        // we've found a contact with a name and
        // a mobile number, so we add it to the list:
        if(fieldIndex != -1) {
          // logically each type of name field will have
          // only one entry, so we take the first one,
          // of index 0:
          names.addElement(contact.getString(fieldIndex, 0));
          phoneNumbers.addElement(phoneNum);
        }
      }
    }
  } catch(Exception e) {
    e.printStackTrace();
    // if an individual contact provokes an exception,
    // we skip it and move on.
  }
} // while(items.hasMoreElements())
myListener.setContactList(names, phoneNumbers);
  }
}
```

As with the communications code, this code should be run in its own thread. The memory access shouldn't be too time-consuming (although on some platforms it is), but there's also a possibility of the initial PIMList access method blocking while the AMS takes over with a system screen asking the user for permission. And if the same thread that should be handling the system screen is stuck on calling this method, the handset will crash. If the user fails to give permission (or in case the search for names and phone numbers fails for any other reason), it's good to maintain the option of allowing the user to type in a phone number as a backup.

The PIMRunner class (Listing 7-4) can be added to the SMS Checkers example from Chapter 6 to create the "Checkers Plus" game by replacing the Checkers.java class in Listing 6-10 with the new version in Listing 7-5. This new version gives the player the option of selecting an opponent from the contact list (or entering the opponent's number manually as in the original version of the Checkers game), and then displays the list of contacts as a GUI List (see Figures 7-2 and 7-3).

Figure 7-2. *The user has the option of selecting an opponent from his address book or entering the opponent's number manually.*

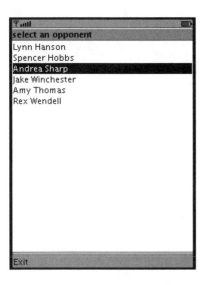

Figure 7-3. *The user is presented with the list of names from his address book.*

Looking at Listing 7-5, you can see one strategy for handling the threading issues regarding when to start the PIMRunner thread and how to synchronize it.

Listing 7-5. *Checkers.java*

```java
package net.frog_parrot.net;

import javax.microedition.midlet.*;
import javax.microedition.lcdui.*;
import java.util.Vector;

import net.frog_parrot.net.*;
/**
 * This is the main class of the checkers game.
 *
 * @author Carol Hamer
 */
public class Checkers extends MIDlet implements CommandListener,
    ContactListener {

  //-------------------------------------------------------
  //     game object fields

  /**
   * The canvas that the checkerboard is drawn on.
   */
  private CheckersCanvas myCanvas;

  /**
   * The class that handles turn taking and communication.
   */
  private MoveManager myMoveManager;

  /**
   * The helper thread to load the contact list.
   */
  private PIMRunner myPIMRunner;

  /**
   * The field that takes in the remote player's phone number.
   */
  private TextField myPhoneNumberField;

  /**
   * The vector listing the contacts' phone numbers.
   */
  private Vector myPhoneNumbers;
```

```
/**
 * The list of the user's initial choices.
 */
private List myStartList;

/**
 * The form where the user can enter an opponent manually.
 */
private Form myInvitationForm;

/**
 * The menu screen where the user selects a friend's number
 * from a list.
 */
private List myContactMenu;

/**
 * The screen where the local player enters a message for
 * the remote player.
 */
private TextBox myTauntBox;

//--------------------------------------------------------
//    command fields

/**
 * The button to exit the game.
 */
private Command myExitCommand = new Command("Exit", Command.EXIT, 99);

/**
 * The button to cancel a message in progress.
 */
private Command myCancelCommand = new Command("Cancel", Command.CANCEL, 99);

/**
 * The button to send the initial invitation.
 */
private Command myOkCommand = new Command("Ok", Command.OK, 0);

/**
 * The button to enter a message for the remote player.
 */
private Command myTauntCommand = new Command("add message",
    Command.SCREEN, 1);
```

```
//----------------------------------------------------------
//    initialization and data

/**
 * Initialize the canvas and the commands.
 */
public Checkers() {
  try {
    // create the canvas and set up the commands:
    myCanvas = new CheckersCanvas(Display.getDisplay(this));
    myCanvas.addCommand(myExitCommand);
    myCanvas.addCommand(myTauntCommand);
    myCanvas.setCommandListener(this);
    CheckersGame game = myCanvas.getGame();
    myMoveManager = new MoveManager(this, myCanvas, game);
    game.setMoveManager(myMoveManager);
    // create the screen where the user can optionally enter
    // a message to send to the opponent.
    myTauntBox = new TextBox("message", null, 100, TextField.ANY);
    myTauntBox.addCommand(myOkCommand);
    myTauntBox.addCommand(myCancelCommand);
    myTauntBox.setCommandListener(this);
    // Start with a screen to offer the the user the choice of
    // whether to enter an opponent's phone number manually or
    // select an opponent from the user's addressbook.
    String[] choices = { "choose from list", "enter manually" };
    myStartList = new List("select an opponent", List.IMPLICIT,
                           choices, null);
    myStartList.addCommand(myExitCommand);
    myStartList.setCommandListener(this);
  } catch(Exception e) {
    // if there's an error during creation, display it as an alert.
    errorMsg(e);
  }
}

/**
 * Create the form for entering the invitations.
 */
synchronized void createInvitationForm() {
  if(myInvitationForm == null) {
    myInvitationForm = new Form("Checkers");
    myPhoneNumberField = new TextField(null, null, 15,
                                       TextField.PHONENUMBER);
    myInvitationForm.append("Please enter the phone number "
                            + "of the remote player:");
    myInvitationForm.append(myPhoneNumberField);
```

```
    myInvitationForm.addCommand(myOkCommand);
    myInvitationForm.addCommand(myExitCommand);
    myInvitationForm.setCommandListener(this);
  }
}


//----------------------------------------------------------------
// implementation of MIDlet
// these methods may be called by the application management
// software at any time, so we always check fields for null
// before calling methods on them.

/**
 * Start the application.
 */
public void startApp() {
  // If the game wasn't launched by receiving an invitation,
  // start with a screen to prompt the user to send an
  // invitation to another player.
  if(myMoveManager.getState() == MoveManager.NOT_STARTED) {
    Display.getDisplay(this).setCurrent(myStartList);
  } else {
    try {
      myMoveManager.wakeUp();
    } catch(Exception e) {
      errorMsg(e);
    }
  }
}

/**
 * Throw out the garbage.
 */
public void destroyApp(boolean unconditional)
    throws MIDletStateChangeException {
  // tell the communicator to send the end game
  // message to the other player and then disconnect:
  if(myMoveManager != null) {
    myMoveManager.shutDown();
  }
  // throw the larger game objects in the garbage:
  myMoveManager = null;
  myCanvas = null;
}

/**
 * End the program now.
```

```
   */
  public void quit() {
    try {
      destroyApp(false);
      notifyDestroyed();
    } catch (MIDletStateChangeException ex) {
    }
  }

  /**
   * Pause the game.
   * This closes the receiving thread.
   */
  public void pauseApp() {
    myMoveManager.pause();
  }

  //----------------------------------------------------------------
  //  implementation of CommandListener

  /*
   * Respond to a command issued on the Canvas.
   */
  public void commandAction(Command c, Displayable s) {
    if(c == myCancelCommand) {
      myTauntBox.setString(null);
    }
    if(s == myTauntBox) {
      if(myMoveManager.getState() == MoveManager.NOT_STARTED) {
        myMoveManager.sendInvitation(myPhoneNumberField.getString());
        myPhoneNumberField = null;
        myCanvas.setWaitScreen(true);
        myCanvas.start();
        myCanvas.repaint();
        myCanvas.serviceRepaints();
        Display.getDisplay(this).setCurrent(myCanvas);
      } else {
        Display.getDisplay(this).setCurrent(myCanvas);
      }
    } else if((c == myExitCommand) || (c == Alert.DISMISS_COMMAND)) {
      if((myMoveManager != null)
          && (myMoveManager.getState() != MoveManager.NOT_STARTED)) {
        myMoveManager.endGame();
      } else {
        quit();
      }
    } else if(c == myOkCommand) {
```

```
      Display.getDisplay(this).setCurrent(myTauntBox);
    } else if(c == myTauntCommand) {
      Display.getDisplay(this).setCurrent(myTauntBox);
    } else if(s == myStartList) {
      // since we've already checked for the exit command,
      // a command action means that the user has selected
      // whether to (0) choose a number from the contacts
      // list or (1) enter a number manually:
      int selection = myStartList.getSelectedIndex();
      if(selection == 0) {
        // Now we start the thread to load the contact list and
        // change the screen.  This could have been loaded in
        // the background at startup time, however accessing
        // the PIM system causes the AMS to ask the user for
        // permission, which may cause confusion if the user
        // hasn't yet requested an action that requires PIM access.
        synchronized(this) {
          // synchronize to avoid accidentally creating
          // multiple threads if the user presses the select
          // key more than once.
          if(myPIMRunner == null) {
            myPIMRunner = new PIMRunner(this);
            myPIMRunner.start();
          }
        }
      } else {
        // set the screen so the user can enter the opponent's
        // number manually:
        createInvitationForm();
        Display.getDisplay(this).setCurrent(myInvitationForm);
      }
    } else if(s == myContactMenu) {
      // since we've already checked for the exit command
      // and taunt command, a command action means that the
      // user has selected a contact:
      int selection = myContactMenu.getSelectedIndex();
      // store the selected phone number in the phone
      // number field, then move on to requesting a message:
      myPhoneNumberField = new TextField(null,
          (String)(myPhoneNumbers.elementAt(selection)), 15,
            TextField.PHONENUMBER);
      Display.getDisplay(this).setCurrent(myTauntBox);
    }
  }
}

/**
 * Set the contact list.
```

```
    */
  public void setContactList(Vector names, Vector phoneNumbers) {
    myPhoneNumbers = phoneNumbers;
    String[] nameArray = new String[names.size()];
    names.copyInto(nameArray);
    myContactMenu = new List("select an opponent", List.IMPLICIT,
                             nameArray, null);
    myContactMenu.addCommand(myExitCommand);
    myContactMenu.setCommandListener(this);
    Display.getDisplay(this).setCurrent(myContactMenu);
  }

  //----------------------------------------------------------
  //  message methods

  /**
   * Displays the remote player's message as an Alert.
   */
  public void displayTauntMessage(String taunt) {
    Alert tauntScreen = new Alert("message");
    tauntScreen.setString(taunt);
    Display.getDisplay(this).setCurrent(tauntScreen,
        myCanvas);
  }

  /**
   * Gets the message that the user has entered for the remote
   * player, if any.  Then clears the text.
   */
  public String getTauntMessage() {
    String retVal = myTauntBox.getString();
    myTauntBox.setString(null);
    return retVal;
  }

  /**
   * Manually set the taunt message to tell the remote
   * player that he has won.
   */
  public void setWinTaunt() {
    myTauntBox.setString("You Win!");
  }

  //----------------------------------------------------------
  //  error methods

  /**
   * Converts an exception to a message and displays
```

```
 * the message.
 */
void errorMsg(Exception e) {
  if(e.getMessage() == null) {
    errorMsg(e.getClass().getName());
  } else {
    errorMsg(e.getMessage());
  }
}

/**
 * Displays an error message alert if something goes wrong.
 */
void errorMsg(String msg) {
  Alert errorAlert = new Alert("error",
                               msg, null, AlertType.ERROR);
  errorAlert.setCommandListener(this);
  errorAlert.setTimeout(Alert.FOREVER);
  Display.getDisplay(this).setCurrent(errorAlert);
  }
}
```

As you're experimenting with the PIM API, keep in mind that you can create or modify contacts as well. In the WTK, the corresponding data files are stored in the following directory:

`WTK2.2/appdb/DefaultColorPhone/pim/contacts/Contacts/`

There you can have a look at them, or delete all the contents of the directory if you'd like to start over with a clean slate.

Using the File Connection API

The File Connection API is the other half of JSR 75. This API allows a Java application to access other parts of the device's memory in addition to just the closed RMS sandbox permitted by the standard MIDP Record Management System (RMS; see Chapter 5).

The real beauty of the File Connection API is that it allows your application to share data with other types of applications (even non-Java applications) on the handset. So, for example, if a given handset allows access to the images folder or to the ringtones folder, it's possible for your game to install a wallpaper or a ringtone *as a wallpaper or a ringtone* that the user can use outside of the game. It's a fun type of perk that your game can give a user for reaching a certain level or just to remind her of your game.

But this API's strategy is the opposite of the PIM API's strategy in terms of finding the data you want. Instead of creating standard constants so that you can find familiar items regardless of the underlying data structure, this API just opens the access door to certain filesystems and lets you explore them as they are.

I like the elegance of the File Connection API, and in particular the way it's designed to function just like the various network connection APIs (using `Connector.open` with a URL, returning a `Connection` with an `InputStream` and an `OutputStream` just as any network connection would). It's a natural way of accessing files both from the Java perspective (where files have traditionally been accessed through the same streams as sockets and other types of network connections and in the general networking universe (where users are already accustomed to reading local files in an Internet browser using a file://-type URL).

Any game that uses the RMS might be modified to use the File Connection API instead (see the "File Connection vs. RMS" sidebar for a discussion of the advantages and disadvantages). So, rather than doing a complete game example for this case, I'll just show you some generic sample code to print out the accessible file folders on the handset and try creating (or overwriting) a test file. This sample code is given in Listing 7-6.

The thing to notice in the example is how closely communicating with the filesystem matches all of the other types of messaging and communications code. The only new point is that you construct the URL with the prefix file:/// followed by the name of a root directory that you get by querying the FileSystemRegistry class for accessible roots. Even the FileSystemRegistry class should look familiar since a lot of communications APIs have you get the list of available connections from some sort of registry.

Listing 7-6. *FCRunner.java*

```java
package net.frog_parrot.net;

import java.util.Enumeration;
import java.io.*;

import javax.microedition.io.*;
import javax.microedition.io.file.*;

/**
 * A simple file Connection testing utility.
 */
public class FCRunner extends Thread {

  FCTest myMidlet;

  FCRunner(FCTest test) {
    myMidlet = test;
  }

  public void run() {
    FileConnection rootdir = null;
    try {
      Enumeration items = FileSystemRegistry.listRoots();

      // Now print the available roots:
      while(items.hasMoreElements()) {
        String rootname = (String)(items.nextElement());
        myMidlet.display("\n *** new root: " + rootname);

        // open the root directory:
```

```
// note there are three slashes before the root name
// because there is no "host" for this connection:
rootdir = (FileConnection)Connector.open(
    "file:///" + rootname);
// List the current files:
Enumeration ls = rootdir.list();
while(ls.hasMoreElements()) {
  String filename = (String)(ls.nextElement());
  myMidlet.display("  file: " + filename);

  // print the contents of the file:
  FileConnection file = null;
  try {
    file = (FileConnection)Connector.open(
        "file:///" + rootname + "/" + filename);
    if(file.canRead()) {
      InputStream is = file.openInputStream();
      byte[] contents = new byte[25];
      int len = is.read(contents);
      is.close();
      myMidlet.display("  contents: "
          + new String(contents, 0, len));
    } else {
      myMidlet.display("  * not readable");
    }
  } catch(Exception e) {
    e.printStackTrace();
  } finally {
    try {
      file.close();
    } catch(Exception e) {}
  }
}

// now try to create a file:
FileConnection newfile = null;
try {
  newfile = (FileConnection)Connector.open(
      "file:///" + rootname + "myNewFile");
  if(newfile.exists()) {
    OutputStream os = newfile.openOutputStream();
    os.write((new String("overwriting old contents")).getBytes());
    os.close();
  } else {
    newfile.create();
    OutputStream os = newfile.openOutputStream();
    os.write((new String("creating new contents")).getBytes());
    os.close();
```

```
        }
      } catch(Exception e) {
        e.printStackTrace();
      } finally {
        try {
          newfile.close();
        } catch(Exception e) {}
      }
    }
  } catch(Exception e) {
    e.printStackTrace();
  } finally {
    try {
      rootdir.close();
    } catch(Exception e) {}
  }
 }

}
```

The corresponding MIDlet class to run this thread is just a simple variant of the other MIDlet classes, such as Listing 7-2. The only difference is that it needs to include a "display" method that writes a string to the screen. This is shown in Listing 7-7.

Listing 7-7. *FCTest.java*

```java
package net.frog_parrot.net;

import javax.microedition.lcdui.Command;
import javax.microedition.lcdui.CommandListener;
import javax.microedition.lcdui.Display;
import javax.microedition.lcdui.Displayable;
import javax.microedition.lcdui.Form;
import javax.microedition.midlet.MIDlet;

/**
 * A simple MIDlet to test which APIs are implemented.
 */
public class FCTest extends MIDlet implements CommandListener {

  private Command myExitCommand = new Command("Exit", Command.EXIT, 1);
  private Command myOkCommand = new Command("OK", Command.OK, 1);
  private Form myResultScreen;

  /**
   * Empty constructor.
   */
  public FCTest() {
  }
```

```java
/**
 * Initialize the Displayables.
 */
public void startApp() {
  myResultScreen = new Form("Results");
  myResultScreen.addCommand(myExitCommand);
  myResultScreen.addCommand(myOkCommand);
  myResultScreen.setCommandListener(this);
  Display.getDisplay(this).setCurrent(myResultScreen);
}

/**
 * Implementation of MIDlet.
 */
public void pauseApp() {
}

/**
 * Implementation of MIDlet.
 */
public void destroyApp(boolean unconditional) {
}

/**
 * Respond to a button push.
 */
public void commandAction(Command command, Displayable screen) {
  if(command == myExitCommand) {
    destroyApp(true);
    notifyDestroyed();
  } else {
    FCRunner runner = new FCRunner(this);
    runner.start();
  }
}

/**
 * Append a string to the current display.
 */
public void display(String str) {
  myResultScreen.append(str);
  myResultScreen.append("\n");
}

}
```

FILE CONNECTION VS. RMS

The File Connection API allows your MIDlet to access the platform's memory in much the same way that a Java program on a desktop computer reads from and writes to the computer's hard disk (and other) drives. This gives you a lot of added power to share memory between applications and even to read and write on removable memory. However, on a small device this leads to the usual disadvantage: you have to know the particular handset very well to know which folders you have access to and how to access them.

The File Connection API is great if your project has a small set of target handsets, and not so great if you want your application to be useful on all MIDP handsets across the board. The RMS has the advantage of always being supported, so it's probably better to use the RMS if all you want is to set some simple data aside and find it again later. The RMS also has the advantage that—unlike with a File Connection—the MIDlet doesn't need to ask the user's permission for access, which makes a big difference for user-friendliness if your game isn't trusted (certified).

Of course, even the RMS isn't as predictable as one might like. There are handsets where RMS access is slower than File Connection access (and some where it's not), and some that handle individual records in unexpected ways (setting aside a big space for each record even if it's not used, or failing to free up the memory of a deleted record). Then there's the fact that the RMS is not convenient for pooling data among multiple MIDlet suites: to share a record store between suites, you need to leave the access door open to every MIDlet on the device. In addition, the record store is deleted when the associated MIDlet suite is deleted even if other MIDlet suites still wanted to access the data. And in high-end platforms where MIDlets can run concurrently, there are sometimes questions about whether one MIDlet suite can access a RecordStore while another has the RecordStore open.

So there's a bit of a trade-off, meaning it's better to know both the File Connection API as well as the RMS, and choose which one to use depending on your application.

More Options

The communications and data sharing APIs in this chapter and Chapter 6 are the ones you'll probably get the most mileage out of when developing MIDP games. But there are others you might end up using depending on your application. Plus, as Java ME evolves, new options are popping up all the time. Fortunately, the designers and architects proposing new JSRs tend to be pretty careful to follow the standard communications patterns fairly closely, so once you've got the idea, you can start using new protocols in your games as soon as you hear about them.

One of the exciting new options in MIDP 3 is inter-MIDlet communication. Before MIDP 3, MIDP devices were permitted to run MIDlets concurrently, but there was no standard way for MIDlets to communicate with one another or exchange data except by writing data to some sort of persistent storage (see the "File Connection vs. RMS" sidebar). One of the main advances in MIDP 3, however, is all the extra support for multitasking. So MIDP 3 includes a new type of connection: the IMCConnection, the inter-MIDlet communication connection.

The beauty of the IMCConnection is how perfectly it fits into the standard Java universe. The MIDlet can act as either client or server, and in terms of the code to open the connection and communicate across it, it's identical to the code you would write for Bluetooth (see the earlier section "Using Bluetooth"). The difference is that registering and finding services is much easier in IMC since the system is designed and optimized for Java, unlike Bluetooth where the registry system (using UUIDs and other attributes) was designed for non-Java applications. With IMC, you build the URL from the standard identifiers for a Java application: the MIDlet name, the vendor name, the version number, and the fully qualified classname of the `MIDlet` class (see Chapter 2).

Another type of connection that fits the same socket programming pattern as Bluetooth and IMC is straight socket programming using a `CommConnection`. This type of connection can be used to communicate with other `MIDlets` or applications on the device or can be used to communicate across the Internet. Support for this type of connection is required by MIDP starting from MIDP 2. However, even though the API classes to support this type of connection are present on all MIDP 2 and 3 devices, the device itself and/or the operator's network aren't always set up to allow this type of communication through. This is another type of communication (like `UDPDatagramConnection`), where it's mostly useful for people who are developing for a particular target device and/or operator (see the "Choosing a Protocol" section in Chapter 6).

Summary

In this chapter you've seen examples of how to use some additional communications and data access options such as Bluetooth, PIM, File Connection, and more. And the cool thing to notice is that the APIs for all of these different protocols have been carefully designed to follow familiar Java patterns, so it's easy to get up to speed on using a new API if you're already familiar with another. Of course, regardless of what type of connection you plan to use, communication entails playing a bit outside of your Java `MIDlet` sandbox, so you'll need permission. Additionally, you may have your own concerns about authenticating the party you're communicating with. Either way, the next item on the agenda is security, covered in Chapter 8.

CHAPTER 8

■ ■ ■

Securing Your Applications

Effective security is one of the main selling points of Java. Java offers consumers the assurance that an untrusted program won't damage their devices or perform any unauthorized actions, and Java offers developers the use of a wide array of security tools that can be easily integrated into an application. The security features offered by Java Micro Edition (Java ME) with MIDP follow the same basic strategies and philosophy as the security features of other Java editions.

The main part of the MIDP security model involves how `MIDlets` are granted access to sensitive operations such as making network connections. This is covered in the section "Understanding Protection Domains and Permissions." Another component of security is securing the connections used for communication, which is explored in the section "Setting Up Secure Connections," where you'll see how to improve the Dungeon game from Chapter 6 by using HTTPS to transmit the game data.

Understanding Protection Domains and Permissions

Java's built-in security is based on a Java application that's run by a virtual machine that prevents the application from breaking certain security rules. The virtual machine allows each Java application access to its own data only, unlike a C program that can more or less read and modify any data anywhere on the machine. The virtual machine's bytecode verifier ensures that the Java application won't get out of its memory area by cheating and adding or removing the wrong data from the stack.

In addition to restricting access to memory, the virtual machine protects the real machine from a potentially malicious application by restricting access to protected resources. A `MIDlet` (like an `Applet`) is run in a "sandbox," which is essentially a place where it has enough room to run around and have fun but can't get out and make trouble. The application management software that runs the `MIDlet` decides which protected resources the `MIDlet` can access.

MIDP 1 security was entirely based on the "sandbox" model. The only part of memory a MIDP 1 `MIDlet` can access is the RMS area set aside for that `MIDlet`'s suite (see Chapter 5), and the `MIDlet` couldn't perform any network operations without the AMS first consulting the user.

A weakness to the MIDP 1 system was that `MIDlets` known to the manufacturer, operator, or user to be safe were made to jump through the same annoying hoops as unknown `MIDlets` downloaded from the Internet. So with MIDP 2 a system of protection domains and permissions was introduced, based on the security model used by other versions of Java such as Java SE and the Connected Device Configuration (CDC) of Java ME.

A protection domain is essentially a mapping between a set of permissions and a set of certificates that can be used to authenticate a given MIDlet. A permission is an object that represents the right to perform a restricted operation (see the "Requesting Permissions" section). When a MIDlet is installed, the AMS places it in a protection domain based on which certificate was used to digitally sign the MIDlet (or into a special domain for untrusted third-party MIDlets if the MIDlet is a MIDP 1 MIDlet and/or not signed). If the MIDlet attempts to perform an action that requires permission, the result depends on whether the permission is one that is granted to the MIDlet's protection domain. If it is (and if the MIDlet correctly requested the permission in its JAD file; see "Requesting Permissions"), then the action is allowed without consulting the user. If not, the AMS will take over the display and show the user a system screen stating what restricted action the MIDlet would like to perform (such as sending an SMS to a given phone number; see Figure 8-1) and asking the user's permission. If the permission is not granted, the method call that required permission throws a SecurityException.

Figure 8-1. *The AMS shows a warning screen if an untrusted MIDlet attempts to perform a restricted action.*

A MIDP 2 or greater handset generally has four protection domains: the manufacturer domain, the operator domain, the identified third-party domain, and the unidentified third-party domain. (It is possible for the manufacturer to define other protection domains as well.) The manufacturer domain is the domain for all of those MIDlets signed by the handset manufacturer, and the operator domain is the domain for all of the MIDlets signed by the mobile network operator who provides the user's phone service. Both of these parties are implicitly trusted, so these two domains are granted the widest range of permissions. (The digital certificates for the operator domain may be stored in the device's smart card to allow the user to switch the device from one operator's network to another.) The identified third-party domain is the domain for MIDlets signed by a certificate that is granted by a recognized Certificate Authority (see the section "Using Digital Certificates"). In MIDP 2, this domain was called the "Trusted Third-Party Domain" but the name was misleading because the only thing the Certificate

Authority can guarantee is that the `MIDlet` provider can be positively identified and not necessarily that the `MIDlet` provider is trustworthy. So from MIDP 2 to MIDP 3 the third-party terminology was changed from trusted/untrusted to identified/unidentified, but the behavior is the same. The fourth protection domain, the unidentified third-party domain, is the domain for unsigned `MIDlets`. These `MIDlets` must get explicit permission from the user to perform any restricted action.

Requesting Permissions

Any restricted action a `MIDlet` might want to perform has an associated "permission." Permissions in Java ME are similar to permissions in Java SE. For CDC and for MIDP 3, they're actually based on the same permission classes as Java SE permissions. That means that each permission is a subclass of `java.lang.Permission`, and each permission class is generally found in the same package as the restricted methods it regulates. Permissions in MIDP 2 aren't defined as classes, although their names look like classnames and they're mapped to permission classes if a MIDP 2 game is played on a MIDP 3 device. A MIDP 2 permission is just a string that looks like a fully qualified classname and represents a restricted action (such as `javax.wireless.messaging.sms.receive`).

Most of the MIDP 2 permissions involve making network connections since network connections may cost the user money. Examples include `javax.microedition.io.Connector.http` and `javax.microedition.io.Connector.https`. Some optional APIs define MIDP 2–style "named permissions" as well, including PIM—where your `MIDlet` naturally needs permission before reading from the user's address book—and File Connection (which may access sensitive areas of the device's memory).

If a `MIDlet` requires a certain permission, it must signal this request in the JAD file. If the permission is necessary in order for the `MIDlet` to run at all, the permission should be declared in the `MIDlet-Permissions` JAD attribute, and if it's merely a nice plus for running the `MIDlet`, it should be declared in the `MIDlet-Permissions-Opt` JAD attribute. Some of the examples in the earlier chapters of this book need to have permission attributes in their JAD files as follows:

Dungeon from Chapter 6:

```
MIDlet-Permissions: javax.microedition.io.Connector.http
```

Checkers from Chapter 6:

```
MIDlet-Permissions: javax.wireless.messaging.sms.receive, \
javax.wireless.messaging.sms.send, \
javax.microedition.io.PushRegistry
```

Checkers Plus from Chapter 7:

```
MIDlet-Permissions: javax.wireless.messaging.sms.receive, \
javax.wireless.messaging.sms.send, \
javax.microedition.io.PushRegistry
MIDlet-Permissions-Opt: javax.microedition.pim.ContactList.read
```

Bluetooth Checkers from Chapter 7:

```
MIDlet-Permissions: javax.microedition.io.Connector.bluetooth.client, \
javax.microedition.io.Connector.bluetooth.server
```

The MIDP 3 permissions allow more precision. Instead of having a choice of granted or not granted, it's possible to request specific cases such as the right to connect to a particular URL or the right to File Connection access for a particular directory in the device's filesystem. Since MIDP 3 permissions can take arguments, each permission must be requested in an individual JAD attribute. So instead of having one `MIDlet-Permissions` attribute, the JAD would contain a list of `MIDlet-Permission-<n>` attributes. For example, if I'm targeting my Dungeon game for MIDP 3 and I only need it to connect with my own server, I would place a `MIDlet-Permission-1` attribute in the JAD with the URL of my server as an argument.

Once your `MIDlet` has requested the permission, it's up to the device and the user to decide whether the permission should be granted. The device's AMS may provide a set of menus to allow the user to grant certain permissions to certain `MIDlet` suites, but usually permissions are determined through protection domains that are associated with digital certificates.

Using Digital Certificates

The MIDP security system is largely based on the X.509 Public Key Infrastructure (PKI). The public key infrastructure is integral to the creation of secure connections, and it's also used in the creation of protection domains.

A *digital certificate* is a set of data containing cryptographic information that allows you to encrypt messages and verify the identity of the sender. A `MIDlet` is signed by encrypting a hash of the JAR file and placing the corresponding encrypted data in the corresponding JAD file. Because the signature is based on a hash of the JAR file, in addition to identifying the `MIDlet`'s origin, the digital signature ensures that the `MIDlet` JAR and everything in it (particularly the properties in the manifest file) are authentic and have not been modified by a third party. In fact, anyone can create a digital certificate containing any name they want, so a certificate must be recognized in order to be useful for identification purposes. In practice, this is accomplished as follows: the handset has a set of root certificates embedded in it that identify the different protection domains. Only someone with access to the right keys can sign a `MIDlet` with a certificate that a handset will recognize. When the `MIDlet` is installed, the signature is verified against the JAR data and against the root certificates on the device, and the `MIDlet` is assigned to a protection domain accordingly.

If you're working for a handset manufacturer or mobile operator, the signature will typically be added as the final step after the `MIDlet` has passed quality control. If you'd like your `MIDlet` to be placed in the identified third-party domain, you can apply for a certificate from a known Certificate Authority (CA) such as VeriSign. For testing and development, you can create your own certificate and embed it in the WTK emulator using KToolbar. KToolbar even allows you to generate the "certificate signing request" file to send to a CA if you'd like to go through the CA's application procedure to get your certificate signed by the CA's certificate so that your `MIDlets` will be installed in the identified third-party domain.

KToolbar makes the signing procedure simple. Once you've opened a project, select Sign from the Project menu, then select New Key Pair in the window that comes up. This generates a new pair of keys that are placed in the WTK's `appdb/main.sks` file. Before it generates the keys, you need to provide some data about who you are (since the point is to authenticate a particular identity). The one thing to keep in mind is that if you'd like to use the same keys for creating an HTTPS connection (as in the improved Dungeon example of this chapter), the `CN` attribute needs to be the host's Uniform Resource Locator (URL).

A key pair can also be created with the `keytool` utility that comes with the Java Software Development Kit (SDK). The following is an example of the command I used to create a certificate for my local testing:

```
keytool -genkey -alias tomcat -keyalg RSA
```

This command creates a digital certificate in the default keystore (`~/.keystore`) using the RSA algorithm. I gave the certificate an alias of `tomcat` because this is the certificate I used to create secure HTTP (HTTPS) connections on my Tomcat server. When you enter the command to create the certificate, `keytool` will prompt you to enter a name ("What is your first and last name?"). This is the prompt for the `CN` attribute where I entered the URL of the host I'm using for my HTTPS connection.

If you've generated your key pair using the Java SE SDK, or you have a key pair from some other source that you'd like to associate with a protection domain for your local testing, then in KToolbar's Sign MIDlet Suite GUI window (that pops up when you select Project ➤ Sign), you click Import Key Pair and KToolbar will prompt you to browse for the keystore file, enter the passphrase and the alias, and choose the protection domain that you'd like to associate with the key pair.

The next step is to sign the `MIDlet` Suite, which is done in the Sign MIDlet Suite GUI window by highlighting the certificate you'd like to use and clicking the Sign MIDlet Suite button. This adds a couple of lines to the `MIDlet`'s JAD file such as the following:

```
MIDlet-Certificate-1-1: ➥
MIICAjCCAWsCBEYM/t8wDQYJKoZIhvcNAQEEBQAwSDEKMAgGA1UEBhMBeDEKMAgGA1UECBMBeDEKMAgG➥
A1UEBxMBeDEKMAgGA1UEChMBeDEKMAgGA1UECxMBeDEKMAgGA1UEAxMBeDAeFwOwNzAzMzAxMjEzMTla➥
FwOwNzA2MjgxMjEzMTlaMEgxCjAIBgNVBAYTAXgxCjAIBgNVBAgTAXgxCjAIBgNVBAcTAXgxCjAIBgNVBA➥
oTAXgxCjAIBgNVBAsTAXgxCjAIBgNVBAMTAXgwgZ8wDQYJKoZIhvcNAQEBBQADgYOAMIGJAoGBAJLyxT➥
TTlAyUDnJAlRylxVsUmEpu3XgcnIth2sz/+cy1mQz7jp8f/5uMS8brri7D1OZ67QBskc2XXP3KYJ6Oxqakn➥
9FPdjQaB+nN/1CR5g/bOy/C/Qh2wOaxTBysnffQCCs3UueB4bEFcWdF9L4/MAIVg7vUNNiLE2a/HfdLAE/➥
hAgMBAAEwDQYJKoZIhvcNAQEEBQADgYEAR565dYadP2RhmRVkBhxnUNlUaRvVNcShpSzvLrUYm5OgjNjBMu➥
VBhgtLJ+Oa4p/dy3EpcwbGHJ4V+Um5S5K9uhuOUCpasuSyZKdMaJnOn2zLaCYh9gvjfcbMAJsBX+zJXVa6➥
5AVoPlRvqc3Ap6COmrcQYfVeaKiXWr/nUg9OFvU=
MIDlet-Jar-RSA-SHA1:➥
WhdYYooHeRmYd7jEhg5eFKZrX886TyaJz1GBMFZ1M5EFXySfAsWdgxUwlJSfF+3iW57bSIDcF477pb2KzX➥
Bv2q4OfuMBLtSyvVkTxDC68urRHYjAs5WV2a4nxV9vO7cHz2YEjtwkAM/Ule2db2DGW2Yu7r6S8pGqvDA8➥
4+GPP/Q=
```

If you'd like to sign your `MIDlet` from the command line or from a script or Ant build file, you can use the JadTool utility that comes with the WTK. The WTK documentation explains how to use it, or you can see the list of possible arguments by running JadTool with the `-help` option.

Then when you install the `MIDlet` in the emulator using Project ➤ Run via OTA, the `MIDlet` will be installed in the protection domain you've chosen for your certificate. In the WTK emulator, you can see whether your `MIDlet` is running as a certified `MIDlet` or not by looking for the tiny certificate icon in the top bar of the screen (see Figure 8-2). The same signature generated in the JAD file by KToolbar is valid on a real device as long as the key pair used is one that is embedded in the device.

Figure 8-2. *The icon that shows that the MIDlet is running as certified*

The Sign MIDlet Suite GUI window also provides a button to allow you to generate a Certificate Signing Request (CSR) to send to a CA in order to get your certificate signed (see Figure 8-3).

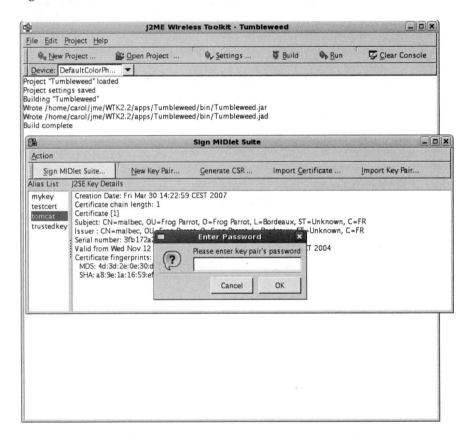

Figure 8-3. *Signing a MIDlet using KToolbar*

If you'd like to get your certificate signed by a CA, you need to contact the CA to find out how to do it. It's not completely simple (because the CA needs to verify your identity), and unfortunately it's not free. Plus you'll need to renew the certificate regularly, which also costs money. But if you need to allow customers to securely contact you, you have no way around this.

OBFUSCATING YOUR CLASSES

The Java class file format is designed to be nice and simple for the Java Virtual Machine to read, and as a side effect it's actually pretty easy to decompile. It doesn't take much to write a program that will parse a `.class` file and return a corresponding `.java` file, complete with the field, method, and variable names.

Obfuscation makes your class files a little less legible and hence adds a layer of protection to hinder people from decompiling your code and altering it. What obfuscation does is take all of the names of methods, fields, and variables and change them to simple strings such as "a," "b," "a1," etc. Since variable and method names take up a lot of room in the class file, obfuscation is as useful for decreasing your JAR size as it is for security. Note that changing the names of anything declared as `public` renders the program unusable as a library, but a typical obfuscator will allow you the option of leaving public variables and methods intact or of obfuscating everything (if you know your JAR will not be called by any other Java code).

Obfuscation is very easy to do. It's just a question of downloading an obfuscator tool such as `proguard.jar` (from `http://proguard.sourceforge.net/`) and dropping it in the WTK's bin directory. Then from KToolbar, the option Project ➤ Package ➤ Create Obfuscated Package will build a JAR containing an obfuscated version of your project. The same obfuscation utility can also be called from an Ant build file (see the "Building with Ant" sidebar in Chapter 1).

Setting Up Secure Connections

Secure connections are extremely easy to program with MIDP because all the work is done behind the scenes for you. The idea is that the application developer doesn't need to be concerned with the details of how the underlying secure socket is created; it's enough to know you want to use one and then leave the details to the application management software.

To use a secure connection, you need to get an instance of `HttpsConnection` instead of `HttpConnection` or get an instance of `SecureConnection` instead of `SocketConnection`. To get the right connection, all you need to do is send the right URL to the method `Connector.open()`. It couldn't be simpler. Once you have a handle to the `Connection`, you can get information about it by calling `getSecurityInfo()` to get the corresponding `SecurityInfo` object. The `SecurityInfo` object will give you more details about the protocol, the cipher suites, and the server's certificate.

Using HTTPS

HTTPS is the standard protocol that most browsers use for communicating securely. It's just the same as HTTP except that communication takes place over a secure connection using the SSL protocol.

Because of MIDP's generic connection framework, switching a game from using HTTP to HTTPS is just as simple as changing the URL. On the client side, that's the only change you need to make. The MIDP classes will take care of creating the right type of connection for you as long as the URL is right. Generally you need to change the `http://` at the beginning of the URL to `https://` and change the port number if the server listens for HTTP and HTTPS messages on different ports. (Consult your server configuration to find out what port it's listening on for HTTPS connections, and keep in mind that many operator networks will not allow HTTP connections on nonstandard ports.) In my test version of the Dungeon game from the previous chapter, the URL changed from `http://frog-parrot.net:8080/games/DungeonDownload` to `https://frog-parrot.net:8443/games/DungeonDownload`. And that was the only change

I needed to make in my client code. (Remember to use your own domain name or Internet Protocol [IP] address instead of `frog-parrot.net` when testing because my `Servlet` isn't usually running on this site.)

On the server side, the code doesn't need to change at all. A `Servlet` doesn't care if it's being served over HTTP or HTTPS. It's just a question of configuring your server to use HTTPS. (Consult the documentation; it shouldn't be very hard.)

The hardest part is setting up the certificate. If you're planning to communicate with real clients over the Internet using HTTPS, then you'll need a real certificate. See the earlier "Using Digital Certificates" section for more information.

If you'd like to test locally, you can just create your own certificate. This is also discussed in the "Using Digital Certificates" section. You have one additional step to perform when using HTTPS with the emulator and a self-signed certificate: you must import the server's certificate into the emulator's keystore. If you don't do this, the emulator won't recognize the server's certificate and will refuse to connect (unless it's a real certificate from a CA and not just a self-signed certificate).

To import the server's certificate into the emulator's keystore, you can use KToolbar as explained in the "Using Digital Certificates" section or use the MEKeytool utility that comes with the MIDP toolkit. With my configuration, the command I used was the following (all on one line):

```
java -jar ~/j2me/WTK2.0/bin/MEKeyTool.jar ➥
-import -alias tomcat -MEkeystore ~/j2me/WTK2.0/appdb/_main.ks ➥
-storepass changeit
```

This command is loaded with options, but most of them are self-explanatory. The beginning (`java -jar ~/j2me/WTK2.0/bin/MEKeyTool.jar`) merely tells the machine to run MEKeytool. The `-import` option gives the command to import a certificate. Since I didn't include the option `-keystore`, MEKeytool assumes that the certificate should be read from the default keystore at `~/.keystore`. The `-alias tomcat` option tells it to use the certificate that has the alias `tomcat`. (The certificate has that alias because it's the certificate that my Tomcat server is using). The `-MEkeystore ~/j2me/WTK2.0/appdb/_main.ks` option tells MEKeytool that the destination keystore is `~/j2me/WTK2.0/appdb/_main.ks`, which is the default keystore for the emulator (assuming that the toolkit was installed in the directory `~/j2me/`). Then, obviously, the option `-storepass changeit` gives the password needed to read from the server's keystore. You'll almost certainly have to modify the options a bit if you run this command on your own system, but if the modifications you need to make aren't obvious, the toolkit's HTML documentation covers MEKeytool.

Once you've made these modifications on both the test client and test server, your development environment will make connections through HTTPS.

USING SECURE CONNECTIONS WHILE SELLING YOUR GAME

Let's face it: if you're giving your game away for free, you probably don't need to worry much about security. But unless you're lucky enough to have an infinite amount of free time for writing games, you're probably writing your games with the intention of making some money from them. The security features of MIDP can help you do that. Unfortunately, it's hard to prevent people from playing your game for free if they're determined to do so. But assuming that you're an independent programmer distributing your game yourself or that you're running a small game business, this sidebar contains some suggestions on how to encourage your customers to pay for your game if they play it.

The simplest business model is to place your JAR file on a secure server and limit access to who can download it. The disadvantage of this one is that it's too easy for one paying customer to give away your game free to others. If the game is good, it will likely start popping up for free download on sites all over the Internet, and it's hard to get all of the unofficial distributors to cut it out.

Probably the most effective way to get paid for your game is to distribute it freely and then require it to call your server at some point. This works especially well if you have a part of the game that can be played for free and another segment that requires payment. People are used to sharing things with their friends on the Internet, so if the free part of your game is interesting, it acts as its own advertisement.

Two principal strategies exist for writing games with a free part and a paying part. The easier approach is to put the entire game in the JAR and just write the game in such a way that part of it won't play until the user calls up your server to unlock it. To "unlock" the game, all you need to do is instruct the game to create a special `RecordStore` when the game calls your `Servlet`, and then later, when the user would like to play the paid part of the game, have the program check that the required `RecordStore` exists before allowing the user to access that part of the game. The other strategy is to do as I did in the Dungeon game, where you write a game in which the various levels or game boards are read from data, and you have the users call you up to download more boards. I'm partial to this second approach because it's flexible. If your game is well written, you can have one game keep bringing in more money just by writing more boards for it. Plus, your game can be elaborate and long running without wasting precious memory on your clients' devices because you can have the program replace the completed boards in memory with the new ones.

Whichever strategy you choose, MIDP makes it convenient for you to require the game to call your server at some point.

Here's a standard scenario: the first step is to run a `Servlet` on an HTTPS web server with a real digital certificate from a CA. Then include a command in your game's command menu that leads to an instruction screen that indicates how to contact your company to purchase the right to play the rest of the game. Most likely, you should instruct the user to visit your (secure) web site with a regular browser in order to pay you through a PayPal account (which is easy to set up). You can also build your site to take credit card information, but that's more complicated, and a lot of people are more comfortable using a standard like PayPal rather than giving their credit card info to a small vendor. In exchange, your server can return a single-use password-type string. Then the user can access a screen on the game to key in the password and call your server. The game should have the correct URL to use to contact your server already built in. Your `Servlet` should read in the password and mark it as used (so that further users can't download again using the same password) and send back either the game data or the instruction to unlock the paying part of the game. Note that it's certainly possible to have the user key his credit card information directly into the device and have the device send that information to your `Servlet` in the same transaction where the `Servlet` sends the data to the device. This has the advantage of simplicity, and it eliminates the step of creating a temporary password. The only disadvantage is that the user may not be accustomed to sending his credit card information that way and hence might hesitate to do it.

The device is using HTTPS to communicate with you, which will ensure that the user (or someone else) isn't just spoofing your site. If you use standard HTTP, a hacker could read all the data being transferred in both directions from a session between your server and a paying customer and then spoof your site and write a `Servlet` that returns the same data your `Servlet` returns. Then nonpaying customers could go around you and get the complete game from the hacker. Such a hack is unlikely to happen or to steal much of your business in practice, but using HTTPS makes it nearly impossible to use such a hack. For additional security, you can have the program examine the site's certificate to make sure it's the right one (see the "Using Other Secure Connections" section for information on how to do that), but with HTTPS it's not really necessary because the application management software verifies the name of the certificate for you.

You may worry that once a user has downloaded the data or "unlocked" the game by contacting you, she may be able to distribute just the data or distribute an unlocked version of the game. This unfortunately is the weak point in the security model. Once the data is on the user's device, the user has access to it for good or for bad. It's true that when a `MIDlet` creates a `RecordStore`, no other `MIDlet` suite can access that `RecordStore` unless the `MIDlet` suite that created the `RecordStore` explicitly grants access to it to other `MIDlets` (to do this, use `RecordStore.setMode()` or create the `RecordStore` with the versions of `RecordStore.openRecordStore()` that takes the argument `authmode`). So you may think that then you could create a `RecordStore` containing secret data that the user can't read or alter. Unfortunately, this isn't possible since the user can read your `MIDlet`'s data and pass data to your `MIDlet` by performing phony updates.

To take advantage of the `MIDlet` suite update function, all the user has to do is create a new `MIDlet` suite and give it the same vendor name and `MIDlet` name as your `MIDlet` suite (since the vendor name and the `MIDlet` name are the parameters that the device uses to identify the owner of a `RecordStore`). If the user's goal is to read the data your program created, she can write a `MIDlet` that will list all the `RecordStores` and their contents. If the user has already installed your `MIDlet` suite on a device and then tries to install another `MIDlet` with the same name and vendor name, the device will view it as an update and ask the user if she wants to make the existing `RecordStores` available to the new version. Thus, the user can give the new (fake) version access to the old (real) version's data even if the URLs that the versions were downloaded from are completely different. Even signing the JAR file isn't sufficient because the user can update a signed JAR with a JAR signed by someone else and still grant the new version access to the earlier version's data. So, a hacker could download your game, pay to download the additional data, and then read the data by "updating" the `MIDlet` suite with a `RecordStore`-reading `MIDlet` that has the same name and vendor name as your `MIDlet`. He could then write a `RecordStore`-writing `MIDlet` (again with the same name and vendor name as your `MIDlet`), which will create exactly the `RecordStores` that your `MIDlet` would normally create after calling your server. The hacker can distribute the `RecordStore`-writing `MIDlet` and then tell people to run it once (to create and populate the `RecordStore`) and then "update" it with a copy of your game. In this way a hacker can grant users access to a cracked version of your game. Unfortunately, you have no way to prevent hackers from cracking your game in this manner. But in practice this exploit is complicated enough that it's not worth the small price charged by a typical game, so it's unlikely to lose you much money. Also note that MIDP 3 allows you to specify RMS files to be downloaded with the `MIDlet`, which can help with this small security hole.

In addition to the trick using "update," some implementations of MIDP allow the user direct access to the MIDP `RecordStores`. According to the rules of MIDP, a record store that's private can't be accessed by `MIDlet` suites other than the `MIDlet` suite that created it. But it's possible to have an implementation that would allow the user to read and modify the MIDP `RecordStores` using a non-Java application such as a text editor! This is probably not typical, but on a MIDP device with this behavior, there's no simple way to keep a nonpaying user from unlocking his game by copying the `RecordStores` from the device of a paying user. Again, though, writing your RMS in binary format (instead of user-friendly text) will hinder the casual user from hacking your game.

The only sure way to obligate users to pay for a game is to force the game to contact your server every time it runs. The disadvantage to such a strategy is that this will annoy your users a great deal, especially if they have to pay for Wireless Application Protocol (WAP) access, which they typically do. In the case of a multiplayer game that passes through a common server instead of connecting peer-to-peer, the user won't mind connecting every time since it's obvious they can't play against other users without connecting. That's why hosting multiplayer games is a good business model. Using HTTPS, you can ensure that the game will contact only your server, and by having the game send you some sort of ID or handle for each player, you can keep track of how much each user is playing (for billing purposes).

Using Other Secure Connections

Like HTTP, some other types of network connections such as Bluetooth and plain sockets offer secure versions. In the case of Bluetooth, again the work is done for you behind the scenes. Authenticating the other party and optionally also encrypting the data transmissions is merely a question of changing some of the connection parameters as long as the device supports authentication and encryption. However, unless your application is transferring billing interactions or other security-critical data through Bluetooth, it generally isn't worth the bother. Connecting to another player in a multiplayer game isn't terribly security critical since the players can tell if they've correctly connected to one another.

In the case of plain sockets, switching a MIDP client program from using a SocketConnection to using a SecureConnection (in other words, switching from using a plain socket to using SSL) is almost as trivial as switching from HTTP to HTTPS. In fact, just as with HTTP versus HTTPS, it's sufficient to just change the URL. (In this case, switch the beginning of the URL from socket:// to ssl://, and change the port number if necessary.)

Even though setting the right URL is all that's required for creating a SecureConnection, you should probably also programmatically verify that the certificate that the server is using is the right one. When you create a SecureConnection, the application management software will accept any valid certificate (as long as it's from a recognized CA). This means that unless you verify the name on the certificate yourself, you still may be making an SSL connection with the wrong host even though the host has a real certificate.

Checking the certificate is quite easy. To demonstrate, I've written a simple verification method (see Listing 8-1).

Listing 8-1. *Verification Method*

```
/**
 * This takes a secure connection and makes sure that
 * the corresponding certificate is the right one.
 * @throws SecurityException if the certificate isn't
 * issued to the correct entity.
 */
private void verifyCertificate(SecureConnection conn)
    throws Exception {
  SecurityInfo info = conn.getSecurityInfo();
  Certificate cert = info.getServerCertificate();
  String sub = cert.getSubject();
  // the subject should end with CN=DOMAIN_NAME where
  // DOMAIN_NAME is the name of the domain that you
  // expect to be communicating with.
  if(! sub.endsWith("CN=" + DOMAIN_NAME)) {
    // you'll give it one more chance in case the CN
    // attribute wasn't the last attribute in the list:
    if(sub.indexOf("CN=" + DOMAIN_NAME + ";") == -1) {
      // if it fails both these tests, then the certificate
      // isn't the right one...
      throw(new SecurityException("Certificate CN wrong"));
```

```
        }
    }
}
```

To understand Listing 7-1, keep in mind that the method getSubject() (of the Certificate interface) returns the name of the certificate owner in Lightweight Directory Access Protocol (LDAP) format. This means that the subject string will look something like this: C=US;O=Any Company, Inc.;CN=www.anycompany.com. The part of the subject you probably want to verify is the value of the CN attribute. This should be the URL of the site that owns the certificate. Technically it doesn't have to be, but in practice it usually is. The CN attribute should appear at the end of the subject string. That's why I used the method endsWith() to check if the CN of the certificate is right. If the end of the subject string isn't what I expected, the certificate owner is probably the wrong one. In Listing 7-1 I give the certificate a second chance to have the correct CN somewhere in it (by using the method indexOf() to determine if the correct CN is present). If you're using SSL in a commercial application, you may not want to be so lenient.

Summary

Java security seems to focus around protecting the device and user from your program, but ultimately it's a good thing, because that means the user won't be hesitating over worries about whether your game is untrustworthy before installing it. If the game has been approved and signed by the manufacturer or operator, it has more permissions than if it is merely identified by a Certificate Authority, and if it's not identified at all, it can still perform restricted actions (such as sending an SMS) as long as the user is aware of the action and clicks OK. Digital signatures and encryption techniques help ensure the integrity of the data as well as authenticate the source and destination of communications.

CHAPTER 9

■■■

The Mobile 3D Graphics API

One of the most exciting optional APIs for game developers is the Mobile 3D Graphics (M3G) API, defined in JSR 184. From a business perspective it's not necessarily the most important optional API because a 3D game is generally costlier to produce than a game without 3D. In addition—although studies show that many people will play games on their handset even at home where they have access to their computers and game consoles—simple, familiar games are typically more popular on handsets than games that boast amazing graphics. It's difficult to impress your players with graphics on a small device because they've seen more impressive graphics on the big screens of their game consoles. I'm not saying that 3D games are never worth the bother on a small device—just that you need to be that much more creative to use 3D in a fun and original way to make it pay.

On the other hand, from the developer's perspective 3D is a gold mine. The 3D API is so rich with possibilities that you can't help but want to try it out and see what it does. It's a nice break from client/server programming where the whole trick is tracking down exactly the right configuration that allows the two to communicate, and once you've got it, you're done. With 3D, even after the program is working, there are a million little things you could add or tweak, and any one of them might produce an interesting result. So it's a fun challenge to learn it, and once you've got a feel for how to use the 3D API, you have a valuable skill because even the simple stuff is tricky enough that even a skilled engineer is unlikely to get a handle on it in one sitting.

In this chapter, I'm going to focus on the fundamentals of the coordinate systems, rendering, and M3G file structure. I'll give an overview of the advanced features that are available, but the bells and whistles are easier to learn from the JavaDoc once you have a thorough grasp of the basics.

Vertex Buffers and Coordinates

A complete three-dimensional scene is a complex object, but it ultimately comes down to sets of coordinates. Understanding how the different coordinate systems work together is the key to navigating your 3D scene with ease.

Defining the Polygon

The most basic object is an array of simple values sitting inside a `VertexArray`, which gives information about how to divide the array into vertices. You would normally expect each vertex would have three coordinates, but there are cases where a vertex may be defined by two or four coordinates, and the `VertexArray` stores that information.

A VertexArray is really a memory-saving device to avoid creating lots of unnecessary objects. Since sets of vertices working together will normally have the same basic properties, the VertexArray stores the common data of the whole group rather than creating a class called Vertex containing the coordinates of each single point and then having the developer create arrays of these Vertex objects. The VertexArray allows you to take an array of simple values and say, "Every three (or two or four) values in this list should be grouped as a single vertex." A VertexArray object also has fields to indicate how many vertices should be read from the underlying data array and the data type, such as float or double, of each individual coordinate. (Technically, it saves the storage size in bytes of the coordinates, not the name of the data type.) The VertexArray is a basic building-block object that can be used as data in other objects.

The VertexArrays are grouped together to describe a complete object through a VertexBuffer. A VertexBuffer is essentially a collection of vertices where each vertex takes data from one or more VertexArrays. A VertexBuffer can contain a VertexArray giving the positions of the vertices, another defining a normal vector for each vertex, another VertexArray giving color information for each vertex, and possibly multiple vertex arrays of texture coordinates. I'll provide more details of what each of these types of coordinates do, but the thing to keep in mind is that all of the VertexArrays in a single VertexBuffer must have the same length (in terms of number of vertices) because the values are lined up to define different aspects of each vertex. Not only does this save memory, but it also makes it easy to change one aspect (such as colors) for all of the vertices in a single action.

I'd like to start with a very simple example—a square-base pyramid—to show how VertexArrays and VertexBuffers work, and in particular to show a polygon is defined in terms of triangles and how the triangles are defined in terms of vertices (see Figure 9-1).

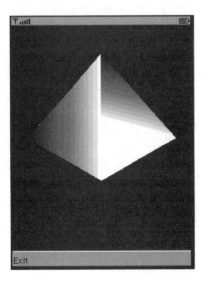

Figure 9-1. *A square-base pyramid created with the Mobile 3D Graphics API*

Position Coordinates

The position coordinates follow the standard conventions of graphs in mathematics. The Y-axis points up, the X-axis points to the right, and the point where they cross is the origin. (This is a little different from the 2D coordinates in the lcdui.Graphics class, where the origin is the top-left corner and the Y coordinate *increases* as you go down.) Then to see where to find the Z-axis, think of yourself as being above the x-y plane looking down on it. Then if you look directly down at the origin, your eye is at some positive point along the Z-axis. So the standard orientation is that you are looking down the Z-axis toward the points with negative Z coordinates. Figure 9-2 shows what a square-base pyramid would look like from this angle. And, as in familiar mathematical notation, the coordinates of each point are given as a 3-tuple in x-y-z order.

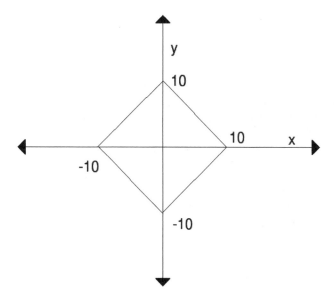

Figure 9-2. *Looking down the Z-axis at a square-base pyramid on the x-y plane*

This sample code fragment shows how to define the vertices of a square-base pyramid with its top point at the point (0, 0, 10):

```
// Every set of three elements of this array
// gives a vertex of the pyramid. The top row gives
// all of the vertices needed, however we include some
// extra copies of some of the vertices to try
// different things with them:
short[] vertices = {
  0, 0, 10,  10, 0, 0,  0, 10, 0,  0, -10, 0,  -10, 0, 0,  0, 0, 10,
  0, -10, 0,  10, 0, 0,  0, 0, 10
};

// Here we construct the VertexArray, which is
// a generic data structure for storing collections
```

```
// of coordinate points:
int numVertices = vertices.length / 3;

// specify how many vertices, plus the fact that
// each vertex has three coordinates, and each coordinate
// is coded on two bytes (a short):
VertexArray va = new VertexArray(numVertices, 3, 2);
// set the data, starting from index 0:
va.set(0, numVertices, vertices);

// Now create a 3-D object of it.
VertexBuffer vb = new VertexBuffer();
// the second and third tell how to scale and translate all of
// the coordinates; for simplicity we set them to identity:
vb.setPositions(va, 1.0f, null);
```

Here, all I've done is write a list of values and define how they should be turned into a set of position coordinates for nine vertices (the points of the pyramid, plus some extras to show how two vertices can be defined differently yet share a location). The next step is to define how to group the vertices into triangles and surfaces made of strips of triangles.

■**Note** Remember that the lowercase f at the end of many primitive values in this chapter means that the primitive is of type `float`. The Mobile 3D Graphics API requires the `float` type for its calculations, which means in particular that it requires CLDC 1.1 instead of CLDC 1.0. When compiling these examples in the WTK, don't forget to set the configuration to CLDC 1.1 under Project ➤ Settings.

IndexBuffers and Triangle Strips

The `IndexBuffer` allows you to define surfaces by selecting vertices by index from a `VertexBuffer`. `IndexBuffer` is an abstract class whose only subclass in the JSR 184 API is `TriangleStripArray`; however, it may be extended in the future to support other types of vertex groupings.

The `TriangleStripArray` is an ordered list of indices to specify which vertices to take from a `VertexBuffer`. The first triangle in the triangle strip is the one whose indices are given by the first, second, and third indices in the `TriangleStripArray`. Then the next triangle in the strip is the one whose vertices are given by the second, third, and fourth indices, and so on. (Technically instead of "first" I should perhaps be saying "zeroth" here, but that's not really a word, and I think it's clear what I mean.) So you see that every triangle in the strip has two corners and one side with the previous triangle in the strip, and also shares two corners and a different side with the next triangle in the strip, thus making a continuous surface.

Figure 9-3 shows one of the triangle strips that will be defined in this example in order to turn this set of vertices into a pyramid. To start with, I'll just define the base with two of the triangular side faces, leaving two of the four faces of the pyramid off for the moment. Also note that in Figure 9-3 the point (0, 0, 10) should be directly above the origin (0, 0, 0,), but in order to see the four triangles of this triangle strip better, for this illustration I've cut the pyramid at the top point and folded the two sides down.

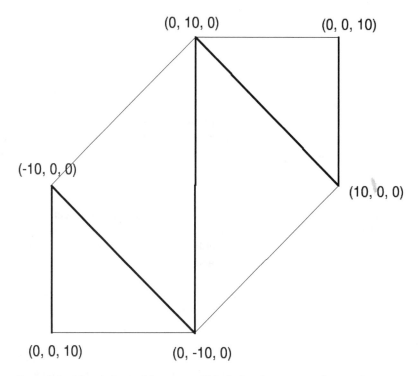

Figure 9-3. *The surface of the pyramid is defined as a strip of triangles.*

The TriangleStripArray can be defined implicitly or explicitly. To define it implicitly, you just give the index of the vertex you want to start with in your VertexBuffer, and the rest of the vertices in the VertexBuffer are assumed to be in the correct order from there. That's the way I've done it in this example. I start by ordering the vertices in the order given by following the bold line in Figure 9-3. You can see from the figure that this ordered set of vertices implicitly defines four triangles. It's also possible to define a TrianglestripArray explicitly. To do that, you construct it with an additional array that gives the order of the indices to use to construct the triangle strip. Then, since it's not usually convenient to create a 3D object from a single strip of triangles, you provide another array to define how many triangle strips you'd like in your TriangleStripArray and how long each one should be. If we call this array stripLengths, then the first triangle strip is made of stripLengths[0] vertices (to create stripLengths[0] - 2 triangles). Then to make the next triangle strip, we move ahead to the next (unused) vertex on the list and make a triangle strip from the next stripLengths[1] vertices, and so on.

The following code defines the square-base pyramid implicitly using a TriangleStripArray. This pyramid can easily be defined using a single strip of triangles, but in this example I'll define it as two separate triangle strips and leave one face off the pyramid so that I can do some tricks with the normal vectors as this example continues:

```
// Here we define the triangle strips
// use the first six vertices to make one strip of triangles,
// then make a triangle strip from the next three vertices:
int[] strip = { 6, 3 };
```

```
// Then construct the corresponding IndexBuffer
// as an implicitly-defined TriangleStripArray
IndexBuffer tsa = new TriangleStripArray(0, strip);
```

The VertexBuffer and the IndexBuffer in our examples can be used together to define the polygon at render time if we're rendering in immediate mode (which we discuss in a moment). You can see that the first triangle strip starts with one of the four top faces of the pyramid, defines the two triangles that make up the base of the pyramid, and then gives the face opposite the first face. The second triangle strip has only one triangle: another of the four top faces. I'm leaving the fourth face off so that we can look at the inside of the pyramid.

Lights, Camera, Render!

In the M3G API, rendering is the act of projecting your three-dimensional object or scene onto a two-dimensional target. Usually the target in question is some region of the handset's screen, accessed through the Canvas class; however, it is also possible in Java ME to render into a mutable Image by getting the associated Graphics object (in exactly the same way you might draw anything else in a mutable Image).

The first step in rendering is to get a handle to the singleton Graphics3D object, which is the class that does the work of rendering. Then bind it to the Graphics object of the target.

To define how your 3D object should be projected onto the target, you obviously need to specify a few things. Where is the camera positioned? What kind of light is lighting the object, and in what direction(s)? What does the background look like? How near or far away must the object be to be visible? Should perspective be employed so that farther objects appear smaller?

The following simple code creates a background and a standard Camera object that defines where the viewer is (at a point in space), and then binds the Graphics3D object to the Graphics object of the Canvas or mutable Image. If this code is in the paint method of a Canvas or Canvas-like object, the Graphics object is retrieved as an argument; in other cases you get it from the getGraphics() method.

```
// Render by getting a handle to the Graphics3D
// object which does the work of projecting the
// 3D scene onto the 2D screen (rendering):
g3d = Graphics3D.getInstance();
// Bind the Graphics3D object to the Graphics
// instance of the current canvas:
g3d.bindTarget(g);
// Clear the screen by painting it with a plain
// black background:
Background background = new Background();
background.setColor(0x000000);
g3d.clear(background);

// Create the camera object to define where the polygon
// is being viewed from and in what way:
Camera camera = new Camera();
// Set the camera so that it will project the 3D
// picture onto the screen in perspective, with a
// vanishing point in the distance. The arguments
```

```
// give information about what region of 3-space is
// visible to the camera:
camera.setPerspective(60.0f,
    (float)getWidth() / (float)getHeight(),
      1.0f, 1000.0f);
```

Here, I'm just rendering my pyramid object directly in what is called "immediate mode" (more on rendering mode in a moment). In immediate mode rendering, the Background and the Camera are set directly for the Graphics3D object after binding to the target Graphics object. At this point, I would normally add some lights to the Graphics3D object as well, but—unlike the Camera and Background—lights are not technically necessary if no special lighting effects are desired. So in this example I'll simply paint the pyramid white against a black background and not bother with lights.

The last thing to take care of before rendering is to define where all of the various items should be placed with respect to one another. By default, the origin of the coordinates in the VertexBuffer to be rendered is the same as the default location for the Camera and the Lights. So we apply a Transform for each object to move it to its proper location and point it in the right direction and rotate it. Fortunately, the Transform object has plenty of convenient methods to translate, scale, and rotate an individual object's coordinates with respect to their original location and orientation.

The Camera is oriented to look down at the negative Z-axis as explained in the "Position Coordinates" section earlier. So we need to translate the camera by moving it up along the Z-axis in order to see the pyramid.

Once we've done all that, we're ready to render. The VertexBuffer and IndexBuffer defining the polygon are passed as arguments to the Graphics3D's render() method along with the appearance and transform information:

```
// Now set where we're viewing the scene from:
Transform cameraTransform = new Transform();
// We set the camera's X position and Y position to 0
// so that we're looking straight down at the origin
// of the x-y plane.  The Z coordinate tells how far
// away the camera is -- increasing this value takes
// you farther from the polygon, making it appear
// smaller.  Try changing these values to view the
// polygon from different places:
cameraTransform.postTranslate(0.0f, 0.0f, 100.0f);
g3d.setCamera(camera, cameraTransform);

// Now set the location of the object.
// If this were an animation we would probably
// translate or rotate it here:
Transform objectTransform = new Transform();
objectTransform.setIdentity();

// Now render: Project from a 3D object to a 2D screen
g3d.render(vb, tsa, new Appearance(),
objectTransform);
```

Once the object is rendered, the only thing left to do is release the target, as shown in the following snippet. This is a necessary step that must be performed for the rendered image to be made visible, so it should appear in the `finally` clause of the `try` block where the target is bound:

```
// Done, the canvas graphics can be freed now:
g3d.releaseTarget();
```

All of our code can be placed in the paint method of a `Canvas`. Figure 9-4 shows what the result looks like in the WTK.

Figure 9-4. *A simple incomplete pyramid viewed from above*

The first thing you should notice is that even though the square base is part of the polygon, it turned out black on the screen. That's because by default the inside faces are invisible—not rendered. In M3G terms, they've been removed, or "culled." If you'd like the inside faces to be visible, then create a `PolygonMode` object for your polygon's appearance, and set the `PolygonMode`'s culling to `CULL_NONE`. The computer determines which side is "inside" and which side is "outside" by determining whether the vertices of the triangle are defined in clockwise or counterclockwise order. If going from the first, to the second, to the third vertex of the triangle means going around the triangle counterclockwise, then you're looking at the outside. (If you don't want the outside to be the counterclockwise side, there's a method to invert the inside and the outside.)

Unfortunately—since each triangle in the triangle strip shares two vertices (in order) with the next triangle—it turns out that if one triangle is given counterclockwise, the next one will be clockwise. So your triangle strip logically would alternate between showing you the inside face of the triangle and the outside face of the next triangle, which isn't what you want in a reasonable surface. Thus, the inside and outside of the entire triangle strip is determined by the inside and outside of the first triangle.

Textures and Lighting

Now that we've covered the basics of how coordinates work in the Mobile 3D Graphics API, let's jazz up this pyramid example by adding some textures and lighting effects. These effects are defined using (what else?) more coordinates!

As discussed in the section "Defining the Polygon," different aspects of the vertices in a `VertexBuffer` can be defined using additional `VertexArrays`. So far we've given each vertex only a position coordinate, but we can also define a normal vector at each vertex as well as color coordinates and multiple sets of texture coordinates. In this example, I'll explain how all of these different types of coordinates work.

First let's have a look at the normal vectors. The whole idea of defining a normal vector seems kind of counterintuitive to me. If you're on the face of one of the triangles of your polygon, the normal vector is logically the vector perpendicular to the flat face of the triangle. So you don't need to define a normal since the normal is determined by the triangle. It makes sense, then, that the places where we get to define the normal vectors are at the vertices. But what does it even mean to be perpendicular to a pointed part of the surface? You might think it would be used to give the graphics functionality a hint as to how to smooth out and round the point, except that the 3D graphics engine doesn't do that.

The normals are used to tell the graphics engine how to make light reflect off the surface. So in a sense it does give information about how to smooth and round off the corners—at least from the point of view of the reflected light. If you define the normal vector to be perpendicular to a triangle face, light will reflect off the triangle as if the triangle is perfectly flat, with a nice, crisp point at the vertex. But if you'd rather smooth out your surface a little—say you're making a ball and you want it to be less obvious that it's constructed of triangles—you can define a normal pointing directly out from the center of the ball toward each vertex, giving what the perpendicular direction (normal vector) would be if the ball were smooth at that point.

The flat-faces-and-sharp-points model requires you to define more vertices than the smoothed/rounded model because when you're smoothing you can reuse the normal vector, whereas to get flat faces you need to define a new normal vector—hence a new corresponding vertex—for each face that meets at a given point.

To see how this works, let's define a set of normal vectors for the pyramid example:

```
// coordinates of normal vectors, each one
// corresponding to a vertex:
short[] normals = {
  0, 0, 10,  10, 0, 0,  0, 10, 0,  0, -10, 0,  -10, 0, 0,  0, 0, 10,
  1, -1, 1,  1, -1, 1,  1, -1, 1
};

// place the values for the normals in a VertexArray:
// note that the number of vertices needs to be the same
// as the number of vertices in the VertexArray of
// position coordinates since they'll be lined up
// in the same VertexBuffer.
VertexArray na = new VertexArray(numVertices, 3, 2);
// set the data, starting from index 0:
na.set(0, numVertices, normals);
```

```
// set the normals for the VertexBuffer:
vb.setNormals(na);
```

Lining these normals up with the location coordinates given here, you can see that the normal vector points straight out from the origin. Thus, light will reflect off the surface as if it were rounded and not flat. Then for the second triangle strip—the one with just one triangle—I've defined all three normal vectors to be perpendicular to the face of the triangle. So light will reflect off that triangle as if it were a flat surface. This example illustrates why it takes more vertices (and more triangle strips) to define a polygon with flat faces than it does to define the same polygon a little bit rounded: the vertices of the last triangle share positions with some of the other vertices, but they need to be defined as separate vertices in order to have normal vectors that are perpendicular to the given face.

The next step is to add some light. Four different types of light are available: ambient (lighting the whole scene equally from all directions), omnidirectional (radiating in all directions from a point), directional (giving parallel rays of light in a fixed direction), and spot (giving a cone of light from a spotlight). Normal vectors are used to decide the angle at which the light bounces off the surface—relevant for all lighting types except ambient. For this example, let's set up an omnidirectional light source along the same axis as the camera:

```
// now add the light:
Light light = new Light();
light.setMode(Light.AMBIENT);
light.setIntensity(20.0f);

Transform lightTransform = new Transform();
lightTransform.postTranslate(0.0f, 0.0f, 50.0f);
g3d.resetLights();
g3d.addLight(light, lightTransform);
```

To show the reflection better, instead of just using a default Appearance as we did in the previous section, let's give the pyramid a shiny surface and turn off culling so you can see the inside. Then let's rotate the pyramid a little and render the following:

```
// Let's try creating a more complex appearance:
Appearance appearance = new Appearance();

// first a reflective material
Material material = new Material();
material.setShininess(100.0f);
appearance.setMaterial(material);
PolygonMode pm = new PolygonMode();
pm.setCulling(PolygonMode.CULL_NONE);
pm.setTwoSidedLightingEnable(false);
appearance.setPolygonMode(pm);
```

```
Transform objectTransform = new Transform();
objectTransform.setIdentity();
objectTransform.postRotate(DEFAULT_DISTANCE, -1.0f, 0.0f, 0.0f);

// Now render, project the 3D scene onto the flat screen:
g3d.render(vb, tsa, appearance, objectTransform);
```

In the `Transform`'s `postRotate()` method, the last three arguments give the axis of rotation, and the first argument is the angle to rotate around that axis (in degrees). You can picture it using the standard "right-hand rule": pointing your right thumb in the same direction as the axis of rotation, your fingers naturally curl in the direction of rotation. Figure 9-5 shows the resulting pyramid.

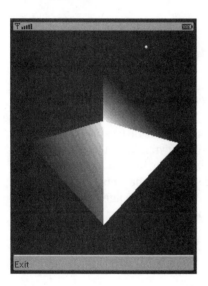

Figure 9-5. *Light reflecting from a pyramid with one flat surface and two curved surfaces*

The thing to notice about the pyramid is how the light reflects off the side with perpendicular normal vectors as if that face is a flat surface, which isn't the case for the other sides.

Since I've disabled "two-sided lighting," the inside of the pyramid is dark. Even if I rotate the pyramid so that my omnidirectional light is shining right on the interior face of the side with normals perpendicular to the face, the surface is completely dark (see Figure 9-6).

Figure 9-6. *The interior of a pyramid without two-sided lighting*

The same normal vector is used for both the inside and the outside face, so in this case, light hits the surface and bounces off toward the outside of the pyramid, not back toward the light source. So if you plan to use lighting effects and show both the interior and the exterior of a polygon, it's better to use two-sided lighting (see Figure 9-7). Note that you can't define the interior normal vector yourself—once two-sided lighting is enabled, the interior normal vector is automatically the opposite direction from the external normal vector.

Figure 9-7. *The interior of a pyramid with two-sided lighting*

The color coordinates allow you to assign an RGB or RGBA color to each vertex and let the graphics engine blend them for you. If you want your whole object to be the same color, just set the VertexBuffer's default color instead of setting an individual color for each vertex. Since the color coordinates are the easiest to understand, I'll skip them in this example and move right on to the far more amusing texture coordinates.

The texture coordinates describe how to paint a two-dimensional image onto the surface of a three-dimensional object. The key to understanding the texture coordinates is to notice that they're not 3D coordinates—they don't correspond to positions in the Graphics3D world. They're 2D coordinates that behave like the coordinates in the lcdui.Graphics class. So in a set of texture coordinates, each vertex gets two coordinates—an X coordinate and a Y coordinate—corresponding to positions on the 2D image, where the origin (0, 0) is at the top-left corner of the image.

To compute texture coordinates beyond the origin, we define the top-right corner of the image to be point (1, 0), the bottom left has position (0, 1), and the bottom-right coordinate is at (1, 1). This may seem limiting since the coordinates are given as whole number shorts, but keep in mind that when you add the texture coordinates to a VertexBuffer, you include a scaling factor (float), so you can think of the texture coordinates as allowing for fractional values.

■Note Any image used as a texture must have its width and height in pixels equal to positive powers of two. The width and height do not need to equal each other.

As an example, let's add a texture to the pyramid, starting by defining and adding a set of texture coordinates:

```
// define the coordinate values
short[] textures = {
    0, 0,  2, 2,  2, 0,  4, 2,  4, 0,  2, 2,
    1, 1,  1, 0,  0, 1
};

// place them in a VertexArray, indicating that
// each vertex gets two coordinates stored on
// two bytes each:
VertexArray ta = new VertexArray(numVertices, 2, 2);
ta.set(0, numVertices, textures);

// set the coordinates in the VertexBuffer with
// the other coordinates, without scaling
// (i.e. multiply only by the identity 1.0f)
vb.setTexCoords(0, ta, 1.0f, null);
```

You may notice that the coordinates in this example aren't all between zero and one. That's because I'm planning to set my texture wrapping as "wrap repeat" so that multiple pieces of my image can appear on each face of the pyramid. Figure 9-8 shows how the texture coordinates correspond to points on my image.

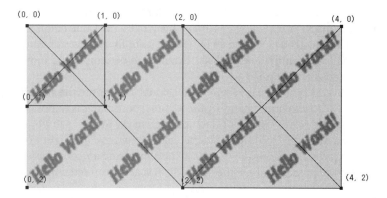

Figure 9-8. *Texture coordinates on an image*

I've used an image that says "Hello World!" not just because of the tradition that basic examples always need to say "Hello World!" but also because I wanted to be sure to use an image with an obvious front and back so that you can see what happens when you put the texture on backward.

Notice what happens when you look at the triangles implicitly defined by these coordinates using the IndexBuffer from the earlier section "IndexBuffers and Triangle Strips." The triangle vertices follow the same counterclockwise-clockwise-counterclockwise pattern as the triangles defined by the corresponding position coordinates (in the section "Position Coordinates") except the last triangle in the first triangle strip. That one is defined with counterclockwise winding just like the triangle before it, but unlike the corresponding triangle given by the position coordinates. Unsurprisingly, as you can see in Figure 9-9, the texture for that face is on backward. Also note that—as expected—"Hello World!" is written backward on most of the inside (back) faces, and the image is scaled differently on the face where the coordinates stayed between zero and one. (I've added the same texture to the background as well.)

Figure 9-9. *A pyramid with a texture*

For my last trick before finishing this example, I'd like to add a second texture to the same pyramid. Texture coordinates are the only type of coordinates where it makes sense to define multiple sets since transparency allows you to see one texture underneath another, so I'll use a second image in which "Hello World!" is written on a transparent background.

For simplicity, I'm just going to use the same coordinates for both textures and then add both textures to my appearance. Note that the way the image is assigned to the corresponding texture coordinates is kind of indirect. The VertexBuffer can have multiple sets of texture coordinates, and each set is assigned an index. Then the Appearance object can have multiple textures (corresponding to different images), and each texture is given an index when it is added to the Appearance. These indices are lined up at render time when the VertexBuffer and the Appearance are sent as arguments to the render function, as you can see in the following code. The result is shown in Figure 9-10.

```
// Start by creating the 2D images to use
Image image = Image.createImage("/images/hello_diagonal.png");
Image2D helloDiagonal = new Image2D(Image2D.RGB, image);
image = Image.createImage("/images/hello_transparent.png");
Image2D helloTransparent = new Image2D(Image2D.RGBA, image);

// create the corresponding texture objects:
Texture2D texture = null;
texture = new Texture2D(helloTransparent);
// set the image to repeat (as opposed
// to stretching the boundary and clamping
// it on when the coordinates are outside
// the image square)
texture.setWrapping(Texture2D.WRAP_REPEAT, Texture2D.WRAP_REPEAT);
texture.setBlending(Texture2D.FUNC_MODULATE);
// set this texture as having index 0 in my appearance
appearance.setTexture(0, texture);

// now create the second texture at index 1
texture = new Texture2D(helloDiagonal);
texture.setWrapping(Texture2D.WRAP_REPEAT, Texture2D.WRAP_REPEAT);
texture.setBlending(Texture2D.FUNC_MODULATE);
myAppearance.setTexture(1, texture);

// wrap the texture coordinates in a VertexArray:
VertexArray ta = new VertexArray(numVertices, 2, 2);
ta.set(0, numVertices, textures);

// set the VertexArray as the texture coordinates
// at both index 0 and index 1
vb.setTexCoords(0, ta, 1.0f, null);
vb.setTexCoords(1, ta, 1.0f, null);

// while we're at it, set the image as a background as well:
background.setImage(helloDiagonal);
background.setImageMode(Background.REPEAT, Background.REPEAT);
```

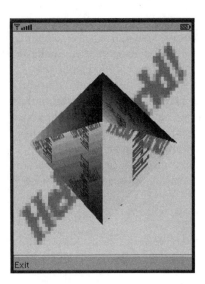

Figure 9-10. *A pyramid with two textures*

Note that all of the code in this example can be placed in the paint method of your Canvas subclass and it's not necessary to implement any other method or define any fields to do it. That's probably not what you would do in practice, but it gives a simple demo to illustrate the fundamentals of the Mobile 3D Graphics API.

The M3G File Format

In most applications, the three-dimensional objects and scenes you'll want to render are too complex to be conveniently defined by hand in the code. JSR 184 defines a special file format to allow the developer to use data created by 3D modeling software.

The M3G File Structure

The M3G file gives you access to 3D objects in the form of serialized Java classes. When you load your M3G file in your Java code (using the Loader class), you get an array of objects of type Object3D.

Object3D is a base class for all of the 3D data objects. Notably, it has VertexArray and VertexBuffer as subclasses. Typically, however, the instances of Object3D that you'll be reading from an M3G file and handling will be more complex objects, such as Nodes. A Node allows you to encapsulate in advance all of the information that was sent to the render method of Graphic3D in the example given in the "Vertex Buffers and Coordinates" section earlier. It also allows you to define how all of the different elements of a 3D scene are related to one another.

The easiest thing to do with an M3G file is to just find the World node and tell the Graphics3D object to render it. Then you'll see the scene rendered exactly as it was created. Otherwise, it's also possible to find a specific instance of Object3D using Object3D's find method and the user-defined ID. This is useful if you'd like to manipulate particular elements in your scene, but to find an instance of Object3D in this way, you need to have a handle to a parent (or other ancestor) node in the same scene graph.

Once you've loaded your M3G file and found the World node, you can traverse your scene graph by querying the World node for its children. If any of the child nodes are instances of Group, these too will typically have children. You'll notice that the graph is a tree (no circuits) like many other data trees you may be familiar with handling (such as a DOM tree you might use when reading data from an XML file). You'll also notice that the World has at most one Background (which is not technically a child Node since it is not a Node—it is a field of the World node). However, it may have multiple Lights and multiple Cameras, which are Nodes that don't need to be immediate children of the World node. They may be children of groups that are further down in the hierarchy. In order to determine which Camera to use when the World node is rendered, only one Camera is active at a time, and the World node has a settable field to keep track of which Camera is the active one.

Every node in the scene graph is a Transformable, which means that it has its own internal matrix keeping track of how its local coordinate system is related to its parent's coordinate system. This is handled through a transformation matrix, as explained in "A Tour of the World Node," later in this chapter.

The most interesting child nodes are probably the Groups and the Meshs. A Mesh is an object that combines all of the different types of polygon data that were earlier covered in the "Vertex Buffers and Coordinates" section. It combines a VertexBuffer with an IndexBuffer and a set of Appearances. The Mesh class allows you to associate these data objects with each other for future use rather than just combining them when sending them to the Graphics3D object for immediate mode rendering. The one difference is that instead of having one Appearance for the whole polygon, each individual triangle strip (also called a submesh) has its own appearance.

A Group node is an invisible node that holds transform information so that an entire subgraph (all of the Group's descendent nodes) can be transformed together as a unit.

Creating an M3G File

Many standard 3D modeling software suites offer the possibility of exporting 3D scenes in M3G format. In this chapter, I'll talk about how to create an M3G file using the free 3D software suite Blender.

Blender is available for download at http://www.blender.org. It is available for many platforms, including Windows, Mac, Linux, Solaris, FreeBSD, and IRIX. Note that Blender doesn't export in M3G format by default; you need to install a separate plug-in (such as the one available at http://www.nelson-games.de/bl2m3g/default.html). This plug-in is fun because it will not only export your 3D scene as an M3G file but will also export it as Java code, so you can see clearly how any scene that can be defined in an M3G file could also be created programmatically in Java (see the sidebar " Exporting a Scene as Java Code with Blender" for more information).

As the Blender documentation freely admits, Blender is not terribly newbie-friendly. It's a powerful tool once you have the hang of it, but the initial hurdle of figuring out how to make your first file with it is not obvious. I'll explain the steps to create a very basic file with Blender (which will be used in a later example), and leave you to see what you can do with the more advanced features from there.

Figure 9-11 shows what you will see when you first open Blender. A new file in Blender starts off with a cube near the origin. You can see what the cube looks like when rendered by selecting render. The Camera used for this rendering is that little line drawing near the bottom-right corner.

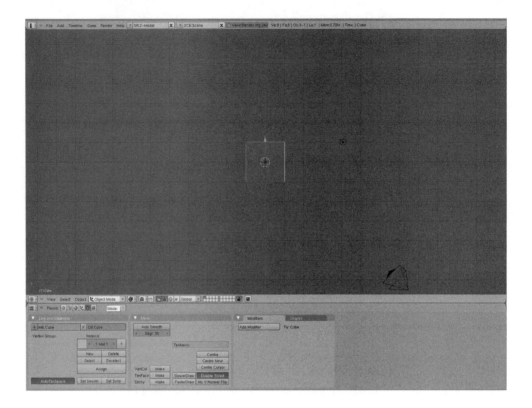

Figure 9-11. *The scene you see when you first launch Blender*

If I don't feel like using the default cube, I just get rid of it by pressing the Delete key. (Since the cube is initially selected by default, pressing the Delete key deletes it.) Instead, for this example I'd like to just move the cube away from the origin.

To move an object, make sure that you're in edit mode (see Figure 9-11; the arrow is pointing at the drop-down menu window where the mode is selected), and then you'll see a set of small buttons with icons: a triangle to translate the object, a donut to rotate it, and a square to scale it. I select the triangle, and little axes appear on the cube allowing me to slide it.

For my example scene, I'd like to have four 3D objects on the x-y plane: a cube, a cylinder, an icosahedron, and a UV-sphere. I add these objects by selecting Mesh from the Add menu, and then slide each one into a different location along the X- or Y-axis, as shown in Figure 9-12. It's also fun to try adding a camera and rotating or pivoting it—that way, you can see how the drawing of the camera indicates its orientation.

Then all you need to do is go to the File menu, and under Export select M3G. If you're using the same plug-in I'm using, it will offer a choice between exporting as M3G or Java code. I recommend trying both, but for this example I'll just be using the M3G file. If M3G doesn't appear as a choice in the Export submenu, make sure your plug-in is installed correctly.

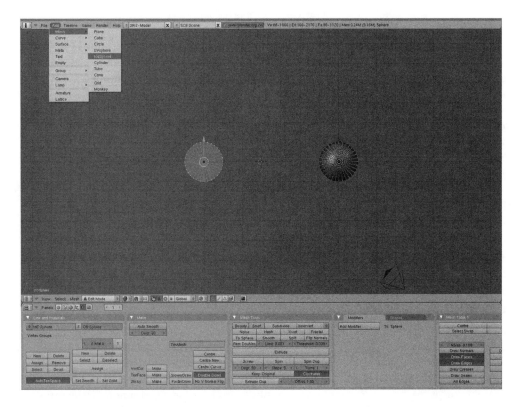

Figure 9-12. *Creating a simple scene with Blender*

EXPORTING A SCENE AS JAVA CODE WITH BLENDER

JSR 184 requires that any object returned by the Loader class be valid in that it must be possible to create the object directly in the code. So you might naturally wonder why the 3D modeling software doesn't just export the scene as Java code instead of as an M3G file. It turns out that you can get the 3D modeling software to export the scene as Java code; for example, the nelson-games.de plug-in for Blender offers this option.

Exporting the scene as Java code is a fun and instructional way to look "under the hood" of how a complex scene is created and tweak it programmatically. Exporting a scene this way can also have real-world applications. The class file will generally be bigger than the corresponding M3G file (even after obfuscation); however, on many devices loading a Java class is faster than loading a resource from a JAR.

The generated class is easy to use, and it's easy to take one version out and replace it with a new version. It creates a final class with one public static method called getRoot() that returns the World node. So all you need to do is call this method and render the result.

Nodes and Rendering

Once you have your scene graph ready and have a handle to the World node, you're ready to render.

Rendering Modes

Immediate mode and retained mode are the two rendering modes available in the Mobile 3D Graphics API. A typical way to think about these two modes is that immediate mode is what you would use when defining a simple object in the code whereas retained mode is what you use for rendering M3G files. That's what it usually comes down to in practice, but that isn't the real difference, especially since you can define a complete scene graph in the code and render it in retained mode. Or you could extract the VertexBuffer and IndexBuffer from a Mesh you found in an M3G file and render it in immediate mode if you like.

   The real difference is just a question of whether you send the data you'd like to render directly to the Graphics3D object (immediate mode) or whether you define all of the scene data (including Lights, Camera, and Background) as a complete data structure in advance and give the root of it to the Graphics3D object to render (retained mode). One advantage to immediate mode is that it's often simpler to have a grasp on the position coordinates since you don't have to take into account the relationship between an object's local coordinate system and its parent's coordinate system (and so forth up the line). Retained mode is more likely to be implemented to take advantage of hardware optimizations.

A Tour of the World Node

To illustrate how to use a scene graph in practice, let's create a fun little example program that allows you to take a tour of any M3G file by navigating around in it. I'm not doing a complete game example in this chapter because the fundamentals of the API are complex enough that I don't want to lose focus by concentrating on the specifics of a particular game. However, this example is relevant to a lot of real-life game applications because it's common for the camera's view to represent the player's view as the player moves around the scene. Figure 9-13 shows the "Tour of the World" program, exploring a 3D scene I created using Blender.

Figure 9-13. *Viewing a Blender-created M3G file using the "Tour of the World" example program*

The first thing I'd like to do is load the M3G file and find the World node. Then I'd like to be able to move all of the World's children together as a Group (I'll explain why in a moment), so I remove all of the children, attach them to a new Group node, and then attach that Group node as a child of the World. Lastly, I define my own Camera at the origin, add it as a child of the World node, and set it to be the active Camera.

```
/**
 * Initialize everything.
 */
public DemoCanvas() {
  try {
    // Load my m3g file:
    Object3D[] allNodes = Loader.load("/fourObjects.m3g");

    // find the world node
    for(int i = 0, j = 0; i < allNodes.length; i++) {
      if(allNodes[i] instanceof World) {
        myWorld = (World)allNodes[i];
      }
    }
    myGroup = new Group();

    // now group all of the child nodes:
    while(myWorld.getChildCount() > 0) {
      Node child = myWorld.getChild(0);
      myWorld.removeChild(child);
      myGroup.addChild(child);
    }
    myWorld.addChild(myGroup);

    // create a new camera at the origin which is
    // not grouped with the rest of the scene:
    myCamera = new Camera();
    myCamera.setPerspective(60.0f,
      (float)getWidth() / (float)getHeight(),
        1.0f, 1000.0f);
    myWorld.addChild(myCamera);
    myWorld.setActiveCamera(myCamera);

  } catch(Exception e) {
    e.printStackTrace();
  }
}
```

Notice that here I'm initializing the fields in my subclass of Canvas for future use.

The reason for grouping all of the World's child nodes is that, as discussed a bit later, a Transformable's transformation matrix tells how to start from the point's local coordinates and get the corresponding coordinates in the parent coordinate system, but not the other way around. This makes sense from the perspective of optimization of the 3D graphics engine because it makes it easy to combine the transformations going up the tree to the root to calculate where all of these nodes (defined locally) should be placed with respect to world coordinates. However, it's annoying in practice because when you apply a rotation to a node's transformation matrix, from the node's perspective it actually looks like the node is staying in place while the World is rotating. This is convenient for animating satellites, but not convenient if you'd like to pivot an object such as a Camera.

The first solution that comes to mind is to take the transformation matrix out, invert it, apply the rotation to the inverted matrix, then re-invert, and install the new matrix back in the Transformable. This is not a good solution because not only does it involve costly matrix operations, but it's not clear that it's even possible since there's a getter for the Transformable's composite matrix but no setter. Another possible solution (which works, but is confusing and kind of costly) is to translate the Camera to the World's origin, then apply a rotation, then translate the camera back to where it was.

The simplest and most efficient solution I've found, however, is to just leave the Camera at the World's origin (see the following code). That way, rotating the rest of the World while the Camera stays fixed is the same as rotating the Camera while the World stays fixed. The problem is that I'd like to be able to move the Camera forward in the direction it is facing in order to explore the World. That's where the trick of grouping everything but the Camera comes into play. Instead of moving the Camera one step forward, I just move everything else one step back. Note that if you'd like the background to move, you need to handle that separately; otherwise, just pick a background image such as distant clouds where it doesn't matter that it's not moving.

```
/**
 * Move the camera or Group in response to game commands.
 */
public void keyPressed(int keyCode) {
  int gameAction = getGameAction(keyCode);
  // to move forward, we get the camera's orientation
  // then move everything else on step in the opposite
  // direction.
  if(gameAction == Canvas.FIRE) {
    Transform transform = new Transform();
    myCamera.getCompositeTransform(transform);
    float[] direction = { 0.0f, 0.0f, DISTANCE, 0.0f };
    transform.transform(direction);
    myGroup.translate(direction[0], direction[1], direction[2]);
  } else {
    // to turn, we pivot the camera:
    switch(gameAction) {
    case Canvas.LEFT:
      myCamera.postRotate(ANGLE_MAGNITUDE, 0.0f, 1.0f, 0.0f);
      break;
    case Canvas.RIGHT:
      myCamera.postRotate(ANGLE_MAGNITUDE, 0.0f, -1.0f, 0.0f);
      break;
```

```
        case Canvas.UP:
          myCamera.postRotate(ANGLE_MAGNITUDE, 1.0f, 0.0f, 0.0f);
          break;
        case Canvas.DOWN:
          myCamera.postRotate(ANGLE_MAGNITUDE, -1.0f, 0.0f, 0.0f);
          break;
        default:
          break;
      }
    }
    // Now that the scene has been transformed, repaint it:
    repaint();
  }
```

The one point I haven't covered so far is how I figured out which direction the Camera is facing. To explain that, let's discuss transformations.

The transformation matrix is composed of a generic matrix, a scaling matrix, a rotation matrix, and a translation matrix multiplied together. You don't necessarily need to use a lot of complex linear algebra in most applications, but it's valuable to have a grasp of how matrices and matrix multiplication works.

Even though the coordinates are three-dimensional, the transformation matrices are four-dimensional to allow translations to be applied through matrix multiplication. The 3D coordinates themselves are actually treated as 4D coordinates where the last coordinate is assumed to be 1 for position coordinates and 0 for direction vectors.

In order to get your bearings, it's easy to figure out where a local coordinate system fits into its parent's coordinate system. Since the transformation matrix takes you from local coordinates to parent coordinates, you can find where the local origin sits by multiplying the transformation matrix by the origin's local coordinates: (0, 0, 0, 1). Similarly, you can get a feel for where the local axes are with respect to the parent coordinate system by multiplying the transformation by a point one unit along each axis: (1, 0, 0, 1), (0, 1, 0, 1), (0, 0, 1, 1). Then, since the Camera is oriented to look down the negative Z-axis, you can find the direction the Camera is facing by multiplying the Camera's transformation by the direction vector (0, 0, -1, 0).

In the previous code, that's the trick I used to figure out which way to translate everything in order to move forward.

For completeness, I'll give the full example code for exploring the World node (Listing 9-1).

Listing 9-1. *The DemoCanvas Class for the "Tour of the World" Example*

```
package net.frog_parrot.m3g;

import javax.microedition.lcdui.*;
import javax.microedition.m3g.*;

/**
 * This is a very simple example class to illustrate
 * how to use an M3G file.
```

```
 */
public class DemoCanvas extends Canvas {

  //------------------------------------------------------
  //   static fields

  /**
   * The width of the camera's pivot angle in response
   * to a keypress.
   */
  public static final float ANGLE_MAGNITUDE = 15.0f;

  /**
   * The distance to move forward in response
   * to a keypress.
   */
  public static final float DISTANCE = 0.25f;

  //------------------------------------------------------
  //   instance fields

  /**
   * The information about where the scene is viewed from.
   */
  private Camera myCamera;

  /**
   * The top node of the scene graph.
   */
  private World myWorld;

  /**
   * The group that will be used to group all of
   * the child nodes.
   */
  private Group myGroup;

  //------------------------------------------------------
  //   initialization

  /**
   * Initialize everything.
   */
  public DemoCanvas() {
    try {
      // Load my M3G file:
      // Any M3G file you would like to
```

```
    // explore can be used here:
    Object3D[] allNodes = Loader.load("/fourObjects.m3g");

    // find the world node
    for(int i = 0, j = 0; i < allNodes.length; i++) {
      if(allNodes[i] instanceof World) {
        myWorld = (World)allNodes[i];
      }
    }
    myGroup = new Group();

    // now group all of the child nodes:
    while(myWorld.getChildCount() > 0) {
      Node child = myWorld.getChild(0);
      myWorld.removeChild(child);
      myGroup.addChild(child);
    }
    myWorld.addChild(myGroup);

    // create a new camera at the origin which is
    // not grouped with the rest of the scene:
    myCamera = new Camera();
    myCamera.setPerspective(60.0f,
                            (float)getWidth() / (float)getHeight(),
                            1.0f, 1000.0f);
    myWorld.addChild(myCamera);
    myWorld.setActiveCamera(myCamera);

  } catch(Exception e) {
    e.printStackTrace();
  }
}


//-------------------------------------------------------
//  painting/rendering

/**
 * Paint the graphics onto the screen.
 */
protected void paint(Graphics g) {
  Graphics3D g3d = null;
  try {
    // Start by getting a handle to the Graphics3D
    // object which does the work of projecting the
    // 3D scene onto the 2D screen (rendering):
    g3d = Graphics3D.getInstance();
    // Bind the Graphics3D object to the Graphics
```

```
      // instance of the current canvas:
      g3d.bindTarget(g);

        // Now render: (project from 3D scene to 2D screen)
        g3d.render(myWorld);

    } catch(Exception e) {
      e.printStackTrace();
    } finally {
      // Done, the canvas graphics can be freed now:
      g3d.releaseTarget();
    }
    // this is not vital, it just prints the camera's
    // coordinates to the console:
    printCoords(myCamera);
  }


  //-------------------------------------------------------
  //  game actions

  /**
   * Move the camera or Group in response to game commands.
   */
  public void keyPressed(int keyCode) {
    int gameAction = getGameAction(keyCode);
    // to move forward, we get the camera's orientation
    // then move everything else one step in the opposite
    // direction.
    if(gameAction == Canvas.FIRE) {
      Transform transform = new Transform();
      myCamera.getCompositeTransform(transform);
      float[] direction = { 0.0f, 0.0f, DISTANCE, 0.0f };
      transform.transform(direction);
      myGroup.translate(direction[0], direction[1], direction[2]);
    } else {
      // to turn, we pivot the camera:
      switch(gameAction) {
      case Canvas.LEFT:
        myCamera.postRotate(ANGLE_MAGNITUDE, 0.0f, 1.0f, 0.0f);
        break;
      case Canvas.RIGHT:
        myCamera.postRotate(ANGLE_MAGNITUDE, 0.0f, -1.0f, 0.0f);
        break;
      case Canvas.UP:
        myCamera.postRotate(ANGLE_MAGNITUDE, 1.0f, 0.0f, 0.0f);
        break;
      case Canvas.DOWN:
```

```
      myCamera.postRotate(ANGLE_MAGNITUDE, -1.0f, 0.0f, 0.0f);
      break;
    default:
      break;
    }
  }
  // Now that the scene has been transformed, repaint it:
  repaint();
}


//-----------------------------------------------------
//  Helper methods for printing information to the console

/**
 * Print the transformable's main reference points
 * in world coordinates.
 * This is for debug purposes only, and should
 * not go in a finished product.
 */
public void printCoords(Transformable t) {
  Transform transform = new Transform();
  t.getCompositeTransform(transform);
  float[] v = {
    0.0f, 0.0f, 0.0f, 1.0f, // the origin
    1.0f, 0.0f, 0.0f, 1.0f, // the x axis
    0.0f, 1.0f, 0.0f, 1.0f, // the y axis
    0.0f, 0.0f, 1.0f, 1.0f, // the z axis
    0.0f, 0.0f, -1.0f, 0.0f, // the orientation vector
  };
  transform.transform(v);
  System.out.println("the origin: " + est(v, 0) + ", "
      + est(v, 1) + ", " + est(v, 2) + ", " + est(v, 3));
  System.out.println("the x axis: " + est(v, 4) + ", "
      + est(v, 5) + ", " + est(v, 6) + ", " + est(v, 7));
  System.out.println("the y axis: " + est(v, 8) + ", "
      + est(v, 9) + ", " + est(v, 10) + ", " + est(v, 11));
  System.out.println("the z axis: " + est(v, 12) + ", "
      + est(v, 13) + ", " + est(v, 14) + ", " + est(v, 15));
  System.out.println("the orientation: " + est(v, 16) + ", "
      + est(v, 17) + ", " + est(v, 18) + ", " + est(v, 19));
  System.out.println();
}


/**
 * A simplified string for printing an estimate of
 * the float.
 * This is for debug purposes only, and should
```

```
   * not go in a finished product.
   */
  public String est(float[] array, int index) {
    StringBuffer buff = new StringBuffer();
    float f = array[index];
    if(f < 0) {
      f *= -1;
      buff.append('-');
    }
    int intPart = (int)f;
    buff.append(intPart);
    buff.append('.');
    // get one digit past the decimal
    f -= (float)intPart;
    f *= 10;
    buff.append((int)f);
    return buff.toString();
  }
}
```

You can see that Listing 9-1 combines the initialization, navigation, and rendering methods I discussed earlier, plus I threw in a couple of helper methods to print coordinates and other data to the console in a nice, readable format so you can get a feel for where you are in your M3G world as you're navigating around. To run this example, of course, you need a simple MIDlet subclass, shown in Listing 9-2.

Listing 9-2. *The MIDletM3G Class for the "Tour of the World" Example*

```
package net.frog_parrot.m3g;

import javax.microedition.lcdui.*;
import javax.microedition.midlet.MIDlet;

/**
 * A simple 3D example.
 */
public class MIDletM3G extends MIDlet implements CommandListener {

  private Command myExitCommand = new Command("Exit", Command.EXIT, 1);
  private DemoCanvas myCanvas = new DemoCanvas();

  /**
   * Initialize the Displayables.
   */
  public void startApp() {
    myCanvas.addCommand(myExitCommand);
    myCanvas.setCommandListener(this);
    Display.getDisplay(this).setCurrent(myCanvas);
```

```
    myCanvas.repaint();
  }

  public void pauseApp() {
  }

  public void destroyApp(boolean unconditional) {
  }

  /**
   * Change the display in response to a command action.
   */
  public void commandAction(Command command, Displayable screen) {
    if(command == myExitCommand) {
      destroyApp(true);
      notifyDestroyed();
    }
  }
}
```

This simple example covers the basics of how to find your way around a mass of 3D data and view it as a recognizable scene. With a little imagination, you can see the beginnings of a 3D game.

Further Tools and Features

Once you've got a grasp of how rendering works with the different coordinate systems, you have the core of the M3G API in hand. But that's not all the M3G API has to offer. There are a bunch of additional goodies to help bring your 3D game to life. Some of the most important ones are explained in this section.

Animations

The M3G API provides built-in support for animating your scene. The classes AnimationController, KeyframeSequence, and AnimationTrack allow you to hook animation data right into your 3D objects. These classes are especially useful for animations that are defined in advance and not dynamically updated. In a game situation, these are more useful for constant repetitive movements, like a planet moving around a star, but less useful for moving objects that must respond to user input, like animating enemy spaceships.

The animations defined in this way operate a little like a movie with specific frames defined. One difference is that the frames don't need to be evenly spaced—the 3D engine can interpolate between them for you. The aptly named KeyframeSequence class only requires you to define those frames that are "key" in that something interesting and new happens. If you'd like an object to just keep going in a straight line, all you need to do is specify two frames (and index them and situate them in world time). Then if you specify linear interpolation, the object will be placed in its correct position along its linear path at any time you choose to display.

Keep in mind that the delta values in the Keyframe sequence are computed relative to the object's original position; they are not cumulative from one frame to the next.

The AnimationTrack is a wrapper class that holds a KeyframeSequence and defines which property the KeyframeSequence can update. Essentially any data property of a 3D object can be updated by an AnimationTrack, from obvious ones like translation and scaling, to items you might not think of updating during an animation such as shininess.

The AnimationController groups a set of AnimationTracks so that they can all be set to the same time and updated together. Note that the AnimationController merely allows you to navigate to different points in time—it doesn't have a built-in timer to set the animation in motion. You can set a Timer and TimerTask to do that.

Let's add a simple animation track to the group in the "Tour of the World" example and set it in motion with a TimerTask. Just add the GroupAnimationTimer class (Listing 9-3) to the same file as the DemoCanvas class, right after the code for the DemoCanvas.

Listing 9-3. *A TimerTask to Advance the Animation*

```
class GroupAnimationTimer extends TimerTask {
/**
  * A field for the World time during the animation.
  */
  int myWorldTime = 0;

/**
  * A handle back to the main object.
  */
  DemoCanvas myCanvas;

/**
  * The constructor sets a handle back to the main object.
  */
  GroupAnimationTimer(DemoCanvas canvas) {
    myCanvas = canvas;
  }

/**
  * implementation of TimerTask
  */
  public void run() {
    myWorldTime += 500;
    myCanvas.advance(myWorldTime);

  }
```

Then, to start the animation, add the startAnimation() and the advance() methods that follow to the DemoCanvas class. Then add a call to startAnimation() as the final line of the DemoCanvas constructor, and the animation will run as soon as the application is launched.

```java
/**
 * Set an animation in motion.
 */
public void startAnimation() {
  // Define a KeyframeSequence object to hold
  // a series of six frames of three values each:
  KeyframeSequence ks = new KeyframeSequence(6, 3,
    KeyframeSequence.LINEAR);
  // Define a series of values for the key frames
  ks.setKeyframe(0, 0, new float[] { 0.0f, 0.0f, -1.0f });
  ks.setKeyframe(1, 1000, new float[] { 3.0f, 0.0f, -2.0f });
  ks.setKeyframe(2, 2000, new float[] { 6.0f, 0.0f, -3.0f });
  ks.setKeyframe(3, 3000, new float[] { 4.0f, 0.0f, -5.0f });
  ks.setKeyframe(4, 4000, new float[] { 1.0f, 0.0f, -6.0f });
  ks.setKeyframe(5, 5000, new float[] { 0.0f, 0.0f, -7.0f });
  ks.setDuration(10000);
  // Make the above series repeat once the duration
  // time is finished
  ks.setRepeatMode(KeyframeSequence.LOOP);
  // wrap the keyframe sequence in an animation
  // track that defines it to modify the translation
  // component:
  AnimationTrack at = new AnimationTrack(ks,
    AnimationTrack.TRANSLATION);
  // have this track move the group
  myGroup.addAnimationTrack(at);
  // initialize an animation controller to run the animation:
  AnimationController ac = new AnimationController();
  at.setController(ac);
  ac.setPosition(0, 0);
  // create a timer and timer task to trigger the
  // animation updates
  Timer timer = new Timer();
  GroupAnimationTimer gat = new GroupAnimationTimer(this);
  timer.scheduleAtFixedRate(gat, 0, 500);
}

/**
 * Advance the animation.
 */
public void advance(int time) {
  myGroup.animate(time);
  repaint();
}
```

Here, you can see that the AnimationTrack has been set to translate the Group node from the "Tour of the World" example. So the data in the KeyFrame sequence will be interpreted to tell the Group where to move. The three arguments of the setKeyFrame() method are the keyframe's index (for ordering the keyframes), the time position of the keyframe (when the frame should be shown in world time), and the data array to be used to transform the node. So, for example, the keyframe set at index 0 says that at time 0 the group should be translated in the direction { 0.0f, 0.0f, -1.0f }.

Once the animation is defined (in the beginning of the startAnimation() method), an instance of the TimerTask called GroupAnimationTimer (Listing 9-3) is created and is set to run at a fixed rate of once every 500 milliseconds. So the GroupAnimationTimer's run() method is called every 500 milliseconds, and each time it is called, it advances the world time by 500. Then it calls the DemoCanvas's advance() method (in the previous code snippet) to set the Group to its new time position and repaint it.

Collisions

The M3G API also has a built-in helper class to give you information about where 3D objects collide with each other: RayIntersection. It looks a little confusing at first, but it's pretty simple to use and quite powerful.

To compute a collision, the first thing you do is create a default instance of RayIntersection and use the pick method from the Group class to fill it with all of the details about the collision. There are two versions of the pick method: one that helps you determine whether random objects in your scene are colliding with one another, and one that is optimized for use with a Camera to tell you what is in the Camera's viewing range.

Both versions of the pick method start with the scope as their first argument. The scope allows you to filter the objects you're checking for collisions with. For example, if your game has a bunch of ghosts floating around that can go through walls and through each other but will possess game characters they come into contact with, then you can set the game characters' scope to something other than the default scope (-1) and then only check for collisions with nodes of that scope. Note that scopes are grouped using bitwise operations: two scopes are considered the same if you get a nonzero result by performing a bitwise & on them. So you can do some bitwise arithmetic to check for several different types of objects at once. A simple technique is to give each type of object a scope that is a power of 2 (for example: walls 1, ghosts 2, player characters 4, treasures 8), then check for collisions by combining them (to check for collisions with walls *or* treasures, pick scope 9). The scope has no relation to the scene hierarchy, so there's no problem grouping objects of different types together to move them as a group. Filtering according to group hierarchy is already built in separately: if you only want to find out about collisions with the descendents of a particular group, then call the pick method on the root of the desired group; otherwise, use the World node.

After the first argument, the first version of the pick method is a little more intuitive. You send the three position coordinates of the point to start from, and the three direction coordinates of the direction to go in, then the RayIntersection instance to store the results in. The camera version is set up to help you detect objects in the Camera's visible range. The two numerical arguments are the viewport coordinates to start the ray from, which are given in the square (0, 0), (1, 0), (1, 1), (0,1) just like the 2D texture coordinates. Then you send the Camera you're interested in and the RayIntersection instance to fill. Typical viewport coordinates to use would be (0.5f, 0.5f) to send the ray right into the center of the direction the camera is facing. However, you can send other values to compute the collisions from the Camera through some other point on the screen (for example, in a shooting game where the gun's line of fire can be repositioned without pivoting the Camera). The least intuitive part is that the collision distance stored in the RayIntersection class is computed from the Camera's near clipping plane rather from its actual location. This is practical because it prevents you from accidentally detecting collisions with objects that are too close to the Camera to be visible, but it's important to take it into account.

Once you've called the pick method to fill your RayIntersection with data, you can read off all sorts of valuable data. Not only does it tell you the distance to the intersection, but it will tell you which Node you've collided with and even the texture coordinates at the point where you've hit. You can also get the coordinates of the normal vector at the point, which will help if you want to calculate how an object should bounce off another object.

The following simple code sample illustrates the use of RayIntersection and pick() to see whether there is an object directly in the line of sight of the Camera and how far away it is. This additional method can be added to the DemoCanvas class of the "Tour of the World" example. This just prints the information to the console—when you write a real application you can decide precisely how to apply the information gathered from the RayIntersection.

```
/**
 * A little method to see how close the nearest
 * object is that the camera sees.
 */
public void getIntersection() {
  // create an empty RayIntersection object
  // to store the intersection data
  RayIntersection ri = new RayIntersection();
  // pick the first element of my world that
  // is in my camera's viewing range
  if(myWorld.pick(-1, 0.5f, 0.5f, myCamera, ri)) {
    System.out.println("intersection at distance "
      + ri.getDistance());
  } else {
    System.out.println("no intersection");
  }
}
```

Optimization

The M3G API allows you to send rendering "hints" to the Graphics3D object. These hints largely concern whether you'd like to sacrifice computing performance in exchange for beautifying the image, and in what ways. They're "hints" in that the virtual machine is at liberty to ignore your recommendations at will, but are helpful for choosing your preferred quality on platforms that have image beautification features available. These hits (antialiasing, dithering, true color) are described in the Graphics3D class. They're set when the Graphics3D instance is bound to its rendering target.

Summary

Understanding how to use the Mobile 3D API is more challenging than a lot of other aspects of mobile game programming because of the mathematics and complex data structures involved. You start with an array of simple data values, and then wrap it in a VertexArray object that defines how the values are grouped to form vertices. A polygon can be defined by grouping a set of VertexArrays in a VertexBuffer object and using a TriangleStripArray to define how the vertices are ordered in strips of triangles to form the polygon's surface. You can render this polygon (project it onto a 2D screen such as a MIDlet's Canvas) in immediate mode, or you can group polygons in more complex objects called Nodes that can be combined into an entire 3D scene graph and render it in retained mode. The Mobile 3D Graphics API allows you to transform 3D objects and offers additional tools to animate your 3D scene and check for collisions.

Once you've created your perfect game—with the M3G API and the other APIs described in this book—the final touch that turns it into a professional game is to add a custom user interface, as you'll see in Chapter 10.

CHAPTER 10

■ ■ ■

Adding a Professional Look and Feel

In Chapter 2, you saw how to create a simple graphical user interface (GUI) using MIDP's built-in `javax.microedition.lcdui` package. The `lcdui` package is a good place to start for a basic game, but for a professional game, you generally don't want to limit yourself to it. The problem is that the `lcdui` classes are designed with a "simplicity over flexibility" philosophy. That means they're easy to use for creating menus and such, but that if you want something more than just a very basic menu (for example, custom fonts or animations related to your game on the menu screen), then you basically have to start from scratch and implement your own menus by drawing them onto a `Canvas`.

An opening animation plus custom menus that match the graphics of the game will make your game a lot more attractive and enhance the player's experience. What's more, professional game studios essentially always customize the look and feel of their games' GUIs, so it's unlikely that players will take your game seriously if it has generic `lcdui` menus instead of a beautiful, professional GUI.

In this chapter, you'll see how to add professional touches to the Dungeon example from Chapter 5 to change it from a hobbyist project to a finished product. Figure 10-1 shows the contrast.

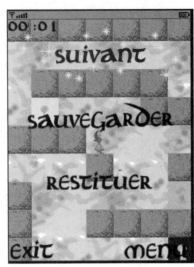

Figure 10-1. *The command menu of the old version of Dungeon and the new version of Dungeon running on a large-screen emulator with Locale (language) set to French*

Customizing for Multiple Target Platforms

As you've seen throughout this book, handling the differences between one platform and the next is a constant problem that you always need to keep in mind. It comes up in obvious ways when writing a GUI as you choose what sizes and kinds of graphics are appropriate and optimize the use of resources for a given handset. Less obvious issues also come up such as identifying different keypress actions using keycodes, as you'll see in the "Implementing Softkeys" section later in this chapter. And while you're customizing your labels and other strings, it's a good time to think about adding custom labels for different languages as well.

Organizing Custom Resources

There are two basic strategies for getting your game to use the correct set of resources for a given platform: (1) in the build stage, you construct different JAR files for different handsets, or (2) at runtime the `MIDlet` queries the platform for information and chooses resources accordingly. Usually it's a good idea to favor the first strategy because it helps you keep your JAR size down by including only the best possible resources for the current platform. Another reason why it's a good idea to build different JARs for different platforms is because it's actually easier for the server to identify which device is requesting the page of game files to download than it is for the `MIDlet` to identify the device once it's installed and running (see the sidebar "Identifying the Platform").

In practice you'll usually use a combination of both strategies, especially to provide multiple sets of labels in case the user changes the language settings of the handset. Since arranging your build procedure to create a series of different JAR and JAD files is very straightforward (see the sidebar "Building with Ant" in Chapter 1); this chapter will mostly focus on the second strategy where a single JAR file is capable of correct customized behavior for a range of possible target handsets.

Most customization is done by having the MIDlet consult resource files (instead of hard-coding custom instructions) so that the customization can be updated without recompiling. A simple technique is to have the MIDlet read data from property files in its JAR. Unfortunately, CLDC's java.util package doesn't provide a built-in class to parse a Java-style properties file. This is quite annoying because it's something that you'll want immediately as soon as you start doing any kind of customization. The good news is that it's not too hard to write a properties parser, as you can see from Listing 10-1.

Listing 10-1. *Properties.java*

```java
package net.frog_parrot.util;

import java.io.*;
import java.util.Hashtable;
import javax.microedition.lcdui.Image;
import javax.microedition.lcdui.game.Sprite;

/**
 * This class is a helper class for reading a simple
 * Java properties file.
 *
 * @author Carol Hamer
 */
public class Properties {

  //-------------------------------------------------------------
  //    instance data

  /**
   * The Hashtable to store the data in.
   */
  private Hashtable myData = new Hashtable();

  //-------------------------------------------------------------
  //    initialization

  /**
   * load the data.
   * This method may block, so it should not be called
   * from a thread that needs to return quickly.
   *
   * This method reads a file from an input stream
   * and parses it as a Java properties file into
   * a hashtable of values.
   *
   * @param is The input stream to read the file from
   * @param image for the special case where the properties
   *        file is describing subimages of a single image,
```

```
 *          this is the larger image to cut subimages from.
 */
public Properties(InputStream is, Image image)
    throws IOException, NumberFormatException {
  StringBuffer buff = new StringBuffer();
  String key = null;
  char current = (char)0;
  // read characters from the file one by one until
  // hitting the end-of-file flag:
  while((byte)(current) != -1) {
    current = (char)(is.read());
    // build a string until hitting the end of a
    // line or the end of the file:
    while((byte)(current) != -1 && current != '\n') {
      if(current == ':' && key == null) {
        key = buff.toString();
        buff = new StringBuffer();
      } else {
        buff.append(current);
      }
      current = (char)(is.read());
    }
    // continue only if the line is well formed:
    if(key != null) {
      // if there is no image, then the keys and values
      // are just strings
      if(image == null) {
        myData.put(key, buff.toString());
      } else {
        // if there's an image, then the value string
        // contains the dimensions of the subimage to
        // cut from the image.  We parse the data string
        // and create the subimage:
        String dimStr = buff.toString();
        int[] dimensions = new int[4];
        for(int i = 0; i < 3; i++) {
          int index = dimStr.indexOf(',');
          dimensions[i] =
            Integer.parseInt(dimStr.substring(0, index).trim());
          dimStr = dimStr.substring(index + 1);
        }
        dimensions[3] = Integer.parseInt(dimStr.trim());
        Image subimage = Image.createImage(image, dimensions[0],
            dimensions[1], dimensions[2] - dimensions[0],
            dimensions[3] - dimensions[1], Sprite.TRANS_NONE);
        myData.put(key, subimage);
      }
    }
```

```
      // clear the data to read the next line:
      key = null;
      buff = new StringBuffer();
    }
  }

  //------------------------------------------------------------
  //   data methods

  /**
   * Get a data string.
   */
  public String getString(String key) {
    return (String)(myData.get(key));
  }

  /**
   * Get a data int.
   */
  public int getInt(String key) throws NullPointerException,
      NumberFormatException {
    String str = (String)(myData.get(key));
    return Integer.parseInt(str);
  }

  /**
   * Get an image.
   */
  public Image getImage(String key) throws NullPointerException,
      IOException {
    String str = (String)(myData.get(key));
    return Image.createImage(str);
  }

  /**
   * Get a pre-initialized subimage.
   */
  public Image getSubimage(String key) throws NullPointerException,
      IOException {
    return (Image)(myData.get(key));
  }
}
```

The parsing algorithm in Listing 10-1 is fairly standard: read the characters from the properties file stream one by one into a byte array, cutting the strings in response to encountering the separator characters. The reason for using a byte array instead of a StringBuffer is so that you can keep track of the string encoding when converting the data into a Java string object. You don't usually have to worry about the character-encoding scheme when using strings that are in English since all of the characters fall into the ASCII range, which is always encoded in the same way. But since these properties files may contain strings to be displayed in other languages, they may contain non-ASCII characters. The standard encoding scheme that must be supported by MIDP devices is UTF-8, so that's the encoding that this example chooses when transforming the byte array read from the properties file into a string. Just remember that when the properties files are generated, they need to be saved in the UTF-8 encoding. A standard text editor (such as Emacs) will allow you to specify the encoding.

The one feature that is a little special in this properties class is that I figured that, while I'm at it, I might as well throw in some additional functionality to cut subimages from a larger Image. The reason for cutting smaller images from a larger Image is the following: since the PNG image format includes a color palette for the image, a single image file made up of a bunch of smaller images that all use the same set of colors takes less memory than storing the smaller images in individual files. It can speed up the resource-loading procedure as well since each individual request for a resource stream from the JAR file takes time. (Note that the image-cutting functionality requires at least MIDP 2, but you can use the rest of this utility class on a MIDP 1 handset by removing the else block from the constructor.)

In the Dungeon example, the images of the strings used in the GUI menus are grouped in larger image files that are cut into smaller images. The Dungeon example has four sets of label images (large English, small English, large French, and small French), as shown in Figure 10-2. (I've included a "download" label in the menu images so this example could be easily modified to use the download feature from the Dungeon example of Chapter 6.)

Figure 10-2. *Four images containing sets of labels: labels_en_lg.png, labels_en_sm.png, labels_fr_lg.png, and labels_fr_sm.png*

When used with the properties class (Listing 10-1) to create a `Properties` instance populated with label images, you can see that you construct it using one of the image files from Figure 10-2 as one argument and a properties file as the other. The properties file consists of the tags to be used to identify each label and then the corners of the subimage in terms of the coordinate system of the larger image (only the top-left and bottom-right corner are required to define the subimage). Listing 10-2 gives the contents of the properties file corresponding to the large English labels.

Listing 10-2. *en_large.properties*

```
next:0,0,179,32
save:0,42,159,69
restore:0,73,199,101
download:0,101,166,138
exit:0,146,57,171
menu:66,148,152,169
ok:158,139,198,170
title:0,172,199,218
```

Note that this same technique could be used to create a custom font for displaying arbitrary strings. That would be more efficient in a case where the game has a large number of messages to display. But since there are only a few labels in this example, it was simpler to just store the labels as whole images.

The next step is to create a class that loads all of the correct properties files that correspond to the current handset. I've called this class `Customizer` (see Listing 10-3). It loads three properties files: one set of general data based on whether the handset has a large screen or a small screen (explained in the "Applying Custom Resources to the Game" section later in this chapter), one set of label strings for labels that are displayed as strings instead of as images, and one set of label images.

Listing 10-3. *Customizer.java*

```java
package net.frog_parrot.util;

import java.io.*;
import java.util.Hashtable;
import javax.microedition.lcdui.Image;

/**
 * This class is a helper class for storing data that
 * varies from one handset or language to another.
 *
 * @author Carol Hamer
 */
public class Customizer {
```

```java
//-----------------------------------------------------------
//   Constants

/**
 * a flag.
 */
public static final int SOFT_NONE = 0;

/**
 * a flag.
 */
public static final int SOFT_LEFT = 1;

/**
 * a flag.
 */
public static final int SOFT_RIGHT = 2;

//-----------------------------------------------------------
//   instance data

/**
 * The width of the handset's screen.
 */
int myWidth;

/**
 * The height of the handset's screen.
 */
int myHeight;

/**
 * Whether to create the softkeys for the current handset.
 */
boolean myUseSoftkeys;

/**
 * A keycode for the current handset.
 */
int myLeftSoftkey;

/**
 * A keycode for the current handset.
 */
int myRightSoftkey;
```

```
//-----------------------------------------------------------
//   data for internal use

/**
 * The custom data corresponding to the current handset.
 */
Properties myProperties;

/**
 * The labels corresponding to the current language.
 */
Properties myLabels;

/**
 * The image file containing all of the labels for the
 * current handset.
 */
Image myLabelImage;

/**
 * The names of the image files for the current language
 * and handset.
 */
Properties myLabelImages;

//-----------------------------------------------------------
//   initialization

/**
 * construct the custom data.
 * @param width the width of the display.
 * @param height the height of the display.
 */
public Customizer(int width, int height) {
  myWidth = width;
  myHeight = height;
}

/**
 * construct the custom data.
 */
public void init() throws IOException {
  InputStream is = null;
  // step 1 is to determine the correct language:
  String locale = System.getProperty("microedition.locale");
```

```
try {
  // Here we use just the language part of the locale:
  // the country part isn't relevant since this game
  // doesn't display prices.
  locale = locale.substring(0, 2);
  // Attempt to load the label strings
  // in the correct language:
  StringBuffer buff = new StringBuffer("/");
  buff.append(locale);
  buff.append(".properties");
  is = this.getClass().getResourceAsStream(buff.toString());
} catch(Exception e) {
  // If the handset's language is not present,
  // default to English:
  locale = "en";
  is = this.getClass().getResourceAsStream("/en.properties");
}
myLabels = new Properties(is, null);
// Since some of the labels are drawn as images,
// here we load label images for the correct language.
// At the same time, load all of the graphical properties
// for the given screen size:
StringBuffer buff = new StringBuffer("/");
buff.append(locale);
// Here only two screen sizes are implemented, but this
// could easily be extended to support a range of sizes:
if((myWidth > 250) || (myHeight > 250)) {
  is = this.getClass().getResourceAsStream("/large.properties");
  myProperties = new Properties(is, null);
  buff.append("_large.properties");
  is = this.getClass().getResourceAsStream(buff.toString());
} else {
  is = this.getClass().getResourceAsStream("/small.properties");
  myProperties = new Properties(is, null);
  buff.append("_small.properties");
  is = this.getClass().getResourceAsStream(buff.toString());
}
myLabelImage = myProperties.getImage(locale);
myLabelImages = new Properties(is, myLabelImage);
// Last, see if we can create custom softkeys
// instead of using lcdui commands:
try {
  // Get the system property that identifies the platform:
  String platform
      = System.getProperty("microedition.platform").substring(0,5);
  // check if the platform is one that we have softkey
  // codes for:
```

```
      String softkeys = myProperties.getString(platform);
      if(softkeys != null) {
        int index = softkeys.indexOf(",");
        myLeftSoftkey
            = Integer.parseInt(softkeys.substring(0, index).trim());
        myRightSoftkey
            = Integer.parseInt(softkeys.substring(index + 1).trim());
        myUseSoftkeys = true;
      }
    } catch(Exception e) {
      // if there's any problem with reading the softkey info,
      // just don't use softkeys
    }
  }


//----------------------------------------------------------
//    data methods

/**
 * Return whether to use softkeys instead of commands.
 */
public boolean useSoftkeys() {
  return myUseSoftkeys;
}


/**
 * Return a data value of type int.
 */
public int getInt(String key) {
  return myProperties.getInt(key);
}


/**
 * Return a label.
 */
public String getLabel(String key) {
  return myLabels.getString(key);
}


/**
 * Return an image.
 */
public Image getImage(String key) throws IOException {
  return myProperties.getImage(key);
}
```

```
/**
 * Return a label image.
 */
public Image getLabelImage(String key) throws IOException {
  return myLabelImages.getSubimage(key);
}


//----------------------------------------------------------
//   utilities

/**
 * Check if the given keycode corresponds to a softkey
 * for this platform, and if so, which one.
 */
public int whichSoftkey(int keycode) {
  if(myUseSoftkeys) {
    if(keycode == myLeftSoftkey) {
      return SOFT_LEFT;
    }
    if(keycode == myRightSoftkey) {
      return SOFT_RIGHT;
    }
  }
  return SOFT_NONE;
}

}
```

You can see that this simple class checks the screen size and the `microedition.locale` system property and then loads the corresponding properties files. The value returned by the `microedition.locale` property gives a string that consists of a language code (given by two lowercase letters) optionally followed by a hyphen and then a country code (given by two uppercase letters). Some examples would be `en-US` for U.S. English, `fr-FR` for French as spoken in France, or `en` for arbitrary English, not specifying the country. The format is the same as for locales in Java SE, except that the two parts are separated by a dash instead of an underscore. For more precisions on this format, see Chapter 5 of the MIDP 2.0 specification.

The labels in the Dungeon example aren't specific enough to warrant using the country code, so only the first two characters are used, and if the language code doesn't match a set of resources present in the JAR, a typical save strategy (as in this example) is to default to English.

Since most of the labels are painted on the screen as images, there are only three items in the label strings properties files: the English (or French) for OK, Exit, and Menu. These are used for the command labels for platforms where the softkey codes can't be determined. All of the softkey-related functionality is explained in the section "Implementing Softkeys."

IDENTIFYING THE PLATFORM

It's often useful to tailor a special version of your game to a specific device or vendor. This can be because of platform-specific optimizations, workarounds of known bugs, keycodes (as in the example in this chapter), and so forth.

It's sometimes possible for the `MIDlet` to determine what platform it's running on by calling `System.getProperty` and getting the `microedition.platform` property. Some handsets return a string giving detailed information about the vendor and model, but unfortunately there are many that just return the generic string "j2me", which tells you nothing. The Dungeon example uses just the first five characters of the `microedition.platform` property (see Listing 10-3) because that is all that's needed to determine if the handset is perhaps made by Nokia or Sony Ericsson, which are manufacturers that I know the keycodes for (see Listings 10-9 and 10-10 later in this chapter).

It's actually easier to identify the platform before the `MIDlet` is downloaded. (Plus, looking at the device's specs sometimes gives more accurate information than querying the device; for example, some handsets' `numAlphaLevels` method returns fewer alpha levels than the handset can actually handle.) A common strategy is to optimize the game with different versions of the JAR file for different devices, saving space by not including resources that won't be used. It's not too hard to set up your build process to create a series of different binaries optimized for different devices (see "Building with Ant" in Chapter 1). J2ME Polish uses this strategy (see the sidebar "Using J2ME Polish" later in this chapter).

Once you have your different versions ready, you create different WML or HTML pages for each device category containing the links to the right JAD files that point to the correct JAR files. When the device's browser requests your game page from your site's server, just configure the server to read the `user-agent` header and serve the right page accordingly. The `user-agent` header will give you precise information about which device is making the request.

Modifying Image Colors and Transparency

Another trick to save space in the JAR file is to modify the color of an image if the same image is used with more than one coloration. In the Dungeon example, all of the menu items are written in black. However, as the user moves up and down the menu to select a choice, there has to be some way to indicate which item is currently highlighted. One way to do this is to change the color of the focused item—in the Dungeon example it will be bright blue.

It wouldn't be terribly efficient to store black versions of all of the labels in the JAR and also blue versions of the exact same images. So in the Dungeon example, for each label image, you create a second image, swapping out the black color and exchanging it with blue.

In the code for the menu, you'll see that it's convenient to have each menu item be a `Sprite` so that in a single method call (`setCell()`) you can switch from the unfocused (black) image to the focused (blue) image. And since a `Sprite` requires all of its cells to be read from a single image object, it's necessary to create a new image object that has both colored versions together, as seen in Listing 10-4.

Listing 10-4. *ColorChanger.java*

```
package net.frog_parrot.util;

import javax.microedition.lcdui.*;
```

```java
/**
 * This class modifies the colors and transparency
 * of an image.
 *
 * @author Carol Hamer
 */
public class ColorChanger {

  //------------------------------------------------------------
  //   Constants

  /**
   * A color constant.
   */
  public static int TRANSPARENT_WHITE = 0x00ffffff;

  /**
   * A color constant.
   */
  public static int OPAQUE = 0xff000000;

  //------------------------------------------------------------
  //   utilities

  /**
   * This method changes the transparency of the Image.
   *
   * @param image the source Image to modify
   * @param color the color value that the new transparency
   * is read from in ARGB.  The RGB part is ignored.
   */
  public static Image modifyTransparency(Image image,
      int color) {
    int transparency = color & OPAQUE;
    int width = image.getWidth();
    int height = image.getHeight();
    int[] imageData = new int[width * height];
    image.getRGB(imageData, 0, width, 0, 0, width, height);
    for(int i = 0; i < imageData.length; i++) {
      // only modify pixels that aren't already
      // fully transparent:
      if((imageData[i] & OPAQUE) != 0) {
        imageData[i] = transparency
            + (imageData[i] & TRANSPARENT_WHITE);
      }
    }
    return(Image.createRGBImage(imageData, width, height, true));
  }
```

```
/**
 * This method doubles the size of the image by
 * adding a second copy of the image to the image file
 * with a new color.  This is used to create Sprites
 * with a "focused" and "unfocused" version of
 * the same image.
 *
 * @param image the source Image to modify
 * @param oldColor the color to replace.
 * @param newColor the color to replace it with.
 */
public static Image createFocused(Image image,
    int oldColor, int newColor) {
  int width = image.getWidth();
  int height = image.getHeight();
  int simpleSize = width * height;
  int[] imageData = new int[simpleSize * 2];
  // make two copies of the image data one
  // after the other in the byte array:
  image.getRGB(imageData, 0, width, 0, 0, width, height);
  image.getRGB(imageData, simpleSize, width, 0, 0, width, height);
  for(int i = 0; i < simpleSize; i++) {
    // change the color in the first of the two copies:
    if(imageData[i] == oldColor) {
      imageData[i] = newColor;
    }
  }
  return(Image.createRGBImage(imageData, width, height * 2, true));
}

}
```

The part of this class that requires some further explanation is the part that modifies the transparency.

Each pixel of an image has a color value given in ARGB format. ARGB stands for alpha, red, green, blue. So when you write the color value as a hexadecimal integer, you think of it as 0xaarrggbb. For example, if the color value is 0x33451027, then the color has 0x27 units of blue, 0x10 units of green, 0x45 units of red, and 0x33 units of alpha.

I assume you're familiar with red, green, and blue, but you might not know what alpha means in this context. Alpha refers to how transparent the pixel is. As you might guess from the constants in Listing 10-4, 0xff000000 gives a fully opaque pixel and 0x00000000 gives a fully transparent pixel, and the intermediate values give semitransparent pixels. A transparent pixel is completely invisible when painted over an opaque pixel. Fully opaque and fully transparent are the only two possibilities that a MIDP device is required to support; however, if some blending is supported, then two semitransparent pixels will have their colors blended (according to their relative opacity) when painted on top of one another. If the platform doesn't support any alpha blending, then semitransparent pixels will be treated as fully transparent.

One thing to note about the ColorChanger utility (Listing 10-4) is that it requires at least MIDP 2. If your target platform has only MIDP 1, it's still possible to modify the colors of an image by reading the PNG file into a byte array and modifying the data before converting it into an Image object. The PNG image format contains a palette of colors that the image uses, and the pixels of the image are mapped to different colors in the palette. So you can change a particular color everywhere it appears in the Image merely by changing one value in the color palette. This is actually more efficient (even on handsets that support MIDP 2 and greater) because all you have to do is change one value in the color palette rather than modifying the whole image pixel by pixel. The drawback is that there's a little more work to do to parse the PNG file data. The technique shown here is a little simpler and more intuitive for the programmer. And when I ran this version on my Sagem my700x, I didn't have any performance problems, so for this example I decided to go with the simpler technique.

JSR 238: THE MOBILE INTERNATIONALIZATION API

If your target platform supports the Mobile Internationalization API (JSR 238), you can save effort as well as memory by using it to sort resources by locale.

This API works by placing the resources in .res files, which are a little like properties files except that they're less human-readable and more efficient for the computer to read. Each resource inside a .res file is identified by an integer key instead of being identified by a String key. Then, instead of using a format of key-separator-value-separator like a properties file, a .res file has a header section, which uses an efficient binary format to map the keys to the offsets where the corresponding data can be found in the data segment of the file. Since the file is already binary, the values can also be binary, which means that you can store a complete image file as a resource inside a .res file (instead of storing just the name of the image and then loading the image data as a separate step). The disadvantage is that you can't just update the .res files in an ordinary text editor—you need to generate the files programmatically.

Using this API saves you the effort of getting the locale string and parsing and interpreting it yourself. All you need to do is organize your .res files in a standard way in the JAR. All of the .res files go under a root directory called global (an immediate child directory of the JAR root). The default resource files go directly in the global directory, and resources for specific locales go in subdirectories of the global directory, and the subdirectories' names are just the locale strings corresponding to the resources in the directory. These can be either short (language only) locale strings or complete (language + country) locale strings or some of each. Then when you load the resource file (using ResourceManager.getManager), the API finds you the correct resource file for the current locale. So if my handset is set to the locale fi-FI and a MIDlet calls ResourceManager.getManager("MenuLabels"), then the ResourceManager that is returned would contain the data of the file /global/fi-FI/MenuLabels.res. Or if that file wasn't present in the JAR, it would use the data from /global/fi/MenuLabels.res. Failing to find even that file, the data would be loaded from /global/MenuLabels.res.

Then, as an added bonus, the Mobile Internationalization API includes a formatter utility that automatically formats currencies and dates according to the current locale. The currency formatting is only a last step for beautification: no currency conversion is performed based on exchange rates, so your game needs to compute the correct value for the current currency before calling the format function; otherwise, there's a risk that you might mean to be selling a new feature for three euros, but on the user's handset it shows up as costing three Canadian dollars or something.

The API also offers methods that allow the MIDlet to choose the locale for the requested resources or formatting task in the case where you want to use a particular locale other than the platform's current locale.

Creating a GUI

Now that you've loaded the resources, the next step is to use them to create a beautiful user interface. This example covers the fundamental components of a professional finish: the opening sequence, the softkeys, and the menu of options.

Starting Off on the Right Foot

Your game should draw the player in right from the start. That's why it's nice to start off with a short but catchy animation. Additionally—even before the opening animation—it's common to put up a simple company logo on the screen as soon as the game is launched and before doing anything else. This initial screen serves the dual purpose of promoting your company's brand and masking the time it takes to load the custom resources. If your target platform is very slow at loading resources from the JAR, you can sometimes speed things up by hard-coding the image data byte array into a Java class. Listing 10-4 gives examples of how to turn Images into byte arrays and vice versa. The trade-off is that it's an extremely inefficient way of storing the data and hence should only be used for very small images. MIDP 2 devices aren't usually low-end enough in terms of screen-size and resource-loading speed for hard-coding the opening image to be useful.

In the Dungeon example, the first step is to color the screen white and paint a small logo over it (Figure 10-3).

Figure 10-3. *The initial splash screen*

The custom resources are then loaded in the background, and when they're ready, the game-specific opening animation begins. This opening animation consists of the title of the game and a drawing of some keys appearing over a background image, as seen in Figure 10-4.

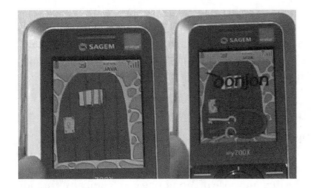

Figure 10-4. *The first screen and the last screen of the opening animation*

If the handset supports alpha blending, the title and keys fade in by gradually turning the transparency from fully transparent to fully opaque. Otherwise, the two components slide in from opposite sides of the screen. Both of these openings looked nice on my Sagem my700x. Even though the fading in animation involves creating a series of Image objects on the fly, there were no speed or memory problems. The splash screen code is shown in Listing 10-5.

Listing 10-5. *SplashScreen.java*

```
package net.frog_parrot.util;

import java.io.IOException;
import javax.microedition.lcdui.*;

/**
 * This class displays the opening sequence.
 *
 * @author Carol Hamer
 */
public class SplashScreen extends Canvas {

  //----------------------------------------------------------
  //   Constants

  /**
   * color constant.
   */
  public static final int WHITE = 0xffffff;

  /**
   * color constant.
   */
  public static final int GRAY = 0x9b9999;
```

```java
/**
 * The distance to move during animation.
 */
public static final int INCREMENT = 10;


//----------------------------------------------------------
//    instance data

/**
 * The customizer giving the data about the image sizes
 * to use for this platform.
 */
Customizer myCustomizer;

/**
 * What step in the opening animation we're on.
 */
int myStep;

/**
 * The step value that indicates that the opening
 * animation is done.
 */
int myLastStep;

/**
 * whether the animation makes the title fade in
 * instead of sliding in.
 */
boolean myUseAlpha;

/**
 * An image used in the opening animation.
 */
Image myBackground;

/**
 * An image used in the opening animation.
 */
Image myKeys;

/**
 * An image used in the opening animation.
 */
Image myTitle;
```

```
/**
 * A screen dimension.
 */
int myWidth;

/**
 * A screen dimension.
 */
int myHeight;

/**
 * A screen dimension.
 */
int myHalfHeight;

/**
 * A screen dimension.
 */
int myHalfWidth;


//----------------------------------------------------------
//   initialization

/**
 * Set the initial data
 *
 * @param numAlphaLevels how much blending is supported.
 */
public SplashScreen(Customizer customizer, int numAlphaLevels) {
  myCustomizer = customizer;
  setFullScreenMode(true);
  myWidth = getWidth();
  myHeight = getHeight();
  myHalfHeight = myHeight >> 1;
  myHalfWidth = myWidth >> 1;
  // if the platform supports a sufficient amount of blending,
  // we set the opening animation to fade in the title and
  // the keys, otherwise we slide them in:
  if(numAlphaLevels > 15) {
    myLastStep = 15;
    myUseAlpha = true;
  } else {
    myLastStep = myHalfWidth / INCREMENT;
  }
}
```

```
//------------------------------------------------------------
//    business methods

/**
 * Advance the animation and return whether
 * the animation is done.
 */
public boolean advance() {
  myStep++;
  return (myStep < myLastStep);
}

/**
 * Paint the screen.
 */
public void paint(Graphics g) {
  try {
    switch(myStep) {
      // the initial step is to quickly cover the screen
      // with a very simple opening image to look at while
      // the Customizer is loading the rest of the data
      // behind the scenes:
    case 0:
      g.setColor(WHITE);
      g.fillRect(0, 0, myWidth, myHeight);
      Image logo = Image.createImage("/images/logo.png");
      g.drawImage(logo, myHalfWidth,
                  myHalfHeight, Graphics.VCENTER|Graphics.HCENTER);
      break;
      // by step 1, the Customizer has found the right
      // data for the opening animation that fits this
      // platform, so it is loaded and displayed:
    case 1:
      myBackground = myCustomizer.getImage("splash.background");
      myKeys = myCustomizer.getImage("splash.keys");
      myTitle = myCustomizer.getLabelImage("title");
      // paint gray over everything in case the background
      // image isn't quite big enough for the whole screen:
      g.setColor(GRAY);
      g.fillRect(0, 0, myWidth, myHeight);
      // Center the background image
      // (Note that some handsets don't implement VCENTER
      // and HCENTER correctly, so in general it's safer
      // to use TOP|LEFT and do your own calculation for
      // for how to place the corner.)
      g.drawImage(myBackground, myHalfWidth,
                  myHalfHeight, Graphics.VCENTER|Graphics.HCENTER);
```

```
          break;
        default:
          // move the title and the keys from the edges to
          // the middle of the screen or fade them in:
          int move = myStep * INCREMENT;
          g.setColor(GRAY);
          g.fillRect(0, 0, myWidth, myHeight);
          g.drawImage(myBackground, myHalfWidth,
                    myHalfHeight, Graphics.VCENTER|Graphics.HCENTER);
          if(myUseAlpha) {
            int transparency = 0x11000000 * myStep;
            myKeys = ColorChanger.modifyTransparency(myKeys, transparency);
            myTitle = ColorChanger.modifyTransparency(myTitle, transparency);
            g.drawImage(myTitle, myHalfWidth,
                      myHalfHeight >> 1, Graphics.VCENTER|Graphics.HCENTER);
            g.drawImage(myKeys, myHalfWidth,
                      myHalfHeight + (myHalfHeight >> 1),
                      Graphics.VCENTER|Graphics.HCENTER);
          } else {
            g.drawImage(myTitle, myWidth - move,
                      myHalfHeight >> 1, Graphics.VCENTER|Graphics.HCENTER);
            g.drawImage(myKeys, move,
                      myHalfHeight + (myHalfHeight >> 1),
                      Graphics.VCENTER|Graphics.HCENTER);
          }
          break;
      }
    } catch(IOException e) {
      // the game should continue even if
      // the opening animation fails
    }
  }
}
```

The opening animation is advanced using the same thread as the game thread. Since the opening animation and the game-related animations don't take place at the same time, it's safer and more efficient to use a single thread for both rather than creating separate threads (see Listing 10-6).

Listing 10-6. *GameThread.java*

```
package net.frog_parrot.dungeon;

import net.frog_parrot.util.*;
```

```java
/**
 * This class contains the loop that keeps the game running.
 *
 * @author Carol Hamer
 */
public class GameThread extends Thread {

  //-----------------------------------------------------------
  //   fields

  /**
   * Whether or not the main thread would like this thread
   * to pause.
   */
  boolean myShouldPause;

  /**
   * Whether or not the main thread would like this thread
   * to stop.
   */
  static boolean myShouldStop;

  /**
   * A handle back to the splashscreen.
   */
  SplashScreen mySplashScreen;

  /**
   * A handle back to the graphical components.
   */
  DungeonCanvas myDungeonCanvas;

  /**
   * A handle back to the MIDlet object.
   */
  Dungeon myDungeon;

  /**
   * The System.time of the last screen refresh, used
   * to regulate refresh speed.
   */
  private long myLastRefreshTime;

  /**
   * The minimum amount of time to wait between frames.
   */
  private static long MIN_WAIT = 100;
```

```
//-------------------------------------------------------------
//    initialization

/**
 * standard constructor.
 */
GameThread(SplashScreen ss, DungeonCanvas canvas,
    Dungeon dungeon) {
  mySplashScreen = ss;
  myDungeonCanvas = canvas;
  myDungeon = dungeon;
}


//-------------------------------------------------------------
//    utilities

/**
 * Get the amount of time to wait between screen refreshes.
 * Normally we wait only a single millisecond just to give
 * the main thread a chance to update the keystroke info,
 * but this method ensures that the game will not attempt
 * to show more than 20 frames per second.
 */
private long getWaitTime() {
  long retVal = 1;
  long difference = System.currentTimeMillis() - myLastRefreshTime;
  if(difference < MIN_WAIT) {
    retVal = MIN_WAIT - difference;
  }
  return(retVal);
}


//-------------------------------------------------------------
//    actions

/**
 * pause the game.
 */
void pause() {
  myShouldPause = true;
}

/**
 * restart the game after a pause.
 */
synchronized void resumeGame() {
  myShouldPause = false;
```

```
    notify();
  }

  /**
   * stops the game.
   */
  synchronized void requestStop() {
    myShouldStop = true;
    this.notify();
  }

  /**
   * start the game.
   */
  public void run() {
    try {
      // first initialize the custom data while the
      // simple splashscreen is on the screen:
      myDungeonCanvas.getManager().init();
      // once the initialization is complete,
      // play the opening animation:
      while(mySplashScreen.advance()) {
        mySplashScreen.repaint();
        synchronized(this) {
          try {
            wait(getWaitTime());
          } catch(Exception e) {}
        }
      }
    } catch(Exception e) {
      myDungeon.errorMsg(e);
    }
    // wait a full second at the end of the
    // animation to show the final image:
    synchronized(this) {
      try {
        wait(1000);
      } catch(Exception e) {}
    },
    // since the splashscreen is done, let go
    // of the data:
    mySplashScreen = null;
    // now the actual game begins
    // flush any keystrokes that occurred before the
    // game started:
    try {
      myDungeonCanvas.start();
```

```
    } catch(Exception e) {
      myDungeon.errorMsg(e);
    }
    myDungeonCanvas.flushKeys();
    myShouldStop = false;
    myShouldPause = false;
    // this is the main animation loop of the
    // game which advances the animation
    // and checks for keystrokes:
    while(true) {
      if(myShouldStop) {
        break;
      }
      myLastRefreshTime = System.currentTimeMillis();
      myDungeonCanvas.checkKeys();
      myDungeonCanvas.updateScreen();
      // pause to make sure not more than 20 frames
      // per second are shown:
      synchronized(this) {
        try {
          wait(getWaitTime());
        } catch(Exception e) {}
      }
      // don't advance while the game is paused:
      if(myShouldPause) {
        synchronized(this) {
          try {
            wait();
          } catch(Exception e) {}
        }
      }
    }
  }

}
```

In this example, the main MIDlet class (Dungeon.java, see Listing 10-7) handles the initialization, game state changes, and error alerts. Looking in the startApp() method, you can see the timing on how the splash screen and game thread are started up, keeping in mind that the call that loads and initializes the custom data is the first call in the game thread's run method (see Listing 10-12 later in this chapter for the implementation of the DungeonManager.init method). So the resource-loading procedure isn't done by the AMS thread that calls startApp() (and which needs to return quickly); rather, it is the first action performed on the game thread once it is started. It's OK to do some resource loading from calls within the startApp() method (in this example, the simple logo is loaded before spawning a new thread), but extensive resource loading (as done by the Customizer and the DungeonManager's init() method) should be done on a new thread, as in this example, because some platforms will crash if the startApp() method takes too long before returning.

Looking at Listing 10-6, you might notice that the splash screen is set to null after being used so that its data can be garbage collected, but the Customizer is held in memory for the duration of the game. I could have written the game in such a way that the Customizer is no longer used after the initialization phase (and hence can be garbage collected), but I didn't bother because the Customizer really isn't holding all that much data. It might be useful to add a step that throws away the label images Hashtable after it is used (since the label images aren't reused once the label sprites are created; see Listing 10-8 in the next section).

Listing 10-7. *Dungeon.java*

```java
package net.frog_parrot.dungeon;

import javax.microedition.midlet.*;
import javax.microedition.lcdui.*;

import net.frog_parrot.util.*;

/**
 * This is the main class of the dungeon game.
 *
 * @author Carol Hamer
 */
public class Dungeon extends MIDlet implements CommandListener {

  //-------------------------------------------------------
  //    game object fields

  /**
   * The canvas that the dungeon is drawn on.
   */
  DungeonCanvas myCanvas;

  /**
   * the thread that advances the game clock.
   */
  GameThread myGameThread;

  //-------------------------------------------------------
  //    initialization

  /**
   * Initialize the canvas.
   */
  public Dungeon() {
    try {
      myCanvas = new DungeonCanvas(this);
    } catch(Exception e) {
      // if there's an error during creation,
```

```
      // display it as an alert.
      errorMsg(e);
   }
}


//-----------------------------------------------------------------
//  implementation of MIDlet

/**
 * Start the application.
 */
public void startApp() throws MIDletStateChangeException {
  if(myCanvas != null) {
    if(myGameThread == null) {
      // put the simple logo splashscreen up first:
      Display d = Display.getDisplay(this);
      SplashScreen ss
          = new SplashScreen(myCanvas.getCustomizer(),
              d.numAlphaLevels());
      d.setCurrent(ss);
      // create the thread and start the game:
      myGameThread = new GameThread(ss, myCanvas, this);
      myGameThread.start();
      // it's not technically necessary to clear the
      // splashscreen, but may help in garbage collection:
      ss = null;
    } else {
      // in case this gets called again after
      // the application has been started once:
      myCanvas.flushKeys();
      myGameThread.resumeGame();
    }
  }
}

/**
 * Stop the threads and let go of data.
 */
public void destroyApp(boolean unconditional)
    throws MIDletStateChangeException {
  myCanvas = null;
  if(myGameThread != null) {
    myGameThread.requestStop();
  }
  myGameThread = null;

}
```

```java
/**
 * Pause the game.
 */
public void pauseApp() {
  if(myGameThread != null) {
    myGameThread.pause();
  }
}

/*
 * End the game.
 */
public void quit() {
  try {
    destroyApp(false);
    notifyDestroyed();
  } catch(Exception e) {
  }
}

/*
 * restart after a pause.
 */
public void resumeGame() {
  myGameThread.resumeGame();
}

//------------------------------------------------------------------
//  implementation of CommandListener

/*
 * Respond to a command issued on an error alert.
 */
public void commandAction(Command c, Displayable s) {
  if(c == Alert.DISMISS_COMMAND) {
    // if there was a serious enough error to
    // cause an alert, then we end the game
    // when the user is done reading the alert:
    // (Alert.DISMISS_COMMAND is the default
    // command that is placed on an Alert
    // whose timeout is FOREVER)
    quit();
  }
}
```

```
//---------------------------------------------------------
//  error methods

/**
 * Converts an exception to a message and displays
 * the message.
 */
void errorMsg(Exception e) {
  e.printStackTrace();
  if(e.getMessage() == null) {
    errorMsg(e.getClass().getName());
  } else {
    errorMsg(e.getClass().getName() + ":" + e.getMessage());
  }
}

/**
 * Displays an error message alert if something goes wrong.
 */
void errorMsg(String msg) {
  Alert errorAlert = new Alert("error",
                               msg, null, AlertType.ERROR);
  errorAlert.setCommandListener(this);
  errorAlert.setTimeout(Alert.FOREVER);
  Display.getDisplay(this).setCurrent(errorAlert);
}

}
```

One additional point that sets this version of the MIDlet subclass apart from other examples in the book is that this time the commands, and all command actions except for dismissing an error alert, have been moved to the Canvas class because they're handled by a custom menu.

Creating Custom Menus

Conceptually, a custom menu is pretty easy to implement. Basically, you draw the user-interface components onto the Canvas and navigate around them in the same way that you would draw and manipulate any other game graphics. It's just a question of doing it from scratch instead of using built-in widgets.

In the Dungeon example, there's one softkey that pops the menu up and down, and then the user navigates around the menu and makes selections using the usual navigation and fire/select keys. The advantage to the custom menu in this example is the fact that the background of the menu is just the current game canvas, which is something you can't do with an lcdui menu. Also the menu is animated: the focused menu item has a three-frame sprite painted behind it made up of stars that give a sparkling effect when the sprite is advanced from one frame to the next (see Figure 10-5).

Figure 10-5. *The image that gives the three frames of the sparkling animation as horizontal strips*

If you want an animated menu without drawing the entire thing from scratch, it is possible to add animated `CustomItems` to an `lcdui` `Form`. However, in that case you have to implement the `CustomItem` yourself, so it's really no easier than painting the whole menu as in the Dungeon example. Another possibility in MIDP 3 is to associate an animated image with each item in a list. But again the platform decides how to display the list and will insist on displaying the corresponding strings in one of the platform's fonts and without giving you the option of placing a background image behind it. So the built-in `lcdui` widgets simply don't give you control over the look of the menu. When you write the code yourself to draw the whole menu onto a `Canvas`, you can give it whatever look you want. Figure 10-6 shows the result for the improved Dungeon example.

Figure 10-6. *The Dungeon game in menu mode on a small-screen emulator*

The menu works by having a menu softkey switch the `DungeonCanvas` in and out of menu mode (just toggling a boolean field `myMenuMode` in the class). When in menu mode, the current game canvas is painted on the screen as usual, but then the menu items are painted on top as sprites. The menu item sprite images are words written on a transparent background (so the game screen is visible between and around the letters) and the letters appear in black or blue depending on whether the item is currently the focused item (as discussed in the section

"Modifying Image Colors and Transparency" earlier in this chapter) and the animated sparkling sprite is painted behind the focused item. The focus can be moved from one menu item to another using the arrow keys, and the focused item is the item that will be selected when the player clicks Select. In menu mode the game thread continues advancing as usual and querying for keystrokes, but the keystroke information is interpreted by the menu command code and the game loop advances the sparkling animation of the star sprite instead of advancing the game ticks and game animation. All of this is seen in Listing 10-8.

Listing 10-8. *DungeonCanvas.java*

```java
package net.frog_parrot.dungeon;

import java.util.Vector;
import java.io.IOException;
import javax.microedition.lcdui.*;
import javax.microedition.lcdui.game.*;

import net.frog_parrot.util.*;

/**
 * This class is the display of the game.
 *
 * @author Carol Hamer
 */
public class DungeonCanvas extends GameCanvas
    implements CommandListener {

  //-----------------------------------------------------------
  //    dimension fields
  //    (constant after initialization)

  /**
   * the top corner x coordinate according to this
   * object's coordinate system:
   */
  static int CORNER_X = 0;

  /**
   * the top corner y coordinate according to this
   * object's coordinate system:
   */
  static int CORNER_Y = 0;

  /**
   * the width of the portion of the screen that this
   * canvas can use.
   */
  static int DISP_WIDTH;
```

```
/**
 * the height of the portion of the screen that this
 * canvas can use.
 */
static int DISP_HEIGHT;

/**
 * the height of the font used for this game.
 */
static int FONT_HEIGHT;

/**
 * the font used for this game.
 */
static Font FONT;

/**
 * color constant
 */
public static final int BLACK = 0;

/**
 * color constant
 */
public static final int WHITE = 0xffffffff;

/**
 * color constant
 */
public static final int OPAQUE_BLACK = 0xff000000;

/**
 * color constant
 */
public static final int OPAQUE_BLUE = 0xff0000ff;

//------------------------------------------------------------
//    game object fields

/**
 * a handle to the display.
 */
Display myDisplay;

/**
 * a handle to the MIDlet object (to keep track of buttons).
 */
Dungeon myDungeon;
```

```java
/**
 * the LayerManager that handles the game graphics.
 */
DungeonManager myManager;

/**
 * the Customizer.
 */
Customizer myCustomizer;

/**
 * whether or not the game has ended.
 */
static boolean myGameOver;

/**
 * The number of ticks on the clock the last time the
 * time display was updated.
 * This is saved to determine if the time string needs
 * to be recomputed.
 */
int myDisplayGameTicks = 0;

/**
 * the number of game ticks that have passed since the
 * beginning of the game.
 */
int myGameTicks = myDisplayGameTicks;

/**
 * An array of number sprites to hold the digit images
 * for the time display.
 */
Sprite[] myNumberSprites = new Sprite[5];

/**
 * The button to exit the game.
 */
Command myExitCommand;

/**
 * The button to display the command menu.
 */
Command myMenuCommand;

/**
 * The button to go to the next board.
```

```
 */
Command myOkCommand;

//----------------------------------------------------------
//   menu-related fields

/**
 * Whether the menu is currently displayed.
 */
boolean myMenuMode;

/**
 * The index (in the menu vector) of the currently focused
 * command.
 */
int myFocusedIndex;

/**
 * The images to use for the current menu items.
 */
Vector myMenuVector = new Vector(5);

/**
 * The space between menu items.
 */
static int MENU_BUFFER;

/**
 * The animated sprite that indicates the selected item
 * in the menu.
 */
Sprite myStars;

/**
 * Menu sprite constant.
 */
int FOCUSED = 0;

/**
 * Menu sprite constant.
 */
int UNFOCUSED = 1;

/**
 * a menu image.
 */
Sprite myNext;
```

```java
/**
 * a menu image.
 */
Sprite myRestore;

/**
 * a menu image.
 */
Sprite mySave;

/**
 * a softkey image.
 */
Image myExit;

/**
 * a softkey image.
 */
Image myMenu;

/**
 * a softkey image.
 */
Image myOk;

//-------------------------------------------------------
//    gets/sets

/**
 * This is called when the game ends.
 */
void setGameOver() {
  myGameOver = true;
  myDungeon.pauseApp();
}

/**
 * Get the DungeonManager.
 */
DungeonManager getManager() {
  return myManager;
}

/**
 * Find out if the game has ended.
 */
static boolean getGameOver() {
```

```
  return(myGameOver);
}

/**
 * Get the Customizer.
 */
public Customizer getCustomizer() {
  return myCustomizer;
}

//-------------------------------------------------------
//    initialization and game state changes

/**
 * Constructor sets the data, performs dimension calculations,
 * and creates the graphical objects.
 */
public DungeonCanvas(Dungeon midlet) throws Exception {
  super(false);
  myDisplay = Display.getDisplay(midlet);
  myDungeon = midlet;
  // calculate the dimensions based on the full screen
  setFullScreenMode(true);
  DISP_WIDTH = getWidth();
  DISP_HEIGHT = getHeight();
  if((!myDisplay.isColor()) || (myDisplay.numColors() < 256)) {
    throw(new Exception("game requires full-color screen"));
  }
  if((DISP_WIDTH < 150) || (DISP_HEIGHT < 170)) {
    throw(new Exception("Screen too small"));
  }
  if((DISP_WIDTH > 375) || (DISP_HEIGHT > 375)) {
    throw(new Exception("Screen too large"));
  }
  // create the class that handles the differences among
  // the various platforms.
  myCustomizer = new Customizer(DISP_WIDTH,
      DISP_HEIGHT);
  // create the LayerManager (where all of the interesting
  // graphics go!) and give it the dimensions of the
  // region it is supposed to paint:
  if(myManager == null) {
    myManager = new DungeonManager(CORNER_X, CORNER_Y,
    DISP_WIDTH, DISP_HEIGHT, myCustomizer, this);
  }
}
```

```
/**
 * Once the customizer has been initialized, this
 * method loads and initializes the graphical objects
 * for the timer and the menu.
 */
void start() throws IOException {
  myGameOver = false;
  // initialize the graphics for the timeclock:
  Image numberImage = myManager.getNumberImage();
  int width = numberImage.getWidth() / 11;
  int height = numberImage.getHeight();
  for(int i = 0; i < 5; i++) {
    myNumberSprites[i] = new Sprite(numberImage, width, height);
    myNumberSprites[i].setPosition(width*i, 0);
  }
  // frame 10 is the colon:
  myNumberSprites[2].setFrame(10);
  // if the customizer identifies the platform as
  // one we have keycode data for, we can implement
  // the softkeys with images
  if(myCustomizer.useSoftkeys()) {
    setFullScreenMode(true);
    DISP_WIDTH = getWidth();
    DISP_HEIGHT = getHeight();
    myExit = myCustomizer.getLabelImage("exit");
    myMenu = myCustomizer.getLabelImage("menu");
    myOk = myCustomizer.getLabelImage("ok");
  } else {
    // if the customizer doesn't have keycodes
    // for the current platform, then lcdui
    // commands must be used:
    setFullScreenMode(false);
    myExitCommand = new Command(myCustomizer.getLabel("exit"),
        Command.EXIT, 99);
    addCommand(myExitCommand);
    myMenuCommand = new Command(myCustomizer.getLabel("menu"),
        Command.SCREEN, 1);
    addCommand(myMenuCommand);
    myOkCommand = new Command(myCustomizer.getLabel("ok"),
        Command.SCREEN, 1);
    setCommandListener(this);
  }
  // Now that the timer and softkeys are ready,
  // this screen can be displayed (since the menu is
  // not shown initially)
  myDisplay.setCurrent(this);
  // initialize the menu graphics:
```

```
  MENU_BUFFER = myCustomizer.getInt("menu.buffer");
  // stars gives a sparkling animation shown
  // behind the selected menu item:
  Image stars = myCustomizer.getImage("stars");
  width = stars.getWidth();
  height = stars.getHeight() / 3;
  myStars = new Sprite(stars, width, height);
  myStars.defineReferencePixel(width/2, 0);
  // now load the images of the menu choices
  // make sprites with selected and unselected
  // versions of the image and add them
  // to the menu vector:
  myNext = menuSprite("next");
  myRestore = menuSprite("restore");
  mySave = menuSprite("save");

  myMenuVector.addElement(myNext);
  myMenuVector.addElement(mySave);
  myMenuVector.addElement(myRestore);
}

/**
 * Internal to start.
 *
 * Creates and initializes a menu item Sprite.
 */
private Sprite menuSprite(String key) throws IOException {
  Image tempImage = myCustomizer.getLabelImage(key);
  int width = tempImage.getWidth();
  int height = tempImage.getHeight();
  Sprite retObj = new Sprite(ColorChanger.createFocused(tempImage,
      OPAQUE_BLACK, OPAQUE_BLUE), width, height);
  retObj.defineReferencePixel(width/2, height/2);
  return(retObj);
}

/**
 * sets all variables back to their initial positions.
 */
void reset() throws Exception {
  // most of the variables that need to be reset
  // are held by the LayerManager:
  myManager.reset();
  myGameOver = false;
}
```

```java
/**
 * sets all variables back to the positions
 * from a previously saved game.
 */
void revertToSaved() throws Exception {
  // most of the variables that need to be reset
  // are held by the LayerManager, so we
  // prompt the LayerManager to get the
  // saved data:
  myGameOver = false;
  myDisplayGameTicks = myManager.revertToSaved();
}

/**
 * save the current game in progress.
 */
void saveGame() throws Exception {
  myManager.saveGame(myDisplayGameTicks);
}

/**
 * clears the key states.
 */
void flushKeys() {
  getKeyStates();
}

/**
 * Switch to showing the game action menu.
 */
void setMenuMode() {
  myMenuMode = !myMenuMode;
}

/**
 * If the game is hidden by another app (or a menu)
 * ignore it since not much happens in this game
 * when the user is not actively interacting with it.
 */
protected void hideNotify() {
}

/**
 * There's nothing to do when it comes back into
 * view either.
 */
protected void showNotify() {
}
```

```
//--------------------------------------------------------
//  graphics methods

/**
 * paint the game graphics on the screen.
 */
public void paint(Graphics g) {
  // The LayerManager paints the
  // interesting part of the graphics:
  try {
    myManager.paint(g);
  } catch(Exception e) {
    myDungeon.errorMsg(e);
    return;
  }
  // the timer is painted on top of
  // the game graphics:
  for(int i = 0; i < 5; i++) {
    myNumberSprites[i].paint(g);
  }
  // paint the menu on if in menu mode:
  if(myMenuMode) {
    int y = MENU_BUFFER;
    for(int i = 0; i < myMenuVector.size(); i++) {
      Sprite item = (Sprite)(myMenuVector.elementAt(i));
      if(i == myFocusedIndex) {
        myStars.setRefPixelPosition(DISP_WIDTH / 2, y);
        myStars.paint(g);
        item.setFrame(FOCUSED);
      } else {
        item.setFrame(UNFOCUSED);
      }
      y += myStars.getHeight()/2;
      //System.out.println("item: " + i + ": " + item);
      item.setRefPixelPosition(DISP_WIDTH / 2, y);
      item.paint(g);
      //g.drawImage(item, DISP_WIDTH / 2, y,
      //    Graphics.VCENTER|Graphics.HCENTER);
      y += myStars.getHeight()/2;
      y += MENU_BUFFER;
    }
  }
  if(myCustomizer.useSoftkeys()) {
    g.drawImage(myExit, 2, DISP_HEIGHT - 2,
        Graphics.BOTTOM|Graphics.LEFT);
    if(myGameOver) {
      g.drawImage(myOk, DISP_WIDTH - 2, DISP_HEIGHT - 2,
          Graphics.BOTTOM|Graphics.RIGHT);
```

```
      } else {
        g.drawImage(myMenu, DISP_WIDTH - 2, DISP_HEIGHT - 2,
            Graphics.BOTTOM|Graphics.RIGHT);
      }
    }
    // write "Next Board" when the user finishes a board:
    if(myGameOver) {
      myNext.setFrame(UNFOCUSED);
      myNext.setRefPixelPosition(DISP_WIDTH / 2, DISP_HEIGHT / 2);
      myNext.paint(g);
    }
  }

  /**
   * a simple utility to make the number of ticks look
   * like a time...
   */
  public void setTimeSprites() {
    // we advance the display ticks once
    // for every twenty game ticks because
    // there are twenty frames per second:
    if(myGameTicks % 20 == 0) {
      // the number sprite is designed so that
      // the frame number corresponds to the
      // actual digit:
      myDisplayGameTicks++;
      int smallPart = myDisplayGameTicks % 60;
      myNumberSprites[3].setFrame(smallPart / 10);
      myNumberSprites[4].setFrame(smallPart % 10);
      int bigPart = myDisplayGameTicks / 60;
      myNumberSprites[0].setFrame((bigPart / 10) % 10);
      myNumberSprites[1].setFrame(bigPart % 10);
    }
  }

  //---------------------------------------------------------
  //   game movements and commands

  /**
   * update the display.
   */
  void updateScreen() {
    if(! myMenuMode) {
      myGameTicks++;
      setTimeSprites();
    } else {
      // in menu mode the game doesn't advance
```

```
    // but the sparking animation behind the
    // selected item must advance:
    myStars.nextFrame();
  }
  // paint the display:
  try {
    paint(getGraphics());
    flushGraphics(CORNER_X, CORNER_Y, DISP_WIDTH, DISP_HEIGHT);
  } catch(Exception e) {
    myDungeon.errorMsg(e);
  }
}

/**
 * Respond to keystrokes.
 */
public void checkKeys() {
  if(! myGameOver) {
    // determine which moves the user would like to make:
    int keyState = getKeyStates();
    if(myMenuMode) {
      menuAction(keyState);
    } else {
      int vertical = 0;
      int horizontal = 0;
      if((keyState & LEFT_PRESSED) != 0) {
        horizontal = -1;
      }
      if((keyState & RIGHT_PRESSED) != 0) {
        horizontal = 1;
      }
      if((keyState & UP_PRESSED) != 0) {
        vertical = -1;
      }
      if((keyState & DOWN_PRESSED) != 0) {
        // if the user presses the down key,
        // we put down or pick up a key object
        // or pick up the crown:
        myManager.putDownPickUp();
      }
      // tell the manager to move the player
      // accordingly if possible:
      myManager.requestMove(horizontal, vertical);
    }
  }
}
```

```java
/**
 * Respond to keystrokes on the menu.
 */
public void menuAction(int keyState) {
  try {
    if((keyState & FIRE_PRESSED) != 0) {
      Sprite selected = (Sprite)(myMenuVector.elementAt(myFocusedIndex));
      if(selected == myNext) {
        reset();
        myDungeon.resumeGame();
      } else if(selected == myRestore) {
        revertToSaved();
      } else if(selected == mySave) {
        saveGame();
      }
      myMenuMode = false;
    }
    // change which item is selected in
    // response to up and down:
    if((keyState & UP_PRESSED) != 0) {
      if(myFocusedIndex > 0) {
        myFocusedIndex--;
      }
    }
    if((keyState & DOWN_PRESSED) != 0) {
      if((myFocusedIndex + 1) < myMenuVector.size()) {
        myFocusedIndex++;
      }
    }
  } catch(Exception e) {
    myDungeon.errorMsg(e);
  }
}

/**
 * Respond to softkeys.
 * The keystates value won't give information
 * about softkeys, so the keypressed method
 * must be implemented separately:
 */
public void keyPressed(int keyCode) {
  int softkey = myCustomizer.whichSoftkey(keyCode);
  if(softkey == Customizer.SOFT_LEFT) {
    // left is exit:
    myDungeon.quit();
  } else if(softkey == Customizer.SOFT_RIGHT) {
    // right either pops the menu up and down
```

```
      // or advances to the next board if a board
      // is done:
      try {
        if(myGameOver) {
          reset();
          flushKeys();
          myDungeon.resumeGame();
        } else {
          setMenuMode();
        }
      } catch(Exception e) {
        myDungeon.errorMsg(e);
      }
    }
  }


  /**
   * Respond to softkeys in the case where
   * lcdui commands are used instead of custom
   * graphical softkeys.
   */
  public void commandAction(Command c, Displayable s) {
    try {
      if(c == myMenuCommand) {
        setMenuMode();
      } else if(c == myOkCommand) {
        removeCommand(myOkCommand);
        addCommand(myMenuCommand);
        reset();
        flushKeys();
        myDungeon.resumeGame();
      } else if(c == myExitCommand) {
        myDungeon.quit();
      }
    } catch(Exception e) {
      myDungeon.errorMsg(e);
    }
  }

}
```

You can see that another advantage of this version over the version in Chapter 5 is that the timer is also drawn with a set of five sprites (all using the same image) instead of being drawn with one of the platform's built-in fonts onto an ugly black bar drawn across the bottom of the screen. Figure 10-7 shows the difference.

Figure 10-7. *The difference in how the timer number appears in the two versions*

The trickiest part of the menu code in Listing 10-8 is the implementation of the softkeys, explained in the next section.

Implementing Softkeys

Nearly every MIDP device uses a system of softkeys to drive its built-in GUI. A softkey is a physical button on the device whose function changes depending on the context. The button corresponding to the softkey is generally placed right next to the screen so that the program can display the current label for it such as Exit, Options, or OK. A typical platform has two softkeys—a right softkey and a left softkey—at the base of the screen.

When writing your own custom GUI, naturally you want to be able to implement the softkey functionality so that you can be sure that the softkey labels match the look of the rest of the graphical components. Unfortunately, the designers of MIDP decided that they didn't want to make it easy for you to do this. The philosophy seems to be that the softkeys are a platform-specific implementation detail that you don't need to know about, and if you start fiddling with them, you can mess up the platform's consistent user experience by perhaps putting your Exit key on the left when the platform normally puts it on the right, or you might assume the softkeys are at the bottom of the screen when for a particular platform they're at the top. So MIDP encapsulates softkeys (and possibly other related input features) in Command objects and says in essence "We'll handle them—you don't touch them."

However, since so many devices use this same consistent design of placing the softkeys at the bottom left and bottom right of the screen, it's natural to want to try to implement them yourself to create a consistent, attractive look for your game. It would have been nice if the designers of MIDP had at least thrown in some minimal support such as a system property you can query to determine whether the platform uses standard (bottom left and bottom right) softkeys, and then provide the corresponding key constants in the GameCanvas class. As it is, it's possible to receive and interpret the softkey events, but you have to do some additional work, and the resulting code isn't terribly portable. Essentially you have to customize the JAR file for every target device (or at least every manufacturer) that you'd like to use custom softkeys on.

Here's how to do it. If you look at Listing 10-8, you'll see that in addition to querying for key states (as in the corresponding class in Chapter 5), the keyPressed() method is also implemented. This is because the return value of the getKeyStates() method only returns information about the standard Java key constants. However, the AMS calls the keyPressed() method with the platform's raw keycode integer corresponding to the key that was pressed. Since these keycodes vary from one device to the next, you usually follow with the getGameAction class to translate the platform-specific keycode into a recognizable Java constant (as explained in the section "Using the Graphics and Canvas Classes" from Chapter 2). But if you happen to know the current device's codes for the left and right softkeys, this is where you use that information.

Figuring out what keycodes your game should be using at any given moment is a two-step process: (1) identify the platform, and (2) load and use the correct keycode values for the current platform. Identifying the platform is a challenge all its own, discussed in the "Identifying the Platform" sidebar earlier. Then figuring out the keycodes for all of your target devices is a separate challenge. Some manufacturers (Sony Ericsson, for example) publish developer guides that contain the keycodes. Additionally, there are online databases listing the keycodes for many popular devices, such as the device database on the J2ME Polish web site (see the "Using J2ME Polish" sidebar).

Many devices follow the WTK's example for their keycode mapping: -6 for the left softkey and -7 for the right softkey. (These are the values used by Sony Ericsson, for example.) But many don't. My Sagem my700x, for example, uses exactly the reverse.

Once you know the keycodes for the current device, implementing the softkeys is a snap. As you can see in Listing 10-8, you set your canvas to full-screen mode, then paint on the softkey labels in the lower right and left corners of the screen, and handle the softkey actions in the keyPressed() method.

However, it's good to provide a fallback for the case where the game is running on a device that you can't identify and/or don't have the keycodes for. In this case, we can still use the custom menu code, but the menu screen is put up and down using standard lcdui Command objects, implemented in the commandAction() method of Listing 10-8. It's not quite as pretty, but it's not the end of the world. Figure 10-8 shows what that looks like.

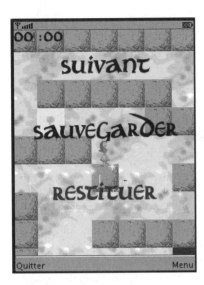

Figure 10-8. *A custom menu using lcdui commands instead of softkeys*

USING J2ME POLISH

If creating a custom GUI seems like more work than it's worth, one alternate strategy is to use J2ME Polish (http://www.j2mepolish.org). J2ME Polish won't give you quite as much freedom as you can get from doing the whole thing yourself, but it will allow you to do a lot of things you can't do with lcdui components, such as controlling the colors of your menus, making menus entirely out of images in various configurations, and painting the menu over an image. And the beauty of it is that you write your program code using the standard lcdui classes. J2ME Polish parses your code and writes a new version, replacing the lcdui calls with calls to corresponding J2ME Polish classes. So from a single code base you can build both a version that uses J2ME Polish menus as well as one that uses plain lcdui menus. It's especially convenient for existing projects that have a series of menus that you'd prefer not to have to entirely rewrite.

Another nice thing about J2ME Polish is the fact that it's based on familiar standards such as Cascading Style Sheets and Ant. You define the look and feel of the GUI for each device using Cascading Style Sheets, and since the code preprocessing and resource selection are done with Ant, the build process is easy to integrate into an existing Ant build process. Plus the system for organizing the resources by manufacturer and device model has already been worked out (including an extensive online database of device specifications) so you don't have to reinvent the wheel to generate versions for a wide range of target devices.

Applying Custom Resources to the Game

The last step in the Dungeon example is to see how to apply the remaining custom resources. One of the first things the Customizer does (in Listing 10-3) is to load a set of properties from a file resource in the game's JAR, either /large.properties or /small.properties, depending on the screen size. These two files are given as Listings 10-9 and 10-10.

Listing 10-9. *large.properties*

```
crown:/images/crown.png
princess:/images/princess_36.png
keys:/images/keys_36.png
stone:/images/stone_36.png
square.width:36
move.length:6
move.buffer:4
jump.int:2
jump.frac.numerator:1
jump.frac.denominator:2
background:/images/interior.png
back.tiles:6
numbers:/images/numbers_lg.png
stars:/images/stars_lg.png
en:/images/labels_en_lg.png
fr:/images/labels_fr_lg.png
menu.buffer:10
splash.background:/images/dungeon_door.png
splash.keys:/images/keys_drawing.png
Nokia:-6,-7
SonyE:-6,-7
```

Listing 10-10. *small.properties*

```
crown:/images/crown.png
princess:/images/princess_24.png
keys:/images/keys_24.png
stone:/images/stone_24.png
square.width:24
move.length:4
move.buffer:3
jump.int:1
jump.frac.numerator:2
jump.frac.denominator:3
background:/images/interior.png
back.tiles:4
numbers:/images/numbers_lg.png
stars:/images/stars_sm.png
en:/images/labels_en_sm.png
fr:/images/labels_fr_sm.png
menu.buffer:10
splash.background:/images/dungeon_door.png
splash.keys:/images/keys_drawing.png
Nokia:-6,-7
SonyE:-6,-7
```

When deciding what should go in these property files, I started with the new graphics files for a larger-screen version of the game, and took every piece of data (images as well as values) that needed to be changed for the new version and threw it in here. Then I changed the code to get these values through the `Customizer` class using the strings such as "crown" or "jump.int" as keys. Figure 10-9 shows the contrast between the smaller-screen version of the game and the larger-screen version.

Figure 10-9. *The two versions of the Dungeon game, depending on screen size*

The first set of values in this list relate to the game itself, starting with the `Images` that correspond to playing in a dungeon built of 24×24-pixel stones or a dungeon built of 36×36-pixel stones. The `move.length` and `jump.frac.numerator` values all relate to how many pixels the princess can move for each game tick, which clearly vary depending on the size of the playing field. `move.length` tells how far she can go horizontally for each game tick, `move.buffer` is how close she's allowed to get to the walls, and the three `jump.*` values relate to how high she can jump.

In this new version, I've completely changed the formula for how high she can jump for each game tick since Chapter 5 (see Listing 5-9). In the earlier version, the formula was exponential; here it's a parabola. The new version of the "game movements" methods of the `DungeonManager` class are given in Listing 10-11. The reason for the change was partially to try something new, and partially because the parabola formula seemed easier to plug the custom values into for the varying screen size. On the other hand, the exponential formula had the advantage that the character goes up high quickly and hovers longer in the top part of the jump sequence, making it easier to jump and move onto a higher block in a single action. One thing I'd like to emphasize by including both algorithms is that there isn't really a canonical formula for how to make game characters move. In the Dungeon example, I started with a general idea of how I wanted the character to move and took some basic formulas and tweaked them until I got the result I wanted in terms of how the player moves around.

Listing 10-11. *The Methods of DungeonManager.java Replacing the "Game Movements" Code from Listing 5-9*

```java
//----------------------------------------------------------
//   game movements

/**
 * respond to keystrokes by deciding where to move
 * and then moving the pieces and the view window correspondingly.
 */
void requestMove(int hdirection, int vdirection) {
  // vdirection < 0 indicates that the user has
  // pressed the UP button and would like to jump.
  // therefore, if we're not currently jumping,
  // we begin the jump.
  if((myIsJumping == NO_JUMP) && (vdirection < 0)) {
    myIsJumping++;
  } else if(myIsJumping == NO_JUMP) {
    // if we're not jumping at all, we need to check
    // if the princess should be falling:
    // we (temporarily) move the princess down and see if that
    // causes a collision with the floor:
    myPrincess.move(0, 1);
    // if the princess can move down without colliding
    // with the floor, then we set the princess to
    // be falling.  The variable myIsJumping starts
    // negative while the princess is jumping up and
    // is zero or positive when the princess is coming
    // back down.  We therefore set myIsJumping to
    // zero to indicate that the princess should start
    // falling.
    if(! checkCollision()) {
      myIsJumping = 0;
    }
    // we move the princess Sprite back to the correct
    // position she was at before we (temporarily) moved
    // her down to see if she would fall.
    myPrincess.move(0, -1);
  }
  // if the princess is currently jumping or falling,
  // advance the jump (change the vertical distance
  // the princess is supposed to move)
  if((myIsJumping <= MAX_FREE_FALL) && (myIsJumping != NO_JUMP)) {
    myIsJumping++;
  }
  // also accelerate the horizontal motion if the princess
  // runs in the same horizontal direction for more than
  // one game tick:
```

```
myIsRunning++;
// But don't accelerate past the maximum speed:
if(myIsRunning > MAX_SPEED) {
  myIsRunning = MAX_SPEED;
}
int horizontal = MOVE_LENGTH * myIsRunning;
// if the princess is currently jumping or falling,
// we calculate the vertical distance she should move.
// This is a parabola given by y = (x*x) * (a + b/c)
// where x is how far we have advanced in the jump
// or fall (myIsJumping), and a, b, and c are constants
// based on the screen size. (The actual values are
// read from a properties file and were originally
// computed through trial and error.)
int vertical = 0;
if(myIsJumping != NO_JUMP) {
  vertical = myIsJumping * myIsJumping * JUMP_INT
    + (myIsJumping * myIsJumping * JUMP_FRAC_NUM)
        / JUMP_FRAC_DENOM;
  // for the first half of the jump we go up,
  // then for the second half go down:
  if(myIsJumping < 0) {
    vdirection = -1;
  } else {
    vdirection = 1;
  }
}
// set the sprite to the correct frame based
// on the princess's current motion:
updateSprite(hdirection, vdirection);
boolean vcrash = false;
boolean hcrash = false;
// now calculate the motion one pixel at a time
// (vertically then horizontally) to see precisely
// how far the princess can move in each of the
// requested directions:
while((vertical >= 1 && !vcrash)
    || (horizontal >= 1 && !hcrash)) {
  myPrincess.move(0, vdirection);
  if(checkCollision()) {
    myPrincess.move(0, -vdirection);
    vcrash = true;
  } else {
    vertical -= 1;
    vcrash = false;
    myViewWindowY += vdirection;
  }
```

```java
    myPrincess.move(MOVE_BUFFER * hdirection, 0);
    if(checkCollision()) {
      myPrincess.move(-MOVE_BUFFER * hdirection, 0);
      hcrash = true;
    } else {
      myPrincess.move(-MOVE_BUFFER * hdirection, 0);
      myPrincess.move(hdirection, 0);
      horizontal -= 1;
      hcrash = false;
      myViewWindowX += hdirection;
    }
  }
  // If the princess is blocked vertically,
  // then the jump or fall in progress stops:
  if(vcrash) {
    myIsJumping = NO_JUMP;
  }
  // If the princess is blocked horizontally,
  // forget any horizontal acceleration:
  if(hcrash) {
    myIsRunning = 0;
  }
}


/**
 * Internal to requestMove.  Set the princess sprite
 * to the correct frame depending on her movements.
 */
private void updateSprite(int hdirection, int vdirection) {
  // if the princess is moving left or right, we set
  // her image to be facing the right direction:
  if(hdirection > 0) {
    myPrincess.setTransform(Sprite.TRANS_NONE);
  } else if(hdirection < 0) {
    myPrincess.setTransform(Sprite.TRANS_MIRROR);
  }
  // if she's jumping or falling, we set the image to
  // the frame where the skirt is inflated:
  if(vdirection != 0) {
    myPrincess.setFrame(0);
    // if she's just running, we alternate between the
    // two frames:
  } else if(hdirection != 0) {
    if(myPrincess.getFrame() == 1) {
      myPrincess.setFrame(0);
    } else {
      myPrincess.setFrame(1);
```

```
        }
      }
    }
```

The next set of lines in the properties files of Listings 10-9 and 10-10 concern the background image that is shown behind the dungeon layer during game play. It looks nicer to have a background image during game play, but since the background is rather bland, I was able to save space in the JAR by using a trick to use the same image file for the smaller screen and for the larger screen. The width and height of the dungeon layer is the size of the square stone (in pixels) times the number of stones (16 across as well as 16 down). So for the larger-screen dungeon, the width (and height) is 384 pixels, and for the larger-screen dungeon, it's 576. So I created a background image that has size 96×96 pixels—a multiple of both dungeon sizes. For the larger screen, a six-by-six grid of background images covers the whole background and for the smaller screen, it's covered by a four-by-four grid of background images. So the back.tiles property tells how large a tiled layer to use for the background. The construction of the additional background layer is shown in Listing 10-12.

After the background properties, there's the image for the number sprite (Figure 10-10), then the data used to construct the custom menu (discussed in the "Creating Custom Menus" section earlier), then the images used for the splashscreen (discussed in the "Starting Off on the Right Foot" section), and finally the keycodes for some known handsets (discussed in the "Identifying the Platform" sidebar and the "Implementing Softkeys" section).

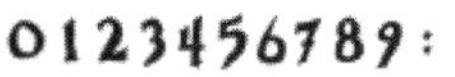

0123456789:

Figure 10-10. *The image file used for the Sprites that make up the game timer*

Most of this custom data is requested by the DungeonManager after it is loaded by the Customizer. Aside from the change to the game movements algorithm (Listing 10-11), this initialization step is the biggest difference between the version of DungeonManager given in Chapter 5 (Listing 5-9) and the new version.

Listing 10-12. *The Initialization Methods of DungeonManager.java Replacing the Constructor from Listing 5-9*

```
/**
 * Constructor merely sets the data.
 * @param x The x-coordinate of the place on the game canvas where
 * the LayerManager window should appear, in terms of the
 * coordinates of the game canvas.
 * @param y The y-coordinate of the place on the game canvas where
 * the LayerManager window should appear, in terms of the
 * coordinates of the game canvas.
 * @param width the width of the region that is to be
 * occupied by the LayoutManager.
 * @param height the height of the region that is to be
 * occupied by the LayoutManager.
 * @param customizer the object that loads the correct
 * custom data for the current platform.
```

```
 * @param canvas the DungeonCanvas that this LayerManager
 * should appear on.
 */
public DungeonManager(int x, int y, int width, int height,
    Customizer customizer, DungeonCanvas canvas) {
  myCustomizer = customizer;
  myCanvas = canvas;
  CANVAS_X = x;
  CANVAS_Y = y;
  DISP_WIDTH = width;
  DISP_HEIGHT = height;
}

/**
 * Set up all of the data.
 *
 * This is called from a separate init method in order
 * to limit the amount of resource loading that is done
 * by the thread that called the startApp method.
 */
public void init() throws Exception {
  myCustomizer.init();
  MOVE_LENGTH = myCustomizer.getInt("move.length");
  MOVE_BUFFER = myCustomizer.getInt("move.buffer");
  SQUARE_WIDTH = myCustomizer.getInt("square.width");
  BACK_TILES = myCustomizer.getInt("back.tiles");
  JUMP_INT = myCustomizer.getInt("jump.int");
  JUMP_FRAC_NUM = myCustomizer.getInt("jump.frac.numerator");
  JUMP_FRAC_DENOM = myCustomizer.getInt("jump.frac.denominator");
  // create a decoder object that creates the dungeon and
  // its associated Sprites from data.
  BoardDecoder decoder = new BoardDecoder(myCurrentBoardNum,
      myCustomizer);
  // get the dungeon walls layer:
  myWalls = decoder.getLayer();
  // the background behind the walls is a single image,
  // so the easiest way to add it to the layer manager
  // is to make it a sprite:
  Image bi = myCustomizer.getImage("background");
  myBackground = new TiledLayer(BACK_TILES, BACK_TILES,
      bi, bi.getWidth(), bi.getHeight());
  // set all cells to use tile 1 instead of the default
  // (blank) tile 0:
  myBackground.fillCells(0, 0, BACK_TILES, BACK_TILES, 1);
  // get the coordinates of the square that the princess
  // starts on.
  int[] playerCoords = decoder.getPlayerSquare();
```

```
// create the player sprite
myPrincess = new Sprite(myCustomizer.getImage("princess"),
                        SQUARE_WIDTH, SQUARE_WIDTH);
myPrincess.setFrame(1);
// we define the reference pixel to be in the middle
// of the princess image so that when the princess turns
// from right to left (and vice versa) she does not
// appear to move to a different location.
myPrincess.defineReferencePixel(SQUARE_WIDTH/2, 0);
// the dungeon is a 16x16 grid, so the array playerCoords
// gives the player's location in terms of the grid, and
// then we multiply those coordinates by the SQUARE_WIDTH
// to get the precise pixel where the player should be
// placed (in terms of the LayerManager's coordinate system)
myPrincess.setPosition(SQUARE_WIDTH * playerCoords[0],
                       SQUARE_WIDTH * playerCoords[1]);
// we append all of the Layers (TiledLayer and Sprite)
// so that this LayerManager will paint them when
// flushGraphics is called.
append(myPrincess);
// get the coordinates of the square where the crown
// should be placed.
int[] goalCoords = decoder.getGoalSquare();
Image crownImage = myCustomizer.getImage("crown");
myCrown = new Sprite(crownImage);
myCrown.defineReferencePixel(crownImage.getWidth()/2,
    crownImage.getHeight());
myCrown.setRefPixelPosition(
    (SQUARE_WIDTH * goalCoords[0]) + (SQUARE_WIDTH/2),
    (SQUARE_WIDTH * goalCoords[1]) + SQUARE_WIDTH);
append(myCrown);
// The decoder creates the door and key sprites and places
// them in the correct locations in terms of the LayerManager's
// coordinate system.
myNumberImage = myCustomizer.getImage("numbers");
myKeyImage = myCustomizer.getImage("keys");
myDoors = decoder.createDoors(myKeyImage);
myKeys = decoder.createKeys(myKeyImage);
for(int i = 0; i < myDoors.length; i++) {
  append(myDoors[i]);
}
for(int i = 0; i < myKeys.length; i++) {
  append(myKeys[i]);
}
// append the background last so it will be painted first.
append(myWalls);
append(myBackground);
```

```
    // this sets the view screen so that the player is
    // in the center.
    myViewWindowX = SQUARE_WIDTH * playerCoords[0]
      - ((DISP_WIDTH - SQUARE_WIDTH)/2);
    myViewWindowY = SQUARE_WIDTH * playerCoords[1]
      - ((DISP_HEIGHT - SQUARE_WIDTH)/2);
    // a number of objects are created in order to set up the game,
    // but they should be eliminated to free up memory:
    decoder = null;
    System.gc();
  }
```

The init() method in Listing 10-12 is the method called by the run() method of the GameThread object (see Listing 10-6).

Aside from the changes noted in Listings 10-11 and 10-12, the only other changes to make in the DungeonManager class for this new version are to declare all of the additional fields that are clearly necessary to make this code run. Also, for simplicity I've eliminated the optimization of only repainting if there is a change. Since the clock is now painted directly onto the game play area, it needs to be repainted every time. I could go through the code and keep track of exactly what part of the screen changes (if any) at each tick, and then carefully only repaint that part, but that level of optimization isn't terribly helpful for this game since the whole screen changes on most ticks.

To complete the beautified version of the Dungeon example, a few more classes are required from back in Chapter 5. Some require no change such as DataConverter.java (Listing 5-3) and GameInfo.java (Listing 5-4). Some others require some simple, obvious changes to get their images through the Customizer class instead of loading them directly: the only change needed for DoorKey.java (Listing 5-10) is that the image is sent in the constructor instead of being loaded; similarly, BoardDecoder.java (Listing 5-5) must be changed to get the images it needs from the Customizer and then pass them along when constructing the DoorKey objects.

Summary

Creating a professional GUI for your game is more complex than just using MIDP's built-in GUI classes. It means drawing the menu and softkey labels onto a blank canvas and implementing the menu navigation functionality yourself. It also means you need to do far more platform-by-platform customization. Yet it's worth the effort because adding the beautiful custom interface is the finishing step that makes it clear that your game comes from the big leagues even if you're working independently or as part of a small game studio. And as you can see, every step from beginning to end of creating a professional game—fun to play and ready to sell—is something you can do yourself.

Index

Numbers and symbols

3D API. *See* M3G API
3D object, 322–324
3D software suite, 333–334
| (or) operator, 29–30
% (percent) operator, 46
>> << (shift operators), 137

A

acceptAndOpen method, 275
advance() method, Tumbleweed game, 62–69
Alert, 27–28
AlertDISMISS_COMMAND, 28
AMS. *See* application management software (AMS)
animated menu, adding, 381
AnimationController class, 345–346
animations, M3G API support for, 345–348
AnimationTrack class, 345–346
Ant, building games with, 13
Antenna, JAR of Java-ME-specific build tasks by, 13
Apache server, 17–18
append() method, 29
Applets, 22
application management software (AMS), 22–26, 210
applications
    building for MIDP, 5–6
    securing, 305–316
Apress web site, Source Code/Download, 53
ARGB format, 365–366
arrays, converting between ints, 135–136
asynchronous communications, 195
audio files, 128–129
augmented BNF notation format, 122
available() method, 196

B

bitwise &, 46
Blender software, 333–335
blocking method, 104
Bluetooth, 263–285
BNF notation format (augmented), 122
BoardDecoder.java
    changes in, 205
    converting array of bytes to dungeon, 149–154

BoardReader class, 199–205
br.start() method, 199
buttons and menus, in MIDlet subclass, 28–29
byte arithmetic and data types, 136–143
byte arrays, converting between ints, 135–136
byte values and int values, converting between, 135
bytes
    converting integers to, 131
    signed and unsigned, 137–138

C

Camera and Lights, defining placement of, 323
Camera object, 322
Canvas class
    Camera object, 322
    Canvas object, 34
    vs. GameCanvas class, 62–69
<card> tag, 15
CDC (Connected Device Configuration), 1–2
cell phones, running games on, 14–19
Certificate Authority (CA), applying for, 308
Certificate Signing Request file, generating, 308
character encoding, in Java, 3
Checkers game
    Bluetooth protocol for, 264–285
    Checkers.java code, 256–261
    CheckersCanvas class code, 234–241
    CheckersGame class, 242–255
    creating multiplayer, 212–261
    game state flags, 212
    initial communications steps in, 220–222
    piece move considerations for, 256
    writing communications code for, 212–234
    writing game logic for, 234–261
checkKeys() method, 62
child nodes, Group and Mesh, 333
ChoiceGroups, 33
Class.getResource() method, 78
classes, obfuscating, 311
CLDC (Connected Limited Device Configuration), 1–3. *See also* Java Community Process (JCP)
    secure, 311–316
    threads vs. standard Java threads, 95–104
clientRun() method, 275
collidesWith() methods, 80
collisions, M3G API helper class for, 348–349

color coordinates, assigning color to vertex with, 329
ColorChanger.java, 363–366
colors and transparency, modifying images, 363–366
Command objects
    arguments for, 28–29, 51
    MIDP encapsulation of softkeys in, 396
commandAction() method, 104, 199
CommConnection, 303
communications and business strategy, 285. *See also* network communications
Connected Device Configuration (CDC). *See* CDC (Connected Device Configuration)
Connected Limited Device Configuration (CLDC). *See* CLDC (Connected Limited Device Configuration)
Connector.open() method, 194
ContentLength HTTP header, 196
cowboy Sprite, 78–80
Cowboy.advance(int tickCount, boolean left) method, 80
Cowboy.checkCollision(Tumbleweed tumbleweed) method, 80
Cowboy.java file, 81–89
createAnimatedTile(int staticTileIndex) method, 91
currency formatting, 366
custom menus. *See* menus
CustomItems, adding in MIDP 2, 33
Customizer class, loading handset properties files with, 357–362

D

daemon threads, 95
data
    compacting, 137–143
    saving simple, 131–135
    serializing complex, 135–136
    storing and retrieving, 131–192
data access and messaging, 263–303
data arrays, 132
data storage, applying to Dungeon game, 143–159
data types and byte arithmetic, 136–143
data-transfer protocols, 193–194
DataConverter, integer compression utility class, 137–143
deadlocks, avoiding race conditions and, 115–117
deallocate() method, 129
defineReferencePixel(int x, int y) method, 80
destroyApp() method, 22, 104
digital certificates
    using, 308–310
    verification method for, 315–316

DiscoveryAgent, 265, 275
DiscoveryListener, 265
Display class, 26–28
Display.getDisplay() method, 27
Displayable class, 26–28
domain name vs. numerical IP address, 197
doors and keys, 188–189
drawString() method, Graphics class, 43–44
Dungeon class, 198
Dungeon game
    adding professional look and feel, 351–407
    applying data storage to, 143–159
    creating, 159–192
    creating custom menus in, 380–396
    downloading next board for, 197–198
    Dungeon.java, 376–380
    in action, 143
    initial splash screen, 367
    multiple boards for, 136–137
    programming to sell, 313
    versions depending on screen size, 400
    writing client code for, 198–205
    writing server code for, 206–209
DungeonCanvas.java, 382–395
    GameCanvas subclass, 164–171
DungeonDownload servlet, 206–209
DungeonManager class
    changes in BoardReader.java, 205
    "game movements" methods of, 400–404
DungeonManager.java
    initialization methods, 404–407
    LayerManager subclass, 171–188

E

else if block, adding to commandAction() method, 199
EMS (Enhanced Messaging Service). *See* Enhanced Messaging Service (EMS)
emulators, default in WTK, 13
EncodingUtils.java, 154–159
Enhanced Messaging Service (EMS), 209
enumerateRecords, 132

F

FCRunner.java, 298–300
FCTest.java, 300–302
File Connection API, 297–302
FileSystemRegistry class, 297
fillRoundRect() method, 34
float (f) type, M3G API graphics, 320
flushGraphics() method, 62
Form class, creating GUI screen with, 29–33
formatter utility, Mobile Internationalization API (JSR 238), 366
Forms, adding items to, 33

G

g.drawString() method, 70
g.fillRect() method, 70
game logic, writing for Checkers game,
    234–261
game state flags, Checkers game, 212
GameCanvas class
    Graphics class use with, 69–70
    subclass, 164–171
    vs. Canvas class, 62–69
GameInfo class, 143
    GameInfo.java, 143–148
games. *See also* Checkers game; Dungeon
    game; maze game; mobile games;
    Tumbleweed game
    adding professional look and feel, 351–407
    applying custom resources to, 398–407
    complete Dungeon game, 159–164
    programming to sell, 312–314
    storing and retrieving data, 131–192
GameThread subclass, Tumbleweed game,
    58–62
GameThread.java file, 59–62, 372–376
    Thread subclass, 189–192
GET request method, 209
getGameAction class, 397
getGameAction() method, 34
getKeyStates() method, 62
getLength() method, 196
getRecord() method, 132
getSquareSize() method, 135
gimp (the), image making software, 19
global directory, .res files under, 366
graphical layers, organizing for Tumbleweed
    game, 71
Graphics class
    built-in shapes in, 34
    drawString() method of, 43–44
    using with GameCanvas class, 69–70
Graphics.drawImage() method, 94
Grass subclass, Tumbleweed game, 89
Grass.java file, Tumbleweed game, 91–94
Grid.java file, 46–51
Group node, 333
GroupAnimationTimer class, 346–348
GSM/GPRS, 14
GUI (Graphical User Interface), creating,
    367–397

H

handsets, data-transfer protocols for, 193
HEAD request method, 209
Hello, World application
    creating, 6–10
    hello.jar file, 5–6
    Hello.java file, 7–9
    HelloCanvas.java file, 9–10

hello.png icon, 6
hello.wml file, 15
    web page, 18–19
HelloCanvas.java file, 9–10
hideNotify() method, 25, 113
.htaccess file, 17–18
HTTP (Hypertext Transfer Protocol)
    changing to HTTPS from, 311–312
    for communicating with server, 195–209
    required by MIDP 1 and MIDP 2, 193
    request method, 209
HttpConnection
    creating an instance of, 195–197
    HttpConnection class, 209
HTTPS, 311–312
Hypertext Transfer Protocol (HTTP). *See*
    HTTP (Hypertext Transfer Protocol)

I

IANA Port Number Registry, web site, 216
identified third-party domain, 306
Image, rendering into mutable, 322
image colors and transparency, modifying,
    363–366
image files
    software for creating, 19
    used for sprites, 404
IMCConnection, new in MIDP 3, 302–303
immediate mode
    in Mobile 3D Graphics API, 336
    rendering, 322–323
IndexBuffer class and Triangle strips, 320–322
init() method, 407
InputStream classes, in Java ME network
    communications, 194–195
int values/byte values, converting between, 135
integer compression utility class, 137–143
integer record ID. *See* record ID
integers (ints)
    converting between arrays and, 135–136
    converting to bytes, 131
inter-MIDlet communication option, in
    MIDP 3, 302–303
IP (Internet Protocol) address, domain name
    vs. numerical, 197
isColor() method, 27
isShown() method, 25
Item class, for GUI screen, 29–31
Item.addCommand() method, 31
ItemCommandListener, setting, 31
itemStateChanged() method, 31

J

J2ME Polish, using, 398
JAD (Java application descriptor) files
    declaring permission in, 307–308
    in demo applications, 5

JadTool utility, 309
JAR files
    customizing, 397
    in demo applications, 5
Java Community Process (JCP), downloading
        JSRs from, 2
Java ME (Micro Edition)
    network communications in, 194–195
    understanding, 1–4
Java ME Wireless Toolkit. *See* Sun Java
        Wireless Toolkit for CLDC
Java Micro Edition (Java ME). *See* Java ME
        (Micro Edition)
Java SE SDK, handling of key pair by, 309
Java Specification Requests (JSRs), 2
Java threads vs. CLDC threads, 95–104
Java Virtual Machine (JVM), 1–3
java.io.ByteArrayInputStream class, 135
java.io.ByteArrayOutputStream class, 135
java.io.DataInputStream class, 131–135
java.io.DataOutputStream class, 131–135
java.microedition.lcdui package, writing Java
        GUI with, 21
java.microedition.lcdui.command, instances
        of, 28–29
java.util package, classes in, 44–51
javax.microedition.io.Connection, 194
javax.microedition.io.HttpConnection
        interface, 195
javax.microedition.lcdui.CommandListener,
        29–51
javax.microedition.lcdui.game, MIDP-2, 4
javax.microedition.lcdui.game.*, 53
javax.microedition.lcdui.game.GameCanvas
        class, 62
javax.microedition.media.control.
        ToneControl class, 122
javax.microedition.media.Manager.
        playTone() method, 118
javax.microedition.rms package, 131
JCP. *See* Java Community Process (JCP)
JSRs. *See* Java Specification Requests (JSRs)
jump.frac.numerator value, 400
Jump.java file
    Tumbleweed game MIDlet subclass, 54–58
    updated version of, 96–104
JumpCanvas class, 70
JumpCanvas.checkKeys() method, 71
JumpCanvas.java file
    additions and changes to, 114–115
    Tumbleweed game, 63, 69
JumpManager subclass, LayerManager class,
        70
JumpManager.java file
    additions to, 112–113
    Tumbleweed game, 72–77
JVM. *See* Java Virtual Machine (JVM)

K

key pairs, creating, 309
key states, querying for Tumbleweed game,
        62–63
keycodes, for game, 397
KeyframeSequence class, 345–346
keyPressed() method, 34, 397
keyPressed(int keyCode) method, 62
keyReleased() method, 34
keyRepeated() method, 34
keys. *See* doors and keys
keytool utility, creating key pairs with, 309
KToolbar, 11–13
    generating Certificate Signing Request file,
        308
    in Java ME Wireless Toolkit, 5
    MIDlet running on WTK emulator with, 21
    preverifying and building project, 13
    setting up new project, 12–13

L

large.properties file, for loading properties,
        398–399
LayerManager class, 71–72
LayerManager subclass,
        DungeonManager.java, 171–188
LayerManager.paint(Graphics g, int x, int y)
        method, 71
LayerManager.setViewWindow(int x, int y, int
        width, int height) method, 71
libraries, Java ME's vs. standard Java, 3
lighting effects, adding to pyramid, 326–328
lighting effects and textures. *See* textures and
        lighting effects

M

M3G API, 317–350
M3G file, creating, 333–334
Manager.getSupportedContentTypes()
        method, 129
manufacturer domain, 306
matrix multiplication, 339
maze game
    creating maze for, 45–46
    maze generation algorithm, 44–45
    Maze.java file, 22–25
    on Sagem my700x, 35
    on small device emulator's screen, 34
MazeCanvas class
    modifying for game, 132
    MazeCanvas.java file, 34–43
media, using, 118–129
MEKeytool utility, 312
menus
    creating custom, 380–396
    custom using lcdui commands, 398
    making each item a Sprite, 363–365

Mesh node, 333
messaging and data access, advanced,
    263–303
microedition.locale property, 362
microedition.platform property, 363
MIDI. *See* Musical Instrument Digital
    Interface (MIDI)
MIDlet, listing in registry, 211
MIDlet class, 22–29
    code for Checkers.java, 256–261
    Tumbleweed game, 53–58
MIDlet lifecycle methods, 6
MIDlet Suite
    issues with update function, 314
    signing, 309
MIDlet-Jar-Size property, 6
MIDlet-Jar-URL property, 6
MIDlet-Name property, RecordStore
    identified by, 131
MIDlet-Permission-<n> attributes, MIDP 3,
    308
MIDlet-Permissions JAD attribute, 307
MIDlet-Permissions-Opt JAD attribute, 307
MIDlet-Vendor property, RecordStore
    identified by, 131
MIDletM3G class, for "Tour of the World"
    example, 344–345
MIDlets
    lifecycle of, 22–26
    lifecycle methods, 6
    listing in registry, 211
    using, 21
MIDPAPI, 195–197
    building application for, 5–6
    playing tonal music with, 118–122
    security, 305
    versions, 3–4
MIDP 2
    permissions in, 307
    security, 305
    using games API, 53–94
MIDP 3
    inter-MIDlet communication option in,
        302–303
    permissions in, 308
MIDP games, communications and data
    sharing APIs, 302
MIDP Record Management System (RMS), 131
MIDP RecordStore, for unlocking games, 313
MIDP security model, for Java ME
    applications, 305–316
MMS (Multimedia Messaging Service). *See*
    Multimedia Messaging Service
    (MMS)
Mobile 3D Graphics API (JSR 184). *See* M3G
    API
mobile games, creating in Java platform, 1–19

Mobile Information Device Profile (MIDP).
    See MIDP API
Mobile Internationalization API (JSR 238),
    366
Mobile Internet Device Profile (MIDP). *See*
    MIDP; MIDP 2; MIDP 3
Mobile Media API (JSR 135), 4, 118
move.length value, 400
MoveManager class, 227
    Checkers game, 213
    code for, 228–234
Multimedia Messaging Service (MMS), 209
multiplayer game example, creating, 212–261
multiple target platforms, customizing, 352–366
music
    disadvantages of playing files, 128
    figuring integer values for notes, 118–119
    finding public domain, 128
    pausing and unpausing, 96–104
    playing, 118–122
    playing tones with a player, 122–128
Musical Instrument Digital Interface (MIDI),
    118
MusicMaker.java file, 122
myAlertDoneCommand, 27

N

network communications, 193–262
    for Checkers game, 213–216
    programming techniques, 194–195
nextFrame() method, Tumbleweed game, 79
nodes and rendering, 335–345
normal vectors, 325–328
Notify.acceptAndOpen method, 275
notifyDestroy() method, 26
numColors() method, 27
numerical IP address vs. domain name, 197

O

obfuscator tool, 311
Object.finalize() method, elimination of in
    CLDC, 2
Object3D class, 332
operator domain, 306
optimization, of Graphics3D objects, 349
or (|) operator, 29–30
OutputStream classes, Java ME network
    communications, 194–195
Over the Air (OTA) provisioning, 16–18

P

<p></p> tags, 16
paint() method
    calling, 27
    implementing, 34
    in Checkers game, 241
paint(getGraphics()) method, 62

paint(Graphics g) method, 70
pauseApp() method, 22, 104
PDA Optional Packages, JSR 75, 285
permissions, 307–308. *See also* protection domains and permissions
phone number, entering for Checkers game, 216
PIM API, 285–297
PIM.getInstance() method, for Bluetooth Checkers game, 286–288
PIMRunner class
    adding to create Checkers Plus game, 289
    code for Bluetooth Checkers game, 286–288
PIMRunner thread, starting and synchronizing, 290–297
platform, identifying, 363
Player, for playing tones, 122
playTone() method, 118–119
polygon, defining, 317–322
PolygonMode object, creating and setting culling, 324
port number, Checkers game, 216
position coordinates, setting pyramid's, 319–320
POST request method, 209
prefetch() method, 129
PrefStorage class, 132
PrefStorage.java, code for, 133–135
preverification process, 3
prevFrame() method, Tumbleweed game, 79
Professional Information Management (PIM) API. *See* PIM API
profiles, configuring, 193–194
properties
    file for large English labels, 357
    parser, writing, 353–355
properties.java file, 353–355
protection domains and permissions, 305–310
protocols. *See* data-transfer protocols
push registration, static vs. dynamic, 211
push registry, for inbound communications, 210–211
PushRegistry.listConnections() method, 210
PushRegistry.unregisterConnection() method, 211
pyramid
    adding textures and lighting, 325–332
    creating with M3G API, 318–322
    effect of putting image on backward, 330

R

race conditions, avoiding deadlock and, 115–117
RayIntersection class, for computing a collision, 348–349

read() method vs. readFully() method, 196
readUTF() method, 136
realize() method, 129
record ID, assignment of, 132
RecordComparator, creating to traverse records, 132
RecordEnumerator, 132
RecordFilter, creating to traverse records, 132
RecordStore class
    creating, 131–135
    for unlocking games, 313
RecordStore.openRecordStore() method, 132–135
render() method, Graphics3D's, 323–324
rendering
    immediate and retained modes, 336
    pyramid object in M3G API, 322–324
repaint() method, 34, 62
.res files, 366
ResourceManager.getManager, 366
resources, organizing custom, 352–362
retained mode, in Mobile 3D Graphics API, 336
RMS vs. File Connection API, 302
run() method, 115–117
runGame() method, 275

S

saving simple data, 131–135
scene graph, illustrating use of, 336–345
searchServices() method, 265
security, MIDP for Java ME applications, 305–316
Security Exception, 306
SelectScreen class, modifying for game, 132
SelectScreen.java file, maze game, 31–33
selectService() method, Bluetooth client-side use of, 275
server. *See* Apache server; web server
server-side code, Dungeon game, 206–209
serverRun() method, 275
serviceRepaints() method, 62
setCell(int col, int row, int tileIndex) method, 91
setColor() method, 34
setCommandListener() method, 27
setContentLength() method, 206
setCurrent() method, 27
setCurrentItem() method, 27
setFrame(int sequenceIndex) method, 79
setFrameSequence(int[] sequence) method, 79
setGameOver() method, 113
setLayout() method, 29
setLoopCount() method, 123
setMode() method, 275
setRecord() method, 132
setRefPixelPosition(int x, int y) method, 80
setRequestMethod(), 209
setSequence() method, 122

setSquareSize() method, 135
setTransform(TRANS_MIRROR) method, 80
setTransform(TRANS_NONE) method, 80
setViewWindow(int x, int y, int width, int
        height) method, 71
shift operators (>> <<), 137
Short Message Service (SMS) protocol. *See*
        SMS (Short Message Service)
        protocol
showNotify() method, 26, 113
Sign MIDlet Suite GUI window, 309–310
small.properties file, for loading properties,
        399–400
SMS (Short Message Service) protocol
    drawback of, 194, 209
    for handsets, 193–194
    vs. User Datagram Protocol (UDP),
        209–210
SMSManager class
    Checkers game, 213
    code for, 222–227
SMSReceiver class
    Checkers game, 213
    code for, 217–220
SMSSender class, Checkers game, 213–216
softkeys, 396–397
Source Code/Download section, Apress web
        site, 1
splash screen
    initial for Dungeon game, 367
    SplashScreen.java, 368–372
Sprite class, Tumbleweed game, 77–89
sprites, image file used for, 404
square-shaped pyramid. *See* pyramid
start() method, 22
startAnimation() method, 346–347
startApp() method, 104
    adding code to download boards, 198–199
    starting MIDlets with, 22
static method, for creating RecordStore, 131
streams, serializing complex data with,
        135–136
subimages, cutting from larger images,
        356–357
Sun Java Wireless Toolkit for CLDC
    adding directories to, 13
    downloading and installing, 4–5
synchronization, avoiding race conditions
        and deadlock with, 115–117
synchronized keyword, 115–117
synchronous communications, 194–195
System.getProperty, 363

T
TabbedPane, grouping GUI screens in, 33
TextFields, 33
texture coordinates, understanding, 329–332

textures and lighting effects, adding to
        pyramid, 325–332
Thread class, Tumbleweed game, 58–62
Thread subclass, 58–59
Thread.yield() method, 59
ThreadGroup class, eliminated in CLDC, 96
threads
    avoiding race conditions and deadlock,
        115–117
    CLDC vs. standard Java, 95–104
    daemon, 95
    reusing, 104
    spawning new, 104–115
threads and media, improving Tumbleweed
        game with, 95–129
TiledLayer class
    creating for Tumbleweed game, 89–94
    vs. Sprite class, 77
Timer, advancing an automation with, 105
TimerTask class, advancing an automation
        with, 105, 346–347
Tomcat, web site, 197
ToneControlMusicMaker.java file, 123–128
tones, playing simple, 118–122
tools and features, for bringing 3D games to
        life, 345–349
"Tour of the World" example
    adding animation track to, 346–348
    DemoCanvas class for, 339–344
    MIDlet subclass to run, 344–345
    viewing M3G file with, 336
Transform object, 323
Transformable, in scene graph, 333
transformation matrix, 337–339
transformations, in Tumbleweed game,
        80–81
transparency, ARGB format, 365–366
Triangle strips and IndexBuffers, 320–322
TriangleStripArray, 320–322
Trusted Third-Party domain, MIDP 2, 306
Tumbleweed game, 53
    adding new threads, 95–117
    applying transforms, 80–81
    Class.getResource() method, 78
    Cowboy.java file, 81–89
    creating TiledLayer class in, 90–91
    GameThread.java, 59–62
    Graphics class in, 69–70
    Graphics class in, 69–70
    Grass.java file, 91–94
    image file for cowboy Sprite, 78
    Jump.java MIDlet subclass, 54–58
    JumpCanvas class, 69–70
    JumpCanvas.java file, 63–69
    JumpManager.java file, 72–77
    keeping cowboy in middle of screen, 71–72
    LayerManager class, 71–77

numbering system for cowboy Sprite cells, 79–80
pausing and restarting, 113–115
pausing and stopping, 96–104
querying key states, 62–63
selecting frame to show in, 78–79
Sprite class in, 77–89
Thread class in, 58–62
threads spawned in, 105
TiledLayer class, 89–94
tumbleweed image for, 78
updating and repainting screen, 62
TumbleweedThread class, 105–113

U

UDP protocol. *See* User Datagram Protocol (UDP)
Unicode characters, CLDC support for, 3
unidentified third-party domain, 307
Universally Unique Identifier (UUID), 264
User Datagram Protocol (UDP) vs. SMS protocol, 210
user-agent header, 363
UTF-8 encoding, saving properties in, 356
utility class, converting integers to bytes, 131
UUID. *See* Universally Unique Identifier (UUID)
uuidgen command, creating client-side UUID with, 264

V

vectors, normal, 325–328
verification method, for digital certificates, 315
VeriSign, applying for certificate from, 308

vertex buffers and coordinates, 317–332
VertexArray, defining the polygon, 317–318
VertexBuffer, 318, 329
VolumeControl, 123

W

WAP. *See* Wireless Application Protocol (WAP)
web server, 19
configuring, 16–18
using Tomcat as, 197
Wireless Application Protocol (WAP), 193
accessing Internet with, 14–15
adding multiple game links in page, 16
verifying phone access configuration, 18
Wireless Messaging API (WMA), 209
WML file
accessing and downloading applications, 18–19
preparing, 15–16
tags, 15
World node
exploring, 339–344
moving child nodes as a group, 337
rendering, 332–333
tour of, 336–345
writeUTF() method, 136
WTK emulator
checking MIDlet certification in, 309–310
HTTPS used with, 311–312
MIDlet running on with KToolbar, 21
WTK's BluetoothDemo, 265

X

X and Y coordinates, 43
X.509 Public Key Infrastructure (PKI), 308

You Need the Companion eBook

Your purchase of this book entitles you to buy the companion PDF-version eBook for only $10. Take the weightless companion with you anywhere.

We believe this Apress title will prove so indispensable that you'll want to carry it with you everywhere, which is why we are offering the companion eBook (in PDF format) for $10 to customers who purchase this book now. Convenient and fully searchable, the PDF version of any content-rich, page-heavy Apress book makes a valuable addition to your programming library. You can easily find and copy code—or perform examples by quickly toggling between instructions and the application. Even simultaneously tackling a donut, diet soda, and complex code becomes simplified with hands-free eBooks!

Once you purchase your book, getting the $10 companion eBook is simple:

❶ Visit **www.apress.com/promo/tendollars/**.

❷ Complete a basic registration form to receive a randomly generated question about this title.

❸ Answer the question correctly in 60 seconds, and you will receive a promotional code to redeem for the $10.00 eBook.

2560 Ninth Street • Suite 219 • Berkeley, CA 94710

eBookshop

Offer valid through 2/20/08.